# The Psychoanalytic Study
# of the Child

## VOLUME XIX

# The Psychoanalytic Study

# of the Child

VOLUME XIX

INTERNATIONAL UNIVERSITIES PRESS, INC.

New York                                                New York

HEINZ HARTMANN

# DEDICATION

This nineteenth volume of *The Psychoanalytic Study of the Child* is dedicated to Heinz Hartmann on his seventieth birthday. It is but a token of the deep appreciation, esteem, and gratitude which we feel for the man and his work. This publication would not have been born without his vision, nor would it have lived and grown without his interest, guidance, and active participation in the editorial work. His scientific contributions have given basis, form, and structure to this Annual and have set the standards which authors and editors have tried to adhere to.

*Felix qui potuit rerum cognoscere causas!*—Virgil: *Georgica*

Ruth S. Eissler

# CONTENTS

# Clinical Contributions

Contents of Previous Volumes

# CONTRIBUTIONS TO PSYCHOANALYTIC THEORY

# CONCEPT FORMATION IN PSYCHOANALYSIS

HEINZ HARTMANN, M.D. (New York)

*Author's Note.*—The following essay is a first English translation of the two introductory chapters of a book, *Die Grundlagen der Psychoanalyse,* which I wrote and which was published in German in 1927. When I was asked some years ago to agree to an English edition of the *Grundlagen,* I did not see my way clear to accepting this suggestion; obviously, since 1927, the theories of psychoanalysis had undergone considerable change, and so had my knowledge and understanding of analysis. However, the book was actually written with a twofold aim in mind. It was to present an outline of psychoanalytic theories, but also to attempt a methodological study of psychoanalysis as a science and of the formation of its basic concepts. My objections were directed against the republication of the whole book because this would have meant the presentation today of a survey of psychoanalytic theories that was written in the 20s. The objections are not valid in the same degree so far as the methodological chapters are concerned. As a matter of fact, when I returned to these problems in later years (e.g., 1958 and 1959), I still found myself in agreement with the approach and with many of the points made in the earlier work. Recently friends again prevailed on me to publish at least a few of those chapters, using the argument that there may be some historical interest in reading now what was one of the first, maybe the first, explicit approach by an analyst to this particular aspect of psychoanalysis. It is for this reason that hardly any changes have been made in the text.

## I

### PSYCHOANALYSIS AS A NATURAL SCIENCE

The source materials of psychoanalytic investigation are highly complicated psychic structures and developments: complex thoughts or wishes, affects, dreams, neurotic symptoms and their genetic his-

Translated by Lottie M. Newman from a draft by Ernest Kafka, M.D.

tory. Besides, there are certain individual and collective documents such as diaries, poems, works of art, myths, and social, legal or religious phenomena; we use these to the extent to which we can infer specific psychic processes from them. That observations on mentally ill persons have become the starting point for psychoanalytic theory is no accident, since certain basic characteristics of psychic events are most clearly visible in pathological phenomena; on the other hand, the differences between normal and pathological processes are not of primary importance in collecting analytic material or in its scientific elaborations, in so far as they concern psychoanalytic theory. Since psychoanalysis is no longer confined to the explanation of neurotic symptoms, its ultimate task has become the formulation of basic concepts which can encompass the whole manifold range of psychic events, in health and illness, in the civilized and the primitive individual, in the adult and the child. This is to say: scientific analysis is now moving in the direction of becoming a general theory of human behavior.

The foundations which psychoanalysis has worked out in this way may appear to be primitive when we compare them to those of the empirically richer, methodologically purer natural sciences which deal with the lifeless material world. But if we stop to think of the methodological difficulties, e.g., in biology, we will no longer have the impression that we face a completely unbridgeable gulf. Certain difficulties of theory building are in fact inherent in biology no less than in psychology. On the other hand, other difficulties are inextricably bound up with the most general characteristics of psychic life. Still others are due to the gaps in our empirical knowledge and will be eliminated as these gaps are filled in.

We will have to examine the means and ways by which psychoanalysis attempts to approach its goal of becoming a theory of mental life, how far it has accomplished this task, and what difficulties stand in the path of realizing this goal.

To begin with and quite apart from any theoretical considerations, psychoanalysis has enormously increased our factual knowledge of psychic events—and the substance of this knowledge forms the foundation for scientific elaboration with respect to normal and pathological phenomena. Significant areas of infantile and psychotic mental life were even, so to speak, "discovered" by analysis. The knowledge

of this observational material is absolutely necessary for an understanding of the various aspects of analytic theory, though not for its
logical foundations. Each psychoanalysis provides the investigator
with a plenitude of psychological discoveries which no other method
can yield. Here, then, in the collecting and ordering of significant
observational material is the first task of psychoanalysis—first not in
the temporal but in the methodological sense. The aim of this task
is not the singling out of particularly striking, e.g., pathological
processes; rather, the first methodological task is to perform systematic and classificatory work. This aspect of analytic investigation is
frequently misunderstood by its opponents. Much of what is again
and again referred to as "analytic speculation" is, while certainly
often surprising and strange, actually nothing else but the result of
extensive and intensive especially penetrating observation. How
analysis succeeded in so considerably enlarging the field of psychological observations and how it made accessible to systematic scientific investigation certain processes which hitherto had been gleaned
by only a few intuitively gifted persons—these problems can be
understood only through an elucidation of the psychoanalytic method,
its relation to unconscious processes as well as to the dynamics of
mental life. The answers to these questions would involve going to
the core of analytic theory. However, the systematic classification of
each new territory of psychic life definitely belongs, from a methodological point of view, to that area which we generally term descriptive science and which we usually distinguish from explanatory
science (see Hartmann, 1927b).

This type of collecting and classifying, however, is for psychoanalysis not the goal but a preparation; the goal is rather, as we shall
see, the formulation of a system of rules or laws that govern psychic
events. This circumstance also explains the position of psychoanalysis
with respect to the so-called phenomenological school of psychology.
The principal difference is the following: when psychoanalysis refers
to the content of symptoms or the modes in which obsessional neurotics experience the world in terms of specific libido positions, this
represents an attempt to organize the qualitative manifoldness of
psychic data by "reduction" of the qualities; thereby psychoanalysis
accomplishes what Rickert (1921a, 1921b) recognized as the essence
of concept formation in the natural sciences. In contrast to psycho-

analysis, the phenomenologically oriented school set itself the task of studying and conceptualizing these very qualities and their manifoldness—in our example, this would be the different shades in the *experience* of a compulsion—thus dispensing with questions relating to causality. The evaluation of the two methods naturally differs according to the point of view one entertains with respect to the possibility of a merely descriptive insight into psychic life on the one hand, or to psychic causality and the possibility of basing psychology on the natural sciences on the other. No doubt, the facts established by phenomenological psychology are significant and valuable for psychoanalysis; and so are the results of Baade's (1916, 1918) "representational [*darstellende*] method" whose findings psychoanalysis can utilize as the starting points of investigations and which complement it. On the other hand, analysis itself has contributed a considerable number of fine "phenomenological" observations. Yet, in psychoanalysis, the significance of minute *descriptive* observations of many discrete qualities has today largely been relegated to second place; moreover, analytic *descriptions,* compared to phenomenological descriptions, often appear to be sketchy and less subtle. This is natural if we consider the ultimate goal of analysis and the stage of development it has reached. Certainly an exact descriptive conceptualization of those modes of experiencing that were first made accessible to scientific scrutiny by analytic work would also be a significant task for the analytic investigation in a narrower sense. The distinction between a primarily descriptive and a primarily explanatory treatment of the same factual material has its analogue in the sciences dealing with the physical world. Here, too, one often finds both approaches side by side, and it is hardly possible to view them as opposites which preclude each other. One point must be immediately clarified: psychoanalysis always deals with *real* psychic events in *real* persons, and whatever insights can be gained with the aid of so-called "phenomenological reduction" (Husserl, 1921) lie strictly outside its field of investigation. Its logical task is not to find connections of "essences" but causal connections.

If, as we said, the ultimate goal of psychoanalysis is to be a general theory of mental life, in what way does it propose to deal scientifically with the manifoldness of mental life? First of all, like all natural sciences, it develops general concepts, and endeavors to formulate generally applicable laws on the basis of information derived from individuals. As a science committed to formulating laws, psycho-analysis views mental facts from the angle of causality. We do not conceal the difficulties inherent in the problem of psychic causality, but at this point I cannot discuss the many viewpoints which are conceivable and actually have their proponents with regard to this problem. Suffice it to characterize our own standpoint: it is that all temporal changes, the psychic no less than the physical ones, not only can but must be investigated with respect to the category of causality, regardless of the possibility that with a different scientific goal in mind, the same material may lend itself to different kinds of scientific elaboration.

Psychoanalytic concepts, then, should be capable of encompassing the lawful relationships of psychic events. Such concepts as repression, resistance, etc., combine elements which regularly belong together. The rules thus gained are then applied to still strange and unordered material in which one seeks to find familiar elements.[1] One of many such examples would be the application of concepts derived from dream interpretation to the content of the psychoses; psychoanalysis uses the same method that every science uses in inferring rules and laws from the observation of single events. An event is explained to the extent that one succeeds in classifying it under such a rule. For psychoanalysis, for example, the appearance of a specific symbol in a dream is explained when one succeeds in finding, among the latent dream thought having a share in the formation of the dream, one thought as a consequence of whose presence the symbol often appears in the manifest content of the dream. The mere demonstra-tion of a logical connection, however, cannot be considered to con-stitute an explanation in this sense. This fact is of fundamental significance for an understanding of the psychoanalytic method and must immediately and emphatically be stressed.

Whether the science of mental life can ever aspire to formulate generally valid laws, in the strict sense of the term, will not be dis-cussed here. But it is important to make clear that the striving to

---

[1] This should hardly have to be said since it is self-evident. It must nevertheless be stated explicitly because of the repeated attempts to prove that the logical assumptions of the natural sciences cannot be applied to the "higher" mental life. It is precisely the methods of psychoanalysis which have so frequently—and erroneously—been singled out as being in opposition to the natural sciences.

approximate such laws is basic to psychoanalytic investigation. Kant's statement about the regularities which we find in the events themselves is as valid with regard to mental life as it is in the physical sphere. But as every science concerned with genuine lawfulness, psychoanalysis reaches beyond what is immediately given; and it does so via reasoning by analogy: more generally, by inductive inferences. For example, all analytic statements about unconscious processes depend on reasoning by analogy. It does not thereby transgress the limits set for an empirical science. The psychoanalytic theory of sexuality, of the etiology of neurosis, of transference, resistance, etc., was gained by inductive reasoning. In addition, deductive conclusions naturally also play a role; they lead back from the found regularity to the concrete single event. In contrast, the axiom of lawful regularity of psychic events is to be designated a nonempirical aspect. However, such an assumption of lawfulness forms the basis of every inductive science.

Because of the causal point of view, psychoanalysis does not stop at the psychic qualities; rather, in speaking of psychic processes, it proceeds to the building of concepts which transcend the qualitative aspects. It develops concepts of mental factors which group themselves in a number of ways: in such a manner that the resulting complex structures can be different with regard to all manifest characteristics. What differs phenomenologically may nevertheless belong together if viewed in causal-genetic terms, and vice versa. On the other hand, from the interaction of such structures of a higher order it is possible conceptually to isolate specific elements. Only this kind of analysis enables us to find regularities in psychic life which have a more general validity than those which we may find without such abstraction. An essential difference between the psychoanalytic and the experimental-psychological approach—if we here disregard the differences in their methods of proof—lies in the fact that psychoanalysis considers the factors which render the most central parts of personality accessible to scientific investigation. Natural science in general, and thus also scientific psychology, can forego the use of such "elements" on which explanations are based. This is often not sufficiently appreciated today when psychology has reached a stage of development which in the history of science can be viewed as a reaction against the absolute predominance of association psychology.

Different schools of scientific psychology differ with respect to the elements which for purposes of explanation they single out from the stream of psychic events as relatively independent units. It is only the choice of these elements and the way in which they are related to each other which can decide whether a school of scientific psychology is to be labeled mechanistic, biologistic, etc. Not even the theories of the Gestalt psychologists are able to change that basic state of affairs.

The methodologically most advanced natural sciences dealing with the physical world have in the course of their development learned more and more to exclude qualities from their conception of the world. This represents a deliberate restriction of the task of representing reality as it appears to us, but it facilitates the most significant advances in the field of measuring reality. For qualities as such are inaccessible to every approach from the natural sciences. It is in principle impossible to prove, by means of the natural sciences, why precisely this quality and not another corresponds to a certain condition which is characterized in physical or chemical terms; all we can say is that there is a correspondence.

Different natural sciences can carry out this reduction of qualities to a different extent and need to do so to a different degree. But in no science is this reduction complete. If, as a famous physicist said, the atoms of chemistry are no less real than, for instance, the sun, then we have to assign qualities to them as well. Nevertheless, and this is decisive, they have fewer qualities than those manifold phenomena for the conceptual mastery of which atomic theory has been created. For the accomplishment of theory building in the natural sciences is, according to Rickert, that it can overcome "the disarray of the extensive and intensive manifoldness of the immediately given material." But we can in no way equate these atoms of chemistry, the reality of which the chemist does not doubt, with atoms in a logical sense. When I referred to the atoms of chemistry as having relatively "few qualities," I mean to imply only what atomic theory states, that different combinations and interactions of the same types of atoms may correspond to different qualities. However, the reduction of those qualities which we must still attribute to the chemical atoms has so far had little relevance for science.

The atom theory interests us here only in this one respect and only as an example of the fact that theory building in the natural sciences leads to a reduction in qualities, though this reduction is not complete even in such a methodologically advanced science as chemistry. Psychoanalysis as a natural science of mental life in this respect has chosen a logically related path—that of every explanatory natural science. The theory of psychodynamics, the libido theory and others are the foundations of this approach. A chemist characterizes a body not by enumerating its qualities but by referring to the elements which are its constituent parts and by describing the position of its atoms in relation to each other. In the same way psychoanalysis deals with certain areas of psychic life. It characterizes conditions and changes of conditions not in terms of the corresponding experiential qualities but in terms of the cooperation or opposition of (relatively) elementary psychic operations whose dynamics are known to us.

Based on our knowledge of certain psychic mechanisms, we can say that if specific psychic tendencies oppose each other in a specific way, there is a high probability that this will lead to a mental condition which is characterized by the quality "anxiety experience." Other constellations create an energic-dynamic change which corresponds to the experience "compulsion," and so forth. In these examples, too, we cannot "explain" the fact that a specific interaction of psychic processes which is characterized in terms of its dynamics corresponds to this particular quality and no other. This fact remains essentially "unexplainable," and we can merely note their coincidence.

If psychoanalysis states that the ego ideal does not permit certain objectionable drive tendencies to appear undisguised in the dream, and by means of the dream censorship forces them to be distorted in a characteristic way, then the essential aspect of the concept "ego ideal" in the psychoanalytic sense is neither the "ego" *experience* nor the "ideal" *experience,* though the term "ego ideal" is of course derived from certain connections with phenomenological givens. The essential aspect is rather the characterization of the ego ideal in terms of topographic, dynamic, and energic factors; that is to say, in terms of its conscious or unconscious aspects, its effects (in our example, the censorship), and its position in the psychic economy. This reminds us of the state of affairs, e.g., in chemistry. For the chemist the essential factor characterizing the substance called chlorine is not the fact that its color is green (*chloros* means yellow-green) but its atomic weight and atomic number—that is to say, conceptual elements which are far removed from what is actually observable. Thus, in this field, the characteristics which are most essential for science are not always represented in the scientific terms;[2] it is of course true that in the sciences dealing with the physical world this circumstance is of little relevance because they have for a long time taken it for granted that scientific concepts are at a distance from observable facts.

Matters are different in psychology, because in this field the necessary distinction between experiencing (*erleben*) and knowing (*erkennen*)—a basic premise of the psychoanalytic method—is by no means systematically made or generally accepted. In finding names for its concepts, psychoanalysis could avail itself (with few exceptions) of no other designations than those which are derived from the world of mental qualities. For this reason psychoanalysis has repeatedly encountered misunderstandings which arise from the fact that its generalizing concepts, which are characterized by few qualities, are erroneously taken for descriptions of phenomenologically observable facts. This error has resulted in the criticism that psychoanalysis views facts in a onesided and arbitrary manner. On the other hand, the frequency of this misunderstanding justifies the construction of a specifically analytic terminology.

The type of concept building which, as we have pointed out, is essential in analytic work must by its very nature break up the unity of experience. Yet this way of concept formation permits not only a better classification but also a more exact prediction of psychic processes. The "onesidedness" for which psychoanalytic explanations are criticized over and over again would constitute a methodological defect only if the task of psychoanalysis were the description of psychological conditions in all the diversity in which they are experienced; but since its goal is that of the natural sciences, namely, the setting up of rules or laws, the decisive factor is not just the recording of subjective experience but the explanatory value of its hypotheses. Still another frequently occurring misunderstanding should be countered here: psychoanalytic theory in no way aims at somehow "deriving"—in certain circumstances—the experience "anxiety" from the experience "sexual excitement"; nor do modes of experience having a "high complexity" such as artistic and religious experiences

2 One could also think of the word "electricity"—amber (*electrum*).

originate from a combination of "simple" mental *qualities;* neither can these "simple" *qualities* be pieced together like a mosaic. If "reduction of qualities" were to be understood in this sense, one would indeed be faced by an impossible undertaking. This cannot be the task of natural science, nor is it a task of the physical sciences. Who would try to "derive" the red color of mercuric oxide by "piecing together" the metallic color of mercury and the colorlessness of oxygen?

Let us further exemplify the foregoing discussion. With an admirable sensitivity for mental subtleties and meaningful connections, Scheler (1923) attempted to classify and to distinguish from each other the manifold forms of sympathy and love. Such work is also significant for psychoanalysis, because it confronts us with an abundance of phenomenologically neat descriptions of psychic qualities which today certainly could not yet be completely classified by our method and which offer many stimulating ideas that are also highly pertinent to specific psychoanalytic problems. But psychoanalysis must adopt an entirely different position with regard to Scheler's attempt to give an *explanation,* indeed, a theory of the facts of love and sexual life. I will touch upon precisely this aspect of Scheler's work because it promises to throw some light on the only position that mental qualities can have in a scientific theory of psychic processes. For Scheler, empathy [*Nachfühlen*] and sympathy [*Mitfühlen*] are primary phenomena, in other words, manifestations which cannot genetically be derived from simpler factors. He then attempts to refute genetic theories by demonstrating that the phenomenological findings do not correspond with the content of their concepts (which were after all formulated, at least in so far as these theories are systematic, to *explain* psychic processes). Thus Scheler is bound to reject a genetic theory of sympathy which rests its explanation, e.g., on the mechanism of identification, because it is not always possible to demonstrate in the phenomenologically observable facts a *feeling* of being at one with the individual with whom sympathy is felt. From my previous discussion it must be obvious that a natural science approach—and hence also a psychoanalytic approach—to mental phenomena cannot be committed to this type of reasoning. The psychoanalytic concept of identification refers to a specific energic and dynamic relationship to ego and superego on the one hand, and to the object on the other, but not to the *experience* of feeling at one, though this experience may be responsible for the name of this particular relationship without, however, being connected with it in a simple way.

The same argument is valid also with respect to Scheler's objections to the attempts to "derive," or to "make understandable," the phenomena of spiritual [*geistig*] and sentimental [*seelisch*] love from sexual love. If it were really the intent of the psychoanalytic theory of sexuality to derive the *experience* of "holy" love from voluptuous sensations, this attempt would in principle be doomed to failure. In this respect we fully agree with Scheler. The fact, though, is that Freud never made such an attempt, which would definitely be beyond the boundaries of psychoanalysis.

For psychoanalysis, the world of qualities is a premise: analysis does not derive the ways of experiencing from each other, but notes their appearance in the course of development and specifies their lawful relationship to psychic states which are characterized in terms of their dynamic and energic aspects. Neither can there be any question of deriving qualities from these natural science concepts of psychic situations. The concept of libido on which psychoanalysis also bases its explanation of those phenomena which Scheler calls "holy" and "soulful" love takes its name, it is true, from the manifest feature characterized by the quality of voluptuous sensations. However, these voluptuous sensations, and in general the *qualities* which we subsume under sexual *experience* in a narrower sense, are not essential characteristics of the psychoanalytic *explanatory* concept of libido. Psychoanalysis has consistently avoided the mistake of many psychological schools, which view the phenomenologically particularly vivid and striking experiences as being the most essential ones also from the causal-dynamic point of view. The circumstance that some have not recognized the natural science character of psychoanalytic theories on the one hand, and the fact that concepts formed with a view toward establishing rules and laws have been erroneously thought to refer to phenomenological data on the other —these facts are responsible for such pronouncements as the recent one by Spranger (1924): that psychoanalytic psychology is "primitive." With respect to this objection psychoanalysis is fully justified in pointing out that a natural science theory of psychic life does not have the task of portraying psychic qualities.

As a matter of fact, in so far as one is dealing with complex psychic phenomena, psychoanalysis represents a first step in that direction. The explanatory concepts available to psychoanalysis are in part not yet sharply defined and are still in the process of being revised; its empirical foundation still requires, but is also amenable to, much supplementation. For these reasons it is obvious that analysis today is by no means in a position to order and classify, in the sense outlined above, the entire range of psychic qualities.

The personality structure of an adult is different from that of a child, a European's is different from that of an Australian Negro, and finally neuroses and psychoses change it in characteristic ways. Different personality structures—and we naturally include among them what we know as individual differences—lead to the emergence of different qualities. In both ontogeny and phylogeny new qualities emerge. In this respect the analogy with chemical theory building which to some extent we have previously followed breaks down. This fact, however, does not in principle constitute an obstacle to a natural science approach to psychic phenomena. On the contrary, since psychoanalytic theory explicitly emphasizes the interdependent relationship of certain ego and superego structures to consciousness, perception, and of reality,the emergence of new qualities does not present any fundamentally new difficulties to theory building in psychoanalysis.[3]

At this point we should stop to consider an objection that could be made to our reflections and therefore also to the logical basis of psychoanalysis, and for this reason deserves our attention. We have more than once compared the methods of psychoanalysis with the methods of those natural sciences whose subject matter is the physical world. Indeed, we have taken it for granted that the most general viewpoints of theory construction are the same in both. That is to say, we made the assumptions that a natural science approach to psychic phenomena is possible and that in the field of psychology the relationship of generalizing concepts to qualities does not fundamentally differ from that obtaining in the natural sciences dealing with the physical world. These premises are debatable.

3 For a discussion of value problems, see Hartmann (1928, 1960).

We must therefore try to clarify, at least in its essential aspects, the difference between physical and mental in terms of the theory of science. Our question therefore is: in which way does the uniqueness of psychic material determine its scientific conceptualization? We expect the methods of a particular science to be extensively shaped by its subject matter, but does this dependent relationship also obtain with regard to the most general basic principles of its working method? This question, in so far as it is pertinent to the contrast between the physical and the mental, has actually been answered in the affirmative by many philosophers and psychologists who frequently based their arguments—and I select the most important one—on an idea according to which physical and psychic phenomena differ fundamentally with respect to the ways in which they are "given" [*Gegebenheitsweise*] to the observer. They reason that only the psychic is immediately given, whereas the physical world is given only mediately and requires mediation by psychic processes. All actuality is content of conscious processes; conscious processes, however, are psychic processes. In rejecting this reasoning, we follow Rickert's (1921a, p. 95ff.) critique which convincingly demonstrated that this philosophical viewpoint confuses the psychological subject with that of the epistemology. I want especially to underscore this critique because only through it can we find the methodological path to a natural science of psychic life. I fully agree with Rickert's proof that the dictum, "psychology deals with 'subjects,' whereas natural science deals with 'objects,' " in so far as this dictum is correct, has no bearing upon the logical structure of concept formation. Psychology too must turn everything it investigates into "object"; and "the objectivized psychological world can in its entirety be investigated in the same way as the objectivized physical world; moreover, it can be subjected at least to a generalizing 'description' in the manner of the natural sciences and eventually also to a natural science 'explanation' which applies to all psychic realities and hence must proceed by means of generalizations" (Rickert, 1921a, p. 113). A natural science concept formation, however, is for psychology not only possible but indispensable "as soon as psychology strives to attain knowledge of the entire psychic life in all its incalculable manifold aspects" (Rickert, 1921a, p. 128).

The essence of a natural science concept formation has been

characterized as a tendency toward the general. Generalization over-comes the "extensive and intensive multiplicity of the heterogeneous continuum" in which form all actuality is given. In the natural sciences, however, the purely classificatory treatment of material is regarded strictly as preparatory work and "whenever some elements are subsumed under a concept, we presuppose that these elements either are directly related to each other in terms of a necessary natural law—i.e., that their relationship must be generally valid—or that their grouping will at least permit the first steps toward such concepts as will express a relationship necessary in terms of a natural law"(p. 145). "Observing" ["*Anschauen*"] or "experiencing" is certainly not yet recognizing; observation is necessary in so far as it must be the starting point of conceptualization. Scientific man "therefore takes leave from observation as soon as he has succeeded in being explicitly clear about, and fully aware of, the precise relationship of his observations to the content of his concepts" (p. 32). It is true that concepts pertaining to observable phenomena play an important role in all natural sciences; yet each such concept carries with it, in principle, the possibility of further resolution.

While the various natural sciences differ with respect to the degree to which they have reached this stage of theory building, I am only concerned with demonstrating that the same logical goal is valid for all of them. As a consequence, psychoanalysis, if it is a natural science of mental life, must of necessity take that position with regard to the problem of qualities which we have attributed to it. That its concepts must be at a distance from the experienced givens of psychic life is therefore determined by its logical character as a natural science. For "an unmediated and observable means of obtaining knowledge is as little possible in psychology as it is in the physical sciences" (Rickert, 1921a, p. 117). That which has been attained by knowledge can never preserve the full immediacy of what has been experienced. It is a great misconception under which so many psychologists labor that this statement does not apply to the psychic sphere. Münsterberg (1900, p. 332) stated: "The psychological will, which still wills, is no better than the physical atom, which is still fragrant and glimmers." This methodological insight is valid for every generalizing psychology, though of course not to the same degree for every conceivable psychology.

In this respect there can be only differences of degrees among the various schools of natural science psychology—that is, degrees of generality of concept construction and, in connection with it, the extent to which qualities have been eliminated from these concepts. Several concepts of experimental psychology such as the concept of "determining tendencies" can on a logical basis be placed on exactly the same level as those of psychoanalysis. However, if the objections that are made to natural science psychology as such have been leveled with particular sharpness against psychoanalysis, we have to seek one of the reasons for this in the following circumstances: unlike experimental psychology which concerns itself only with the peripheral facts of mental life, psychoanalysis strives to comprehend in the manner of natural science the very core of personality—in other words, that sphere which one believes not only to experience most immediately but also in general to comprehend immediately. Besides the scientific objections, there are purely emotional ones which are aroused by this kind of description of the central problems of personality.

Naturally, the concepts of psychoanalysis are not all equally far removed from experiential qualities. How far their reduction must go in an individual case depends on the partial goal of an investigation. In dealing with specific problems such as, to give an example, in the explanation of a parapraxis, it is not necessary to invoke the most general theory of mental life. On the other hand, if the problem concerns the interrelation of the instinctual drives, or the drive dependence of "higher" psychic functions, then the solution of these problems requires the construction of more general concepts which contain little of what can be immediately experienced.

It has frequently been proposed that the term natural science psychology be reserved for those attempts which establish the dependence of psychic processes on brain physiology, and which transfer the laws governing physiology to the psychic sphere. Such a restriction is misleading, for, as we have seen, a generalizing conceptualization of psychic life is possible and no less "natural" scientific than the conceptualization of the physical world. There are also some schools of psychology that attempt to build a theory of psychic life without crossing the boundaries of conscious psychic processes. It is possible in this way to formulate rules, but at the cost of blocking the way to rules of more general validity.

If we have been able to establish that the most general principles of concept construction and the logical goals are shared by natural science psychology and the generalizing natural sciences dealing with the physical world, then we must immediately add that this common ground extends only to these most general principles. A schematic transposition of physical—or biological—theorizing to the sphere of psychology is bound to be sterile and is in no way being aspired by psychoanalysis. Its theory is not burdened by the far too extensive dependence on physical or chemical analogies which marred the older theories of association psychology. Not only the collection of material but also its conceptual treatment are, as I said before, co-determined by the subject of investigation. The manner in which the subjects are "given" also influences the structure of the theories. Consequently, psychoanalysis is not, as is sometimes assumed, a mechanistic theory of psychic life; its natural science character should not be equated with what one calls "mechanistic." In fact, one might even say that to some extent psychoanalysis came about as a reaction to the all too "mechanistic" viewpoints of older psychologies.

A difficulty which confronts every psychological theory rests in the problem of the quantifiability of psychic life. In everyday life we say that this event gave more pleasure than another, we speak of stronger and weaker passions, and so forth. Furthermore, analytic theory distinguishes quantities of libido and affect intensities, it follows the fate of quantities of cathectic energy, and concepts of stronger or weaker repressions or resistances are familiar in psychoanalytic dynamics. The question, however, is: to what extent can such quantifying conceptualizations be justified? With regard to sensations, one can distinguish between "more" and "less," but not "how much." Most psychologists would agree that one cannot measure the intensity of experience as such. What is measured in such attempts are frequently nothing but the physical accompaniments. It nevertheless is meaningful to speak of "stronger" and "weaker" in relation to psychic phenomena, and psychic structures can be ordered according to their intensity. One can, for instance, using Ach's (1905) method, establish the associative equivalent of determining tendencies; i.e., one establishes that strength of reproduction tendencies which is just overcome by a determining tendency, and since the former are gradated one derives a measure of the latter.

Yet, reproduction tendencies and determining tendencies are concepts of explanatory psychology. What we measure is not the intensity of experiences. The statements psychoanalysis makes about quantitative relations are to be understood exactly in the sense of this example. We derive a measure of the dynamics of psychic processes from the repression of a specific instinctual tendency, the overcoming of a particular resistance, the extent of reactive changes. Furthermore, the time factor plays a role in energy considerations. In this way the surprising persistence of the effects of repressed instinctual tendencies has become a datum of fundamental significance for the analytic theory of the distribution of quantities of psychic energies—that is to say, for a quantifying view.

We see that psychoanalysis cannot dispense with quantitative concepts; on the other hand, since we can in no case speak of exact measurements, the quantitative factor cannot in our theory construction attain the eminent role it plays in the natural sciences dealing with the physical world. The latter, in the final analysis, achieve the conceptual mastery of qualities by means of "reducing" them to quantitative relationships, the existence of which can be proved only by virtue of the fact that matter occupies space. This path is in principle closed off to all psychological sciences. Yet even in psychology quantitative *temporal* differences can be measured.[4]

With regard to theory building, there exists a second complication which does not affect all subdisciplines of psychology in an equal measure but especially affects those which, like psychoanalysis, investigate highly complex psychic processes. This difficulty is due to the fact that in these branches of psychology one has not many possibilities of intentionally setting up psychic situations which are sufficiently comparable. But this would be the premise of "planned experimentation." Consequently psychoanalysis must rely on other inductive methods of proof. The relative incompleteness of its inductions is not the result of some methodological flaws; rather it is an inherent difficulty of every psychology which, in dealing with

4 We cannot here investigate to what extent it is possible, in principle, to base a general theory of psychic life on differences in duration and rhythm, but Rickert (1921a, p. 125) rightly noted that such an attempt would not be logically untenable.

higher mental processes, reaches beyond what is experimentally demonstrable. But science cannot ignore the most important processes of mental life merely because experimentation cannot yet accommodate them.

On the other hand, some specific problems in psychoanalysis are amenable to experimentation. We can consider the theory of symbolization to have been experimentally proven, and experimental procedures are in principle applicable to several specific problems. An approach related to experimentation consists in observing the presence or absence of reactions to certain typical, repetitive experiences and, more important, in noting those changes which have been brought about, in a specific way and at a particular time, by a deliberate intervention of the analyst; for example, when the analyst gives or withholds interpretations; when he encourages or inhibits the formation of transference; or when in general he utilizes some of the manifold possibilities for intervention which the analytic situation puts at his disposal. One might object that this kind of "experiment" already *presupposes* certain assumptions. We would reply that experimentation without "assumptions" is not possible, though one can of course experiment without being aware of them. However, in this I would see a danger to scientific investigation, but not in the conscious use of hypotheses on the basis of which the experiment has been designed (cf. Poincaré, 1906).

Unlike most natural science psychologies, psychoanalysis does not disregard the *content* of psychic phenomena and does not restrict its investigations to the formal aspects of psychic processes. It studies specific instinctual drives with respect to their specific aims and objects, and their developments with respect to their direction toward specific objects. This does not limit the character of psychoanalysis as a natural science; a generalizing psychology which does justice also to the content of psychic phenomena is certainly possible.

The psychoanalytic method is further characterized by its genetic procedure. It is a developmental psychology in the sense that it makes psychic ontogenesis the subject of causal-psychological investigation. Consequently, the psychoanalytic classification of mental structures is often genetic rather than purely descriptive. That is to say, from the angle of classification, psychoanalysis considers as belonging together such psychic processes which in the developmental history of an individual have a common origin. In this area, too, the classification is based on the assumption of lawful connections between the elements. This assumption is founded on the laws of psychic development which psychoanalytic developmental psychology has established.

With this type of genetic classification the analytic method comes close to certain biological approaches, which also regard a common developmental history as the criterion of the relatedness of species. In both approaches, phenomenologically completely different structures may turn out to be very close to each other when viewed from a causal-genetic perspective. In a general way, psychoanalysis examines mental life with respect to its biological functions; its concept of the person is constructed much like the biological concept of the organism. "Fitting together," usefulness, and unity are not restricted to the psychological person, they beckon to us wherever we look at the living world.

The source materials of analytic investigation are individual mental states of individual persons. But we have repeatedly called attention to the fact that essentially psychoanalysis does not just aim at comprehending in an immediate way the subjective experience of a specific person at a specific moment. Its primary goal is rather to establish general laws which go beyond the individual in whom the existence of such laws was discovered, and which can claim to be valid for other human beings.

We must be quite clear about the fact, however, that even the most complete knowledge of lawfulness in nature cannot by itself tell us anything about a single specific event. Such a statement presupposes a further requirement, namely, an exhaustive knowledge of the factualities of the preceding "world events" (and not only of the cross-section of the psychic event, because, as I shall further elaborate, psychic causality cannot be viewed as "closed"). The validity of every law refers to specific givens which cannot themselves be derived from that law; the essence of lawfulness rests precisely in the fact that quite generally and independent of a specific moment in time, a given set of circumstances must have certain consequences. Or, in Windelband's (1915) words, "the totality of what is given in time appears in irreducible independence from the general law according to which it nevertheless proceeds." Here knowledge based on natural law comes up against a boundary which *no* science of lawfulness can cross.

The generalizing conceptualizations have created a gulf between what is immediately given and the natural science conceptual system. We now must ask whether and to what extent it is possible to bridge this gulf and to find the way back from the conceptual systems to their concrete individual point of departure. We ask whether it is possible with the help of a natural science approach to comprehend individuality. The answer to this question, apart from its general importance for the methodology of the natural sciences, is of special interest to us because in the field of psychology more than in any other field of the sciences, we accord far greater significance to the differences between the individual objects investigated.

We must agree with Rickert (1921a) who says that natural science can "never completely, in conceptual terms, account for all the peculiarities of the object examined because their number is limitless in any heterogeneous continuum." On the other hand, there can be no doubt that characteristics which distinguish one object from another can be conceived of as points at which planes of lawfulness intersect. We must therefore say: no natural science approach can ever fully comprehend individuality because *each* object has an infinite number of diverse characteristics; there always remains an unsolved residue. This residue, however—and this is the most important for us—is reduced to the extent to which a natural science succeeds in penetrating its subject matter by means of laws. This is to say: the extent to which the individual factor can be solved depends upon the stage of development a science has reached.

Rickert's statement "that every *real* tone, like every *real* person, exists but once, that every single *real* sense quality differs from all the others" is basically correct. But it is equally true that on the basis of physical considerations, one can succeed in producing a tone whose qualitative characteristics can to a certain degree be calculated. That qualities themselves cannot be derived from natural science concepts has been repeatedly emphasized; on the other hand, they can be coordinated with certain processes operating according to laws, and this fact makes it possible for us in some measure to predict their occurrence. This circumstance in turn yields a further result: it becomes possible to construct a world of qualities on the one hand on the basis of our knowledge of the laws of nature and on the other by coordinating their points of intersection with the qualities. The degree of diversity of such constructions has in principle no limit—unless it is the qualitative individuality in the strict sense, that is to say, the infinite qualitative diversity inherent in everything that is real.

If we say that psychoanalysis can in principle attain knowledge about the individual, this statement can mean only that it is possible to comprehend what is "relatively" individual in terms of points at which planes of lawfulness intersect and we must concede that we here face an unending task. It is a different matter, however, if we use the psychoanalytic method to determine characteristics which actually differentiate specific individuals from each other—that is, specific distinguishing characteristics and *not* the infinite qualitative diversity which of necessity and in principle makes each individual different from all others. Actual differences between two persons or between two psychic states are thus to be conceived of as points at which psychological laws intersect, and in this sense psychoanalysis can certainly make contributions to the knowledge of the individual.

Psychoanalysis is not a closed system. Its theories are still undergoing lively changes; it "gropes its way forward by the help of experience, is always incomplete and always ready to correct or modify its theories" (Freud, 1923, p. 253). Nevertheless it has come closer to the logical ideal of a natural science of complex mental life than other psychological disciplines. In the course of its development psychoanalysis has repeatedly discarded some of its hypotheses when it turned out that experience did not confirm them. So did it happen with the initial conception of the etiology of the psychoneuroses. Other assumptions of analytic theory, for example, those concerning repression, resistance, infantile sexuality, symbolism, and many others, have increasingly been supported by experience and today psychoanalysis can compete with every other psychological theory as far as the security of its foundation is concerned.

As we have already said, psychoanalysis is a biologically oriented psychology. As a matter of fact, it regards itself as a branch of biological investigation; this does not mean that psychoanalysis transcends the subject matter of psychology in the direction of organic biology, rather it views the psychic as a biologically active agent. It would be unreasonable to expect the laws of analysis to attain that degree of validity which the physical-chemical sciences have reached. Psychoanalysis has often been condemned for proceeding too quickly with its generalizations; we can counter this argument by pointing out that the inductive basis of psychoanalytic theories is much broader than one tends to assume if he has not himself worked with the analytic method. And the task of scientific theory is not only to summarize what is known but to stimulate the raising of new questions. These new questions, in turn, open up fresh perspectives on already established findings. What Rickert said about psychology in general applies in an even higher degree to psychoanalysis precisely because it has made the most inaccessible area of mental life the subject matter of its investigative work: "In so young a science 'çaution' may not always be the mother of the wisdom which leads to valuable hypotheses." Natural science not only may but must construct hypotheses, and one misjudges the function of hypotheses if one demands that science proceed in a strict sense without premises. As Poincaré correctly noted, almost every science, regardless of the stage of its development, has been criticized for prematurely making generalizations; there is no justification for adopting this argument in a critique of the fruitfulness of such generalizations. Even the most exact sciences go beyond what is immediately given when they reason by analogy or make constructions, for "the scientist should categorize; science is made out of facts as a house is built out of stones. Yet, a mere accumulation of facts is no more a science than a pile of stones is a house" (Poincaré, 1906, p. 143).

## II

### PSYCHOANALYSIS AND THE CULTURAL SCIENCES

Psychoanalysis endeavors by scientific means to comprehend the depths of mental life that have previously been inaccessible. It is therefore understandable that, being a new method, psychoanalysis eventually had to make the attempt to test the extent of its applicability to the cultural sciences. Having clarified its most general logical foundation, we shall now try to obtain a picture of the scope and significance of this science. To this end we ask what position psychoanalysis occupies, or can occupy, among all the sciences; or, to put it more precisely, whether and to what extent we are justified in expecting that its application to the cultural sciences will result in an enrichment of these disciplines. I shall retain the term "cultural sciences" because it is most commonly used, though some objections to this terminology deserve serious consideration. My decision to adhere to this nomenclature should therefore not be regarded as my taking a stand for or against those principles of classification on the basis of which one can delimit the sciences from each other, for I am here not primarily concerned with the classification of sciences in terms of their subject matter and method. But we are interested in determining the nature of the relationships which psychoanalysis, by virtue of its subject matter and method, has with regard to the other sciences; whether these are incidental relationships or whether this new science occupies the place of an ancillary science which is absolutely necessary for the other sciences. In other words, the question is whether psychoanalysis occupies a "topologically central" position.

We must first attempt to get a general idea of the role which a generalizing psychology can play in the field of the cultural sciences. In this way we shall gain various points of view which in their broadest formulation can be significant for psychoanalysis as well, because, as we have seen, the ultimate logical goals of psychoanalysis are the same as those of every psychology operating as a natural science. Psychoanalysis and experimental psychology complement each other on a large spectrum; and while their results may occasionally contradict each other, there is no contradiction in the most general foundations of their working methods.

The science of history—which can serve as the representative of the cultural sciences here—has as its subject matter changes in time that happen but once. The developments are not repeatable in their entirety, and therefore cannot be accounted for by generalizing conceptualizations, unless one is inclined to apply to history those biological concepts which were gained from the comparative study of the evolution of animal species. We do not have to decide to what extent such a transfer is possible or can be fruitful; in any event, it is clear that this would lead us far afield from what today we are accustomed to call historical investigation, and this question therefore need not be considered here. On the other hand, the generalizing method can be used with respect to sectors of historical development. Historians have made efforts in this direction; since methodology does not prescribe how individual sciences *should* proceed but merely determines how they *actually* proceed, such attempts will have to be recognized as historical investigations. The science of history has in this way established the existence of certain rules[5] governing historical events; these rules, to the extent to which their elements are mental in nature, must be regarded as *hypotheses* of generalizing psychology. On the other hand, we must realize that in establishing such rules the historians work with *prescientific* concepts and their results require confirmation or refutation by scientifically purified psychological knowledge. Here we have an area which in principle constitutes a point of departure for the fruitful application of the concepts of generalizing psychology to history.

The realm in which the generalizing method can be applied, however, extends much further. Here we come back to our previous deliberations concerning the possibility of accounting for individual events in terms of generally valid statements. The infinite diversity of each actual occurrence, its individuality in the strictest sense, can never be completely accounted for by generalizing conceptualizations. This infinite diversity is also not reflected in the concepts of history. Beyond this, however, the subject matter of history as a whole is, as we have seen, "individual" as a development occurring but once. Furthermore, the material of history is "individual" in so far as it deals with the representation of psychic events, in the sense that even before we start conceptualizing, the differences between individual human beings seem to us to have far greater significance than the differences between various animals belonging to the same species or the differences between various characteristics of lifeless matter. History has this "individuality" of material in common with psychology. Finally, the working method of history is "individual" in so far as it cannot be disputed that its research trend is more concerned than the natural sciences with depicting unique events. This does not mean that an event occurring but once is of no interest to the natural sciences. While there is a large group of instances in

5 In this area we cannot speak of laws in the strict sense of the term.

which our interest, focused on the unique event as the point at which planes of lawfulness intersect, is basically generalizing (here belongs, e.g., the anticipated confirmation or invalidation of physical theories through a single astronomical event), there is another group in which the interest of the natural scientist (that of the physician in the unusual case, of the psychologist in extraordinary mental phenomena) would be incompletely understood if one construed it to be an exclusive interest in the general significance of the single case. But these are exceptions; the dominant research concern in the natural sciences is unquestionably with the general; that of the historian, with the special case. That much must be conceded even if one does not share Rickert's view according to which the essence of conceptualizations in history is a value-oriented individualizing procedure. The historian can certainly use the history of the Roman empire to compare the Roman emperor as a type with other types of rulers and on this basis reach some general conclusions concerning the special psychological and behavioral characteristics of powerful leaders; but even in such cases the historian will have to focus on the special events to a far greater extent than any investigator in the natural sciences would.

The psychological differences of actual individual beings are, as we already noted, to a large extent understandable if we conceive of them as points at which planes of lawfulness intersect. This is as true for human "characteristics" as it is, to choose an example from pathology, for neurotic symptoms: neurotic symptoms can perfectly well be explained on the basis of what we know about the laws of neurosis. What we comprehend here is something that differentiates, though it is not individuality in the strict sense; we determine something that is relatively individual—relative because what has been determined *actually* can be found only in that one individual, though we must admit that it may also occur in others. Of course, from a purely historical viewpoint unique actions are of interest even though the possibility exists that they might "in the same way" be carried out by other individuals; that is to say, if they can also be conceived of as points at which generally valid concepts intersect. Hence we maintain that a specific action carried out by a specific person can in this sense become the subject of psychological investigation using the methods of the natural sciences.

The picture which a historian draws of a historical personage
is a reconstruction. He forms this picture on the basis of documents
left by that person and others, from actions recorded in writing or
by word of mouth, and his knowledge of the cultural, economic,
and social conditions of the period. If it is not to remain patchwork
but present a well-rounded picture of the whole personality, the
historian must resort to a psychological scheme because only that
will allow him to integrate the individual traits into a coherent
whole. His work is comparable to that of the archaeologist who is
faced with the task of reconstructing a statue from a few fragments;
only in this case the schemata which must complete the restoration
also consist of artistic norms (in addition to the viewpoints derived
from the history of art). Such normative schemata can become significant also for the historian, e.g., when he attempts to re-create
the logical content of a philosophical system from various details
that have been handed down to us. An understanding of logical
meaningful connections is also indispensable for the comprehension
of historical personages because in many respects psychological
processes become manifest in them; but alongside these schemata,
those which we have previously called the psychological schemata
gain in importance.

The historian, in so far as he is concerned with the portrayal of
historical personages, must work on the premise that certain mental
attitudes are *possible;* he must make judgments about the psychological significance which specific experiences had for specific persons; he must know to which character types one can ascribe specific
actions and which mental structures do not permit such an attribution; in short, he must have knowledge of a standard scale which
enables him to make a decision about which mental conditions,
characteristics, and actions are compatible in that unit we call personality and which exclude each other. The historian takes this
standard scale from prescientific psychology, from what we call his
"capacity to empathize." This ability to empathize enables him to
"understand" historical personages; and it has often been claimed
that this is the real goal of historical psychology. While we shall still
have to deal with the concept of "understanding," I want to make a
few remarks here. Simmel (1921) said: "Whether the psychological
links which the historian applies to events are objectively true, i.e.,

whether they really portray the mental activities of acting persons, would have no interest for us if we could not *understand* the course and content of these processes." This statement requires the following qualification: we assume that there always exists a multiplicity of possible understandable connections; among these, the historian can accept only those which he can assume to have the greatest probability of *actually* operating in a given case; in making this decision he will also utilize his knowledge of the historical period, of the social and other conditions existing at the time, and of the particular individual. The decisions involved here also concern, at least in part, questions of causal connections, i.e., psychological constructions having the character of *hypotheses*. Consequently a generalizing psychology can attain a position of basic importance in the significant area of historical research concerned with portraying historical persons; in this field too it can serve as a control for a prescientific representation of mental connections.

Whatever one may think of the "essential nature" of historical development, it is certain that the historian is *directly* and predominantly concerned with actions of human beings. With this reason as well as those detailed above, we have clearly established that it is possible for history to make fruitful and extensive use of psychological theory as an auxiliary science. I shall come back to the reason why this possibility was, actually had to be, of little consequence to history until now. First I explicitly want to make the following clarification: the insight into the significant role that psychological theory is basically capable of playing should definitely not lead to a view according to which the task of historical research would be applied psychology. No psychology can ever become the "basic science" of history—in addition to some obvious reasons, because not all mental phenomena are of equal importance to history; on the contrary, its logical foundation requires history to make a choice—regardless of whether it seeks "the criterion of selecting the most essential" in the concept of "culture" (Rickert, 1921b) or in the concept of the "historically effective" (Meyer, 1902). We are particularly interested in the question whether the cultural sciences can find a conceptual foundation in the investigation of mental life for the following reason: based on his conviction that psychology does indeed have a dominant position among the cultural sciences and with due regard for the discrepancies which exist in this area with respect to potential and actual significance, Dilthey (1924) could make the demand for a new psychology which he characterized as "descriptive" and which he distinguished from the constructing "explanatory" psychologies. The difficulties inherent in the application of explanatory psychology to the cultural sciences can, he thought, be solved only by a descriptive and dissecting psychology; that is to say, by "describing those components and connections which occur regularly in the psychic life of every fully matured individual; by describing how they are conjoined in a single connection which is neither superimposed nor inferred but directly experienced." The significance of this psychology was thought to reside in the fact "that each connection it utilizes can unequivocally be verified by inner perception and that each such connection can be demonstrated to be a component of a more global connection which has not been deduced but is immediately given." This attempt of Dilthey's has for the first time[6] illuminated the basic problem of psychological methodology which is inherent in the question whether psychological understanding is possible and significant, a question which is of fundamental importance for psychoanalysis as well.[7]

For the time being, therefore, we shall disregard the possibility of a descriptive psychology in Dilthey's sense. But we are immediately faced with a further question: can the task set for psychology by its application to the cultural sciences really and in principle not be solved by any explanatory psychology? In this context we can point to our earlier deliberations on the basis of which we established that it is possible for a generalizing psychology to meet these demands, though the historian has in fact not yet found it essential to evaluate his material in terms of the findings of this psychology. Hence we maintain, in contrast to Dilthey, that what prevented this psychology from attaining significance for the cultural sciences was not its character as a science of lawfulness but rather the stage of development it had reached, its methodological immaturity, and its preoccupation with a limited area of facts.

That the historian to a large extent no longer expects his science

---

6 We may here pass over the "forerunners" of this theory.

7 For a discussion of this question, see Hartmann (1927b).

to be furthered by the findings of explanatory psychology is due less to methodological considerations than to the actual uselessness of experimental psychology for his purposes. "Thought psychology" is, according to a statement by one of its founders, "so bold as to wish to shed light on legal proceedings and the secrets of artistic creativity, the venerable problem of free will and the most intimate processes of religious conversion and ecstasy, the practice of education and teaching, and on the premises of all sciences" (Külpe, 1912); I would further concede that the newer experimental psychology, quite apart from the enormous fruitfulness of its methods and results in the *psychological* area, has, by applying itself to the phenomena of "higher" psychic life, also made advances in terms of its possible application to the cultural sciences; nevertheless even its "boldest" applications do not yield those psychological insights which the historian needs in his scientific work, or do so only to a very limited degree.

Psychoanalysis is in a much more favorable position with respect to the demands of the cultural sciences. Its investigative interest concerns those parts of the human personality which, though most deeply hidden, are also the most central ones—that "innermost" area from which the totality of psychic phenomena can be comprehended in their mutual interdependence and position with respect to each other. In the concept of "instinctual drive" psychoanalysis has found the key which enabled it to subject the "full and entire nature of man" to scientific investigation. Here I cannot detail the foundations for this statement[8] but will merely assert that the analysis of instinctual and affective processes and the tracing out of positions and drive-determined attitudes through all their vicissitudes and their tiniest arteries branching out into memory, perception, and action were, for psychoanalysis, the means of ordering complex mental phenomena. Only after this key had been found was it possible to uncover connections linking an individual's experiences most widely separated in time, to examine the mutual dependence of character and experience, and conceptually to approach that oneness which contains within it the most varied psychic manifestations of a person.

[8] For a discussion of the reasons for this statement, see Hartmann (1927a, Chapter 8; and 1948).

In contrast to other schools of psychology which investigated partial aspects of psychic life and disregarded the structure of the whole, psychoanalysis always placed special emphasis on the unity of personality; and it is not without interest that psychoanalysis, by virtue of concepts grounded logically in the natural sciences, has contributed infinitely more to the insight into this unity than those schools which proclaimed the unity of the whole person as their program but were entirely unable to conceptualize it. Also in the area of pathology, psychoanalysis views a symptom not merely as a sign of disease processes foreign to the personality but rather traces the formation of a symptom to its most minute personal roots. But whenever psychology deals with wholes, scientific research must still investigate the boundaries of these wholes and their structure. In doing so, it must distinguish sharply between experiental units and explanatory elements.

Psychoanalysis investigates the psychological organism in terms of its typical modes of operations and the nature of their mutual interdependence; this preparatory work permits us to recognize how these processes combine themselves into functional units and form a structure; based on this knowledge of mental connections we can construct the picture of human personality. The psychoanalytic concept of personality is similar to biological concepts. What other authors have referred to as the "total personality" frequently has different implications; this type of "totality" can never be represented in psychoanalytic concepts. For psychoanalysis, too, unity of person is not the sum of psychic formations added to each other— this would not be unity. In psychoanalysis unity means the interrelationship of mental activities in terms of *psychic functions*. On the other hand, all types of unity derived from viewing psychic phenomena in terms of value criteria are beyond the purview of psychoanalysis. Psychoanalysis is concerned with *real* mental life, not with the unity of "meaning-connections."

We have asserted that psychoanalysis is oriented toward establishing the lawfulness of mental processes. This statement must not be misunderstood to mean that even in investigating its material psychoanalysis invariably starts with the formal characteristics of this material to the exclusion of all others. On the contrary, psychoanalysis—unlike the other natural science psychologies—puts the main emphasis primarily on the content of mental phenomena. One of the most essential tenets of psychoanalysis is that in psychology a point of view concerned exclusively with purely formal aspects is bound to remain incomplete and must be supplemented by investigations of the relationship between form and content. Hence, psychoanalysis takes notice not only of the formal characteristics of instinctual drives which Freud (1915) distinguished in terms of motor pressure, aim, object, and source, but also of instinctual vicissitudes which derive from the investment of drives in typical objects; furthermore, these object cathexes are in turn determined by specific characteristics of the concrete object. Psychoanalysis investigates not only man's affectivity per se, but also its relationship on the one hand to the structure of instinctual drives and on the other to the structure of reality and, moreover, what we generally subsume under the term "character." When psychoanalysis scrutinizes thought sequences it is less interested in establishing the nature of the relationship between imagery and thought, regardless of those tendencies which one could define only in terms of their content; the accent is rather on analyzing how specific ideas are determined by specific (frequently unconscious) instinctual tendencies. One more example, this time from psychopathology: the analyst's interest in the psychoses is focused not primarily on the formal elements of the thought disorder but rather on the extent to which thought content can be derived from specific drive tendencies and the extent to which it is possible to establish that certain elements of content determine the formal elements of the disorder.

By now it must certainly be clear that, as I said before, it is completely wrong to label psychoanalysis as a "mechanistic" psychology. On the other hand, the fact that psychoanalysis focuses on mental content does not change its character as a natural science or its ultimate goals in that direction. Even content-characterized psychic processes can be subjected to a generalizing approach. The fact that psychoanalytic psychology is founded on the concept of instinctual drive both facilitates and necessitates its investigation of content.[9]

It has often been assumed that there exists an unbridgeable gap

9 For a detailed discussion of these problems, see Hartmann (1927a, 1948).

between "understanding of other persons" ["*Menschenkenntnis*"][10]
and scientific psychology. This assumption is only partly justified.
The fact that prescientific and scientific concepts cannot be brought
closer to each other is determined not by the nature of these concepts but by the present stage of development of psychology. It cannot be disputed that the majority of politicians, businessmen, physi-
cians (and, for that matter, historians), whose understanding of
people we praise, possess little or only a very superficial knowledge
of scientific psychology; moreover, these persons are scarcely bent on
studying psychology as a means of improving their capacity to judge
and evaluate the intentions and motives of other people. It is equally
true that not every scientist whose field of investigation is psychology
shows a particularly keen understanding of other people in everyday
life. Still, I think that, aided by the concepts of scientific psychology
our knowledge of man can also be increased and perfected in the
area of "understanding of and knowledge about other people." The
theories of psychoanalysis provide for this possibility.

Psychoanalysis made us aware of certain connections, the knowledge of which permits us not only to explain human behavior but,
to a certain degree, even to predict it—human behavior not under
the artificially isolating conditions of the laboratory experiment
but in its living relation to other persons, to professional and sexual
life; psychoanalysis could accomplish this primarily because it recognized the unconscious strivings, the enormous power and pervasive-
ness with which they determine all part aspects of human behavior;
while psychoanalysis made the unconscious strivings accessible to
scientific investigation, they had previously been incorrectly evalu-
ated not only by prescientific but also by preanalytic psychology.
Naturally, the capacity for good everyday understanding of other
people and for work in scientific psychology does not correspond to
the same Anlage. On the other hand, it is commonly assumed that
the capacity to judge and evaluate people in everyday life is wholly
independent of any knowledge of the results of scientific psychology.
It cannot be claimed that this contention, though almost universally

---

[10] There exist no English terms which cover precisely what in German is meant by
*Menschenkenntnis* and *Menschenkenner*. They have been variously translated here as
"understanding of other persons," "practical understanding of and knowledge about
people," "common-sense psychologist," etc.

regarded as correct, is generally valid. True, the study of psycho-analysis will as a rule not turn a bad common-sense psychologist into a good one; but a person having good psychological judgment can, with the help of psychoanalysis, secure, broaden, and correct his insights on a large range.

As the task of creating, filling out, and correcting a system of psychic connections which we call practical understanding of man devolves upon psychoanalysis, the latter may also be trusted to be capable of providing some objective standard as an aid for the cultural sciences. It may also be expected to be capable of occasionally providing an objective standard against which can be tested the truth of those reflections about the nature of man which philosophers have set down. But psychoanalysis cannot provide such standards in all areas to the same degree. It should be obvious, e.g., that philosophical "wisdom," in so far as it contains open or hidden valuations, is not amenable to analytic verification. But it should be equally obvious that value-*oriented actions* of human beings are definitely not beyond the scope of psychoanalytic *investigation*. Finally, it must be emphasized that the criteria of "poetic truth" as we may accept or reject them in characters of a drama or novel differ from the inductively arrived at convictions of the truth of judgments which scientific psychology makes about the reality of psychic connections.

Psychoanalysis is in turn indebted to the writers and philosophers for stimulating reflections and hunches in so far as these may represent hypotheses about possible mental connections. Such hunches about psychic connections are generally considered to have been arrived at by a process and as a result of psychological "intuition." I would agree with this, if intuition is here used to imply no more than a person's ability, through sudden insights, without conscious preparation, and without the aid of the concepts of scientific psychology, to see and single out from among the confusing multitude of psychic peculiarities and details those active forces and connections which can stand the test of empirical verification. One glance at the history of the physical sciences teaches us that this "seeing" of new connections without inductive preparation also plays a role in this area (one might think here of the way in which Robert Mayer arrived at the formulation of the principle of conservation of

energy); but in this field, because of its more advanced methodology, intuitive processes recede into the background and are far
more difficult to detect.

Men possess this psychological aptitude, which, by the way, can
to a certain extent be further developed, in an astonishingly different measure. Many people must simply be called blind to experiential qualities and connections; there are, in contrast, a few in-
genious "psychologists" whose mostly aphoristic pronouncements
disclose a whole world of psychic realities. Every science committed
to investigating the interrelationships of complex psychic phenomena can, in addition to the painstaking work of induction, use
such thoughts as signposts pointing to preliminary psychological constructions, which of course require empirical confirmation. Psychoanalysis can never be exempted from the obligation to use its material
and apply its concepts to the *verification* of such thoughts, no matter
how "convincing" they may be.

This practical understanding of other people and the psychology
of philosophers and writers are closely related to the ability which
the historian needs for his reconstruction of historical personalities.
For this reason the position and potential of psychoanalysis are similar with respect to both areas. Its focus on the core of mental life and
on the content of mental acts, on unconscious processes, and on the
unity of the person permits a fruitful application of its insights also
to those areas of the cultural sciences in which other psychological
methods are bound to fail.

The historian constantly needs to make decisions concerning how
and to what extent certain experiences affected and influenced a
certain type of person. Psychoanalysis enables the historian to make
such judgments on an empirical basis and to free them from the conventional formulae to which the psychology of most historians had
been confined. Within certain limits it is not a utopian undertaking
to study, on the basis of psychoanalysis, the possible attribution of
specific modes of behavior to specific character types and in this way
either to support or to dismiss the exclusively common-sense attribu-
tions of everyday psychology which have passed into most historical
accounts. Psychoanalysis can also make some significant contributions to the field of group psychology where the historian may be
called upon to evaluate the impact of certain events on large masses

of people. Here he can resort primarily to the viewpoints and experiences contained in Freud's study of *Group Psychology and the Analysis of the Ego* (1921). But such psychoanalytic findings can become even more significant for the social scientist, especially of course when he is concerned with the establishment of rules or laws of behavior and with social psychology (see, e.g., the work of Federn, 1919).

The first applications of psychoanalysis to problems of the cultural sciences were in the fields of mythology and religion—more specifically, in what we generally term "the products of fantasy activity," because the characteristic stamp of unconscious mental processes is more apparent in them than it is in reality-adapted actions and thinking. The elaboration which derivatives of instinctual processes generally undergo in the form of secondary rationalization is here less marked. In exploring this particular domain a hypothesis which became fruitful drew an analogy between myths and dream (Freud called myths mankind's secular dreams). In occupying itself with the study of myths, psychoanalysis in turn gained a certain measure of confirmation of some specific analytic theses in so far as even some nonanalytically oriented investigators had pointed to the significance which is to be accorded to incest and castration as "original motives" (psychoanalysis had emphasized their importance in the unconscious mental life of the individual).

Another area to which psychoanalysis has made important contributions is the psychology of the artist.[11] But we must also state that the accomplishments of psychoanalysis in this area, methodologically as well as contentwise, can be regarded as no more than a beginning.

There is one domain which is completely closed to psychoanalysis—that concerned with norms and values. This point can scarcely be emphasized strongly enough. Yet, those mental processes which as facilitating or inhibiting factors lead to the realization of values in the actual mental life of individuals are within the scope of psychoanalytic investigation.

We began our deliberations with the statement that psychoanalysis, in its own field of study where it is not an "applied" science,

11 In addition to Freud (1910), see, e.g., Rank (1912, 1918), Hitschmann (1919), and now Kris (1952), among many others.

investigates individual occurrences with regard to their general validity—in other words, psychoanalysis seeks, via the construction of
generic concepts to which the individual event is subordinated, to
advance to formulations of lawful interconnections of psychic processes. In concluding this chapter we might ask whether psychoanalysis also contains elements which might be called historical in the
sense that they focus our attention especially on events occurring
but once that is to say, whether alongside the methods rooted in the
natural sciences psychoanalysis also uses other working methods. We
have already said that a very considerable amount of psychoanalytic
research deals with the facts of psychic development. One of the
primary interests in psychoanalysis is the temporal sequences in which
the various drive components manifest themselves and establish
definite relations with other psychic processes. This circumstance,
however, must not mislead us to assuming that the unique development as such is deemed to be of significance; rather psychoanalysis
strives to establish the *laws* of development; moreover, its genetic
concepts were formed in a way that they can claim to be generally
valid. Hence there is no reason not to call this developmental psychology a natural science.

In summary, we can say: psychoanalysis by itself can never solve
the problems which are set for the cultural sciences, but as an ancillary science many opportunities are open to it which so far have
scarcely been tapped.

## BIBLIOGRAPHY

Ach, N. (1905), *Über die Willenstätigkeit und das Denken.* Göttingen: Vandenhoeck
    und Ruprecht.
Baade, W. (1916), Über psychologische Darstellungsexperimente. *Arch. ges. Psychol.,* 35.
—— (1918). Selbstbeobachtung und Introvokation. Z. *Psychol.,* 79.
Dilthey, W. (1924), Ideen über eine beschreibende und zergliedernde Psychologie.
    *Gesammelte Schriften,* 5. Leipzig: Teubner.
Federn, P. (1919), *Zur Psychologie der Revolution: Die vaterlose Gesellschaft.* Vienna:
    Anzengruber-Verlag.
Freud, S. (1910), Leonardo da Vinci and a Memory of His Childhood. *Standard Edition,*
    11:59-137. London: Hogarth Press, 1957.
—— (1915), Instincts and Their Vicissitudes. *Standard Edition,* 14:109-140. London:
    Hogarth Press, 1957.
—— (1921), Group Psychology and the Analysis of the Ego. *Standard Edition,* 18:67-
    143. London: Hogarth Press, 1955.
—— (1923), Two Encyclopaedia Articles. (A) Psycho-Analysis. *Standard Edition,* 18:235-
    254. London: Hogarth Press, 1955.
Hartmann, H. (1927a), *Die Grundlagen der Psychoanalyse.* Leipzig: Thieme.

—— (1927b), Understanding and Explanation. In: *Essays on Ego Psychology*. New York: International Universities Press, 1964.
—— (1928), Psychoanalyse und Wertproblem. *Imago*, 14.
—— (1948), Comments on the Psychoanalytic Theory of Instinctual Drives. In: *Essays on Ego Psychology*. New York: International Universities Press, 1964.
—— (1958), Comments on the Scientific Aspects of Psychoanalysis. In: *Essays on Ego Psychology*. New York: International Universities Press, 1964.
—— (1959), Psychoanalysis as a Scientific Theory. In: *Essays on Ego Psychology*. New York: International Universities Press, 1964.
—— (1960), *Psychoanalysis and Moral Values*. New York: International Universities Press.
—— (1964), *Essays on Ego Psychology*. New York: International Universities Press.
Hitschmann, E. (1919), *Gottfried Keller*. Vienna: Internationaler psychoanalytischer Verlag.
Husserl, E. (1921), *Logische Untersuchungen*. Halle: Niemeyer.
Jaensch, E. (1920), *Einige allgemeine Fragen der Psychologie und Biologie des Denkens*. Leipzig: Barth.
Kris, E. (1952), *Psychoanalytic Explorations in Art*. New York: International Universities Press.
Külpe, O. (1912), Über die moderne Psychologie des Denkens. *Int. Mschr. Wiss.*, 6:1069-1110; also in: *Vorlesungen über Psychologie*. Leipzig: Hirzel, 2nd ed., 1922.
Meyer, E. (1902), Zur Theorie und Methodik der Geschichte. *Geschichtsphilosophische Untersuchungen*. Halle: Niemeyer.
Münsterberg, H. (1900), *Grundzüge der Psychologie*. Leipzig: Barth, 1910.
Poincaré, H. (1906), *Wissenschaft und Hypothese*. Leipzig: Teubner, 1914.
Rank, O. (1912), *Das Inzest-Motiv in Dichtung und Sage*. Leipzig: Deuticke.
—— (1918), *Der Künstler: Ansätze zu einer Sexualpsychologie*. Vienna: Heller, 2nd & 3rd ed.
Rickert, H. (1921a), *Die Grenzen der naturwissenschaftlichen Begriffsbildung*. Tübingen: Mohr, 3rd & 4th ed.
—— (1921b), *Kulturwissenschaft und Naturwissenschaft*. Tübingen: Mohr, 4th & 5th ed.
Scheler, M. F. (1923), *Wesen und Formen der Sympathie*. Bonn: F. Cohen.
Simmel, G. (1921), *Die Probleme der Geschichtsphilosophie*. Leipzig: Duncker & Humblot, 4th ed., p. 35.
Spranger, E. (1924), *Psychologie des Jugendalters*. Leipzig: Quelle & Meyer.
Windelband, W. (1915), Geschichte und Naturwissenschaft. *Präludien*, 2. Tübingen: Mohr.

# REMARKS ON GENESIS, STRUCTURALIZATION, AND FUNCTIONING OF THE MIND

JEANNE LAMPL-DE GROOT, M.D. (Amsterdam)

In psychoanalysis the genetic approach to mental phenomena has proved its intrinsic value for the understanding of the human mind. For the explanation of adult behavior, normal as well as pathological, the tracing back to its origins in early childhood is a necessary procedure. However, the genetic approach is only part of the picture. Without taking into account the maturational processes, including the development of the different functions, the structuralization and the differentiation of the mind, the influence of the environment and the inner and outer conflicts which give rise to reactive and defensive processes, the explanation remains one-sided and incomplete.

I am aware of the fact that these statements are self-evident and generally accepted. The reason I mention them here lies in the fact that though they are common knowledge, they nevertheless are often neglected. I am referring to those authors who do not clearly distinguish between genetic determinants (to borrow a term of Hartmann's) and developmental end products of mental processes, especially in connection with the structuralization into id, ego, and superego with their different functions. This lack of distinction may lead to oversimplifications in two opposite directions. On the one hand, functions and activities of an adult's ego organization are sometimes described as if they were merely a defense against "oral," or "anal," or "phallic" tendencies, which may be genetic determinants, but certainly do not cover the whole picture. This lack of a clear distinction between function and genesis is repeatedly stressed and criticized by Hartmann (1955), by Hartmann and Loewenstein (1962), etc. On the other hand, processes occurring in infancy are sometimes described in terms of an adult's (pathological) behavior

(Melanie Klein, e.g.). Some authors speak, for instance, of an infant's
or toddler's "schizophrenic ego split." It is quite clear that an infant's ego organization does not yet exist as a system and therefore
cannot yet be "split." This kind of confusion is mentioned by me in
connection with the antedating of the system superego in the infant's
first months of life (1939). Thus I am in agreement with Hartmann
that it is necessary to distinguish clearly between genesis and function and I think all psychoanalysts should take his warning to heart.

However, a number of questions arise in view of this general
statement. I shall try to enter into a few of them. What happens to
the different mental functions in the course of the maturation and
development into adulthood? For the sake of clarification it seems
preferable to examine the substructures of the mind separately although we are quite aware of the fact that development occurs in a
constant mutual interplay.

We begin by examining the id, the area of the instinctual drives.
Freud pointed out at an early stage of psychoanalysis that the
id functions according to the pleasure principle. The drives strive
for instinctual gratification. This basic id function remains in existence during an individual's whole life. However, the shape of the
drives changes in the course of the development. In infancy we observe the *Teiltriebe*, the partial oral, anal, and phallic drives, which
gradually develop into the mature genital drive. I need not go
further into this part of psychoanalytic theory which is well known
and affirmed by numerous observations.

We next turn to the ego. Nowadays we prefer to speak of the
"system" ego as an organization of a number of functions. In the
earliest stages of psychoanalytic theory formation Freud used the
term "ego" in different, not always clearly defined, ways. However,
in *The Ego and the Id* (1923) he definitely describes the ego as a
structured part of the mind, as a "coherent organization of mental
processes." It comprises consciousness, it controls partial processes,
it is master of motility, and it is the agency which makes use of
repression (and defense) in cases where instinctual strivings cannot be discharged or are not allowed to become conscious. The ego
is that part of the mind which has direct contact with the outer
world and acts according to the reality principle. Its basic functions
are mediation between inner and outer world (passive and active),

adaptation, and, finally, synthetization (or harmonization) of the various demands from inside and from the environment. The mature ego has developed a large number of singular functions, which may participate in the achievements of the basic functions of adaptation and integration. With Hartmann we distinguish between primary autonomous ego functions, e.g., perception, memory, reality testing, judging, etc., and other ego functions, which develop as reaction to or defense against instinctual tendencies and environmental demands. The latter group of functions may obtain a "secondary" autonomy in case they are able to solve the conflicts with the id and the milieu and to enter into the "sphere free of conflict." However, both the primary autonomous and the secondary autonomous functions may be drawn into the sphere of conflict at a later stage and in pathological development the ego may not be able to get back its ability to master the conflicts, at least not without impairment of the ego organization itself.

We now return to our question: what happens to the different functions (and here we speak of ego functions) in the course of life? Ego functions are not yet present in the newborn child, though we assume with Freud and Hartmann that the individual potentialities out of which they are to develop are present in the archaic inheritance; but they come into being only after birth and under the influence of experience and learning processes. The infant is also in need of support of his mother's love and care in order to develop them in a favorable way. An organization of the ego functions into the system ego finds place only in a much later stage. In order to explain the great and obvious differences between the adult's and the little child's ego activities Hartmann has introduced the new concept of "change of function," a very valuable concept indeed. However, I think we have to investigate to which ego functions this concept applies. In examining those ego functions which emerge in the conflictual sphere, that means, e.g., in a conflict between instinctual tendencies and the ego we have to accept that a change of function takes place if the ego succeeds in mastering the id striving that cannot be discharged directly. I shall give two examples out of many that could be described: (1) During the anal phase of instinctual development the little child has to learn to abandon the pleasure of messing and soiling himself, his clothes and his surroundings. The child's ego may reach this achievement by developing reaction formations of cleanliness, orderliness, and economy (the well-known "anal triad"). These reaction formations may gradually become character traits, automatisms. Later on these character traits, though originated as a defense against id strivings, may change their function and, for instance, enter into hygienic or economic activities which serve quite different purposes of a personal as well as of a social kind. They may have their share in processes of adaptation and organization and sublimated activities. (2) Compassion can genetically be traced back to a reaction formation to strong sadistic impulses. As a character trait in later childhood and adulthood it does not function any longer as a defense, but it may serve social adaptation, integration, and contact with fellow men. At least, this state of affairs applies to "normal" development, where the ego's original defensive function may gain secondary autonomy. In pathological cases the conflict fails to be solved and the ego has constantly to ward off the pressing instinctual demands. To summarize: change of function in defensive processes can be observed in normal development; in pathology the defensive function persists.

In regard to the primary autonomous ego functions I think we observe the reverse situation. Perception and reality testing, for instance, continue to exist throughout life, though their contents may be enlarged by learning processes. More knowledge about the real facts of life may widen the scope of the fields covered; the functional side of the processes, however, need not be changed in "healthy" development. On the other hand, in pathological cases the autonomous functions may be drawn into the conflictual sphere with the consequence of a change of function, e.g., in being employed for defensive purposes. This is most clearly observed with psychotics. A case in point is a patient suffering from a jealousy delusion. During a walk with his wife, he perceives an acquaintance greeting them and for a few seconds looking at his wife, whom he had never met before. This perception is instantly drawn into the patient's delusional system; it is used for accusing his wife of infidelity and functions as a warding off of his own impulses to commit adultery. The patient's reality testing is distorted in a way similar to his perception and both have changed their original function of learning about the real facts of life into the defensive function against unacceptable instinctual tendencies.

Regarding the "basic" (or general) ego functions of mediating between the inner world and environmental influence, of adaptation and integration, I think we meet with equal conditions. In "normal," harmonious development those basic functions persist essentially unchanged throughout life, though they become more consolidated and cover a larger field of knowledge through learning. Under pathological conditions the functions may be changed, probably mainly to be used in warding-off processes.

If this train of thought should prove to be correct, we may summarize as follows: under "normal" conditions a change of ego functions finds place in the area of secondary autonomy, whereas the general, basic functions and the primary autonomous singular functions keep to their original aims. Under pathological conditions, however, every ego function is exposed to change by being drawn into the pathological process. It is decisive for the form and the severity of the mental illness how many and which functions share this fate. Here emerges the necessity for detailed, clinical research, which I cannot pursue at this time. A single tentative remark suggests that a contribution to the theme of "choice of neurosis" (*Neurosenwahl*) is to be expected from these considerations. In all mental disturbances the basic functions of adaptation and integration are affected, though in psychoses they are much more severely affected and lead to a more or less complete withdrawal from the outer world, whereas in neurotic disorders a certain contact with the object world is maintained.

Could it be that one important factor in these differences is to be found in the fact that in neuroses *secondary autonomous* ego functions lose their autonomy on re-entering the sphere of conflict and are subject to change, whereas in psychotic disorders the *primary autonomous* ego functions are impaired from the very beginning of the illness and therefore lose their original function? Several authors have described this process as occurring on the basis of an irregular, faulty, or interrupted development of ego functions in very early childhood and a regression to these points of arrest.

This seems to be the place to recall to mind an early paper of Freud's (1911) in which he describes how the pleasure principle, which originally governs the mental life, is gradually replaced by the reality principle as a consequence of disappointments and frustrations. At that time there did not yet exist a workable psychoanalytic theory of ego development. Nowadays we know that the substitution of the reality principle for the pleasure principle occurs in connection with the growing organization of ego functions, a process which under normal conditions is stimulated by frustrations. We should not forget that in the same paper Freud states that this substitution does not abolish the pleasure principle. In fact, Freud says, the reality principle is its safeguard: an immediate, but in its consequences uncertain pleasure experience is renounced in order to gain a later, but certain one acquired along new paths. We may add: not only along new paths, but also with new means, new contents, and last, but not least, with a new mode of satisfaction. Though ways, means, contents, and modes of satisfaction change during the course of development, the original tendency to gain some kind of gratification is retained. Maybe we could assume that no mental action whatsoever is taken without the (often unconscious) expectation of acquiring some kind of gratification or of avoiding unpleasure. It is hardly necessary to recall that under the pressure of overpowering forces in the outside world it may happen that neither goal is attainable to the slightest degree. On the other hand, even neurotic suffering, which originates in the person's own mental life, contains some mode of satisfaction. In a paper (in press) on "Superego, Ego-Ideal and Masochistic Fantasies" I give an example of "pleasurable" suffering in the shape of grandeur fantasies of being an exceptional and very great martyr.

This idea brings us to our next point, the examination of the third mental substructure: the superego and ego ideal system. On a previous occasion (1962) I tried to investigate the precursors (or, to use Hartmann's term, the genetic determinants) of both conscience and ideals. I preferred to examine them separately because their original functions are opposite to each other, the conscience (superego in a narrower sense) coming into being as a restricting and prohibiting agency, whereas the ego ideal emerges as an agency providing satisfaction through hallucinating, magical wishful thinking, and fantasies of omnipotence. I also drew attention to the fact that in the course of development, that is, at the time of the passing of

the oedipus complex, both agencies merge together in one substructure of the mind, the superego in a wider sense. This close contact
necessarily provokes a mutual influence so that ideals may become
"oughts" (you "ought" to live up to a certain ideal, instead of you
"wish" to live up to it), and prohibitions may become ideals, e.g.,
complete obedience to the demands of an authority may be idealized. However, they show a compulsive character and are used as a
defense against anxiety-provoking impulses. As far as they limit the
person's inner freedom to choose his own ideals and restrictions, we
are entitled to see them as having entered the realm of pathology.

   In connection with the merging into one mental substructure of
ideals and prohibitions during the passing of the oedipus complex
Hartmann and Loewenstein (1962) prefer to speak of the superego
system *tout court* and to distinguish between the idealizing and the
self-criticizing functions of the superego. I agree with the authors,
that their conceptualization is simpler, more in line with the concept of the ego, being an organization of functions and therefore
more appropriate than the one, used by me so far, which conceived
of the ego ideal and the restricting superego as two sides of the
"superego in a wider sense."

   In another context Hartmann and Loewenstein propose to apply
the concept of "change of function," used in ego psychology, to the
system superego as well. However, the authors do not indicate which
functions are subject to such a change and under which conditions
the changes take place. I shall try to make some remarks to this point
in following a path similar to my previous one regarding ego functions. As a matter of fact it is quite obvious that a number of a "normal" adult's ideals are very different from the little child's grandeur
and omnipotence fantasies and the idealization of his parental
images, though we should not overlook the fact that much of the
original magic and wishful thinking is still present in the conscious
or unconscious mind of a "healthy" adult. Hartmann and Loewenstein also mention this fact.

   However, I think we are entitled to put the question: *what* has
changed in the more mature ideal functioning? Obviously the *contents* have changed, under the influence of the total personality as
it increasingly takes reality factors into account. I also suggest that
the mode of satisfaction provided by living up to the ideals has

changed. Gratification drawn from thinking, from intellectual activities, from scientific and artistic, in short from sublimated performances, is clearly different from direct instinctual satisfaction as well as from the narcissistic gratification provided by imagining oneself omnipotent.

But has the original *function* of procuring some kind of satisfaction really changed? I do not see that this is the case, at least not in harmonious development. Hartmann and Loewenstein (1962) describe as an example of a "change of function" in the superego system the more mature ego ideals "striving after perfection," "a direction-giving function, which is relatively independent of the objects and relatively independent also of the instinctual precursors." I quite agree with the authors as to the description of the possible shape of an adult's ego ideal. However, is "striving after perfection" not a search for satisfaction? And, after all, as long as a person believes more or less that "perfection" can really be achieved by any human being, is it so far away from magic, wishful thinking?

My notion is that the *basic* function of ideal formation—the aiming at narcissistic gratification and the attempt to guide the ego's activities in that direction—has not been changed in principle. The little child also, though not very successfully, tries to realize his wishes of being as powerful and perfect as he imagines his parents to be. What has undergone a transformation are the form and contents of the ideals and the paths along which the person attempts to gain satisfaction. The transformation, I think, has become possible in connection with the development of ego functions through learning and experience in contact with the outside world, in short, under the impact of the reality principle. Among the many special ego qualities which are of importance for this transformation process is the ego's capacity for neutralizing drive energy, which then may allow the superego system to make use of more or less neutralized energy. This point is more extensively elaborated by Hartmann and Loewenstein.

Under pathological conditions, however, e.g., in the above-described case where ideals have a compulsive character, the function may have changed from a pleasure-providing into a restricting one. In a similar way the "oughts" and "ought-nots" of the restricting superego which have become ideals may give satisfaction, but both processes, in adopting each other's original functions, have caused a distortion of the system superego and cannot be looked at as a harmonious developmental outcome.

Therefore I propose the following summary: if functions of the superego system are drawn into the sphere of conflicts for which the personality is unable to find a "sound" solution, pathological conditions have entered the picture with the consequence that a change of superego functions may take place. In harmonious development the *original* functions persist, though their *contents* and the *modes* of both gratification and unavoidable renunciation may be subject to transformations. This train of thought seems to be in line with Freud's statement that the superego is closer to the id than is the ego. This is valid not only as to the dynamics and economics in mental life, which are clearly described by Hartmann and Loewenstein in connection with aggression; it seems to apply also to the functions of *pleasure-seeking* and *renouncing* under the pressure of object relations. The superego has no direct contact with the real factors in the environment. It is only the ego that through its different functions, i.e., perception, action, reality testing, etc., can react upon the outer world, and learns to store knowledge about all kinds of reality factors. And only through the mediation of the ego organization is the superego indirectly influenced by the environment, as is the id.

We here touch upon a field in need of thorough research, namely, on the influence which the mutual *interplay* between id, ego organization, and superego system exercises upon the various functions of the substructures of the mind as well as upon their contents and the modes of satisfaction. Many investigations in this field have already been carried out by Freud and others in a general way. However, more detailed research is still needed to gain a deeper insight into the manifold conditions which lead to the development of a harmonious personality, respectively to pathological disturbances. I do not intend to go into this topic at this time. I am quite aware of the fact that the propositions brought forward here are of a tentative nature and in need of either confirmation or substitution by more appropriate ones.

BIBLIOGRAPHY

Freud, S. (1911), Formulations on the Two Principles of Mental Functioning. *Standard Edition,* 12. London: Hogarth Press, 1958.
—— (1923), The Ego and the Id. *Standard Edition,* 19. London: Hogarth Press, 1961.
Hartmann, H. (1955), Notes on the Theory of Sublimation. *This Annual,* 10.
—— (1960), *Psychoanalysis and Moral Values.* New York: International Universities Press.
—— & Loewenstein, R. M. (1962), Notes on the Superego. *This Annual,* 17.
Lampl-de Groot, J. (1939), Considerations on Methodology in Relation to the Psychology of Small Children. *Int. J. Psa.,* 20.
—— (1962), Ego Ideal and Superego. *This Annual,* 17.
—— (in press), Superego, Ego-Ideal and Masochistic Fantasies.

# SOME HYPOTHESES REGARDING THE SIGNIFICANCE OF INDIVIDUAL DIFFERENCES AT BIRTH FOR LATER DEVELOPMENT

ANNELIESE F. KORNER, PH.D. (San Francisco)

In the last twenty years an increasing number of investigators have become interested in research with infants. This interest has sprung from two different concerns. One group of investigators has tried to explore the earliest environmental impact on the child's development. Under this rubric are the numerous contributions on the effect of differences in mothering, of early mother-child separation and institutionalization on infant development (see, for example, A. Freud and Burlingham, 1944; Spitz, 1945; Brody, 1956; Rheingold, 1956; Bowlby, 1960; Provence and Ritvo, 1961; Provence and Lipton, 1962; and many of the recent contributions in this Annual). Another group of investigators has become increasingly interested in the primary endowment with which infants are born. In one of his last contributions, "Analysis Terminable and Interminable," Freud (1937) stated his conviction that "each individual ego is endowed from the beginning with its own peculiar dispositions and tendencies." Hartmann (1950) expanded on this, linking individual differences in the primary ego apparatuses to later choice of defense and by implication to choice of illness. Hartmann introduced the hypothesis that there are individual differences at birth in "state of adaptedness" (1939) and in the "core of differentiation between the ego and the id" (1950). Margaret Fries and Woolf (1953), in their observations of what they termed "congenital activity types," were among the first investigators who tried to capture cer-

From the Mt. Zion Psychiatric Clinic, San Francisco, Calif. Now at the Department of Psychiatry, Stanford University School of Medicine, Palo Alto, Calif.

This investigation was supported by Public Health Service Research Grant M-5980 (A) from the National Institute of Mental Health.

tain variations in primary ego endowment and to relate them to later personality development. More recently, Meili (1957) has studied what he called *"Reizverarbeitung"* in infants ("mechanisms of working through stimuli") which he used to delineate the earliest characterological differences among individuals. Escalona and Heider (1959) studied individual differences in sensory responsiveness among infants. Alpert, Neubauer, and Weil (1956) reported on children with unusual variations in drive endowment. Bridger and Reiser (1959) and Lipton, Steinschneider, and Richmond (1960), among others, have investigated individual variations in autonomic reactivity among neonates.

## SIGNIFICANCE OF PRIMARY EGO AND DRIVE ENDOWMENT FOR LATER DEVELOPMENT

A systematic exploration of this relationship may clarify many problems which now confront the fields of child development, pedagogy, diagnosis, and treatment, and may aid in the development of individualized methods of child rearing. In a very special way, primary endowment variations may influence even environmental experiences, for what an infant presents to his mother will determine to some extent her response. Benjamin (1961) described the reciprocal relationship between primary endowment and experience in another way. As he put it: "Not only can innate differences in drive organization, in ego functions and in maturational rates determine different responses to objectively identical experiences, but they can also help determine what experiences will be experienced and how they will be perceived." Earlier, Hartmann (1950) made a related point, offering the hypothesis that the infant's congenital equipment will from birth on influence the nature of his self-experience and the attitudes of his developing ego, and that both will be preserved in his system of memory traces. Thus it is likely that genetic differences in the biological sense may help create genetic differences in the psychoanalytic sense. It is equally plausible that differences in primary endowment may throw a unique cast on the manner in which a child will experience and master each developmental step.

My interest in this problem originated from the difficulties one encounters in differential diagnosis. Psychological tests (and diagnostic interviews), like all cross-sectional observations, are ill-equipped to differentiate between differences in origin of any particular difficulty and to reconstruct their genetic development. As I have stated elsewhere (1962a), test results largely reflect end products. Yet, for an accurate diagnosis, prognosis, and possibly for an appropriate choice of treatment methods it is extremely important to know the origin of a particular difficulty. For these purposes, we need to differentiate between the products of defensive elaborations of unresolved maturational tasks posed by the various psychosexual stages and the manifestations of basic ego and drive variations. This differentiation is very difficult to make since the end products of both developments often look very much alike, particularly when the innate ego and drive variations are reinforced through secondary neurotic elaborations. For example, there is a diagnostic and prognostic difference if a child's hyperactivity is an expression of what Fries calls his "congenital activity type" or if it is a function of a frantic fear of passivity and of castration anxiety, or whether one is superimposed on the other. There is also a diagnostic and prognostic difference between the child who, from birth, has high stimulus barriers which limit his sensory experiences and the child who, for reasons of fear of curiosity originating from experiences in the oedipal phase, has a reduced capacity to see, to hear, and to take in. Theoretically, it is easy to see how the first child might be predisposed to experience the onslaught of the oedipal phase as potentially traumatic, simply because he is already handicapped in integrating stimuli of any variety and intensity. He may therefore neurotically elaborate what was a problem long before the advent of a neurotic conflict. Our therapeutic methods deal primarily with the products of neurotic conflict and the neurotic elaborations of ego deviations rather than with the modifications of basic ego characteristics. Often treatment alters the former, and what seem to be residuals are expressions of the latter. Possibly, by better understanding the influence which primary endowment factors and deviations exert on the timing, the intensity and the mode of expression of conflict, we shall develop different and more effective treatment methods for dealing with these residuals.

The learning problems, in their diagnostic variety, clearly demonstrate this admixture of primary ego deviations and neurotic conflict as each contributes in varying degrees to the difficulty. We can readily identify the consequences of conflict on the ego's development. While the primary endowment factors may originally have constituted a specific predisposition to the choice of conflict, their recognition must frequently await the successful resolution of that conflict. Through diagnostic testing, for example, it is not difficult to observe the imprint of psychosexual fixations on perceptual style and, by implication, on modes of thought. It is much harder to detect the nonconflictual factors which may have predisposed the child to these fixations. In more concrete terms, when we talk about stimuli being retained, taken in, digested, warded off, diffused, or ejected, we conceive of perceiving as partaking in what Erikson (1950) calls "organ modes." The preponderant use of any of these modes suggests that the perceptual and cognitive processes are colored by psychosexual fixations. When, after resolution of the conflicts pertinent to the fixations, the previous perceptual and cognitive styles persist, the theoretical question arises whether these structures are of a primary or secondary autonomous order (Hartmann, 1939, 1952). Certainly, from a developmental point of view it is conceivable that the quality and mode of an infant's way of perceiving and experiencing may influence the course of his psychosexual development and may predispose him to certain psychosexual fixations. There is confirmation of this hypothesis in some of Benjamin's longitudinal observations (1959). For example, he described an infant of six months as retentive and as "holding on" in his behavior. He accurately predicted that this child would develop anal retentiveness during the period of bowel training. In discussing some of his other cases, Benjamin pointed out that this early tendency is not a sufficient condition for anal retentiveness, but rather a highly contributory one.

## An Approach to the Study of the Influence of Primary Endowment Factors on Later Development

The logical beginning for an investigation of the reciprocal relationship between the primary ego and drive variations and their influence on later development is the study, as soon after birth as possible, of an infant's modes of dealing with internal and external

stimuli. Such an assessment may give clues about individual variations in the "original state of adaptedness" and the "core of differentiation between the ego and the id" in Hartmann's sense (1939,
1950). This kind of evaluation may also tap the earliest core of the
infant's affective and cognitive developmental potential and may
disclose the preconditions for both.

Many longitudinal studies reflect how methodologically difficult
it is to find a bridge between neonatal and later behavior. This is
really not surprising in view of the fact that development proceeds
toward an ever-increasing complexity and differentiation with constantly changing behavioral contents which obscure continuities. To
overcome this difficulty the variables to be studied should reflect the
formal characteristics of behavior rather than the continuously
changing content. Thus, it is the study of the *style* of development
rather than of the developmental process itself which may provide
the continuities in behavior for which we are searching.

With these stipulations in mind I wish to propose certain neonatal variables to be studied before the infant has much opportunity
to accommodate to, or identify with, parental modes of stimulus
dosage. All these variables involve the neonate's responses to internal
and external stimuli. They all involve behavioral manifestations
which may become part of later developmental acquisitions and may
thus reflect individual style. Furthermore, all the variables are derived from observations which have already been made by others,
albeit for different purposes. This implies that methods for this
type of observation already exist.

What follows are descriptions of the variables and statements
regarding the hypothetical directions in which these variables may
find expression in later development. The methods designed to obtain data on the variables are described elsewhere (Korner, 1963).
Nevertheless, it will be possible to get a glimpse of the methods to
be used from the description of the variables and from reference to
the work of others.

*The Variables*

1. *Frequency and length of periods of alert inactivity: an index
of availability to external stimuli.* Peter H. Wolff (1959) noted, in
the first five days of life, periods of alert inactivity in which the

infant's eyes are wide open and appear to focus. There are individual differences in the length and frequency of these periods in a twenty-four-hour interval as well as in the infants' capacity for visual and auditory pursuit movements. In full-term, normally delivered babies in whom the effects of anesthesia and medication have worn off, such individual differences may reflect relative degrees of autonomy from the pressures of internal stimuli. As such they may reflect a greater or lesser need for a stimulus barrier or *Reizschutz*. Wolff offers the hypothesis that the state of alert inactivity may be a precondition for a later capacity to pay attention and to concentrate. Assessing these periods at birth may thus give a base line of an enduring ego variable.

2. *Singular or global versus multiple response to external stimuli.* Auditory stimulation experiments of my own (1962b) and of others have shown that some babies respond with a larger repertoire of reactions, others with single responses. Still others respond globally with their whole bodies. Hypothetically, it is conceivable that the neonatal characteristics expressed in this variable may find expression in subsequent ego qualities. They may, for example, favor later adoption of certain cognitive control principles and certain kinds of defenses. Thus, singular and global responsiveness may be a sensorimotor antecedent to later "leveling" and to repressive tendencies. This variable may also relate to later diversification of ego mechanisms and to qualitative aspects of the synthetic functions of the ego.

3. *Response to multiple or competing external stimuli.* Individual variations in this variable have been noted during ophthalmological examinations on neonates. In this examination the physician looks at the eyegrounds by shining a light into the baby's eye after the nurse restrains him and offers her finger with a sterile nipple as a pacifier. Some babies suck more strenuously when the eye examination begins, others stop completely. A modification of this technique can be used to test a baby's response to competing external stimuli. Hypothetically, this variable, like the previous one, may tap predispositions to later defense choice. This variable may relate to later tendencies toward motor discharge or displacement behavior aimed at tension reduction; it may foreshadow the need of

warding-off mechanisms or propensities toward flooding of the ego apparatuses in the face of massive stimulation.

4. *Influence of internal state on behavior, particularly sensory responsiveness.* Peter H. Wolff devised an experiment which very clearly demonstrates the relative strength of response to external and internal stimuli. He elicited smiles and visual pursuit in response to the voice during the first minute of feeding on the bottle in four-week-old infants. Babies probably vary in this autonomy from internal state. In the immediate postnatal period the relative strength of internal and external stimuli can be inferred from the baby's response to external stimuli while under various degrees of hunger tension and during various states of arousal. Sensory thresholds vary greatly with deep sleep, irregular sleep, drowsing, alert inactivity, waking activity, and crying.[1] They probably also vary with hunger, thirst, fatigue, and discomfort. These variations in threshold due to internal state have been a major impediment in determining the sensory sensitivity of infants. Bergman and Escalona (1949) first pointed to the importance of unusual sensitivity as an etiological factor in the development of major psychopathology. Ever since that time investigators have been trying to assess variations in sensitivity fo the various sensory modalities among infants. Invariably, the problem of state at the time of stimulation was an insurmountable technical obstacle to the determination of thresholds.[2] After struggling with this difficulty in the course of sensory stimulation experiments (Korner, 1962b), it occurred to me that instead of battling this problem, I should study it. It is assumed that the degree to which an infant is subject to influence of internal state has biochemical, endocrinological, and neurophysiological roots, and may thus be an expression of constitutional individuality. Thus degrees of state-boundness may be an important variable to be studied in its own right.

Hypothetically, one may expect a negative correlation between this variable and variable 1: the more state-bound the infant, the less available he might be to external stimuli. In time this may affect the maturational rates of a host of developmental acquisitions.

[1] Peter Wolff (1961) has given elaborate descriptive criteria for differentiation of these states of arousal.

[2] See Escalona's discussion of the problem of state (1962).

For example, will the state-bound baby smile later or less frequently than the baby who is more available to external stimulation? Will the onset and resolution of stranger anxiety be delayed? Benjamin (1959) noted that stranger anxiety occurs with the maturation of the perceptual apparatuses which allow the baby to differentiate mother from nonmother. He further noted, as had Katherine Wolf, that babies who are highly responsive to visual stimuli experience stranger and separation anxiety earlier and more severely. Will the state-bound baby be more protected against the experience of "out of sight, out of mind"? Will such babies be less apt to acquire transitional objects, depending perhaps less on tactile and visual reassurance than do babies who rely heavily on these modalities for purposes of tension reduction? Furthermore, will the state-bound baby be delayed in learning to consider himself dependent on laws external to himself which would explain to him his mother's appearances and disappearances? Will he be delayed in gaining an internal representation of the mother which is essential in the acquisition of object constancy and the resolution of separation anxiety? All these hypotheses can be tested by using Piaget's (1936) techniques which reveal clearly when renunciation of omnipotent thought and object constancy are achieved.

5. *Distinctness of state.* Some babies demonstrate more clearly than others when they are hungry or sleepy. Some pass from one state of arousal to another without spending much time in transitional, indeterminate states; others convey a much greater indistictness of internal state. Hypothetically, this quality of distinctness of internal state may influence the development of such ego functions as the capacity to communicate, anticipate, and discriminate. Babies whose need states are clear-cut and predictable can convey their needs more readily to their caretakers than babies who are not. They probably also can develop internal sets of expectations earlier than those infants who are unpredictable and indistinct in their experience of various internal states. Indistinctness of state may delay discrimination between external and internal reality and may predispose to later regression in this discrimination. Are these the babies who later are more prone to develop fears about going to sleep? Also, does distinctness of state facilitate a greater awareness and expression of needs and a clearer distinction between likes and dislikes?

6. *Zone reliance.* Drive tension may originate from internal stimuli other than hunger. Psychoanalytic theory postulates that there are individual differences in the strength and direction of instinctual drive endowment. Already at birth one can observe individual differences in the babies' mouthing activities. Some babies mouth much more than others irrespective of hunger. Erections are common among baby boys; their incidence may differ too. Some of the spontaneous discharges occurring during deep sleep also use the erogenous zones as a channel. Peter H. Wolff (1964), in a systematic study of this phenomenon, noted that during deep sleep spontaneous discharges occur without the benefit of an external stimulus. The most common of these periodic discharges is the startle. He observed that as soon as the startle ceased it was supplanted by other discharges, some of which involved the erogenous zones (e.g., erections, mouthing, reflex smile). Wolff found that individual differences exist in the choice of discharge channels. Hypothetically, this choice may reflect a zone preference which may predispose to greater difficulties in resolving certain phase-specific conflicts and possibly to psychosexual fixations.

7. *Mode reliance.* Another approach to the problem of individual differences in instinctual drive organization is through observation of the earliest manifestations of Erikson's "organ modes" (1950). This concept involves anatomically determined, inborn mechanisms of particular body zones for the discharge of drive tension. Observations of neonates show that there are individual differences in the quality of mouthing; some are primarily sucking or tonguing, others are chewing. Some infants are spitters, others droolers, still others hardly ever spit. Some are vigorous suckers, others are more passive. In Erikson's terms, the infant's mouthing may primarily be incorporative, retentive, eliminative, or intrusive in character. Hypothetically, the question arises whether early preferential mode reliance reflects a lasting and distinctive drive quality which may find expression in later developments. To name a few: will early mode reliance be transferred to later psychosexual stages? Will mode fixation influence character development in the directions outlined by Erikson in his "eight stages of man"? Does early organ-mode reliance favor later manifestations of organ-mode estrangement? The first step in this development may be observable in what Peiper

(1956) calls *"Ausbreitungsreaktion"* ("spread reaction"). In this reaction the modes become generalized as motor patterns for other body zones (e.g., the baby listens, his mouth also opens as do his eyes; or a baby sucks on the bottle and his hand moves rhythmically as if sucking also). Much later one can study organ-mode estrangement in its effects on areas of mental functioning. As mentioned above, perceptual style may retain the organ-specific characteristics of early preferential modes (Korner, 1962a).

8. *Dedifferentiation of behavior.* Within a few days after birth the neonate shows variations in the differentiation of behavior. For example, Peter H. Wolff (1964) noted that, up to a point, hunger tension improves hand-mouth coordination, but with hunger beyond a certain point coordination breaks down. He gauged hand-mouth coordination through the ratio of hand-mouth to hand-face contacts under varying intensities of hunger. Similar variations in differentiation of behavior can be noted in the ratio of smooth versus diffuse motility. Quite likely, individual differences exist in these ratios and in the point in time when one type of activity changes to the other. This implies that under hunger tension, between two feedings, babies vary in the time and the degree to which they become vulnerable to dedifferentiation of behavior. Hypothetically, these indices of dedifferentiation of behavior may be the earliest manifestations of vulnerability to regression, a variable which is considered a very important and lasting component of ego functioning.

9. *Self-consistency.* Auditory stimulation experiments (Korner, 1962b) revealed that some infants responded very predictably, and others did not. It will be of interest to examine the behavior of the neonate in all the previous variables from the point of view of self-consistency and inconsistency. One may find some babies predictable in every respect, others only in certain areas, and still others consistently unpredictable. Hypothetically, this variable may be crucial for the ease with which a mother can learn to understand her infant's needs. It may affect not only communication between mother and child but also the acquisition of internal sets of expectations. Possibly, unpredictability is a function of fluctuations in the strength of internal stimuli impinging on behavior. If so, such variability may be reflected also in later developmental acquisitions. Furthermore,

self-consistency in many areas may reflect internal conditions for a later need of sameness and routine, and, if excessive, may be a precondition for rigidity in development.

The methods designed to gather data on the variables will be used under dual conditions. Observations will be made under conditions free from experimental interventions and during periods of standardized experimental procedures. During the neonatal period this is a necessary division, for experimental interventions may alter the state of the baby to varying degrees. Thus, to obtain a base line of behavior, periods free from interventions will have to precede experimental sessions. During later periods of development, this division will reflect the baby's differential response to familiar stimuli and to novel situations created by the experiments.[3] These are two additional variables tapping differences in adaptive mechanisms under novel, possibly threatening, circumstances and under familiar ones.

## Longitudinal Goals

The third and fourth postnatal days appear to be optimal for an assessment of these variables. Greater behavioral stability has been found on these days than on the first two, and yet the baby is young enough that one may discount the impact of environmental handling. Later observations will be timed to coincide with periods found to be significant by other observers rather than at random periods. Thus, Benjamin (1961) noted that during the third and fourth postnatal week the infant's sensitivity to external stimuli markedly increases, and that, in fact, babies tend to be overwhelmed with overstimulation unless a mothering person acts as a tension-reducing agent. He attributes this "crisis" to a maturational spurt of the sensory apparatuses, and he suggests that its outcome may have important implications for the predisposition to anxiety. In subsequent months the emergence of the social smile and the beginning of stranger anxiety can be studied as can any of the later developmental acquisitions. In trying to trace continuities between the neonatal characteristics and later developments, the hypotheses outlined above should be explored and the style with which a baby deals

---

[3] Thomas et al. (1960) used response to novel situations as one of their variables in a longitudinal study of infants and found it to be persistent in character.

with each developmental step should be studied. The stylistic aspects most consistent with the neonatal observations involve a comparison of (1) a baby's mode of dealing with familiar and with novel stimuli; and (2) a baby's behavior while subject to drive tension with his behavior under optimum conditions of internal equilibrium. These comparisons can be made, no matter what the developmental task.

It would be of particular theoretical interest to explore the relationship between the neonatal modes of dealing with internal and external stimuli and the formation of cognitive control and defense structures. The continuity between the early modes and the cognitive control principles seems particularly plausible, because cognitive functioning is largely determined by the way stimuli are taken in, internally elaborated, organized, and synthesized. Gardner and his collaborators (1959) have found a definite correlation between the cognitive controls and the defenses. From much of their evidence, Gardner et al. suspect that the cognitive control principles are structures antecedent to the formation of the defenses. The study of neonatal variations, in dealing with external and internal stimuli, may carry us back one step further: it is conceivable that these variations involve structures which are antecedent to the cognitive control principles.

*Evaluation of Environmental Impact*

In any investigation going beyond the neonatal age it becomes imperative to evaluate the impact of parental handling. Sander's scheme (1962) seems particularly well suited for our purposes. It describes in detail what is involved in the mutual stimulus dosage and regulation between mother and child and how the requirements change with the advent of new developmental steps.

Particularly interesting in Sander's scheme is the fact that several of his phases correspond closely in time and in task with some of Piaget's stages of sensorimotor development. It is probable that both Sander's "issues" and Piaget's stages touch on factors inherent in the maturational process and may thus point to critical periods in infant development and in mother-child interaction. This implies that the appropriateness of a mother's response to her baby is largely a function of his neurophysiological maturation. This is only one example demonstrating the inseparable tie between cognitive, affective, and interpersonal development. Even though, traditionally, these developments are studied separately, on close scrutiny it becomes clear that every emotional development has a cognitive counterpart and that both arise out of a maturational matrix. There is no separation anxiety without maturation of the perceptual functions, and there is no resolution of this anxiety without the help of the cortical capacity of the infant to see himself dependent on laws external to himself. Conversely, as the work of Spitz (1945), Provence and Ritvo (1961), and Provence and Lipton (1962) has shown, the human contact acts as an organizer for the infant's cognitive development. Provence and Ritvo, for example, found that institutionalized infants were maturationally able to vocalize and grasp at the appropriate time; but, without adequate mothering, these functions were not adequately invested and the children did not make use of these capacities. Their eventual retardation thus was initially a function of lacking object cathexis rather than of a maturational deficit. It is obvious that, in order truly to comprehend the conditions for any developmental step or any maturational difficulty, both the cognitive and the affective components have to be understood. Thus, in the future we may diagnose clinical manifestations of regressions, fixations, and progressions not only in libidinal terms but also through an analysis of phase-specific modes of thought.

## Summary

Starting from the assumption that variations in primary ego and drive endowment may color the manner in which a child will experience and master each developmental step, this paper discusses problems in assessing these primary factors and in tracing their continuity in the constantly changing manifestations of later development. It was suggested that individual differences in the neonate's way of dealing with internal and external stimuli may reflect derivatives of these primary endowment factors; also, that the study of the style of development may furnish continuities in behavior otherwise obscured by changing content. Nine neonatal variables, all involving response to internal and external stimuli, were suggested for study and hypothetical directions in which these variables may find expression in later development were outlined.

## BIBLIOGRAPHY

Alpert, A., Neubauer, P. B., & Weil, A. P. (1956), Unusual Variations in Drive Endowment. *This Annual*, 11:125-163.
Benjamin, J. D. (1959), Prediction and Psychopathological Theory. In: *Dynamics of Psychopathology in Childhood*, ed. L. Jessner & E. Pavenstedt. New York: Grune & Stratton, pp. 6-77.
—— (1961), The Innate and the Experiential in Development. In: *Lectures on Experimental Psychiatry*, ed. H. W. Brosin. Pittsburgh: University of Pittsburgh Press, pp. 19-42.
Bergman, P. & Escalona, S. K. (1949), Unusual Sensitivities in Very Young Children. *This Annual*, 3/4:333-352.
Bowlby, J. (1960), Grief and Mourning in Infancy and Early Childhood. *This Annual*, 15:9-52.
Bridger, W. & Reiser, M. (1959), Psychophysiologic Studies of the Neonate: An Approach toward the Methodological and Theoretical Problems Involved. *Psychosom. Med.*, 21:265-276.
Brody, S. (1956), *Patterns of Mothering*. New York: International Universities Press.
Erikson, E. H. (1950), The Theory of Infantile Sexuality. In: *Childhood and Society*. New York: Norton, pp. 44-92.
Escalona, S. K. (1962), The Study of Individual Differences and the Problem of State. *J. Amer. Acad. Child Psychiat.*, 1:11-37.
—— & Heider (1959), *Prediction and Outcome*. New York: Basic Books.
Freud, A. & Burlingham, D. (1944), *Infants Without Families*. New York: International Universities Press.
Freud, S. (1937), Analysis Terminable and Interminable. *Collected Papers*, 5:316-357. London: Hogarth Press, 1950.
Fries, M. E. & Woolf, P. J. (1953), Some Hypotheses on the Role of the Congenital Activity Type in Personality Development. *This Annual*, 8:48-62.
Gardner, R., Holzman, P. S., Klein, G. S., Linton, H., & Spence, D. P. (1959), *Cognitive Controls: A Study of Individual Consistencies in Cognitive Behavior* [*Psychological Issues*, Monogr. 4]. New York: International Universities Press.
Hartmann, H. (1939), *Ego Psychology and the Problem of Adaptation*. New York: International Universities Press, 1958.
—— (1950), Comments on the Psychoanalytic Theory of the Ego. *This Annual*, 5:74-96.
—— (1952), The Mutual Influences in the Development of Ego and Id. *This Annual*, 7:9-30.
Korner, A. F. (1962a), Developmental-Diagnostic Dimensions as Seen through Psychological Tests. *J. Proj. Tech.*, 26:201-211.
—— (1962b), Response to Auditory Stimulation. Unpublished experiments with three- and four-day-old neonates.
—— (1963), Research Proposal. Grant No. HD 00825-01, National Institute of Child Health and Human Development. Unpublished.
Lipton, E. L., Steinschneider, A., & Richmond, J. B. (1960), Autonomic Function in the Neonate. *Psychosom. Med.*, 22:57.
Meili, R. (1957), *Anfänge der Charakterentwicklung*. Bern: Hans Huber.
Peiper, A. (1956), *Die Eigenart der kindlichen Hirntätigkeit*. Leipzig: Thieme.
Piaget, J. (1936), *The Origins of Intelligence in Children*. New York: International Universities Press, 1952.

Provence, S. & Lipton, R. C. (1962), *Infants in Institutions.* New York: International Universities Press.

—— & Ritvo, S. (1961), Effects of Deprivation on Institutionalized Infants: Disturbances in Development of Relationship to Inanimate Objects. *This Annual,* 16:189-205.

Rheingold, H. L. (1956), *The Modification of Social Responsiveness in Institutionalized Babies* [Monograph of the Society for Research in Child Development, Vol. 21, No. 2, Serial No. 63]. Evanston, Ill.: Child Development Publications.

Sander, L. W. (1962), Issues in Early Mother-Child Interaction. *J. Amer. Acad. Child Psychiat.,* 1:141-166.

Spitz, R. A. (1945), Hospitalism: An Inquiry into the Genesis of Psychiatric Conditions in Early Childhood. *This Annual,* 1:53-74.

Thomas, A., Chess, S., Birch, H., & Hertzig, M. E. (1960), A Longitudinal Study of Primary Reaction Patterns in Children. *Comprehensive Psychiat.,* 1:103-112.

Wolff, P. H. (1959), Observations on Newborn Infants. *Psychosom. Med.,* 21:110-118.

—— (1961), Criteria for Judging State of Arousal. Personal Communication.

—— (1964), *The Causes, Controls, and Organization of Behavior in the Newborn.* In preparation, to be published in *Psychological Issues.*

# VARIATIONS OF ARCHAIC THINKING IN NEUROTICS, BORDERLINE PATIENTS, AND SCHIZOPHRENICS

ANDREW PETO, M.D. (New York)

## I

Observations during regressive phases of the transference in neurotics, borderline cases, and schizophrenics led to assumptions about certain aspects of the development of archaic thinking. The four points of departure for the hypothesis presented are the following:

1. Freud's primary and secondary model of thinking in general, and the concept of the positive hallucinatory image in particular.

2. Negative hallucination (Freud, Hoffer) or, in metapsychological terms, archaic denial as a "prestage of defense" (A. Freud, Fenichel).

3. Hartmann's theory of autonomous ego functions, and in particular those aspects of it that relate to the psychology of the thought processes.

4. The fragmentizing function of the ego (Peto), assuming that there is an ego function which aims at the extreme splintering of mental representations. It precedes the various defense mechanisms and prepares those changes in the nature of mental energy which are conceptualized as neutralizations.

1. In 1900 Freud suggested a model for primal thought which is still extremely useful as a working hypothesis for an analytic theory

Presented, in abbreviated form, at the 23rd International Psycho-Analytical Congress in Stockholm, July 30, 1963; and at the New York Psychoanalytic Society on January 28, 1964.

From the Department of Psychiatry, Albert Einstein College of Medicine, New York, N.Y.

of thinking. Under the impact of the drive cathexis reaching thresh-old intensity, and the absence of the primary, need-satisfying ob-ject, the hungry baby hallucinates the breast. "Nothing prevents us from assuming that there was a primitive state of the psychical ap-paratus . . . in which wishing ended in hallucinating.[1]. . . The bitter experiences of life must have changed this primitive thought-activity into a more expedient secondary one." In other words, perceptual identity, under the impact of a reality-adapted child-mother relation-ship, had to be substituted by thought identity, operating with "small cathectic energies."

The concepts of neutralization, differentiation, and adaptation (Hartmann) substantially contributed to a better understanding of the thought processes, but there are still gaps in our conceptualiza-tion of how the positive hallucinatory image of the nonpresent breast changes into the thought of the same.

The problem of dealing with the frustration of the nonpresent object and the path which from here leads to thinking in thought symbols "with small cathectic energies" was dealt with by Bion (1962). He presented a model of thinking which had two important features. (1) The arising of thought brings into existence the think-ing as an apparatus to cope with the arising thought. "Thinking has to be called into existence to cope with thoughts." (2) "The model I propose is that of an infant whose expectations of a breast is mated with a realization of no breast available for satisfaction. . . . If the capacity for toleration of frustration is sufficient, the 'no-breast' in-side becomes a thought, and an apparatus for 'thinking' develops. . . . A capacity for tolerating frustration thus enables the psyche to develop thought as means by which the frustration that is tolerated is itself made more tolerable."

This assumption about the nonautonomous, conflict-determined origin of thinking does not answer just how this "capacity for tolera-tion" is implemented by the psyche.

2. In "A Metapsychological Supplement to the Theory of Dreams" (1917), Freud, while discussing regression as the necessary condition for the occurrence of hallucination, remarks in a footnote

[1] Reports on subjective experiences of sensory deprivations and the accumulating evidence of studies on sensory deprivations support this assumption of Freud.

that "any attempt to explain hallucination would have to start out from *negative* rather than positive hallucination." Thus Freud attributed a decisive role to negative hallucination in archaic thought processes.

Freud's remark on negative hallucination was taken up by Hoffer (1952). Though he first refers to it as "a kind of sensory and affect deafness" and as "raising the physiological threshold of stimulation," later he makes a statement which I consider relevant for the present discussion: "Perhaps it [negative hallucination] is not more than an effect of mobile energy which just *balances the stimulus*" (my italics). Thus Hoffer's approach shows that the problem can be explicitly conceived in terms of energy changes, i.e., within the frame of the economic point of view.

It is essential that the relationship between negative hallucination, archaic denial, and negation should be clarified. Fenichel (1945) stated: "The ability to deny unpleasant parts of reality is the counterpart of the 'hallucinatory wish fulfillment.' Anna Freud has called this type of refusal . . . 'pre-stages of defense' [1936]. The gradual development of reality testing makes such *wholesale falsification of reality* impossible. . . . However, these tendencies toward denial try to remain operative. They succeed best against certain single internal perceptions of a painful nature. Freud explained that the 'negation' of such a perception may be a compromise between becoming conscious of the data given by the perception and the tendency to deny" (my italics).

Thus Fenichel equates negative hallucination with the concept of archaic denial, and stresses that negation indicates a further structural development beyond this archaic denial.

Jacobson (1957) thinks that denial "presupposes an infantile concretization of psychic reality, which permits persons who employ this defense to treat their psychic stirrings as if they were concrete objects perceived." She differentiates neurotic denial, where the quality of the imagelike units of being psychic is not lost, from psychotic denial, where the pathological process leads to lending the image units a truly concrete quality.

De Monchaux (1962), in her discussion of Bion's paper (1962), also quoted Freud's cryptic remark on negative hallucination; she proposed that to tolerate the negative it has first to be denied through

raising the sensory thresholds. "The capacity to perceive the negative event depends on the capacity to inhibit negative hallucination."

The "double negative" as a transition from negation to affirmation was considered by several authors as an important step in
thought development (Kestenberg, 1953).

3. Hartmann's formulations (1939) may serve as a particular
frame of reference to the clinical observations to be presented and
the conclusions drawn from them: "The newborn infant is not
wholly a creature of drives; he has inborn apparatuses . . . which
appropriately perform a part of those functions which, after the
differentiation of ego and id, we attribute to the ego. A state of
adaptedness exists before the intentional processes of adaptation
begin. . . . Differentiation progresses not only by the creation of
new apparatuses to master new demands and new tasks, but also and
mainly by new apparatuses taking over, on a higher level, functions
which were originally performed by more primitive means."

4. In earlier papers (1961, 1962, 1963) I attempted to demonstrate the presence of fragmentizing in the transference neurosis,
in a single analytic session, and in the dream, pointing out superego
fragmentations in the Irma dream.

In a masochist's transference neurosis the threatening mother
image was symbolized in the form of hypochondriac "cancer." The
ego, in this case, attempted to deal with the representation through
extreme splintering of this somatic symbolization, breaking it up
into "smaller cancers," and trying to reduce anxiety through this
extreme splintering of the symbol. The fragmentizing acted upon
an archaic superego structure which came into being through regression.

Similarly, in a single analytic session, I was able to demonstrate
the purposeful splintering of the parental images and of the analyst
as an object. A lasting result of the projective-introjective defenses
is preceded by this extreme fragmentation. The latter seems to represent the initial phase of the process which eventually leads to more
mature identifications and sublimations.

Finally, the Irma dream gave an opportunity to demonstrate
that within the frame of the dreamwork the ego deals with the chang-

ing impact of superego pressure, which develops in the course of regression of varying degree, in such a way that these superego structures are broken down into their elements. This purposeful fragmentizing is then followed by the fortuitous displacements and condensations which are observable and which lead to transient superego configurations.

## II

After outlining the concepts of the positive hallucination in Freud's model, as well as those of negative hallucination and fragmentizing, I shall attempt to illustrate with three examples the following hypothesis: Under normal circumstances the earliest phases of thought formation may proceed from the positive hallucinatory image as follows. This hallucinatory image of the nonpresent, need-satisfying object is subjected to extreme fragmentation; subsequently these fragments are completely decathected. Thus negative hallucination or, in metapsychological terms, archaic denial comes into operation. This negative hallucination paves the way for a new phase of cathexis with changed, more neutralized energy. We may observe the reappearance of fragments which gradually form a new thought symbol. It is assumed that the first phase of fragmentation is an interlude between the positive hallucinatory image and its complete decathexis, caused by archaic denial. This biphasic process is followed by a second stage of fragmentation, which precedes the emerging of the thought symbol instead of the positive hallucinatory image.

If this process is disturbed, archaic denial may prevail and certain forms of faulty thinking may develop. The first development will be illustrated with a case of hysteria; the second faulty development, with a borderline case. Finally, a third form of archaic thinking will illustrate a variation which seems to operate in certain forms of schizophrenia.

*Case 1.* The patient was a twenty-seven-year-old divorced woman, who held· a responsible job with an advertising agency. She sought treatment because of unhappy love affairs, frigidity, emotional tension. She was very intelligent and attractive.

She presented hysterical character traits and corresponding dynamics. The analysis revealed that her main conflicts were centered around the phallic phase with marked bisexual trends. Toward the end of the second year of her analysis she developed a full-blown transference neurosis, which at the time of the phenomena to be reported showed bisexual oscillations with corresponding anxieties. A couple of important screen memories became meaningful in the transference resistance, and their analysis helped to elucidate certain dominant character features of the patient. After partial working through of the phallic aspects of these memories, she experienced vaginal orgasm for the first time.

In the first screen memory, her mother always took her into her bed, while her father, a traveling salesman, was away during the week. She often listened to the noises her mother made while lying in the dark and once told her mother: "You are picking your nose!" Her mother laughed heartily and praised her for her good eyes and hearing. While the screen memory referred to nose picking, the emerging fantasy in the transference referred to repressed thoughts and feelings about the mother's assumed rubbing of her own genitals and breathing heavily in her excitement.

In the second screen memory, her father regularly took her into the shower at the age of three to five. She had to stand with her back to him, since both were naked. A great deal of giggling, heavy breathing, and tickling was involved. Phenomena of the transference were interpreted and led to reconstructions which indicated that her father's erect penis touched and simultaneously excited and frightened her.

These experiences and fantasies, which were condensed into the two screen memories, were also the source of bisexual identifications and of a variety of guilt feelings; in addition, they determined her adult object relationships.

At this stage of her analysis the patient became extremely sensitive to "noises and sounds" originating from me. The changes in the rhythm and depth of my breathing, the movements of my lips, the rustling of my clothes, the movements of my fingers—all these had an upsetting and confusing effect upon her. She begged me to keep quiet, accused me with intentionally irritating her or poking fun at her. She also thought that her talk about her sexual exploits might arouse me and that I could not control my excitement. Another group of fantasies revolved around my assumed aggression. She thought I was about to hit her or to reprimand her because of her promiscuity in the past and her attitude in the sessions. She worried about my intention of dismissing her soon because she was too child-ish for therapy.

In what follows I shall describe some forms of her thinking processes that occurred at these crucial phases of her transference during the sessions.

The screen memories were drawn into the transference and the patient experienced persistent genital excitement during this phase of her treatment. The "noises and sounds" coming from the analyst became, through projection-introjection mechanisms, the representa-tives of the mentioned maternal and paternal activities and sounds. The patient hallucinated the maternal, fantasied masturbation and projected it onto the analyst. She *actually* saw and heard her mother rubbing her genitals while the mother was sitting behind the patient in the analyst's chair.

This was after a while unbearable and the mother representa-tion in the transference, the masturbating mother image, was splin-tered, fragmentized into chaotic "noises and sounds" and visual fragments. This provoked anxiety and archaic defense measures: "negative hallucination," archaic denial, turned these images and thought splinters into nothingness. She cried: "Now you went away, you left me alone." This complete decathexis after the extreme splintering of the representations allowed the ego an archaic denial of the traumatic situation. As a next step the ego recathected the image fragments, which before the denial had been represented by the frightening and exciting noises. The newly formed, recathected visual and auditory fragments turned into words originating from me, namely, the interpretation given earlier or during the phe-nomena. They were repeated by the patient and integrated into meaningful thoughts, which at first were ego alien. She said: "Your words became my words, I talk with them. They are not irritating me any more." Thus she indicated a phase of structuralized negation. This phase subsequently allowed emergence of a fully integrated version: "Your words changed into my words, these are actually my thoughts; my thoughts about my mother and about you."

I suggest that the transition from the positive hallucination of the absent need-satisfying object to thinking in thought symbols

leads first through the extreme splintering of this positive hallucination. This process seems to imply and represent the first manifestation
of far-reaching changes in the energy cathexis of the representation. After the extreme fragmentation of the hallucinated image, a
phase of "negative hallucination" followed, marked by her complaint
about the analyst's absence.

This woman with her well-integrated ego maintained this archaic
denial for a very short while on such occasions. Soon her ego brought
into operation, through recathexis, the reappearance of the fragments
of the hallucinated image and was gradually able to integrate them
into thought symbols invested with a more neutralized energy quality. Inner speech appeared and led to abstract thought symbols.

Jacobson (1957) may have observed similar phenomena of which
she gives the following account: ". . . this concretization of psychic
reality [which, in Jacobson's opinion, precedes denial] . . . involves a
cutting apart of psychic units, on the one hand; but, on the other, a
merging and categorical regrouping of the separated components. . . .
In psychotics, however, the pathological process leads to a real fragmentation, a splitting, a concretization and externalization of psychic
manifestations."

## III

Certain borderline cases show a different form and sequence of
archaic regressive thinking. In the regressive thinking of one male
patient the positive hallucinatory image was, as in the previous case,
followed by extreme fragmentation and subsequent archaic denial
in the form of negative hallucination. This denial, however, persisted and was maintained for a prolonged period of time. It was not
followed by the re-emergence of the fragments and gradual appearance of thought symbols. The patient showed certain forms of faulty
thinking, which were assumed to be caused by the disturbance discussed above, i.e., the maintenance of negative hallucination on the
path from the hallucinatory image toward the abstract thought
symbol.

*Case 2.* The patient was a thirty-four-year-old professional man,
married, with two children. He came into analysis because of a general feeling of aimlessness. He was also worried about his impulsive
activities which, in his own opinion, were aimed at destroying his

private and professional life. At his job he was irresponsible, provocative, and openly disobedient.

Permanent rage, basic confusion about emotional and social values and about his identity were embedded in an essentially chronic state of depression.

His mother exposed him to a great deal of sexual seduction and pampered him in every way until his twelfth year. When the patient was fifteen, she was admitted with hallucinatory psychosis to a mental hospital, where she was still living in autistic withdrawal at the time of the analysis.

The patient's father had a severe personality disorder with depressive and paranoid features. The patient remembered a scene, which was confirmed by an aunt, when his father tried to stab a knife into his mother's throat while attempting to push her out of the window.

This patient became confused whenever he had to cope with an emotional or intellectual task in the analysis or in his everyday life. When he was able to control an immediate outburst of anger or self-destructive clowning or other forms of self-humiliation, his judgment was impaired by thinking in false analogies, false conclusions, and false generalizations. The following examples illustrate his thought disturbances.

*False analogy establishing a false conclusion.* I pointed out to him that, as a form of acting out in his marriage and in the transference, he made every effort to impregnate his Catholic girl friend. This would have created the necessity of a showdown with his wife and two children or with his mistress. Furthermore, it would have precipitated his dismissal from his job and therefore also resulted in termination of his analysis. Though he consciously wanted to avoid this showdown, the underlying, most prominent preconscious fantasy was that of just sitting back, as he had done as a little boy, and watch how the grownups fight it out. I do not wish to refer here to the complex etiology of this fantasy.

My interpretation provoked the following angry response from the patient: "What you tell me means that everybody who has a girl friend and has intercourse with her wants to impregnate her, since he knows that this may occur even with the greatest precaution. So you state that everybody who drives a car wants to die in an accident, since they know that people often die in car accidents."

*False generalization.* I interpreted that when he was worried, he often started clowning in order to avoid the outburst of anxiety and confusion. The reason for this interpretation was that he started talking with a foreign accent so as to ridicule me. His reaction was: "So you tell me that whenever I become anxious, I start talking with a foreign accent." Undoubtedly, this thinking was in the service of resistance and, to put it into his own words, he wanted "to get a rise out of you" through ridiculing me and acting silly. However, there was more to it than mere resistance; if on such occasions I pointed out his faulty thinking and interpreted it as resistance, he became desperate, started yelling, or helplessly crying, and often went into a state of transient confusion. He accused me of confusing him and of deliberately bewildering him. He desperately tried to convince me that this type of thinking was not directed specifically against me or developed during his analysis, but always prevailed and separated him from other people.

*Lack of abstraction ability.* The patient lacked the capacity to shift from one symbolization level to another, from the concrete or special to the abstract and general. He mentioned several times, on occasions similar to the one mentioned above, that he was never able to write a genuine answer to a certain type of examination question or comparable types of questions, e.g., after he visited a theater with friends: What does the author want to express through a certain figure in a play? He felt lost and confused and screamed in his mind: "What should the author express, but the words that are spoken? How should I know what else the author thought of, but what he writes down in a book?" On second thought he was always able to answer the question because he learned to say what was expected of him, but he knew that it was a parrotlike mechanical answer.

One important reason for this inability of oscillating between different symbolization levels was based on the fact that he mainly applied doubt and denial when dealing with the onslaught of traumatic thoughts and emotions in everyday life as well as in the transference situation. He always questioned whether he felt love or hatred toward somebody. "After all, what is love, etc.?" He also tried to evade the impact of the interpretations and his own reactions to them by denying that he understood them "really" or could apply

them to himself. He flatly denied the validity and impact of everything that reached him from within or without.

In the heat of the transference this patient slipped transiently,
in the course of the projective-introjective oscillations, into hallucinating the mother image as represented by the analyst. Such phases
always represented extreme frustration and despair since he was not
able to express his archaic-infantile wishes, which had been partly
gratified, partly thwarted by his psychotic mother. He yelled and
screamed at me as if I were his mother and demanded undefinable
tenderness and care.

This phase of a positive hallucinatory image produced in the
frustration and abstinence of the analytic setup was often followed
by fragmentation of the hallucinatory image of the mother or, less
often, of the father representation. The fragments represented random details of varying aspects of these parental images and precipitated an archaic denial in the form of negative hallucination. The
patient screamed: "Nothing, absolutely nothing!" and quieted down
through this decathexis of the traumatic situation. In many instances
this decathexis was not followed, as it was in the hysterical patient,
by the reappearance of the fragments which would gradually have
led to the emergence of a thought about the primary object or its
derivatives. This patient maintained archaic denial which prevented
him from a better grasp of the traumatic situation and from a verbalization in the form of a higher level of thought formation.

Usually this denial was maintained and developed eventually
into structuralized negation which allowed the emergence of thinking about the object in this form. In most instances not even the
stage of structuralized negation was reached, but the denial ended
in a confusional state of feelings, images, thought fragments, without
any further development toward better integration.

Thus the decathexis of mental representation was maintained
in the traumatic situation and the ego had no opportunity to proceed
along the path outlined in the previous case toward thought symbolization on a more sublimated and better integrated level.

It is assumed that the type of faulty thinking described in the
second patient is, among other factors, caused by a variation in the
sequence from the primary to the secondary model of thinking, i.e.,
persistence of archaic denial. Since this variation implies a deficiency

in neutralization, in change of energy modes, it is furthermore assumed that this variation is at the basis of at least a certain type of thought disturbance.

## IV

*Case 3.* Another form of regressive archaic thinking was observed in a case of schizophrenia. This young man was referred to me when he was twenty, with the diagnosis of an impending schizophrenic episode. He was a senior in college. The year before, after a banal sexual disappointment, he had begun to have difficulties in his studies, although previously he had always been a brilliant student. The presenting symptoms were an increasing depression and ruminations about the futility of life. He was, however, from time to time making an effort to find solace in the literature of idealism, existentialism, etc. He suffered from depersonalizations and sometimes heard a shrill voice (which proved to be that of his mother) that reprimanded and threatened him. Severe anxiety attacks were tied up with a feeling of sinking and giddiness and a "crinkly" feeling of his skin. His thinking became at times "too fast" with concomitant confusion and inability to "think clearly." An inner, pressing emptiness was associated with physical inertia. Prior to his treatment and in its early phases he spent a great deal of his time in bed ruminating and sleeping.

Early in therapy he admitted that he was afraid of policemen and Negroes who might climb into his apartment and might mishandle him and his girl friend.

He proved to be better integrated than the above symptoms would indicate, and the predicted psychotic break did not occur. He kept his appointments and even went out of his way to come to the sessions. The symptoms were present for a further year; nevertheless he graduated from college with honors and took up postgraduate studies on a scholarship. The depression and the ruminations disappeared, and so did the manifest thought disturbances. The anxiety attacks and the body-image disturbances were still present after two and a half years of treatment, and he still hallucinated, when under great strain, his mother's voice. During the analysis he married a Catholic-German girl, one of his reasons being his wish never to be without company at night.

He went through with his marriage despite the analyst's and his orthodox Jewish father's strong objections. He evaded the draft by impregnating his wife in the first month of their marriage and is at the time of this report the loving father of a six-month-old boy and a rather good husband to his wife.

In the first two years of his treatment he often slipped into regression with visual and auditory hallucinations which he was able to interrupt any time by talking to the analyst as a real person. Without going into a further discussion of the course of the treatment and the material that was unearthed, I wish to report certain phases of a single session toward the end of this period, as an example of the kind of regressive archaic thinking he often presented in such transient phases.

The mood of the session was set by the following events: He knew that his father had not yet paid the fees for the last two months of his therapy. This indicated, realistically, that the father wanted to force the discontinuation of the patient's treatment. He was rather upset about this and bitterly attacked me because I would not continue his treatment without fees. He said, with tears in his eyes, "You consider me a professional object. I don't want to continue. Let's have a break."

He was having difficulties in his marital life. His wife complained of pain during intercourse, became frigid, and avoided sexual relations. Simultaneously his potency diminished, he did not feel like masturbating, which had always solaced him in the past. These developments caused him a great deal of anguish. Moreover, his wife persistently belabored him with the idea that his mother was ugly and he did not need to depend on his parents emotionally even though they completely supported him financially.

As an introduction for the material that follows it should be reported that the lobster, tarantula, or black-widow spider played an important role in these phases of the analysis as symbols for the mother image in his fantasies and hallucinations. He often regressed into a fantasy-*cum*-hallucination, which resembled, at its inception, the fantasy play of young children. On such occasions he imagined he turned into a big black spider or into another similar animal, and started, in fantasy, jumping around in my office until I presumably went out of my mind in panic. Then he would tear me to pieces to devour the fragments. It often happened, on these occasions, that in the course of this "play," just as children do, he became so anxious himself that he had to interrupt the fantasy. The fantasy often turned into a hallucination. Either the tarantula turned into an independent being and threatened the patient himself, or I, the therapist, turned into a counter black-widow and tore him to pieces. Analysis revealed, as already indicated, that the animals symbolized mainly the orally devouring and the phallic-castrating mother, while the fangs and arms of the animal represented the caressing fingers of the loving mother, who could not be trusted, since the arms also symbolized the threatening strangulating arms of the bad mother; they also represented the spreading and engulfing legs of the mother imago in the primal scene.

This more recently discovered material as well as the previous oedipal and preoedipal material gave an opportunity to interpret certain of his complicated and ambivalent feelings toward me in the transference. As a matter of course he identified me on several layers with the parental imagos, with his own self, and with his wife. Therefore the transference projections represented several aspects of his intersystemic and intrasystemic conflicts. The interpretation I gave summarized the main resistance and content aspects of his feelings and object relationships in terms of attachment and abandonment, care and neglect. He reacted with an anxiety attack which was followed by an outburst of anger.

He said: "I always knew that I could not trust you, that when I really needed you, you wouldn't be there. I want to tear you to pieces. I feel the strips of your flesh between my teeth. You are a lobster and I taste the shreds of your flesh in my mouth. I taste you in my mouth. I feel like eating and licking honeycomb. I am eating a lobster, or is it you? I am seeing it in isolated film pictures going on, isolated, separated. Click-click-click. Small pieces. No connection."

After the last remark ("No connection") the patient said: "That's the treatment you really deserve." He then switched to integrated thinking and started talking about a relative, who represented the analyst's "bad" traits. Finally, a rational assessment of the analyst as a frustrating person became conceivable.

Thus in the wake of the interpretation which summed up the main trend of the session, a wave of fantasied abandonment and feared closeness precipitated hallucinatory regression in which the symbol of the nonpresent, need-satisfying dangerous mother image was orally torn to pieces. Subsequently the fragments were reintegrated, transiently into a whole symbol, the lobster, which then again was orally torn into its fragments. The next step in this hallucinatory, primary-process thinking sequence was the image of the analyst mother, who was sweet-tasting. It was not clear whether it was still tasted *and* seen as a lobster or as the analyst in separate isolated image sequences of split-second duration (the filmlike sequence in the hallucination). In any event, the image was constantly fluid, not a concrete whole for any but the most limited time sequence. Eventually, after this "click-click" phase of wholeness, which was of extremely short duration, secondary-process thinking came into being, as described in the previous paragraph.

This sequence of regressive archaic thinking contains several elements of the sequences I described in the hysterical and in the borderline patients: (1) the positive hallucinatory image of the nonpresent, need-satisfying object; (2) the alternating stages of fragmentation; and (3) subsequent integration. However, conspicuous by its absence is one phase which was present in the other patients, namely, the phase of negative hallucination, of archaic denial.

### Discussion

Following these observations I went through the case material I published in a paper on "Body Image and Archaic Thinking" (1959). The schizophrenic patients I discussed in that paper went through regressive transference phases which culminated in a variety of blissful confluences with the analyst-mother's body. The self and the nonself were united in a vague and not clearly describable mass of muddy-fluid material. I interpreted these changes in the body image as the earliest forerunners of thinking in the presymbolic phase. Freud's "groping forward" was represented by these attempts of the early ego to search and incorporate the environment. An important reason for this assumption was the fact that after these regressive transient experiences in the transference, the patient's thinking cleared up for shorter or longer periods following this "grasping the world around them" on the presumably most archaic level.

I noticed when I reread these observations, that while the positive hallucinatory image and various phases of fragmentation and reintegration were present in these phenomena, I was not able to trace the operation of negative hallucination. Since this observation corresponds with the record of Case 3 reported above, I feel inclined to assume that *ceteris paribus* this lack of archaic denial is characteristic of archaic thinking in certain forms of schizophrenia. This hypothesis, it must be emphasized, does not state anything about the nature of the thought disorder or about whether this peculiarity is present only in certain types of the disease. My observations were made on relatively well-contained cases, a rapidly deteriorating juvenile paranoid psychosis, and several cases between these two extremes. None of the cases was, at the time of observation, hospitalized and all were able to come for treatment to my private office.

I further suggest that this lack of the operation of archaic denial may represent a serious difficulty for the proper functioning of secondary-process symbolization in these patients. The period of archaic denial seems to be necessary for the transformation of energies, for the proper preparation of economic changes which eventually lead to neutralization and those sublimations which are necessary for synthetic secondary-process thinking (Hartmann, 1952). This assumption corresponds to Freud's hypothesis on negation as the first important step in thinking properly.

The transition from a purely sensorimotor ego toward a "thinking" ego can be visualized, not in terms of defense, but only in terms of inborn coded patterning. Though the functions described are later used by the ego as defenses, they represent antonomous functions in the earliest stages of thinking. I believe this view corresponds to Székely's formulation (1962) which states that in the presymbolic phase the optical experiences are incorporated into the body image and subsequently organized in a meaningful way.

The sequence described marks the transition from the primary to the secondary model of thinking. It indicates the development from a sensorimotor pre-ego toward a "thinking" pre-ego. It is assumed that fragmentizing and archaic denial are manifestations of autonomous ego functioning, though in the course of later developments these "prestages of defense" (A. Freud, 1936) assume the role of introductory steps in the process of defensive mechanisms.

The sequence of the transition from the primary to the secondary model of thinking represents one aspect, among many other facets, of the primary core of ego functioning. Various authors conceptualized the conflictuous aspects of this primary core as true and false self (Winnicott, 1955), the state of primary love (Balint, 1960), the pristine ego's earliest splits (Fairbairn, 1955).

In assessing the limitations and more general applicability of the assumptions presented in this paper, the following considerations may be taken into account.

1. However regressed the thought processes of the cases presented were, they still represented those of adults. Although the regressive thinking of adults, even of schizophrenics, is not identical with that of very young children, it is probable that it represents a new edition of the original pattern with similar economic and dynamic aspects.

2. The important fact is that these "new editions" of archaic thinking show a significant difference in different forms of ego pathology.

3. Although the regression in the sessions may have started from a variety of object relationships, the final, most regressed thinking always indicated that, at the basis of thought symbolization, the child-mother unit serves as the matrix for the primal hallucinatory activity that becomes the stepping stone for further primary- and secondary-process thought.

4. The developmental phase that would correspond to this type of earliest structured precursor of thinking is subject to speculation. Kris (1962) thinks that "Normally, already at three months, this hallucinatory imagination is in certain situations clearly structured by the experience. Perception and memory interact to produce an anticipation of the future when the child learns to wait for its feeding and registers in the mother's preparations the cues for the forthcoming satisfaction."

Spitz (1961) also puts this type of mental activity at an early age: "I believe that hallucinatory wish fulfillment in infancy is probably the earliest mental activity and comes into being at the period at which neonatal sleep turns into regular sleep, which is differentiated from clearly distinguished waking, that is, sleep proper."

Finally, the following technical considerations should be discussed:

1. The process of archaic thinking as it appears in case 1, the hysteria patient, and in other neurotic and so-called "normal" patients, does not need any therapeutic-corrective approach because it develops along lines which lead to adequate sublimation, i.e., thinking in proper thought symbols. The pathology of the neurotic does not affect his thinking, his proper symbolization process. Everyday clinical experience convinces us that the thought processes of the neurotic are intact. It is assumed that one decisive factor in this fact is the intactness of the full sequence. Therefore adherence to the classic analytic technique as conceived by Freud will produce satisfactory results. The core of the symbolization process is intact.

2. In certain borderline and schizophrenic cases, apart from other pathogenic factors, the symbolic function is basically faulty, since the sequence of the component steps is disturbed. There are archaic and basic difficulties in the way of proper neutralization and subsequent sublimation. Certain areas of the thought apparatus do not participate in the perpetual integrating function of the ego.

Thus, while the neurotic patient may be "left alone," in this sphere this does not apply to the other type of patient. Everything has to be done to get as close to this faulty basic thought functioning as possible, in order to change it. There is certainly no lack in suggested and practiced modifications of the classic technique in dealing with these patients. All these modifications aim, based on theoretical assumptions and practical results, at establishing some form of transference situation which is thought to be identical with or dynamically related to an early primary conflict situation that may have affected the developing organism at an extremely tender age. The primary principle of all the pertinent theories is that the course of development ran into a conflict series of the primary object relationship which proved to be too traumatic to be dealt with adequately. The optimistic note of any therapeutic approach is based on the assumption that this conflict can be at least partially undone with some proper modification of the classic technique in the treatment of delinquents, psychopaths, etc. Certain undeniable results encourage this assumption. Nevertheless, everybody agrees that even after relatively satisfactory treatments such patients have their difficulties and present "scars," "pockets," that have to be protected, frailty of emotional life, etc.

I assume that in so-called borderline and schizophrenic cases only the conflictuous aspects of the ego can be drawn into the "heat of the transference," but not the core of the autonomous archaic thinking process. Personally, I am of the opinion that the greater the intensity of the regressive transference at certain phases of the treatment, the better are the chances to penetrate into the sphere of archaic conflicts of the developing ego, the better are the chances that a faulty thinking sequence can be *secondarily* controlled without actually being changed. Regressive transference processes, if they are properly handled at certain decisive phases of the treatment, may affect the defensive aspects of archaic denial. Therefore the patient learns how to bear frustration and to resort to detour functions. These changes of the ego's conflictuous aspects help to isolate and encapsulate those areas of thinking which are affected by the faulty sequence in symbolization. Though the basic symbolization process in these areas does not change, the patient learns how to manipulate his object relations in a more reality-adapted way, and this leaves the faulty symbolization process sealed off.

### BIBLIOGRAPHY

Balint, M. (1960), Primary Narcissism and Primary Love. *Psa. Quart.*, 29.
Bion, W. R. (1962), The Psycho-Analytic Study of Thinking: II. A Theory of Thinking. *Int. J. Psa.*, 43.
de Monchaux, C. (1962), The Psycho-analytic Study of Thinking: III. Thinking and Negative Hallucination. *Int. J. Psa.*, 43.
Fairbairn, W. R. D. (1955), Observation in Defence of the Object-Relations Theory of the Personality. *Brit. J. Med. Psychol.*, 28.
Fenichel, O. (1945), *The Psychoanalytic Theory of Neurosis*. New York: Norton.
Freud, A. (1936), *The Ego and the Mechanisms of Defense*. New York: International Universities Press, 1946.
Freud, S. (1900), The Interpretation of Dreams. *Standard Edition*, 4 & 5. London: Hogarth Press, 1953.
—— (1917), A Metapsychological Supplement to the Theory of Dreams. *Standard Edition*, 14. London: Hogarth Press, 1957.
Hartmann, H. (1939), *Ego Psychology and the Problem of Adaptation*. New York: International Universities Press, 1958.
—— (1952), The Mutual Influences in the Development of Ego and Id. *This Annual*, 7.
—— (1955), Notes to the Theory of Sublimation. *This Annual*, 10.
Hoffer, W. (1952), The Mutual Influences in the Development of Ego and Id: Earliest Stages. *This Annual*, 7.
Jacobson, E., (1957), Denial and Repression. *J. Amer. Psa. Assn.*, 5.

Kestenberg, J. S. (1953), Notes on Ego Development. *Int. J. Psa.,* 34.
Klein, G. S. (1959), Consciousness in Psychoanalytic Theory. *J. Amer. Psa. Assn.,* 7.
Kris, E. (1962), Decline and Recovery in the Life of a Three-Year-Old. *This Annual,* 17.
Peto, A. (1959), Body Image and Archaic Thinking. *Int. J. Psa.,* 40.
—— (1961), The Fragmentizing Function of the Ego in the Transference Neurosis. *Int. J. Psa.,* 42.
—— (1962), Superego Fragmentation in the Irma Dream. Presented at the American Psychoanalytic Association, New York.
—— (1963), The Fragmentizing Function of the Ego in the Analytic Session. *Int. J. Psa.,* 44.
Spitz, R. A. (1961), Some Early Prototypes of Ego Defenses. *J. Amer. Psa. Assn.,* 9.
Székely, L. (1962), The Psycho-Analytic Study of Thinking: I. Meaning, Meaning Schemata, and Body Schemata in Thought. *Int. J. Psa.,* 43.
Winnicott, D. W. (1955), Metapsychological and Clinical Aspects of Regression within the Psycho-Analytical Set-up. *Int. J. Psa.,* 36.

# ASPECTS OF NORMAL AND PATHOLOGICAL DEVELOPMENT

# HEARING AND ITS ROLE IN THE
# DEVELOPMENT OF THE BLIND

## DOROTHY BURLINGHAM (London)

At the Hampstead Child-Therapy Clinic we may soon have the opportunity of following the development of several blind infants. It therefore seems important to become aware in greater detail where their development deviates from that of the seeing infant, since only this knowledge can teach us how best to answer their needs.

When going through the literature concerned with the blind, it is interesting to note how many authors mention the lack of information regarding the blind infant's first months and years of life, a lack of information likewise existing with regard to the deaf. A.-M. Sandler (1963), in her paper on "Passivity and Ego Development in a Blind Infant," was among the first to study this subject.[1] I greatly admire her paper which I consider extremely important for the understanding of the blind child. It stimulates my wish to follow more closely the development of hearing and listening, to go more deeply into the role of these functions, their possibilities and effects, as well as to show the similarities and dissimilarities between hearing and the sense of vision.

A.-M. Sandler stresses in her introduction that her arguments are presented from the point of view of the child's intrapsychic development. Although she is well aware of the importance of the child's object relationship, especially to the mother, she nevertheless expresses the hypothesis that the ego deformation which occurs as a result of blindness does so in its own right.

In what follows, I shall attempt to describe the role played by the

The work with blind children is part of the Educational Unit of the Hampstead Child-Therapy Course and Clinic and as such is maintained by the Grant Foundation, Inc., New York. The research work with the blind is assisted further by the National Institute of Mental Health, Bethesda, Maryland.
[1] See also the papers by Fraiberg and Freedman in this Volume.

mother in furthering, or in failing to further, her infant's innate possibilities to develop. It is my contention that some of the developmental deviations of the blind children and some of the reduction in their ability to enjoy experiences are due to a lack of interaction between child and mother; i.e., they are due to the infant's failure to elicit responses from the mother in certain all-important spheres.

## VISION

Looking up the role of vision in Gesell's developmental tests, one is struck by the variety of "regards" described by him for the infant. According to Gesell, the infant regards after delay, spontaneously, momentarily, starily, consistently, recurrently, prolongedly, predominantly, each type of regard having a bearing for the state of development which has been reached.

According to Gesell et al. (1934):

At 1 week the baby stares without fixation.

4-12 weeks: looks at mother's face, adults' hands and own hands; face brightens.

6 weeks: starey gaze, true inspection, follows retreating figure of mother, a moment of searching, more alert, adaptive.

16 weeks: protracted moment of staring, knows mother, sobers when he sees strangers.

24 weeks: recurrence of regard.

28 weeks: perceptual behavior; interest in own abilities, can be content alone, concentrates on an object.

40-52 weeks: inquisitive visual and motor behavior; intent on regarding what other person does; perceptive moods, gives and takes.

52-56 weeks: imitates.

Compared with these detailed differentiations in the maturing function of looking, the function of hearing does not receive a corresponding amount of attention.

## MOTIONLESS ATTENTION

For some time my interest has been aroused by the immovable attention displayed by seeing infants when looking or listening intently. It is a common observation, also noted many times in our Baby Clinic, that infants of five or six months are found to stare immovably at their mother's face. Several months later this motion-less attention is reserved for strangers, who are looked at with a fixed stare which may be interrupted for a quick glance at the familiar face of the mother, only to be taken up again in the same manner.

It is well known, of course, that motionless attention when look-ing is not restricted to infants, but can be found at all ages in situa-tions which call forth marked interest or surprise. One only needs to watch boys looking at a fast-moving electric train in a shop window, or at acrobats on a trapeze high above the ground. The best example of this behavior at present is people's motionless gazing at television. What I have in mind is the oft-repeated observation of a woman watching television while ironing; the more interesting the picture, the slower her iron goes over the material, stopping entirely at a moment of special excitement when the viewer becomes completely motionless and staring.

Corresponding observations can be made when a child is listen-ing. This is not surprising since discontinuing all activity reduces the sounds made by oneself and concentrates the attention on the noise listened to. I refer here to the observation of a nine-month-old seeing baby who would stop crawling about the room and become motionless on hearing the clock strike. He stayed perfectly still until the clock stopped striking, when he glanced quickly at his mother sharing the experience with her. After several occurrences of this kind the child gradually lost interest and no longer paid attention to the clock. Familiarity had reduced this particular form of attentive listening.

Motionless attention, which is an interesting feature in the seeing, is, of course, of immensely greater importance in the blind. In our nursery school for the blind, we were able to observe various types of it, to which I shall refer later.

## THE DEVELOPMENT OF HEARING IN THE BLIND

Although, so far, our possibilities of observing blind babies have been insufficient, some material has been collected on baby Molly from the age of six months.[2] More detailed notes have been made

2 By Cecily Legg, Doris Wills, Alice Colonna.

concerning Danny from age two years nine months over a period of fourteen months.[3] Other knowledge comes from our nursery school children (from age three years) or from reconstructions in the analysis of the blind.[4] Even with this scarcity of direct material of the earliest years of life, it has been possible to get some idea of how the sense of hearing is used by a blind child.

Molly, at six months, was reported to smile when her mother tickled her on her chest and made a jingling noise with a rattle. When a clock chimed she made a slight movement toward it; when the curtains were drawn, she stopped playing with her hands and seemed to concentrate on what was happening.

At seven months she liked crumpling paper and listening to the sound; she scratched her pillow, listening to the sounds made by her nails.

At eleven months she did not smile when she only heard her mother's voice, but did when she was tickled at the same time.

At one year five months, Molly now had a baby sister. When the baby cried, Molly lay quietly, listening; she banged her feet to make the baby cry, chuckled when she made the baby cry, and banged her feet again.

At one year six months, she imitated the baby's burping and cooing noises.

At one year seven months, she reached out toward a voice and was discouraged when she was not noticed.

The points illustrated by these observations are the following:

that passive intake of noise led to active imitation of it which was enjoyed;

that listening to the baby sister's crying could lead to a purposeful action, the purpose being the repetition of a pleasurable sound;

that cheerful noises were imitated vocally no less than noises signifying distress;

that, perhaps most important of all, no body contact can be made with a voice, and that failure in this respect leads to noticeable discouragement.

3 By Doris Wills. Danny was a defective blind child.

4 Analytic treatments of blind children of various ages were carried out by Hansi Kennedy, Isabel Harris, Agnes Gehr, Cecily Legg, Alice Goldberger, and Dr. Max Goldblatt.

So far as I know, no one has yet explored the difference between an object which can simultaneously be seen and felt and one which can simultaneously be heard and felt. While sight is much more concerned with something material and tangible, a noise, and especially a noise the origin of which is unknown, must seem to the blind child like something disembodied and out of reach.

The following observations made on Danny are extracted from a paper by Doris Wills (1963) on "The Role of Sound in the Development of a Blind Child."

Danny (two years nine months to three years eleven months) examined all objects by banging them, turning them, and banging them on each surface to get as many impressions of the objects through sounds as possible.

He patted his own body, stomach, and legs in such a manner that made it clear that he was interested in the sounds produced thereby. At times, when he was leaning against a wall or door, he would bang his head or back against it, apparently accidentally, the purpose again seeming to be the creation of noise.

The mother reported that when he dropped his bottle he was able to get down and pick it up. This was the first object he went after and retrieved purposefully. When he was on the floor, he would throw a toy across the floor and hitch after it; having found it, he would throw it again, progressing in this way for some distance.

He drummed with his feet when he was sitting and patted cushions on the couch; these activities represented a motor discharge as well as an exercise in producing noise.

He reached for objects that he heard and wanted; when he was unable to get to the object which had produced the sound, he shook his hands and fussed.

He understood certain words ("bottle" and "car") and reacted to them so that the mother was careful not to use them unless she wanted him to have the bottle or to take him to the car. When he was having his bottle and "car" was mentioned, he dropped the bottle to go to the car.

The stages in Danny's use of sound are the following:

producing a sound and pleasure in this;
using sound production for the purpose of recognizing an object;
combining motor discharge with sound production to express
    impatience;

producing purposeful sounds as a means to locate an object;
recognizing isolated words, meaningful to him.

At our nursery school for the blind it is possible to observe how
the older children (three to six years) use their hearing. They have
many different ways of listening, from the taking in of their surroundings to the assembling of facts, to the making of a noise for
experimenting and purposeful activities. Their reaction to what is
heard is of equal interest.

By listening, the children know who is in the room and what
activities are in progress.

They orient themselves in the room, know where objects are
placed, and remember their location. This orientation and locating
of objects are based on listening to conversations, or any slight noise
made by movement, by the running of the water from the tap, the
noise of the heater, etc. Whatever gives them a clue to where the
sound comes from informs them also of their own position in relation to the sound.

They are also aware of sound beyond the room, of a dog barking,
cars passing, i.e., the background noises of everyday life.

They seem to use their sense of hearing more efficiently than the
seeing; it may be that through practice, they are able to hear sounds
which are fainter and less distinct.

By dropping objects, banging them, throwing them against floor
or wall, knocking one piece against the other, and especially by banging an object against their own bodies, as the younger children do,
they add to their knowledge of things and learn a great deal about
shape, consistency, compactness, or hollowness. An accidental happening, such as knocking bricks over, is repeated purposefully to
discover what has occurred. However, hearing is only an accompani-
ment to mouthing, touching, and smelling. It is the combined sense
experience which adds to the child's knowledge. Surprisingly enough,
this type of experimenting, which is repeated endlessly, does not
seem to awaken further curiosity; on the contrary, it often leads
to what appears like boredom or regression to autoerotic manifestations.

The fact that an object has a name attached to it is treated like a
further valuable piece of information concerning it. Listening to

conversations and understanding them are great sources of interest to the children and give them a feeling of power. But listening and hearing without understanding can also lead to confusion and disappointment, as in the case of some of our most backward or disturbed children who merely parrot what they hear.

The children are frequently found to imitate the sounds which they have heard. A child, apparently busy at the far end of the room, was heard to jabber away to himself apparently meaninglessly, but in reality he was reproducing a telephone conversation in the next room which was held in Danish. A boy to whom a lawnmower was explained was interested only in its noise, which he was later heard to imitate. Another child imitated the noise of workmen digging up the street by means of manipulating a plate against different surfaces.

It is also possible to follow the children's experiences in their own homes by understanding the sounds which they produce in school. One child, in whose family a sister had been born, imitated the crying and cooing of the baby, her burping and sucking at feeding time, the noise made by the mother's stirring the formula for the baby's bottle. Another girl of six searched one day in the nursery for what she called her Hoover. As there was no Hoover in the nursery, every possible other object was offered to her without success until at last she came across a small dinky car, called this her Hoover, proceeded to push it on the floor and held it to her ear: the noise it made had reminded her of the Hoover her mother used at home. It is extraordinary how the children find ways of manipulating objects to make the sounds which represent their major interests. In the analysis of several of the children the therapist was able to unravel the experiences of their past by understanding these ways.

Conversations that have made an impression are also often repeated. A boy of four years three months, after a bad experience in the hospital where his eyes had been treated without an anesthetic, repeated how they said: "Lie down," and Mummy said: "I won't have my child upset." She had in fact said this and insisted on taking him away. Another time in the nursery he kept banging doors for no apparent reason; when this was objected to, he said, "That is what my mother does when she is angry," showing how he understood moods by means of sounds.

### LISTENING IN RELATION TO WITHDRAWAL

Withdrawal and apparent lack of interest sometimes prove to be different forms of listening. When a visitor enters the nursery it often seems as if the children did not even notice. Closer observation shows at such times a moment of silent listening on their part which replaces the glance of a seeing child. A child may stand or sit at a table, apparently passive and oblivious to the activities of the other children, but later his questions reveal that he was merely listening to take in what they were doing. It is sometimes days later that a child mentions an important happening in the nursery when it was thought that he had been completely withdrawn and uninterested at the time. Very often the withdrawal serves the purpose of listening more intently. At other times the listening may be a substitute for action. One little girl, when the others were dancing, would sit with her fists in her eyes, completely wtihdrawn; no one could get her to take part until one day when she suddenly got up and danced by herself, making her movements appropriate to the record, showing how well she had been listening.

Even when the children prefer to be active rather than listen, they are often forced into this role. One day an older sister accompanied one of our children to the nursery. She enjoyed the nursery toys and was very active. The blind child tried to join her but was unable to participate actively and was pushed away. The result was that she just tried to stand or sit as near her sister as possible, listening to what she was doing.

A boy had brought a new whistling car to the nursery, another boy took it and made it whistle. The owner remarked softly, "It is my car." He stood in the middle of the room listening but made no effort to claim the car, nor did he make any fuss of any kind. He just stood and listened. The same situation could happen in a nursery of seeing children, but unless the child was very much younger or inhibited, he would certainly raise a great outcry.

Instead of a sound leading to activity it often does the opposite. A blind child may listen to other children playing with a toy, but remain sitting where he is, merely asking what toy they are playing with.

When one of our nursery children drops a toy or any article and it rolls away, the blind child will usually listen to it until it stops rolling; he will not try to retrieve it, but merely ask someone to pick it up for him. The effort to get it himself, to find it, is often very difficult for him, takes a long time, and just is not worth all the trouble to him.

Hearing strange or unexpected noises arouses great fear in the blind children, and in such situations they become motionless, listening. Even slight noises can cause distress. When three of the children were washing dolls which squeaked, the squeak became too much for one of them. She withdrew, sat, and listened. The barking of dogs upsets several of our children; they become anxious, stand still, and listen. Even when they are reassured that the dog is far away and separated by a fence that they have felt, the listening is still continued for a long time; or the child may be filled with terror and in a state of panic, when even listening is no help.

But stillness is also frightening. Hearing someone leave the room causes fear of separation, and the resulting stillness often arouses panic. A little girl clearly showed this when she was in the room with her therapist who happened to be motionless. She called out suddenly in panic, "Where are you? Where are you?" The most striking example of this is reported by Fraiberg and Freedman (1964b) from the analysis of a nine-year-old blind boy:

> On one occasion I employed an innovation in these games [of hide-and-seek] in order to test his ability to follow cues in locating objects. I began the game with the ritual, "Good-by, Peter!" and then walked to a corner of the room clicking my heels on the wood floor to give him an opportunity to trace my movements. Then I waited in my corner, but did not give him the signal of my voice as I usually did. He started in search of me, was obviously not oriented, walked right past me, went through the door of the bathroom that communicates between his room and his parents' room, passed on into his parents' room, and then there was silence. He did not return. After a while his mother and I went in search of him. We found him lying on his mother's bed, his shoulders heaving convulsively and a look of mute terror on his face. . . . I tried to put his feelings into words and I tried to explain what had happened and that I had not been lost at all. But he refused to have anything to do with me for the rest of that

hour and he would not play the hide-and-seek games with me for a very long time.

## HEARING IN RELATION TO THE MOTHER

In our work with blind children we have become convinced that it is possible to observe and understand the use made of the sense of hearing, its variations and advances, in a manner similar to the well-studied development of sight. In what follows I shall attempt to explore the role which the relationship to the mother plays in this development. Since we hope to initiate a study of blind infants in their first year, I shall, in anticipation of these more direct observations, record here material derived from our work with the various mothers of the blind, i.e., their own impressions and memories of the child's earliest stages and of their own feelings and attitudes, past and present. Almost all these mothers had one or more seeing children besides the blind one, either before or after him. We shall have to wait and see whether the expected next step in our work will confirm or disprove the impressions gathered so far.

It is our impression that after a birth, the mother's first concern is to look at the baby, and to know that he is without physical defect. At this early moment only one mother knew about her child's blindness, i.e., the complete lack of eyes. During the early weeks the mothers learn to know their children in many ways, by looking at them, handling them, and recognizing their needs from their manner of crying.

Since infants, whether seeing or blind, react in these first weeks on the basis of reflex patterns and in accordance with satisfaction or dissatisfaction, the differences between them are not very obvious at this time. Hearing in the blind infant develops just as gradually as the sense of sight in the seeing infant. At this stage contact with the mother's body and the situation of nursing or being fed are the closest relationship. It therefore seems likely that the blind infant, as he roots and feels the mother's breast and as he sucks, also gradually notices the sounds which accompany this experience. With a bottle-fed infant the noises of the bottle feeding accompany the closeness of being held.

With the seeing children the mother's wish now is to make contact and to make them smile at her. By smiling and talking she does her utmost to elicit a response. That the blind infant naturally cannot respond as the mother desires or expects does not mean that in his own way he is not responding to the tone of her voice. What confuses the mother is the fact that the more interested the blind child is, the quieter he will become as he listens, the intentness of the listening probably being a clue to the strength of his response. This listening of the blind seems to be on a par with the staring gaze of the seeing infant—what is taken in at this time are probably the noises related to the infant's own body and to the mother's activities, her coming and going.

The mother who is concerned and disappointed because her baby does not react to her in the expected way will become more and more active with him in order to get an answering response. We know from our mothers that they have tickled their infants, even the corner of their lips to make them smile; that they have handled them roughly, done anything to get a show of feeling. According to the mothers, they often found their infants lying quietly and motionless. Possibly it was the approach of the mother to the cot which produced this *in*activity of the infant in order to listen more attentively to her footsteps and to try and differentiate the sounds. The important point here is that the mother would not be aware of the infant's listening, since she herself does not use this sense in the same manner.

While many a mother has made determined attempts to stimulate her infant, it is also natural for the mother of an inactive infant to pay less attention to him. Some mothers said of this period, "He did not seem to need me." Fraiberg and Freedman (1964b) also refer to such a remark by the mother of the boy already mentioned. As a consequence the infants were receiving less stimulation even before the mothers took them to the eye hospital and had their fears confirmed that their children were blind. Often this did not happen before the fourth month, sometimes even later, although the apparent unresponsiveness of the infant and the lack of communication between mother and child may have started much earlier to slow down development. The sense of hearing probably remained unaffected by all this. On the contrary, unobserved by the mother the infant heard more acutely, was more sensitive to noises, and had an excessive ability to differentiate between sounds.

While this was going on, the blind infant was also taking the normal steps from uncoordinated to coordinated movement and to more purposeful activity. Stretching out and thrashing about with arms and legs led to accidental encounters with objects, such as the sides or foot of his cot, which produced sounds, and the further repetition of such accidental happenings led to hitting out for the sake of the resulting noise. Tactile and acoustic impressions of the object seemingly competed for the child's attention and led to repetition. As the mothers reported, and as we could observe with other children, the infants were more active with their legs than their arms and seemed to produce more sounds with them when banging them against the bars of their cots. When the legs are more vigorous and therefore make more noise in kicking, they are naturally favored for this purpose. Interest in the sound produced is followed by interest in its variations, which in turn leads to a discrimination between objects according to the noise connected with them. This was confirmed also by the later observations of our nursery school children at play. The interest in the sounds made by their muscular activity is greater than the urge to use this same muscular power for sitting and standing or other active purposes.

Normal seeing infants during the same stage of development use their arms in preparation for pulling themselves up to sitting positions, and their leg muscles in preparation for crawling, standing, and walking. It is difficult to know how large a part vision plays in propelling them toward an aim, nor do we know how far the passivity produced in the blind by listening is a detrimental factor in slowing up this development. Whatever the answer may be, the greater interest of the blind infant in using his muscular power for making sounds seems to deflect him from using the same muscles equally for locomotion.

The mothers try to help their infants by pulling them up by their arms to create a sitting position, but this does not really remedy the situation, because this occurs in answer to the mother's wish and not in response to a stimulus arising from her child. We often find ourselves in a similar position trying to "stimulate" the interest of our blind children in the nursery school. Whenever such stimulation from our side does not answer to a spark in the child or does not coincide with it, the resulting activity remains abortive. When we give advice to the mothers, we should not forget to make use of this experience. Instead of urging them toward being active with their children, we should be able to teach them to look out for the clues which betray the child's need for activity.

For the seeing this is also the period when they watch with fascinated interest how adults and older children move about, and in play learn to imitate, as, for instance, in the game of pat-a-cake. Imitation plays a role also in the development toward sitting up and standing. I remember in this connection an observation of boy twins in the Hampstead Nurseries; one of them stood up for the first time in his cot, while the other one watched him despairingly, trying over and over again to stand like his brother but falling back. It took him a full day more until he could follow suit.

In contrast, the blind child can imitate only sounds. Although he is aware of the mother's moving from place to place, wishes to follow her, and notices by the position of her voice whether she sits or stands, at this juncture it is impossible for him to imitate her physical postures and movements.

The most difficult period for the mothers seems to be when they learn the fact that their infant is blind. Invariably they fall into a depression and consequently withdraw from the child, instead of stimulating him when he needs it most in order to counteract the other effects of blindness. Moreover, aside from being depressed, the mother does not know how to help the child. All the mothers we have worked with have, after a period of withdrawal, done their utmost to meet the problem confronting them. Some mothers have shown thought and cleverness in the choice of measures they have taken up. They have presented their infants with all kinds of objects and toys that make a noise, given them pots and pans to play with, the noises of which were familiar from daily use; when they were in another room but within earshot, they purposefully made sounds themselves or talked to the children to keep contact, or kept the wireless on to keep the children from being bored. But these well-meaning attempts to help are not necessarily those the best answer to the infant's needs.

The mothers are not the only ones who do not know how best to help these blind children; we are all groping in the dark with the same problem.

The most profitable approach to this investigation may be to try and watch what is found lacking in the development of the blind at a later age and to conclude from this retrospectively where the mother has failed to perceive his needs and therefore was unable to stimulate him appropriately.

There is nothing in the life of the blind infant which can make up for the missing interplay with the mother by means of looking and smiling at each other. For the blind, contact with the mother, apart from touch and smell, is made by hearing; but, although the mother talks and sings to her child, she does not perceive that he is building an inner world made up of sounds. Therefore his listening experience rarely affects both mother and infant in a similar manner, and does not draw them nearer to each other. As a further consequence the infant is not encouraged gradually to give up the enjoyment of the body closeness to the mother and to replace it by other means as the sighted do.

The more the infant turns to his world of sound, the less can his mother follow him. She becomes discouraged when he fails to notice that she looks at him and perhaps enjoys doing so. In her efforts to do the impossible and make the child take notice of her visually, the mother fails to follow what is possible, namely, the infant's growing interest in hearing her. She misses out on the chance to direct the child's hearing toward channels favorable for his development.

The less the infant responds to the mother, the less she enjoys him, and this sets up a vicious circle in which he is left more and more to his own devices.

These two reasons together, the mother's initial depression and her constant inability to share her visual experience with the child, are responsible for making her unable to appreciate his forward movement in development. She may not be alive to her infant's budding pleasures, his ability to notice through listening to the many sounds that make up his world, his enjoyment in the first achievements of producing sounds, banging things together, investigating objects, and exploring distances. She may not realize that his greater activity with his legs may be connected with the fact that she has missed the appropriate moment to give him incentives for using his arms. The innate urge that propels a child toward sitting, to crawling, to standing, does not seem sufficient in itself; the child also needs the mother's active participation and enjoyment in these activities (see Joyce Robertson, 1962).

What is so pleasurable for the sighted child is that his newly developing activities are accompanied by glances of approval and shared enjoyment from the mother's side, signs of approval which are missing for the blind. There is also no substitute for the seeing child's glance at the mother in moments of interest when he wants to share a pleasure. A touch or exclamation are not the same as those quick, fleeting glances accompanying actions.

Moreover, when the blind infant wants reassurance at times of doubt or anxiety, there is nothing to take the place of a reassuring glance. The blind infant probably tries to reach the mother in some subtle way at such moments, but not getting a response leads to disappointment and withdrawal on the infant's side.

Watching the mother and copying her activities are of necessity also missing, as, for instance, the pleasure when instead of being fed the seeing infant one day directs the spoon not to his own mouth but to his mother's, an action to which the mother answers with some appropriate reaction of her own, which again the seeing child watches.

With the blind infant, imitation of sound is present in the realm of speech. Since this is the main acceptable possibility of contact, the mothers pursue it energetically and the infants respond and copy them. Since this form of interplay is of such great importance for both mother and child, the learning of words is accelerated. Unfortunately, as mentioned before, this often results in parroting. The blind child's later difficulty in understanding the meaning and concepts of the language of the seeing impedes his ability to use words meaningfully. But the wish remains and the later parroting and jabbering of many blind children may be a result of this early effort of both mother and child to come close in one of the few contacts possible for them.

## Summary

The mother who can respond only as far as her own perceptual world allows has little conception of what a blind child can do and experience. She does not encourage where it would be necessary, and expects too little in the directions where he functions well. To interrupt a blind child's apparent passivity may mean interrupting an active achivement, namely, listening. The continual shaking of noisy toys and the endless play of the wireless are not what the infant needs. Curiosity is most likely alive, but remains unnoticed. Since it is not shared with the mother, it does not lead further but results in repetitive actions, rhythmic movements (blindisms), or in boredom, at best in a lonely experience. All this leads to a slowing down of development in certain spheres; in the most favorable cases what we find is uneven and unharmonious development.

## Literature

There are a few articles and papers that I would like to mention, because I have found them stimulating and helpful while working on this paper.

First, in an article on "Visual Behavior of Newborn Infants," George W. Greenman (1963) notes that body movements cease when the infant is attentive (looking); that one of the earliest ways in which an infant can communicate with his mother is by looking at her; that it serves the infant "psychologically by giving more pleasure to the nurturing person and thus increases the quality and frequency of his stimulation." As an important help in diagnosis, Greenman suggests that lack of visual response in the newborn would show that something is wrong with the child, not necessarily sight.

In 1953, Peter Hobart Knapp published an article on "The Ear, Listening and Hearing." Although this paper has nothing to do with blindness, Knapp remarks on the little attention given to the ear. After a discussion on the ear as a substitute for the genital, he goes to functions of the ear: that hearing is largely unnoticed but is emotionally charged; that the ear has a remarkable capacity to pick out sound patterns against chaotic background noise; that the "act of listening . . . contributes to superego and ego functions and to instinctual gratification. It remains subordinate to the main sensory representative of reality, vision, but extends its bounds." He stresses that auditory stimuli come in constant flow; that the sense of hearing is acute and selective; and he mentions the ability not to listen so as to prevent being overwhelmed by noise.

In an article on the deaf, Robert L. Sheroff (1959) mentions the lack of information concerning either the normal or pathological development of the deaf child in the psychiatric literature. This paper contains a plea to allow mothers to communicate with their deaf children by means of signs, a communication which is prohibited by some schools for the deaf so as to force the children to speak. Sharoff contends that the child's development is retarded in consequence because of lack of communication between mother and child. He also quotes from Ruesch and Kees (1956) who write concerning a hearing child. "In the first year of life expression necessarily must occur through non-verbal means. The child literally speaks with his whole body. . . . An impoverishment of communication and character development can be observed in those children, who grow up in surroundings, where the verbal was emphasized too early and when messages expressed in non-verbal terms were left unanswered."

In 1961, Evelyn Omwake and Albert J. Solnit presented a detailed report of the treatment of a blind child. In a discussion of this paper, George S. Klein (1962) makes the following points: that blindness isolates the child from his environment and makes for a drastic reduction in opportunities for manipulation and stimulation; "that unless certain forms of stimulation-with-learning take place at certain as yet unknown critical periods of a child's life, it is likely that very intractable consequences for adulthood will result"; that the child has a great need of loving behavior from the mother to give him affective experience.

From what I have extracted from these papers it is clear that many people are occupied with the same problems that I have discussed here and have come to the same conclusions; they also stress the same need for more information about the first years of life of both the deaf and blind.

I would like to mention one more paper which has a bearing on the handling of blind children and seems to me important because of the ideas contained in it. This paper, "Education as Related to Perceptual Experience: Normal Developmental Learning and the Education of the Child Born Blind" (1962) by Warren M. Brodey, was written primarily for the purpose of interesting people in the Pilot School for Blind Children in Washington. The effort in this school seems to be not only to stimulate the potential sensory ability of each blind child but to try and help the teachers as well as the mothers to become aware of what blindness really means, that is, to experience blindness as far as it is possible for a seeing person. Brodey suggests, for example, that the teachers should spend several of the school hours blindfolded and try in this way to identify with the blind. Of course it is impossible for a seeing person to go very far in actually experiencing blindness, but the attempt to do it adds a faint knowledge of some of the sense experiences and concepts of the blind, the importance of listening, the difficulties the blind child meets daily, and the skill and cleverness he needs to assemble, co-ordinate, and use the information collected by the other senses.

This, to my mind, is an idea well worth following. If by this means more detailed information is gathered concerning the inner life of the blind, better communication between mother and child can be established from early on and the blind child's isolation can be lessened.

### BIBLIOGRAPHY

Brodey, W. M. (1962), Education as Related to Perceptual Experience: Part 1. Normal Developmental Learning and the Education of the Child Born Blind. *Gifted Child Quart.*, 6.
Fraiberg, S. & Freedman, D. A. (1964a), Observations on the Development of a Congenitally Blind Child. *This Annual*, 19.
—— (1964b), Observations on a Nine-year-old Blind Child with Arrested Ego Development. *This Annual*, 19.
Gesell, A., Thompson, H., & Amatruda, C. (1934), *Infant Behavior*. New York: McGraw-Hill.
Greenman, G. W. (1963), Visual Behavior of Newborn Infants. In: *Modern Perspectives in Child Development*, ed. A. J. Solnit & S. Provence. New York: International Universities Press.
Klein, G. S. (1962), Blindness and Isolation. *This Annual*, 17.
Knapp, P. H. (1953), The Ear, Listening and Hearing. *J. Amer. Psa. Assn.*, 1.
Omwake, E. G. & Solnit, A. J. (1961), "It Isn't Fair": The Treatment of a Blind Child. *This Annual*, 16.
Robertson, J. (1962), Mothering as an Influence on Early Development: A Study of Well-Baby Clinic Records. *This Annual*, 17.
Ruesch, J. & Kees, W. (1956), *Nonverbal Communication*. Berkeley: University of California Press.
Sandler, A.-M. (1963), Aspects of Passivity and Ego Development in the Blind Infant. *This Annual*, 18.
Sheroff, R. L. (1959), Enforced Restriction and Communication: Its Implications for the Emotional Development of the Deaf Child. *Amer. J. Psychiat.*, 116.
Wills, D. (1963), The Role of Sound in the Development of a Blind Child. Unpublished.

# STUDIES IN THE EGO DEVELOPMENT OF THE CONGENITALLY BLIND CHILD

SELMA FRAIBERG (Ann Arbor) and

DAVID A. FREEDMAN, M.D. (New Orleans)

Our interest in the process of ego formation in the congenitally blind infant originated in our first encounters with certain ego deviations found among blind children. We and other investigators were impressed by the high incidence of ego deviations encountered among children totally blind from birth and the clinical picture presented by such children which closely resembled autism in the sighted child. Since many children blind from birth may achieve a level of ego integration comparable to that of the sighted child we had to conclude that the absence of vision was not in itself the primary predisposing factor to deviant development. The deviant blind children showed a uniform developmental arrest and a freezing of personality on the level of mouth primacy and nondifferentiation. These and certain details in the retrospective histories suggested that the process of ego formation had been impeded during the critical period nine to eighteen months. The role of blindness as an impediment and the unique adaptational problems of the blind infant were yet to be understood.

In a review of twenty-eight blind children who constituted the first year's admissions to a guidance program inaugurated by the Family Service Society of New Orleans in 1959 we found seven cases in the age range three to thirteen who presented an extraordinary picture of developmental arrest. The clinical picture resembled that

This investigation was supported in part by Public Health Service Grant #MH-07329-01 from the National Institute of Mental Health.

Mrs. Fraiberg is Associate Professor of Child Psychoanalysis, Department of Psychiatry, University of Michigan Medical School. Dr. Freedman is Associate Professor of Clinical Neurology, Tulane University School of Medicine, and a training analyst for the New Orleans Psychoanalytic Institute.

of infantile autism, but close examination revealed significant differences as well. Later we will describe these children.

Between 1959 and 1962 the authors engaged in the collaborative treatment of a deviant blind child and his mother. The case of Peter, which is presented in Part I of this essay, is typical of the deviant children we encountered in the agency population. The opportunity for close study of the deviant behavior and development of this child brought our attention to certain critical phases in ego formation during which the absence of vision impedes or may imperil integrative processes. The adaptive failures seen in Peter and other children in the blind group brought forth a large number of unanswered questions regarding the adaptive solutions found by normal blind infants and young children. We must assume from the evidence presented by large numbers of healthy and educable blind children that other sensory modalities can substitute for vision in the process of ego formation. There remain the questions: how are these substitutions made, and how does ego formation take place in the absence of vision? All theorizing concerning the process of ego formation is predicated upon the utilization of vision. It occurred to us that developmental studies of infants should help delineate the role of vision in ego formation and the vulnerable points in this early development which may lead to adaptive failures and ego deviations.

In July of 1961 we began our observations of an infant, then twenty-two weeks old, who had been totally blind from birth with the diagnosis ophthalmia neonatorum. She was followed through monthly observations and a motion-picture film record until twenty-eight months of age. A report and discussion of our findings in the study of the infant, Toni, is presented in Part II of this paper. The blind infant achieved at two years of age a level of maturation that was well within the norms for a blind child. At the time our observations terminated we saw no evidence of ego deviations. But as we followed the development of this child we began to understand how her blindness created a roadblock in her development at certain critical points in ego formation. As we watched this healthy blind child find circuitous routes to get onto the main developmental paths, we understood how, under less than favorable environmental circumstances and with less adaptive capacity than that shown by Toni, the complex solutions may never be found at all.

For these reasons the adaptive solutions found by a blind infant are best viewed against the background of adaptive failure in the cases of the deviant blind children.

The following description of the deviant blind child is based upon the group of cases in our Family Service Society case load together with those reported in the literature by Keeler (1958), Parmalee (1955), and Parmalee, Cutsforth, and Jackson (1958). The striking feature of these cases drawn from three sources is "uniformity." The investigator finds himself with the uncanny feeling that he is reading the same case over and over. In studying our Family Service Society records we had to provide ourselves with artificial memory cues to distinguish one case from another. ("Martin is the one who likes to suck on clothespins; Martha is the one who chews rubber jar rings; Jane is the head banger, and Chrissey bangs her bottom against the wall.")

The child may be two years old, five years, nine, or even thirteen years old and the picture is almost unvarying. Typically the deviant child spends hours in bed or in a chair or lying on the floor, absently mouthing an object. There is no interest in toys or any objects that are not in themselves need satisfying or stimulating to the mouth. Contact with human objects is often initiated by biting and even more often by a primitive clutching and clawing with the hands. For all these children the mouth remains the primary organ of perception. New objects are brought to the mouth and are rarely explored manually.

The behavior of the hand is striking. While many of the children can use the hand for self-feeding and can even use spoons and forks, the hand appears to have no autonomy of its own. It can serve the mouth, it can bring objects to the mouth, but it is not employed for examination or manipulation of objects. Discrimination of objects remains centered in the mouth; however, as already seen, objects are important not for their own characteristics but for their qualities in stimulating the mouth.

What we see in this superficial picture of the deviant blind children is a personality that has remained mouth-centered to an extent that is almost never encountered among sighted children except, perhaps, for certain children who have suffered extreme deprivation in infancy (Provence and Lipton, 1962; Spitz, 1945). And we should note that although mouth-centeredness and failure to achieve hand autonomy are two factors uniformly present in the deviant blind children, these are not characteristics commonly found among sighted autistic children. If we consider, further, that the hand of the blind child must serve as a primary organ for perception, the adaptive failure of the hand in these deviant blind children must be regarded as an important factor in the total picture of adaptive failure.

However, these children do display behavior such as body rocking, head banging, arm and hand waving, and bizarre posturing which is strikingly similar to that observed in the sighted autistic child. Language is rarely employed for communication or expression of need and consists mainly of echolalia and the repetitive use of apparently meaningless words and phrases. Discrimination of "I" and "you" has not appeared and self-reference is made in the third person.

In some cases the mother is not discriminated from other persons in the environment. In other cases an attachment to the mother is demonstrable, and reactions to separation from the mother are discernible through biting or clawing or a frenzied display of the whole repertory of autistic behavior. Still other children who seem to be oblivious to mother's presence and efforts to stimulate them will react violently to any threat of separation.

The early developmental histories of these deviant blind children are not significantly different from those of blind children who have achieved a good level of ego integration. They are described as quiet babies who were content to lie in their cribs for hours, and this is a common description of the infant who is blind from birth. The reports on both groups uniformly stress the mother's guilt and depression at learning of the child's blindness. But, as Keeler has reported, the histories of the deviant blind children often show the failure of the mother to offer stimulation and to make emotional contact with the sensorially deprived infant.

The gross motor development of the deviant children is within the norms for blind infants during the first nine months. Learning to hold up the head, to turn over, to sit independently were usually achieved without marked delay according to the histories. But many of these babies either do not creep, or learn to creep at a very late date, and walking is markedly delayed in nearly every case. Several of the children did not achieve independent walking until the age of four or five. It should be noted that among blind children, walking is normally achieved much later than it is among sighted children. In the Norris (1957) study between 50 and 75 per cent of the 295 blind children achieved independent walking between the ages of two and three, with a range from fifteen months to five years. We have some evidence from our records that those infants who have even a small amount of form perception follow patterns of motor development that are very close to those of sighted children and achieve independent locomotion without significant delays.

One of the striking features of this group of deviant blind children is the picture of developmental arrest. The picture of the thirteen-year-old deviant blind child is not different in any significant way from that of the two- or three-year-old in the deviant group. In one case we were able to compare our picture of a ten-year-old blind boy in the deviant group with home movies of him that dated back to the age of three. Except for some progress in independent locomotion there was almost no difference in the developmental achievements at three and at ten.

The deviant blind children present a picture that begins to lag at the end of the first year and falls off progressively during the second year. In the third year we have the impression that development has come to a standstill. If independent locomotion is achieved at four or five, it seems to have little effect upon the over-all developmental picture.

This clinical picture remained unevaluated until recent years. Speculations regarding possible brain damage have been offered, but the available evidence does not give stronger support for a neurological etiology in these cases than for autism in the sighted. Until the past decade the large number of retrolental fibroplasia cases in the blind child population had further obscured the picture and, in the eyes of many clinicians, weighted the possibilities in favor of a neurological etiology. It was not until the publication of studies by Norris et al. (1957) and Keeler (1958) that a comparison of the children with retrolental fibroplasia and children blind from other causes was made, and the new evidence required a clinical reassessment of the blind child with gross ego deviations.

The Norris report which involved 295 blind preschool children is one of the most extensive studies to date. The sample included 209 children (71%) with the diagnosis retrolental fibroplasia; the remaining 86 cases (29%) included children blind from other causes. Testing was conducted at intervals throughout the first six and a half years of the child's life. Tests included the Cattell, adapted for use with the blind child in this study, and the Interim Hayes-Binet Intelligence Scale for the Blind. It was found that the performance of the children in the retrolental fibroplasia group was well within the range for blind children in general with a distribution pattern that did not distinguish this group from the group of children blind from other causes. Actually, if a correction were made for prematurity, the ratings in the retrolental fibroplasia group would have been better than those in the second group. In summarizing their findings Norris et al. say: "Within the limitations of the methods and subjects employed by this study there is no evidence that retrolental fibroplasia is associated with a specific or a generalized brain defect. When a child with retrolental fibroplasia is retarded in his functioning and there are no specific neurological findings, the retardation must be presumed to be directly related to complex social and environmental factors."

It was necessary, then, to make a new assessment of the retrolental fibroplasia group. Evidently, this group which, until a decade ago, constituted more than 70 per cent of the total blind child population, had distorted the over-all clinical picture by including among their numbers a large group of deviant children whose arrested development and bizarre motility gave apparent support to a neurological etiology. In this comparative study by the Norris group the distortions that were brought about through the impact of numbers were corrected and the clinician was obliged to look for other factors in the development of blind infants which might explain the adaptive failure of a significant number of these children.

Keeler's work in Toronto brought fresh insights to the problem of etiology in the deviant blind group. His investigation began with five preschool blind children who presented a clinical picture that struck him as remarkably similar to that of "infantile autism." The description of these children, as given by Keeler, is incorporated in the profile of the deviant child we have presented earlier in this essay. The cause of blindness in all five of Keeler's cases was retrolental fibroplasia. Keeler then selected a sample of thirty-five additional cases of children with retrolental fibroplasia (total registered in Ontario was 102 cases). He found that the histories and behavior patterns of all thirty-five cases were in many ways similar to those he had seen in the five intensive cases referred to his hospital, but none of the second group of children showed ego deviations to the degree seen in the intensive group, and the ten children in the sample who were in school were up to grade in spite of their disturbances of personality. In order to analyze more closely the factors at work in the ego disturbances found among the retrolental fibroplasia cases Keeler decided to study two other categories of blind children; one group blinded at birth and another group blinded postnatally, in infancy or early childhood. The first group consisted of eighteen children who were congenitally blinded by such conditions as cataracts, familial macular degeneration, buphthalmos, endophthalmitis, etc. It is important to note that in all these cases the amount of vision was much greater than that present in the children with retrolental fibroplasia, but none of them had more than 20/200 vision in the better eye. In this group the developmental patterns more closely approximated those of sighted children; there were not the developmental delays in motor achievements, feeding, toilet training, etc. Among these children Keeler did not find autistic patterns and abnormalities in motility to the same degree that he saw them in the retrolental fibroplasia group. In the second group, which consisted of seventeen children blinded postnatally, abnormalities in development and behavior were least conspicuous. The majority of the children in this group became blinded during the first and second years of life and in many cases motor maturation, acquisition of language, feeding and toilet habits, etc., had been established before blindness occurred.

Keeler's analysis of the developmental histories and behavior patterns of the blind children in each of these three groups focuses clinical attention on these points: the gross abnormalities encountered in certain blind children appear to be associated with total or nearly total blindness from birth and a history of inadequate emotional stimulation in the early months of life. If the incidence of abnormal ego development is conspicuously high in the retrolental fibroplasia group, we are obliged to include in this assessment the fact that it is the largest single category of blindness in which total or nearly total blindness from birth occurs. Each of Keeler's five children who showed gross abnormalities and developmental arrest also had a history of inadequate emotional stimulation in infancy. The number of children in Keeler's retrolental fibroplasia group who were in fact functioning adequately appears to confirm the findings in the Norris study and also shows clearly that blindness from birth is not in itself the predisposing factor to deviant development. Both studies bring attention, finally, to the factor of emotional stimulation and incentives for development in an infant blind from birth.

Our cases at the Family Service Society gave additional support to the findings of both Norris and Keeler as reported here. We may add, however, that the severe ego deviations which Keeler reported only in his retrolental fibroplasia cases appeared in our agency cases outside of this group as well. In the two years following our initial survey we found two such examples among new cases, one a girl of three, the second a girl twenty-two months old. In both cases the diagnosis "optic atrophy" had been made. The clinical picture in these two cases differed in no significant way from that of deviant children in the retrolental fibroplasia group. In each case, too, there was a well-documented history of inadequate emotional stimulation and neglect in infancy. In both cases, of course, we have the factors "totally blind from birth" and "inadequate stimulation in infancy" as Keeler has hypothesized for the etiology of autism in the blind child. In Keeler's own control group (the congenitally blind) the amount of vision present in all cases was greater than that of the cases in the retrolental fibroplasia group.

Our Family Service Society cases provide us with one additional footnote: Among the retrolental fibroplasia cases we were unable to find any correlations between the clinical picture of developmental arrest and such factors as birth weight, degree of prematurity, or length of time in oxygen.

None of these studies, of course, rule out the possibility of brain damage in the deviant blind children. While the question remains to be answered, it should be noted that we and others have found that if the pathological signs are detected in the early months or years, remedial measures can be employed which may bring about dramatic reversal of these tendencies and a favorable ego development. In the case of children under three years of age guidance of the mother may be sufficient. In the brilliant case report of Omwake and Solnit (1961) an educational and psychotherapeutic approach brought about normal ego functioning in a child who, at three years of age, resembled in every way the clinical picture of developmental arrest we have described here.

# I

## A Nine-year-old Blind Boy with Arrested Ego Development

The case of Peter which follows is typical of the group of deviant blind children we have described.

Peter was eight years ten months when his treatment was begun. Some months after the work with Peter was under way, his mother began her own analysis which then made possible a more detailed study of the complexities of the mother-child relationship and illuminated portions of the child's history that had earlier been obscure.

Peter is the youngest child of his family. His mother was thirty-five and his father forty at the time of his birth. The pregnancy had been unplanned and was unwelcome. Peter is a surviving member of a set of identical twins who were born prematurely. His birth weight was 2 lbs. and 2 oz. Immediately after delivery he was placed in an incubator with an oxygen-rich atmosphere. At approximately six months of age the parents became concerned about his lack of responsiveness and his apparent indifference to his surroundings. At this time the child was examined and a diagnosis of retrolental fibroplasia was made.

Both parents are intelligent and well educated. They have demonstrated their capacities for parenthood in the rearing of two older daughters, now in adolescence, who present no unusual problems, have performed well in school, and are attractive and responsive youngsters.

The mother became depressed immediately after learning that
Peter was blind. She remembered the early years of Peter's life as a
kind of bad dream. We have the impression from our observations
of the mother both in analysis and in relation to her child and his
treatment that much of her handling then, as now, was mechanical,
driven by guilt, and that at times when her suffering became too
great for her she simply withdrew. There is evidence that Peter was
in the care of servants a good deal of the time and that there was a
succession of maids, so numerous that their names could hardly be
recalled by the mother when later we needed to verify one or another
of the allusions which Peter made to them in his treatment.

We have very little information, therefore, regarding the early
development of Peter. We are told that his motor development was
a little slow during his first year, but his mother could not give us
dates or approximate dates for any of the achievements. We know,
however, that he never crept, that walking with support was achieved
sometime between two and two and a half, and that even at the age
of three, when he entered a nursery school for the blind, he did not
walk independently and moved from place to place by hanging on
to objects.

When Peter was eight his parents grasped at a new hope for their
apparently uneducable child and arranged for him to be sent to an
eastern community where a new residential program for disturbed
blind children was being set up. Since there were initial difficulties
in establishing the new facility, Peter lived in a foster home for
several months and was finally transferred to the institution, where
he remained for approximately five months. The institution closed
its program unexpectedly at the end of this period and Peter was
returned to his home. We have been unable to obtain any reports
from the clinical staff of this institution and the little we know we
can only piece together from the child's communications to his therapist and from the mother's observations when she visited.

As Peter grew to know his therapist and progressed in his ability
to communicate he gave us vignettes of this year. He re-enacted
nighttime scenes in which he made the noises of crying and imitated
the voice of one or another of the nurses in this institution: "Sh-h!
What's the matter?" "Stop that!" "Stop that crying. You're not a
baby!" "You'll wake up all the boys!" And on other occasions he

would mimic an angry adult voice, "Sit there!" "Just sit there until I come back!" (referring to the toilet) and "You made a mess!" The degree to which he had regressed during this period also came out in unexpected ways. A disgusted voice is imitated, "What! Eating your stool!" and when he was first seen approximately a month after he returned from the institution, he was emaciated and in such poor nutritional state that it seemed certain that this child had been refusing food for some time, for there was no question that in this institution the children were adequately fed. Occasionally one caught a hint from Peter's verbal memories that his nutrition had become of great concern to the staff at the institution for he would repeat in alien voices, "Eat your custard now! Now, come on— just a little bit, just a little bit more!" Variations on this theme were common in his "reports."

*Initial Observations*

When I first visited Peter at his home I saw him on the front lawn with his nurse, entwining himself around her body.[1] He was tall for his age, extremely thin, pale, with an absent self-absorbed look upon his face. His arms and legs seemed to flop like a rag doll's. He walked uncertainly with support and several times his nurse picked him up in her arms and carried him from place to place.

Later we moved to the garden. Peter paid no attention to me or to my voice and sat or lay on the picnic table absently mouthing a rubber toy. Occasionally he made an irrelevant statement. Once he sang, in perfect pitch, "Pussy cat, pussy cat, where have you been?" His mother told me that he spent hours at his record player.

After a while he came close to me and fingered me. Then, without any change of facial expression and without any show of feeling, he began to dig his fingernails into the skin of my arm, very hard, and causing me to wince with pain. From this point on it was nearly impossible to divert Peter from digging his nails into me or alternately pinching me with great intensity. It is impossible to describe this experience. I cannot call it sadistic. It was as if he did not know this was painful to me and I really felt that on the primitive undifferentiated level on which Peter operated he was not able to

1 In the case narrative "I" refers to the child's therapist (S.F.). The mother's analyst was D.F.

identify with the feelings of another person. This digging into me had the quality of trying to get into me, to burrow himself into me, and the pinching had the quality of just holding onto me for dear life.

I observed that when Peter lost an object he was mouthing, he showed no reaction to loss and did not search for it. Repeated observations in this session and in others confirmed this point. Very clearly this child had no concept of an object that existed independent of his perception of it.

While his mother was with us I observed that his reaction to her was in no discernible way different from his reaction to me, to the nurse, or to the dog. At no time, then and for many weeks after I began to work with him, did he ask a direct question, express a need through gesture or language, or answer a question put to him. His mother told me that until very recently he did not call her "Mama" but referred to her as "Too-hoo." She explained that this word derived from her own greeting to him when she entered the house.

Peter always referred to himself in the third person. The word "I," his mother told me, had entered his vocabulary before he had gone to the institution last year, but when I was able to observe him directly I felt that "I" was not employed for self-reference and was mechanically interpolated into speech as if he had been given lessons in "I" and "you."

There were no toys to which Peter had any attachment. When he showed transitory interest in objects he brought them to his mouth, sucked on them, chewed them. He did not explore them with his hands, he did not manipulate them. Prehension was poor and the fingers were rigidly extended. The only well-coordinated movements observed were those employed in bringing an object to the mouth.

Peter's mother reported that he could feed himself adequately and I was able to confirm this through direct observation. He still preferred soft foods, had great difficulty in masticating, and usually spit out the masticated food rather than swallow it.

In speech samples which I obtained in later sessions there were typically much echolalia and toneless repetition of stereotyped phrases.

When my early efforts to work with Peter and his mother began to bring favorable results, I suggested with all necessary caution to the parents that we might attempt a treatment program, that we should have reservations regarding its outcome, but that I thought I could promise some improvement in functioning. The parents were able to accept a treatment program on this basis. Both parents said honestly that they did not expect that Peter would ever be able to go to school, that they did not even know whether he was educable to any extent, but if only he could come alive, be responsive, be a happier child, be a member of the family, they would consider the treatment well worth while.

I shall briefly describe the treatment approach. Peter was visited at his home five times a week. From the beginning I discovered that there were great advantages in having his mother present during my visits with Peter. Not only did it constantly afford me a picture of mother and child together, but the mother could gain insight into Peter's behavior. As Peter began to communicate more and more to me, the mother could share the knowledge and the insight and make use of them in her handling of him.

Peter was in no sense "analyzable," of course. What I attempted to do was to apply analytic insights in a kind of education and therapy for a particular child.

The report that follows is a summary of observations over a two-and-a-half-year period.

## The Mother-Child Relationship

The earliest educational work with the mother was, of course, focused on promoting ties between her and the child who barely discriminated her from other human beings in his environment. Mrs. M. was encouraged to take over a major part of the child's care and she was helped to understand how need satisfaction and constancy were the indispensable first steps in establishing human ties. Gradually in the early months of treatment Peter's attachment to his mother became evident. He showed joy when she appeared and reactions to separation. He began to use the word "Mama" consistently for the first time. Out of the need-satisfying relationship gradually evolved the expression of need in language and there was a rapid expansion of speech.

Concurrent with the work in building the mother-child ties was the education of the mother to the unique needs of a blind child in acquiring knowledge of his world. Ironically, much of this education was not new to the mother, who had read widely in the literature of education of the blind; but until the treatment of Peter was begun and her own analysis was under way, she had been unable to apply this knowledge. Where the blind child is almost entirely dependent upon mobility for discovering a world of objects, Peter had been very largely restricted in his home. As opportunities for free movement and exploration of his environment were opened up to him, and as the range of his experience expanded, his exploration and manipulation of objects became more and more absorbing, the discovery of objects led to naming of objects, and there followed a rapid expansion of his vocabulary.

The mother's own reaction to the child's evolving ties to her was ambivalent. On the one hand, she was gratified by the signs of progress, on the other hand, the demands of the child who had wakened to a human relationship were at times nearly intolerable to her. She confessed to irritation and anger and a longing to have someone else take over. It was as if this treatment which required her to be a mother to the child had evoked an ambivalence that was very close to her experiences in the early months of Peter's life. She had not yet begun her own analysis and in my educational role I could not easily explore the dimensions of this conflict. But one thing became clear as we talked together in the early months. This mother, who had impressed everyone with her devotion to the blind child, had in fact avoided contact with him and had turned over most of his care to servants.

Many months later, when Peter's feeding had become the topic for discussion, I inquired about details and learned that Peter usually ate alone or in the company of a servant. When I encouraged Mrs. M. to join Peter for at least one meal a day and report the results to me, she burst into tears and said, "You don't know what you're asking of me!" He was repulsive at mealtimes, she said. He threw food, spit out food, smeared it. "I feel that if I am paying someone to work here I shouldn't have to put up with that myself!" But behind the complaints about the child's repulsive eating habits was a profound revulsion which was illuminated later in the mother's analysis. This analytic material and her own communications to me revealed that she had avoided the feeding of Peter in infancy and that the revulsion against the infant had expressed itself, among other ways, in an inability to feed him. The pattern of turning over the feeding of the child to servants was a very early one. From the analytic material there was good reason to believe that the mother's inability to respond to her infant had antedated the discovery of his blindness (at six months). Her ambivalence toward the infant was associated with a crisis that preceded the child's birth and which, for various reasons, must be excluded from this report. But it is equally important to note that even before the diagnosis of blindness was made, this baby, like all infants totally blind from birth, had appeared to the mother as curiously unresponsive. He was quiet and content to lie in his crib for hours. "He never seemed to need me!" the mother told us, and because this was a woman whose capacities for relationship were largely called forth by expressed needs of a partner, this baby who did not seem to need her could elicit no response.

With some working through of this material in her analysis, Mrs. M. was able to come to grips with her need to abdicate at the time of Peter's meals. She found, to her surprise, that when she joined him at mealtimes, the repulsive food habits declined in a very short period, and the child's own ties to mother were strengthened by the association of mother with eating pleasures.

Another motive in the mother's avoidance of contact with her child appeared early in treatment. In the period that preceded the mother's own analysis, I saw how typically she employed reaction formations against anger and rage, both in relation to her child and to me. With encouragement she was able to express more and more of her feelings toward Peter and then, on one occasion, was able to admit with considerable anxiety that she was afraid that if she "let go" she might kill Peter. She was able to see how, when her anger became dangerous to her, she avoided contact with Peter. When her guilt about and fear of her destructive feelings became evident to her, she accepted my recommendation of analytic treatment for herself.

The mother's analysis made it possible to conduct my educational work with greater freedom and flexibility. Mrs. M. continued to work closely with me and to be present during Peter's sessions, but it was no longer necessary for me to deal with aspects of her own conflict that impeded the child's treatment. With analytic help the mother demonstrated unusual capacities to support the child's treatment.

## The Mouth and the Hand

I hope my description adequately conveyed the picture of mouth activity as I saw it in Peter at the beginning of treatment. The mouth, it appeared, had remained the center of his primitive personality organization. All objects were brought to the mouth; the mouth was almost never empty. Perception largely centered in the mouth. There was almost no handling or exploration with the hands. We know that this is not typical for normal blind children, and yet it is important to note that for all blind persons the mouth functions as a discriminating sensory organ throughout life. (Villay [1930] describes how, even as an adult, he relied upon his mouth, and particularly his tongue, to make the finest perceptual distinctions.) In Peter the mouth had also remained the center of erotic and aggressive impulses, and when I first knew him it did not even appear that these were differentiated. When he made contact he mouthed, and often the moment after, he bit, and this biting had the quality not of intentional aggression but of incorporation.

Very early in Peter's treatment I began to understand the behavior of the hand in the clutching and clawing, that I described earlier. Peter could at first make contact with me only by clawing me, burrowing his fingers into the skin of my arm and neck. When at such times I moved away from him and maintained contact with him merely through my voice, he would immediately revert to apathy or to autistic mannerisms (rocking, swaying, etc.). But on one such occasion as I withdrew in pain, he stopped his clawing of me, withdrew his fingernails from my arm, then bit me on the head. When I recovered, I was again struck by the fact that there was no sadism in this act—again it had the quality of taking me in so that I could not go away. Then, recalling the sequence of the frustrated digging into me with his fingernails and biting that immediately followed, I understood the fuller meaning of the hand behavior. The hand behaved like a mouth, the fingernails like teeth, and the pinching activity like biting also. The oral-incorporative aspects of mouthing and biting had been transferred to the hand.

When I understood the oral-incorporative significance of this clutching and clawing, I was able to make a useful interpretation to Peter. The next time he seized me and clawed me in this way, I did not immediately extricate myself, but said, "You don't have to be afraid. I won't go away." And with this he released his "death grip" on me. In the same session when he began to claw his mother I repeated the interpretation, "You don't have to be afraid. Mother will not go away," and he released his mother. From this time on we were able to bring about control of the clutching and clawing with these words. His mother was deeply impressed. It was "like magic," she said; but most important of all, she had achieved insight into a piece of behavior that she had always interpreted as aggressive and now began to understand as a kind of inarticulate terror. (Later, when this same hand behavior acquired the significance of intentional aggression, other ways of handling it had to be employed.)

In this connection it is worth mentioning that this biting, clawing, pinching behavior is commonly observed among preschool blind children, and it is retained by the blind children with severe ego deviations. It is as if grasping has not freed itself of the oral mode and the hand has not achieved autonomy from the mouth.

For Peter the progress from mouth to hand was slow and laborious. The mouth retained its primacy as a perceptual organ for most of the first two years of my work with him. Even after he progressed in grasping he was slow to acquire pleasure in manual exploration of objects. For the most part it appeared that an object was desirable or not desirable to the degree that it stimulated the oral cavity in some preferred fashion. When I tried to encourage tactile discrimination by bringing him various textiles and textures for him to handle, he brought them to his mouth and discarded them when the texture or taste was not pleasing to the mouth. When Mrs. M. and I covered bean bags with a variety of materials, velvet, satin, corduroy, he did not discriminate among them on the basis of their qualities. When we introduced him to a "tonette," hoping that mouth satisfaction, audition, and manual proprioceptive experience might make this an attractive object to him, he produced one note and tossed it away. He did the same thing on subsequent attempts.

However, there were small and encouraging achievements along the way. There were periods during which he evidently enjoyed fitting together pots and lids, or jars and covers. He began to enjoy filling and dumping a milk bottle with clothespins and successfully inhibited the impulse to bring the clothespin to his mouth.

A big step was achieved at the beginning of the third year of treatment. He became interested in sea shells and brought a number of them home from the beach. He played with them for long periods, tracing their whorls with his fingers and gradually discriminating among them. In a box of several dozen there were a few that he preferred and he quickly sorted them with his finger tips until he found these. He used his mouth minimally for discrimination. His mother and I encouraged this newly found interest and collected shells for him.

Then, almost as soon as Mrs. M. and I became aware of this new progress in use of the hands, we noticed something else. The clawing and pinching had disappeared altogether! Prior to this period there had been much intentionally aggressive scratching and pinching— a later sequel to the undifferentiated clawing we had seen earlier. The hand, which had largely functioned as an auxiliary mouth, now appeared to be freeing itself of the oral mode, with a corresponding neutralization of drive qualities.

There is nothing in my observations that tells us exactly how this was achieved and why it occurred at this particular time! In the meantime, there was a new behavior toward inanimate objects in general. Objects that had once served only self-stimulation now began to acquire independent values. An old wooden bowl that Peter used to suck on and earlier had used to bang his head with now, for the first time, became a vessel and he spent long periods filling it with shells or other small objects.

During this period I had the feeling that something new was taking place in Peter's personality. And then, at the end of a six-week period, the new behavior was lost, the shells and the bowl were again brought to the mouth to be sucked, the pinching and scratching returned, and the promise of these new developments faded. (This regression will be discussed later along with other data from the same period.)

A number of provocative questions derive from these observations of a personality that has remained mouth-centered, as in the case of Peter and other deviant children. Following a suggestion given to us by Dr. Joseph Michaels at an early stage in this study, we began to consider the implications for ego development when an organ that has retained a high degree of instinctual cathexis also serves as a primary organ of perception. The prolonged mouth-centered perception of the blind infant and young child may impede the development of "conflict-free" perception. In the development of the sighted infant the primary autonomy of vision becomes one of the guarantees of conflict-free perception. In the normal development of blind infants and young children, the hand takes over as the leading organ of perception and achieves autonomy from the mouth.

We are accustomed to speak of the hands as the "eyes" of the blind. Until we studied the infant Toni, we did not understand that the achievement of hand autonomy in a blind infant is a feat of extraordinary virtuosity. *In this healthy, normally developing infant, we saw that perception remained mouth-centered until well into the second year, and the hand did not achieve primacy as a perceptual organ until the last half of the second year.* Where vision mediates the evolution of hand autonomy in the sighted child, the absence of vision obstructed this crucial progress in the healthy blind infant, and hand autonomy was achieved finally through an elaborate detour. From the history of Peter and other deviant blind children we began to understand that in less than favorable environmental circumstances the progress from mouth to hand may not be achieved at all and the personality may remain arrested on the level of mouth-centeredness and nondifferentiation.

*Object Concept*

We have already described Peter's inability to search for lost objects or even to attempt to recover them after he lost contact through mouth or hand. At the same time, he could orient himself to a certain degree in his own room, could find his bed, could make his way from his bed to his record player. When I observed him in the family kitchen at a mealtime it was clear that he was not well oriented there, and his behavior in the downstairs rooms suggested that he had explored them very little. His own room, it is important to know, isolated him to a very large extent from even the ordinary household noises. This was a large house and his room was so situated that very little sound carried from the first floor to the second floor, and a circular staircase broke up sound so successfully that on occasions when I had to call his mother or nurse for assistance, my own voice could not be heard.

Peter had in many ways shown that he had no concept of the existence of an object after he lost contact with it; in the same way he showed that he had no concept of the existence of human objects independent of his perception of them. He did not call for his mother, he did not search for his mother. He showed his concern over the disappearance of persons through repeated questions, "Where is Aunt Cora? Where is Roger? Where is Jonathan?" It did not even matter that some of these people had had only the most casual relationship with him. He would ask one question most urgently, "Laura, Laura! Where is Laura!" Laura was a cousin of his mother's who had died during the time when Peter was in the institution. He of course did not know what "dead" meant, but his mother had told him that Laura could not come back.

The "where is . . ." questions need clarification. "Where is Aunt Cora?" for example, did not mean that Aunt Cora must be "some place," i.e., that she had an existence for Peter when he was not in contact with her. This could be tested by means of Peter's behavior toward inanimate objects during the same period. When Peter dropped his bowl or his block there was no attempt at recovery or even a gesture of recovery. He would say in a flat voice, "Where is my bowl?" and his mother or I would retrieve it. If we did not pick it up for him, he would shift his attention. "Where is . . ." then was a magic formula to bring back the object. The "where is . . ." construction was also the magic formula in peek-a-boo games and hiding games that Mrs. M. and I played with Peter, an incantation that "caused" someone to return. Following Piaget (1937), we should probably take the failure to search for human or inanimate objects after loss of contact as a fair sign that he had not acquired a concept of the independence of objects from his perception. At a later stage in treatment, which will be described, Peter demonstrated active search and with this achievement his behavior toward people and things altered in significant ways.

For many weeks at the beginning of my work with Peter I played hide-and-seek games with him and taught him to find me through tracing my voice. These games gave him enormous pleasure and we played them repetitiously hour after hour after hour. After a while he began to formalize the games, sending me away with a push, saying, "Good-by!" then finding me and spontaneously hugging me in a greeting. I had also encouraged his mother to play these games with him, but during the early months of treatment she had very little luck in engaging him in such games. I soon understood why. Once when I asked her to join in a game during one of our sessions, Peter himself refused to go on. I saw through his behavior that it was too dangerous for him to play "going away and returning" with mother herself. As a neutral object I could serve the game purpose very well; his mother could not.

On one occasion I employed an innovation in these games in order to test his ability to follow cues in locating objects. I began the game with the ritual, "Good-by, Peter!" and then walked to a corner of the room clicking my heels on the wood floor to give him an opportunity to trace my movements. Then I waited in my corner, but did not give him the signal of my voice as I usually did. He started in search of me, was obviously not oriented, walked right past me, went through the door of the bathroom that communicates between his room and his parents' room, passed on into his parents' room, and then there was silence. He did not return. After a little while his mother and I went in search of him. We found him lying on his mother's bed, his shoulders heaving convulsively and a look of mute terror on his face. He could not cry in those days, he could only go through a kind of motor parody of grief. I tried to put his feelings into words and I tried to explain to him what had happened and that I had not been lost at all. But he refused to have anything to do with me for the rest of that hour and he would not play the hide-and-seek games with me for a very long time.

For many months Mrs. M. and I found every means available to us to teach Peter the substantiality and permanence of objects through games and other devices. We taught him to find the cookie jar in the kitchen and get his own cookies. We taught him to find the cracker cupboard. He discovered the joys of the pots and pans cupboards, and then, of course, there came a rapid expansion of searches into everything. From the initial discovery of objects that could always be found in the same place he moved on to the discovery that the

same object could be found in a different place and was still the
object he had known before. And yet it was nearly a year of work
before Peter demonstrated real gains in this area. Then he was
searching actively for objects and if he did not find them in the
expected place, he would search for them in another place. When he
wanted his mother he went in search of her.

There was an interesting corollary in speech development at the
same time. We recall that in the beginning Peter did not call for his
mother and, as a matter of fact, he did not even cry to summon her.
Since his mother did not have a substantial existence for him, speech
did not possess one of its vital functions—to summon the lost object,
to bring back the lost object. But later when Peter clearly demonstrated his ability to search for objects and recover them and when
the concept became stabilized, the change was reflected in speech. He
began calling his mother, summoning her to his side, or even calling
her while she was in the same room in order to locate her. At this
time his incessant calling of mother nearly exhausted her. Mrs. M.
also provided us with an interesting observation. On the one hand,
she understood very well that this was a wonderful achievement for
Peter; on the other hand, she found herself disturbed. For now, she
told Dr. Freedman and me, when he was able to express his needs
for her in words, she felt herself bound to him in a new way and one
that was not altogether satisfying. "When he couldn't express his
need for me before I didn't feel quite so guilty about going out and
leaving him, and now that he puts it into words, I feel torn each time
I go away." While the ambivalence of the mother needs no comment
here, we were struck by the fact that for the first time something
like a genuine human relationship was developing between the child
and his mother.

These observations regarding the emergence of an object concept
raise a number of questions. As Piaget (1937) demonstrated, during
the period nine to eighteen months the sighted child makes a series
of experiments which lead him to discover that an object exists independent of his perception of it. The sighted infant demonstrates
an evolving concept of the object through his behavior toward a
screened object, a failure to search for the object under nine months
of age, followed by recovery of the object in successively complex
situations in which the displacements of the object are traced by

means of visual reconstructions. Somewhere between fifteen and eighteen months the sighted infant demonstrates through his search for screened objects that he has a concept of the object that has achieved independence of his perception of it; when he conducts his searches he demonstrates that he knows the object is "some place." This is, of course, one of the crucial developments in the process of differentiation of self and outer world.

When we consider the role of vision in constructing an object's displacements in space, the parallel achievement in the case of a blind infant must be regarded as an adaptive feat. In the first stage of building the object concept the blind infant must trace the object's displacements by means of perceptual cues that are highly inadequate substitutes for vision. Audition, for example, can substitute in tracing only certain classes of objects—those that have sound-making properties. Tactile experience cannot tell the infant where the object is located when he has lost contact with it. The blind infant, then, has a fragmentary and discontinuous experience with objects during the period of tracing, and probably can evolve a concept of the independence of objects from his own perceptions only after his own locomotion provides him with spatial references and repetitive experiences with object finding.

In all this it is undoubtedly the human object that provides maximum experience for the blind infant's building of an object concept. Where no one sense modality can substitute for vision as a distance receptor and an organizer of perceptual wholes, the mother and other highly invested human objects carry the main burden of "teaching" the blind infant about the permanence of objects and through their own persons offer the possibilities of synthesizing and uniting these impressions. Where cathexis of the human object and nonvisual sensory data have established a stable object representation for the blind infant, the goings and comings of the mother, the tracing of the mother through auditory cues, and later the search for the mother by means of the child's own mobility will all lead the blind child to the concept of a mother who exists even when he has lost contact with her. In the early stages of the evolution of this concept it is unlikely that inanimate objects can serve the blind child's learning in the same way, although the sighted child's learning during the same period is achieved through countless experiments in which both human and inanimate objects are employed. The totally blind infant has a restricted range of interest in inanimate objects, as we saw in the blind infant, Toni, and infants known to us in the Family Service Society project. Within this range (which may in the first year include the bottle, a pacifier, a rattle, or bells) only the noise-making objects are useful in tracing the movements of an object.

It is, then, probably the mother who becomes the center of this learning for the totally blind child and while a parallel development can be constructed for the sighted infant, the functional advantages of vision over other sense modalities and the infinitely larger experience with objects provide the sighted child with rich and diverse data for constructing a world of objects; the mother is not the exclusive teacher. Since the blind child's learning must emanate from the experience with mother, insufficiencies in mothering or deficiencies in the mother-infant ties can cut off all possibilities for learning in this sphere.

The arrested ego development of Peter and other deviant blind children shows, almost uniformly, the failure to acquire an object concept. While this is only one of a number of interrelated problems having to do with differentiation and individuation, the adaptive failure in this area suggests that the absence of vision creates a developmental hazard. The mother's resources must be heavily exploited to compensate for the impoverished fund of information available to a blind infant, and when the mother can provide such compensation a normal sequence in ego formation takes place. In those cases where developmental arrest occurs we also find a tragic failure on the part of the mother to get her blind baby's signals and to serve as the unifier of perceptual experiences. In this way the double handicap of blindness and insufficiencies in the experience with mother may cut off for many blind children the developmental path that leads to the achievement of an object concept.

*Mobility*

The importance of mobility and particularly the achievements of independent locomotion have been stressed by Norris et al. (1957), Burlingham (1961), and other writers and students of the blind child's development. Until the blind infant is free to explore his world, he has very limited possibilities for learning about his world. Peter, we are told, never crept at all. (Many blind babies do not.) In this respect his mother blamed her own ignorance, since she did not put him on the floor and did not give him opportunities for creeping. This is certainly a valid point; but as we observed in the blind infant Toni, in the absence of a visual stimulus there is not a strong incentive for the child to creep. And, as mentioned earlier, the blind child achieves independent walking much later than the sighted child.

Peter was still supporting himself by touching walls and other objects when I first met him. He had had very limited opportunities for exploration of his own house. It was a house furnished with antiques, a house of china lamps and crystal and silver ornaments, and clearly, from the furnishing of the downstairs rooms, it was not expected that a still clumsy blind child would enter them. His mother, who had so much anxiety about his retardation and who tried to employ her own experience as a teacher in educating Peter to handle toys and to manipulate toys, had not understood that a crucial experience had been omitted in learning. He needed mobility and the opportunity to explore.

When Peter's mother fully understood this, she was able to bring about many changes in his life. She and I encouraged independent walking, simple climbing, swimming, playing ball. Within a very short time he was walking independently and motor skills improved rapidly. During this period we saw a great improvement in Peter's over-all physical appearance. He gained weight, he acquired muscle in his pipe-stem arms and legs, and his skin lost its pallor. He was encouraged to explore the house and although his mother had thought that he never had shown interest in exploring, once these opportunities were opened up to him he was very soon "into everything"—cupboards, drawers, all the rooms of the house.

As we would expect, Peter's language began to make tremendous leaps. As he discovered objects, handled them, discriminated and named them, his vocabulary enlarged very quickly. He was actively encouraged, at the same time, to express his needs and wishes in words, and his mother learned to be not so quick in anticipating his gestures and tactfully to postpone gratifications until he expressed his wants in words. While these were good achievements, it is important to note that a good deal of his speech was echolalic and did not, properly speaking, serve communication. Also, for a very long time, his speech had no affective quality.

## Aggression and Motility

As I have mentioned earlier, the biting, pinching, and scratching, which I had observed at the very beginning of treatment, reappeared later in connection with intentional aggression. It was impressive to realize that until the second year of treatment Peter had not used his hands for hitting, or his feet for kicking, in directed aggression. Aggression was expressed either through the mouth or by means of the hand following the oral model. At the same time Peter was reluctant to masticate and only through encouragement by me and his mother did he learn to use his teeth for biting food.[2]

I observed fairly early in treatment that Peter did a lot of throwing of objects, particularly of his blocks, but this throwing was aimless and without energy and reminded me of the way a child throws food or toys in the last quarter of the first year. It seemed as if Peter could do only two things with objects, either put them in his mouth or throw them away. At that time, because I was still groping in my educational and therapeutic approaches, I would, after a certain point, interfere with this aimless throwing of objects. For example, when we were "making cookies" with play-dough and Peter began to throw the play-dough, I would repeatedly remind him that play-dough was for making things, for playing games with me and Mommy, and that when he wanted to throw things he could throw balls. If he was in good rapport with me on these occasions, he would accept the prohibition but almost immediately, I saw, he would revert to passivity and lethargy and begin his swaying, or rocking, or nonsense chants.

I began to understand that this throwing was necessary to him. I then changed my tactics and permitted, even encouraged, the throwing without knowing where this would lead. During these throwing sessions he was undoubtedly in better contact with me and his mother

---

[2] We should note also that repeatedly in our records and those of Keeler (1958), Parmalee et al. (1958), and others the deviant blind children were reported to be unable to masticate. Among our children in the nine- to fourteen-year range at the Family Service Society, many were still on soft baby foods.

and there were evident signs of release in his personality. Yet my conscience as a child analyst troubled me very much during this period as I watched play-dough, blocks, and plastic toys go flying through the air in an apparently meaningless barrage. Never before in my therapeutic career had I given permission for such aimless throwing or ever had the feeling that it was justified for therapeutic purposes. While all of this was going on I would sometimes remind myself that normal infants go through such a phase in the last quarter of the first year, but I had never observed this closely or reflected upon its significance in development.

As I watched Peter in many such sessions I saw that gradually the throwing itself became energized and lost its aimless quality. He was throwing hard, and showed evident satisfaction when the object made contact with the floor or the walls. He began to make noises and to accompany his throwing with little cries and sounds that had an aggressive quality. As the throwing acquired aggressive quality, his mother and I, in self-defense and as part of Peter's education, began to provide him with good substitutes for the blocks and other toys for throwing. His mother made about a half dozen bean bags which had enough weight and made a sufficiently satisfactory noise on contact so that they gave satisfaction to Peter. Gradually we now began to limit the throwing to bean bags and balls, and Peter was able to accept the substitution in a way that earlier he could not.

As I recorded my observations and reviewed notes I saw very clearly another connection that seemed to be very significant. As Peter became more active in throwing, and as throwing became more energetic and more aggressive in quality, the biting, pinching, and scratching diminished markedly.

Circumstances provided me with several good tests of the relationship between the different modes of aggression. On one occasion, for example, I arrived to find Mrs. M. bitten and scratched and she reported that she had had a very bad week end with Peter. In order to get a picture of the week end, I asked to what extent Peter had also been throwing. Mrs. M. became embarrassed by my question and said a little defensively that she had decided to put a stop to it this week end. She knew I had recommended that he be given permission to throw, but it all seemed so pointless and so chaotic. (Naturally, I could sympathize with her in all this.) I then suggested that there was probably a connection between his attacks on her and the deprivation of throwing and asked her if she could bear with us for a while. She agreed. When throwing was permitted again the attacks on the mother ceased.

Somewhat later, however, Peter himself gave up the throwing, without any external prohibition as far as we could judge. He reverted once again to biting and scratching, and at the same time his mother reported a severe eating restriction. He was "eating next to nothing except milk and soft foods." There had been progress in masticating for a while and this was lost entirely. The content of our sessions gave me a few clues. He talked incessantly about Laura and other absent persons. "Where is Laura? Where is Bryan? Where is Aunt Cora?" At the same time he repeated the admonishing voices of adults, "You don't want to bite Aunt Cora! Stop that! Stop that!" And then, "Where's Aunt Cora? Where's Aunt Cora?" Or, "Don't scratch Laura. Don't scratch Laura! Where is Laura? Where is Laura?" During this time I saw how he tried to inhibit his biting and scratching and observed a mouth tic exactly representing the urge to bite and the inhibition of biting. Along with the tic Peter would begin swaying, rocking, or bouncing, or uttering gibberish.

The repetitive content of this period strongly suggested that he thought that he could cause people to go away in analogy with eating. Once he even put it quite exactly, "Laura is dead. Laura is all gone." (All gone, of course, was a phrase he would use when he had eaten all of his food.) I decided to put my understanding of the eating inhibition in the form of an interpretation. I told Peter that when he bites his celery or apple he makes it go away inside of him and it is all gone. "But Mommy is not food. Daddy is not food. I am not food. Laura is not food. You cannot eat a mommy or daddy or me. You can't make me all gone." He listened intently to me. After this session his mother reported that he had a hearty lunch, accepted an apple which he had not done for a very long time, and enjoyed his dinner that evening. The eating inhibition returned several times in the weeks that followed. Each time I made a similar interpretation. Each time the eating inhibition disappeared. Along with this he once again returned to throwing and showed much less biting, scratching, and pinching.

Later he demonstrated a similar fear that his own aggression could destroy objects. He had broken a couple of his favorite phonograph records. In the old days we used to replace these. Now he had made enough progress to begin to learn that breaking is an end to things and that they cannot be magically brought back. He was saddened with this knowledge, of course, but then we noticed that he became very anxious when he accidentally broke things; at such times he would revert to apathy and solitude. We would hear his melancholy chant, "The record is all gone! Mommy's vase is all gone!" Then on one occasion when I found him depressed because his mother had not returned at the time she had promised, he used the same melancholy refrain, "Mommy's gone away. Mommy's all gone." It was very clear that once again he needed help in understanding that while his aggression could destroy phonograph records and certain other inanimate objects, his aggression would not make "Mommy all gone" or other people "all gone." I had to repeat this interpretation to him many times until he appeared to grasp it.

We think we can now understand, or begin to understand, the relationship between the aimless throwing of the early period and the differentiation of the aggression described here. In the sequence from oral-centered and undifferentiated aggression in the early behavior to directed and energetic throwing in the later behavior the aimless throwing forms a bridge. This must represent part of the process of separating the skeletal muscles from the mouth. We would need to make close observations on normal infant development in the last quarter of the first year to carry our thinking further; but if our interpretation of Peter's behavior has any validity, the transfer from the mouth to the skeletal muscles constitutes an essential progress in the differentiation of aggression, and the aimless throwing by infants must signify that the skeletal muscles are beginning to take over. We must remember, however, that in the sighted child progress in locomotion normally is made during the same period—a period in which so many events occur that this transitional state in normal development might ordinarily be obscured. In the blind infant there commonly is a maturational readiness for crawling and a failure, in the absence of vision, to achieve locomotion. The fate of aggression during this crucial period merits careful study. This may be another vulnerable period in the development of the blind child, and the particular fate of aggression may be another of the predisposing factors to deviant ego development.

Is the delay in motor development, specifically in locomotion, a key to the fate of aggression in the deviant children? At the point where the skeletal muscles should take over and serve discharge as well as integration of new patterns, a failure in motor function takes place. The achievement in the deviant child may be delayed for another two years or longer. During this period, if we follow the history of Peter and other deviant blind children, libidinal and aggressive impulses remain undifferentiated and centered in the mouth; perception remains centered in the mouth. By the time locomotion is achieved, a state of oral-centered adaptation may also have been achieved and locomotion can no longer lock in with progressive tendencies in ego development that were in a state of readiness during an earlier stage.

*Body Image*

When I first met Peter he was unable to identify parts of his own body when asked such questions as "Where is your nose?" "Where is your ear?" He had so little awareness of internal sensations that he gave neither sign nor signal when he was about to urinate and defecate, and of course could not be trained to use the toilet. He showed little interest in his penis. As we should expect, there was no awareness of sexual differences. As our work progressed it was evident that some crude image of his own body began to emerge. He was able, at the end of the first year of treatment, to identify parts of his own body and to find the corresponding parts (nose, ear, fingers, etc.) on his mother and me. He was able to ask to go to the toilet for urination and defecation.

The discovery of sexual differences took place in an extraordinary way around the eighteenth month of treatment. He had walked into the bathroom as his mother was emerging from the bath. According to the mother's report, he began to explore her body with his hands. The mother chose to use this occasion to enlighten Peter on sexual differences. She allowed him to explore her breasts and the genital area and told him that she had breasts but she did not have a penis. The mother said that Peter showed no reaction at the time.

Peter's mother was much pained when I raised questions about these means of enlightening her child in sexual differences. How else, she wanted to know, could a blind child learn about body differences? There were no good answers to this question, but I recommended verbal explanation along lines that we were following in Peter's treatment sessions.

Following the anatomy lesson in the bathroom, I began to see Peter's reactions very clearly in my sessions with him. I saw him make reaching gestures for his mother's breasts, giggling with excitement when he made contact. On two occasions he reached boldly into her blouse and his mother explained to me with some embarrassment that he had recently discovered that she wore "falsies" in her bras and had even succeeded in removing them in one swift gesture. He called them "little hats" and searched them out in her drawers, bearing them off as trophies.

During the same period Peter began to suffer from constipation. He would withhold for days in evident discomfort. When he sat on the toilet he was visibly frightened, but could not put his fears into words. At the same time his mother reported that he had been wandering around the house for several days searching for "something," but he could not say what he was looking for, and in fact did not seem to know. In a session during this period I saw Peter jumping wildly on his bed and saw his hand move furtively to his penis. His mother then told me privately that the night before Peter had been snuggling close to her at bedtime and had suddenly taken her hand and put it on his penis. She had withdrawn her hand and said, "But you may put your own hand there." Today, as I watched Peter, he was evidently preoccupied with his penis and more than once I saw his hand move to his penis and move away. When I made a neutral comment to Peter on his wish to touch his penis—as a way of opening up the topic for discussion—he suddenly switched to "The hat! I want the little hat!" His mother asked whether it would help if she brought in one of the "falsies" and I agreed. When Peter was given "the little hat" he became completely preoccupied with it, brought it to his mouth, and explored it manually.

Clearly, the anatomy lesson had added to Peter's confusion. He behaved toward "the little hats" as if they were breasts and could be removed. And there was the strong suggestion in his switch from penis to little hats that he believed that a penis could be removed in

similar fashion. Since his exploration of his mother's body in the
bathroom had already confirmed for him that she did not have a
penis, he could only conclude that a penis, too, was portable and
removable. And when we add to this his most prominent symptom
at this time, the retention of his stool, it seemed most probable that
fear of loss of a body part was operating in all these spheres.

In this session Peter and I talked a little about "the little hats."
I told him that the little hats were something that Mommy wore
inside her clothes. The little hats were not breasts. Mommy had
breasts and all ladies had breasts. They belonged to a mommy and
stayed right on her. He listened to me without comment. At the end
of the session his hand moved to his penis once again and then he
said enigmatically, "The ski is all gone." I asked him what a "ski"
was and he did not answer. But in Peter's magic language I knew
that he sometimes substituted one word for another when he needed
to disguise a painful thought or memory.

For several weeks Peter's concerns with penis, no penis, loss, and
breaking became repetitive themes. He began a chant in his hours
with me. "Where's your penis, where's your penis, where's your
penis?" I used the opportunity to clarify his mother's earlier statements in the bathroom and told him that boys and girls and men
and women were made differently. Peter was a boy, made just like
Daddy. Margaret (older sister) was a girl, just like Mommy. After
a while new chant made an appearance, "I am a she. I am a he.
I am a he. I am a she."

Stool retention continued off and on during this period, but there
was no opportunity to make a meaningful connection between the
fear of loss of his stool and fears regarding his own penis. Then in
one session I arrived to find Peter disturbed and almost immediately
ambivalent toward me. He first reached out for my hand and stroked it
softly, then began to bite it. Suddenly, most urgently he asked, "Where
is Laura? Where is Laura?" (the dead cousin). And scarcely waiting for
an answer he began a recital of the names of absent or long-forgotten
people. Then again in an urgent voice, he began to inquire about
lost and broken phonograph records. "Where is Hokey Pokey? Where
is Genie?" "Where are they, Peter?" "Broken. All gone. Broken"
(sadly). I said, "Records can be broken. But people can't be broken."
As I said this Peter's hand went swiftly to his penis. I said, "Peter

can't be broken. A penis can't be broken." He seemed not to take this in.

But now for many sessions the theme of "broken" appeared as a refrain. In the session following the one reported above, Peter began by uttering the single word "tooth" and showed me the place where he had lost a tooth several weeks ago. We talked about the tooth, and how another would grow. I spent a great deal of time in this session telling him how a nose could not go away, a finger could not go away, etc. They belonged to Peter. "Laura?" he said plaintively. "Where is Laura?" (Laura, of course, belonged to the category of objects which go away and cannot be restored.) Once more we talked about Laura. At the end of the hour he said, again with some urgency, "Where is the penis?" and made a tentative reaching gesture toward me. Again I told him that I knew he had found that Mommy and ladies do not have a penis and that it was very hard for him to figure out. Again I gave the explanations, and again I said explicitly that nobody could make a penis "all gone." Peter's penis would always stay with him.

For many weeks the anxiety about "broken" and "all gone" was dealt with in ways very similar to those I have described. I was present on one occasion during a period of stool retention when Peter asked to go to the toilet and I could see the anxiety on his face. I used the occasion to make a connection between his fear of losing the feces and his fear of losing his penis and again gave reassurances. His mother reported that soon after I left that day he asked to go to the toilet again and had a bowel movement. There were to be a number of occasions thereafter when I was able to handle the stool-retention problem through such interpretations. However, I should mention that this problem was very complex; a number of other motives were uncovered before the problem finally cleared up.

The inadequacies of Peter's speech were serious handicaps to an investigation of his blind-child's version of castration anxiety. It was impossible, of course, to get details of his fantasies or to get him to elaborate his cryptic comments. I employed an approach which is of course very different from child analysis. I had to use "educational" techniques to deal with his body concerns, to promote, if possible, the integration of each piece of knowledge into a stable body image.

There were other observations of anxiety in connection with the penis. Though the meaning of these observations remains obscure, I believe they should be reported. On several occasions both his mother and I saw that Peter was manifestly anxious when he had an erection. Erections typically occurred while he was straining for a bowel movement or when he was about to void. The moment the erection appeared he became frozen and immobilized. At these times he would never touch his penis, nor did he do so when erections appeared spontaneously on other occasions. It seemed to me that he then avoided touching his penis.

He refused to hold his penis under any circumstances when he was voiding. For long periods during the two and a half years that I knew Peter he avoided handling his penis. In the early days of treatment I discerned some prohibitions in an alien voice, "Uh! Uh! Uh!" which Peter chanted in a warning voice when he chanced to touch his penis. When this and similar material was handled with Peter he would take a more relaxed attitude toward touching his penis, but before long the avoidance was manifest again. After many months of observations I was unable to come up with a better explanation than that offered by his manifest anxiety in connection with erections. Was the experience of erection and detumescene an equivalent of loss or "castration," the "disappearance" of the penis? Was the loss of sensation that accompanies detumescence a disturbance to this deviant child for whom strong sensations were an affirmation of self? I do not know. Occasionally when I talked with Peter about how sometimes his penis got big and sometimes quite small I had the impression from his response that I was on the right track, but I never received any positive confirmation from him or further material that permitted investigation. Perhaps the only justification for including this in the record is the possibility that such a detail may be useful to another investigator.

*Grief, Pain*

When I now describe and bring together data relating to the affective disturbance in Peter it is with some uncertainty and incompleteness of observations.

When I first became acquainted with Peter, he was incapable of expressing grief. If he reacted at all to loss or the danger of loss, it was through the convulsive heaving of shoulders and distortion of face which I described earlier in the hide-and-seek game. We do not think that such behavior is typical of the deviant blind children.

The measures by which Peter warded off grief, however, were similar to those that he employed in warding off any strong undesirable or unpleasurable stimulus, external or internal as judged by the observer. His reaction to pain may be considered a model. (And here, incidentally, we do have parallels with other deviant blind children and autistic children in general.) Initially Peter showed no reaction to pain. When he injured himself, even badly, he did not cry out, did not complain, but typically reverted to autistic mannerisms. Once when he burned himself severely his mother, who was with him in the kitchen, had no way of telling the moment at which the burn occurred and discovered it only later on. Once when he had the flu we inferred that he had severe stomach pains and internal distress because he waved his hands in a gesture of warding off an external bothersome stimulus. More typical, however, was his attempt to ward off the perception of the painful stimulus—a device he adopted with regard to pain and a variety of other stimuli originating within or without.

I have already reported that he would ward off an aggressive impulse by means of repetitive speech or nonsense words. He employed identical mechanisms in the warding off of grief. His mother and I would sometimes see him with shoulders heaving and the tic-like grimacing of the mouth. We would encourage him to cry, tell him it was all right to cry, that all boys cried sometimes. And sometimes we would see the muscles of his face reacting to our words, giving us the impression that he was on the verge of tears, but suddenly he would come forth with a repetitious phrase like, "I want a triangle cracker, I want a triangle cracker, I want a triangle cracker" and would repeat this sometimes for as long as fifteen minutes.

We cannot attribute to this primitive personality anything like repression. In my notes I employed the provisional term "blocking" of affect, but finally discarded this, too, as being not descriptive. Even blocking has the connotation of a countercathexis, and nothing in my observations of Peter suggested that his ego at that time was capable of forming countercathexes. What I saw could best be described as simple shifts of attention cathexis, a withdrawal of cathexis from a painful perception and an indiscriminate shift to another perception.

The repetition of such a phrase as "I want a triangle cracker" showed that the original impulse was still active while the goal had shifted. When the impulse had exhausted itself the repetitious phrase would cease. I could bring about a complete repetition of the whole sequence if, after Peter became quiet, I should say, "I still think that you want to cry." What I have described here, then, is a very primitive mechanism for warding off a disturbing stimulus. Such shifts in cathexis are not, properly speaking, "displacements," for in displacement the original impulse would break through since only the goal is changed. What we see in Peter is something close to what we mean in laymen's language by the term "distractions." It is what the patient does in the dentist chair when he counts the squares on the ceiling to take his mind off the drilling.

Very early in treatment my efforts to help Peter to express his grief were rewarded by several episodes in which grief broke through. This was during a period in which Peter expressed his fear that he was bad and would be sent away (to the institution). Then, following a real but brief separation from his parents when they took a holiday over a week end, these favorable signs disappeared and it was actually many months before he could again express grief with genuine emotion. When grief emerged once again it took the form of a series of emotional storms all in connection with his fear that his mother would go away and be "all gone." One of these episodes appeared during one of my sessions with him, the others took place with his parents at times of leave-taking.

In this essay I shall not go into the details of but only comment on a significant change which occurred in Peter when he once more acquired the ability to express grief. For the first time he began to react to physical pain. There were several episodes in which he cried after an injury. He even acquired the word "hurts" and was able to say on several occasions when he was constipated and could not expel his stool, "It hurts! It hurts!"

*Differentiation, Separateness*

While in the two and a half years of treatment a slow progress toward separateness and a sense of identity could be observed, the boundaries between "me" and "other" remained unstable and were easily blurred or temporarily lost. As late as the third year of treatment Peter could occasionally lapse into states of confusion between his body and his mother's body. For example, when Peter and his mother were swimming in a pool, she said, "Peter, come here and pour some water on my feet." Peter came over and carefully poured water over his own feet.

The use of "I," which appeared to have stability at the end of the first year of treatment, became a kind of barometer for the whole period I knew Peter. "I" could disappear from his vocabulary for days or even weeks and self-reference in the third person would come back. After a while "I" would emerge once again, stay with us for weeks, and mysteriously disappear once again. At such times I studied my notes for cues regarding the conditions under which "I" became lost or re-emerged. At first I thought I saw patterns related to separation. Following the parents' short holidays there was nearly always some regression accompanied by loss of "I." But after I had accumulated more observations I saw that the loss of "I" occurred just as frequently when no separation had taken place. At the end of the second year of treatment I could trace another pattern that I had missed throughout. "I" disappeared just as frequently immediately following a period of relatively good integration and functioning, often accompanied by healthy strides in the direction of independence!

I saw this most clearly toward the end of the second year of treatment. We had made good progress in reducing the anxieties in connection with separation from mother. Bowel and bladder control were good and Peter was now dry at night for the first time in his life. Peter was often in good contact with me and could now even put into words some of the things he was afraid of. "What are you afraid of, Peter?" "I'm afraid of Mommy" (i.e., "I'm afraid *about* Mommy"). "What woke you up last night, Peter?" "I had a dream." "Tell me a story about the dream." "The garage was all gone." (On the dream day the garage *had* been torn down in order to enlarge the garden.)

Peter now had a new awareness of states of waking and sleeping. At the same time he showed reluctance to go to sleep. Often Peter was wakeful until 12:00 or 1:00 in the morning, bringing frequent requests for food or soft drinks or playing with his phonograph. In part the reluctance to go to sleep may have been the warding off of a disturbing dream. Moreover, since being awake now brought pleasure and satisfactions to Peter, the wish to prolong contact with his family must have been another motive. But there was also something else. Peter had a favorite shell which he now took to bed with him; when he awakened at night and could not find it, he was greatly disturbed until it was restored to him. The shell, like the transitional objects of children in their second year, appeared to symbolize the absent mother and also affirmed his own identity, a substantial something that could be clutched in the hand when the insubstantial self feelings dissolved in sleep. From this and a number of small details I inferred that one of the motives in the reluctance to go to sleep was the fear of loss of identity. I suggested that at such times his mother tell him stories about how Peter goes to sleep, but he doesn't lose Peter. He's always there. And when he wakes up he is still Peter and he will find Mommy and Daddy and everyone waiting for him. These little stories seemed to help him go to sleep.

With all these small signs of an emerging sense of identity the use of "I" appeared to have more stability for a time. Then new anxieties appeared. Suddenly in the midst of play in the garden, with mother and me present, he would stop, go indoors, and climb the stairs to his room. When we followed him we could see his tremendous relief at entering his own room. Typically he would then go to his bed, cover himself up, ask for his favorite shell, and lie there in complete self-absorption. In a very rapid development, he now became reluctant to leave his room and would have been content to stay there all day if we had not encouraged him to come down for meals or go for walks. This behavior was not connected with fear of loss of mother, because at these times his mother was usually present and he knew it. It seemed rather to be associated with an urgent need to establish the connections with a base, the room which affirmed his own unstable core of identity. And during this period "I" was lost again, his contact with mother and with me was poor, there was regression in eating and toilet habits. After a period of weeks the anxieties diminished and he climbed back to a level of integration that was fairly close to the one preceding the regression.

It was during this period that I began to see the pattern that I had missed. There was no apparent external reason for the regression. It struck me that each time Peter had achieved a new level of integration around "I" and separateness, there were fresh anxieties and

regressions which I was helpless to prevent. It was as if the achievement of separateness, of aloneness, was in itself a state of danger that
promoted regression to the tension-free state of nondifferentiation.

## Termination

Peter's treatment was terminated after two and a half years, when
Peter was eleven. While his over-all functioning was greatly improved, the limits of therapeutic possibility seemed to have been
reached. Now, too, an early puberty added its own complications to
the picture of this unstable personality organization. Growth of pubic
hair and changes in the size of the genitals had been noticeable
already at the age of ten. As puberty advanced we saw increased
excitement and indiscriminate discharge through gross body activities, e.g., jumping on his bed with wild hilarity and a sustained erection until he reached exhaustion. This behavior was not, strictly
speaking, new but now appeared more frequently and with a marked
increase in excitement. We could foresee the difficulties ahead for
Peter and the entire family, and the family had already made extraordinary sacrifices in accommodating itself to Peter's unique demands.
I began to prepare the parents for the possibility of institutional care
for Peter and to help them accept the fact that we had gone as far
as we could in treatment in the home.

## Summary

The clinical picture of Peter and that of other blind children
with arrested ego development shows certain resemblances to the
picture of autism in sighted children, but there are significant differences as well. We are struck by the fact that these deviant blind
children show a picture of uniform developmental arrest. The mouth
has remained the center of this primitive personality; perception is
largely mouth-centered and those qualities that we call "aggressive"
and "erotic" remain mouth-centered and appear to be undifferentiated. Tactile perception is minimal; in fact, the hand appears to
have no autonomy from the mouth. These characteristics of the blind
deviant child have no parallel among sighted autistic children.

The unique characteristics of the blind deviant group and the
uniformities encountered in the clinical picture must be linked to
the common defect in the group—blindness from birth. We must

assume that during critical phases of ego formation the blind infant is faced with unique problems of adaptation which have led, in these cases, to adaptive failure.

Each of these deviant blind children had a mother who felt estranged from her blind baby, who could not establish a "dialogue" (in Spitz's terms [1963]), and who became in this way one of the tragic determinants in the child's adaptive incapacity. But we must give equal attention in studies such as these to the adaptive problems presented by blindness itself. When we consider our present knowledge of the role of vision in ego formation, the substitutions and circuitous routes required of the blind infant must be regarded as adaptive feats.

The observations of Peter and other deviant blind children open up two lines of inquiry: (1) blindness as a communications barrier between mother and infant with extraordinary demands upon the mother's own adaptive capacity; (2) blindness as an impediment during critical phases of ego formation with extraordinary demands upon an infant's adaptive capacity. (The two problems are, of course, interdependent.)

1. Many of the mothers of the deviant blind children, like Peter's mother, were adequate or more than adequate mothers in rearing their other children. While we may suppose that in each of these mothers the blind baby struck old wounds in personality, we need to be attentive to blindness as a barrier in the establishment of the mother-child dialogue. Before the diagnosis of blindness was made (usually around five or six months among the retrolental fibroplasia cases) the mother was already aware that this baby did not respond in expected ways. He was strangely uninterested in his surroundings; the unseeing eyes made the face seem blank and remote. When the mother sought contact with him through her eyes the child's eyes did not meet hers, which feels curiously like a rebuff if you do not know that the baby is blind. The appearance of the mother's face did not cause the baby to smile. All those ways in which the eyes unite human partners were denied to this mother and baby. It seems reasonable to suppose that when these early signals between mother and child failed, the dialogue between mother and child became halting and uncertain. A mother might still carry on a tactile and auditory dialogue with the baby whose eyes never met hers, and

some mothers succeeded in this even before the diagnosis of blindness was made. (In those cases where the diagnosis of blindness was made soon after birth, as in the case of the infant, Toni, the mother could more easily exploit the nonvisual repertory that was open to her.) But many of the mothers of the deviant blind children seemed unable to find some bridge of communication, and the estrangement of mother and child began in the early months. When the diagnosis of blindness was made, depression and a sense of hopelessness completed the estrangement for some mothers.

While it is true that the mothering of the deviant blind babies was deficient, the successful mothering of a totally blind infant requires extraordinary qualities indeed. And while the developing ego of the sighted infant is insured when the mother is unexceptional or even less than adequate, the blind infant's ego development is imperiled when his mother does not have adaptive capacities which are exceptional.

Omwake and Solnit (1961), in discussing the case of Ann, point out that "The absence of a visual representation of the mother may seriously impair the capacity to form a useful memory of the mother if the mother is unable to provide other modes of libidinally cathected perceptual experiences, especially touching, to compensate for the absence of the visual experiences."

While the histories of Peter and other deviant blind children show marked deficiencies in the earliest ties with mother, other deviant blind children achieve a demonstrable human tie by the seventh or eighth month which is then followed by a developmental impasse during the crucial nine- to eighteen-month period. Typically the child regresses, reverts to passive postures, exhibits autistic behavior, and remains frozen on the level of mouth-centeredness and nondifferentiation. Clearly there are a number of points in the process of ego formation where blindness creates hazards.

2. The specific ways in which blindness may impede the process of ego formation can be inferred from the characteristics of the blind children with arrested development.

*Perception remained mouth-centered.* The hand appeared to have no autonomy from the mouth, and tactile discrimination was minimal. The mouth, as a strongly endowed instinctual zone, is ill adapted for the achievement of conflict-free perception. The adaptive substitution of the hand as a primary organ of perception is an indispensable step in the development of the blind child. However, our study of the development of Toni, a healthy blind infant, shows that hand autonomy evolves very slowly during the first two years and that the hand did not achieve primacy over the mouth as a perceptual organ until twenty months of age. Clearly, since vision mediates adaptive hand behavior in the sighted infant, the adaptive use of the hand as a primary organ of perception requires the blind infant to make an elaborate detour, even under the most favorable circumstances. Under less favorable circumstances, as in the case of Peter and other deviant blind children, there may be no incentives for this complex adaptive task. Perception remained mouth-centered and the adaptive failure had a morbid significance for the future of these children. When the mouth remains the primary organ of perception the distinctions between "inner" and "outer," "self" and "not self" will not emerge. Perceptual experience is restricted to a narrow range of objects— those that stimulate the mouth in some preferred way. The qualities of objects cannot be known. The failure to achieve hand autonomy was one of the crucial factors responsible for maintaining these personalities on the level of nondifferentiation.

*Those qualities that we call "erotic" or "aggressive" remained mouth-centered and were in fact not differentiated.* The biting and oral-incorporative behavior of the mouth in relation to human and nonhuman "objects" had, as its corollary, a hand behavior in which scratching, clawing, and pinching were employed in a frenzied seizing and holding of human objects. In the case of Peter we saw that this behavior was not intentionally aggressive; the hand had not freed itself of the oral mode and oral-incorporative characteristics of the mouth had been transferred to the hand.

*There was a striking failure to employ the skeletal muscles for the discharge of aggression.* Dorothy Burlingham (1961) reported that nondeviant blind children show an inhibition in the expression of aggression, but we cannot suggest parallels here because of the great difference in ego organization between the children studied by her and our deviant blind children. That which is clearly "inhibition" in Burlingham's group actually appears to be a developmental failure in our group. In the case of Peter, for example, we saw inhibitions in expression of aggression only after he had made considerable progress and after aggression had become linked to specific intentions.

Peter affords an extraordinary insight into the process of differentiation of aggression which may have implications for general studies of early ego development. The work with Peter demonstrated that as opportunities for motor discharge were provided (throwing, large muscle activity), the biting-pinching-scratching behavior receded and patterns that were recognizably "aggressive" emerged from the undifferentiated behavior of the mouth and hand which had previously not been intentionally aggressive.

*A significant delay in the achievement of independent locomotion was reported in nearly all of our deviant blind cases.* Many of these children did not crawl at all and most of them did not achieve independent walking until the age of three, four, or later. We have mentioned that for all blind children independent walking is a late achievement by the standards of the sighted child. In our study of the blind infant Toni we found that the delay in creeping was closely linked with the absence of an external stimulus usually provided by vision. Nonvisual stimuli did not provide the same incentives for reaching and, by extension, crawling. The healthy blind infant with good adaptive capacity and very good mothering found the route to these later motor achievements by means of a detour which we describe.

Our deviant blind children were immobile during the first three or four years of life. There may be a close connection between the failure to discharge aggression through the skeletal musculature and the inactivation of the apparatus during a crucial period in development. When independent locomotion was finally achieved a critical period in ego formation and drive differentiation was lost, and it may no longer have been possible for the components of this process to lock in and produce new patterns.

The delayed locomotion may be another factor in maintaining the personality on the level of nondifferentiation. Until the blind child achieves independence in locomotion he cannot fully experience separateness. Nor can he, in the absence of vision, construct a world of objects until he has made physical contact by means of his independent locomotion.

*The failure to acquire an object concept* was demonstrable in the case of Peter and other deviant blind children. The concept of an object that exists independent of the field of perception is achieved among sighted children by means of a visual construction of its displacements in space. In our earlier discussion we described the unique adaptive problems presented to the blind child in making such a construction on the basis of nonvisual information. This is another of the adaptive feats which fell beyond the capacity of the deviant blind child and another of the factors that maintained the personality on the level of nondifferentiation.

## II

### DEVELOPMENTAL PATTERNS IN A BLIND INFANT

With the picture of the deviant children in the background of our thinking we approached our developmental study of blind with the following propositions. There are certain characteristics found uniformly in the deviant blind children that are not found uniformly among sighted children with severe ego deviations. The uniform characteristics in these blind children must be linked to the defect that the children have in common—blindness from birth. If blindness has led to adaptive failures in this group, there should be correlates in the development of all blind children in the form of specific adaptational problems. With this view we began the first of our developmental studies.

Toni R. was the youngest of six children, the illegitimate child of a Negro mother. The father of the older children had deserted the family some time after the birth of the next older sibling. When the mother learned of Toni's blindness soon after birth, she became depressed. She told us that she had no hopes for the child's future until the family agency social worker gave her assurance that Toni had excellent chances of becoming a normal and healthy child and offered the help of the agency in understanding the special problems of rearing a blind child. The family agency has continued its educational work with the mother throughout the period we have known the family.

Toni was observed at monthly intervals from twenty-two weeks through twenty-eight months of age. A film record was maintained throughout the study which we refer to in this report.

## Smiling Response

In our first visit at twenty-two weeks we found Toni in her crib in the tiny family living room, very much in the center of family noise and family activities and keenly attentive to the variety of sounds around her. In the midst of the pleasant confusion we observed that when Toni discriminated her mother's voice she broke into an enthusiastic smile accompanied by joyful kicking. We were impressed to find that our observation at five months as well as the social worker's report from three months showed a *selective smiling response* to the sound of mother's voice. Mrs. R. told us that Toni smiled only for her and for no one else in the family. Our film shows her in games with the mother in which the mother chants nonsense to the baby and the baby's whole face radiates anticipation and joy. The uninformed observer could not easily guess that the child is totally blind.

## Stranger Anxiety

As we followed Toni's development we were impressed by the fact that her blindness per se was not an impediment to the establishment of the vital human connections. At eight and nine months we saw in the film that she clearly discriminated between her mother and a stranger (one of the investigators) on the basis of auditory and tactile cues. She showed a strong anxiety reaction at eight months and violently clutched at the stranger's arm; at nine months she cried as soon as the stranger made contact with her, and we saw her fingering the stranger's face with mounting anxiety and turning her head as if in search for the mother.

It is apparent, then, that if cathexis of the object is achieved, a mental representation of mother can be formed on the basis of a variety of nonvisual sensory data. The retrospective histories of some of the deviant blind children indicate that a smile did not emerge in infancy and that discrimination between the mother and a stranger was not demonstrable in infancy or later in development. Other data in these records show that the mother failed to respond to and stimulate her blind infant and help him utilize perceptual capacities that could lead to an image of mother. Omwake and Solnit (1961) gave emphasis to the same point in their discussion of Ann.

It should be mentioned, however, that there are other cases among the deviant blind children in which the establishment of preobject and object ties followed an apparently normal sequence during the first year, and then reached an impasse, for causes unknown, resulting in developmental arrest or even regression and a freezing of personality at these points. It seemed likely to us that there were a number of vulnerable phases in the process of ego formation for the blind child.

## An Impasse in Motor Development

Toni's motor development during the first eight months was good and even precocious judged by standards for sighted children. At seventeen weeks the social worker observed that Toni could turn herself over and at twenty-two weeks she could sit briefly without support and could stand for one minute with slight support. At seven months when we arrived for our visit we found Toni sitting confidently without support at the open front door. During the same visit one of the investigators observed Toni supporting herself briefly on hands and knees. An observer, judging by experience with sighted children, would say that Toni was on the verge of crawling.

And then for the last third of the first year, this picture of an unimpeded maturational progress began to change and we saw patterns in development that are not familiar to the observer of sighted children.

There was maturational readiness for creeping as evidenced by Toni's ability at seven months to support herself on hands and knees and at eight months to lower herself unassisted from a sitting position in a chair to a standing position on the floor. Yet, until she was fourteen months old she was unable to creep in directed linear fashion. At that time creeping actually coincided with the beginning of walking. At eight months we first observed a form of locomotion that persisted for months. (Actually it had appeared earlier but had not been observed by us.) We have described it as a kind of "pinwheel locomotion" resembling, in some features, the pivoting that typically initiates the sequence that leads to creeping, yet it was distinctly inappropriate in this child whose postural behavior placed her within the forty-week norms for sighted children. The "pinwheel locomotion," a rotating which brought her around full circle,

remained Toni's only form of locomotion on the floor until she was
fourteen months. We learned that this behavior could be set in motion by either pleasurable or unpleasurable excitement. In our films
we have an unforgettable picture of the blind child in futile naviga-
tion of a circle. It is as if the machinery has been set in motion, but
the child has no place to go. The apparatus appears to function in a
vacuum.

We have since uncovered other examples of this pinwheel locomotion among blind infants, but until we have made further direct
observations we cannot generalize. We do know from the extensive
study of Norris et al. (1957) that locomotion is markedly delayed for
all blind children. Many observers of blind infants attribute the delay
in locomotion to "lack of opportunity" provided by the environment,
the undue anxiety of the mother, and the frequent failure to permit
the child to get on the floor. But our observations of Toni showed
no such lack of opportunity. The pinwheel locomotion points clearly,
we think, to the importance of the absence of an external stimulus,
usually provided by vision.

The attraction of the visual stimulus leads the sighted child to
directed linear creeping. At the time when there is maturational
readiness for creeping he is already expert in reaching for an object
in space, and the attraction of the object stimulates a sequence of
motions that can be described as a reach and a collapse, a reach and a
collapse, each time accompanied by some progression. This gradually
evolves into a smoothed-out rhythm in which the reaching gesture
of the hands coordinates with the legs and the whole body takes over
the function of reaching, leading to continuous directed movement.

The sighted child reaches for objects and secures them as early
as twenty-four weeks. Toni could grasp an object on contact at thirty
weeks but made no attempt to reach for an object in space until ten
months of age. When we experimentally jangled keys or bells within
the range of her grasp, she did not reach for these. She made no attempt to recover an object which had fallen from her mouth or her
grasp; the object had no existence in space for the blind child at this
stage. (As a conceptual problem it corresponds to the sighted child's
behavior toward a screened object at the same age; here blindness
itself constitutes the screen.) We understood then that until Toni
could reach for an object in space, there could be no incentive to

linear creeping. But here, too, Toni's blindness created a tragic dilemma, for until she could achieve some degree of mobility, the concept of an object in space would be difficult to achieve.

During the same period (the eight- and nine-month observations) we had the general impression of an impasse in development. Toni now appeared dull and lethargic. She still showed no interest in toys or any objects except her bottle and her pacifier. And there was one new behavior that gave us concern. *In the absence of any other stimulation Toni was content to lie passively on the floor, for long periods, face down, smiling softly to herself.*

Mrs. R., we observed, was now often out of rapport with the child. She was anxious, irritable, and inclined to push Toni toward performance. Toni's pinwheel locomotion was baffling to her. The passive prone position was disturbing to see, and the baby wasn't doing anything "new," she complained. To the mother, who had reared five healthy children, the blind baby now appeared "different" and even dull. All the old fears that Toni might never be normal seemed to rise to the surface again.

Yet there were, in fact, evidences of progressive maturation during these two months, although they were not meaningful to the mother. Toni had learned to lower herself from a chair to the floor. We observed that when she dropped her pacifier she now made tentative reaching gestures for it, although she did not search for it. We watched a feeding in which Toni grabbed the spoon from her mother and inserted it in her own mouth. And, in spite of evidence of the disturbance in the mother-child relationship, we also observed that when the mother actively stimulated her in games, Toni responded with the joyfulness and excitement that we had seen in earlier months. But none of these things were reassuring to the mother. The baby didn't "look" normal to her.

In assessing this period we had to take into account those impediments to maturation that were directly or indirectly related to blindness, and those impediments that were now presented by a disturbance in the mother-child relationship. Clearly they were mutually reinforcing in an intricate pattern. Blindness was an impediment to the achievement of locomotion. Until mobility could be achieved, the blind infant could not make discoveries that would lead her to explore, to discover objects, or to manipulate them. Until objects acquired a value independent of need satisfaction or self-stimulation, Toni could not move beyond the bottle and pacifier. All of this added up to a picture of arrested development to the mother, who reacted with anxiety and withdrawal.

From the standpoint of Toni, who was almost exclusively dependent on stimulation provided by her mother and other human objects for the maintenance of interest in the outside world, inevitable periods of nonstimulation seemed to leave her in an exteroceptive vacuum. At such times she assumed the prone position and fell back on proprioceptive experience, which to us seemed to be erotically stimulating.

During this period Mrs. R. was given guidance and support by her social worker. We ourselves felt it necessary to depart from a neutral position and give reassurance. In addition, we felt that our study was itself a factor in increasing the mother's anxiety about the child's achievement. Toni, in her mother's eyes, had become a movie star and the pressure for performance was increased by our visits and filming. The educational work of the social worker was chiefly in the area of promoting the positive ties between mother and child and of diminishing the mother's anxiety.

At ten months the picture changed again. Toni was not yet able to creep in a linear fashion, but she now strongly resisted being placed in the prone position. Concurrently she achieved mobility of another kind through a walker which her mother had purchased for her. We saw her "scooting" about the room with great energy and enthusiasm. When her mother called to her she could steer her walker in the direction of the mother's voice. This was accomplished through reaching her body in the direction of mother's voice, and the reach of course propelled her. The reaching of the body toward a desired object had a correlate in another behavior. We saw in the same session that Toni could now reach for an object in space. In two experimental situations, one involving a bunch of keys and one a candy cane, she recovered the object by reaching out into space even after she had lost physical contact with it.

It is of interest that the presence or absence of auditory cues seemed irrelevant in this situation. We have no observations indicating that she was able to reach for and recover a noise-making object earlier than a nonnoise-making object.

During the same ten-month observation we saw that Toni and her mother had recovered their old rapport. The mother reported with pride that Toni was "getting into everything," scooting about the house in her walker, exploring rooms, kitchen cupboards. The passive prone position was no longer in evidence.

We observed Toni's behavior toward inanimate objects. Among a series of toys presented to her, cloth dolls, stuffed animals, and a plastic hourglass-shaped rattle, she examined each with her tongue and lips and minimally with her fingers and clearly discriminated among them, choosing and discarding on what seemed to be a basis of "least desirable" and "most desirable."

We asked the mother, "What does Toni do when she gets mad?" (We had no direct observations.) The mother gave some examples. If Toni was in her walker, she began to scoot around the house with great energy. If she was frustrated by a member of the family, she might pinch, and her pinching, we gathered in response to questions, was specifically directed toward the person who was frustrating her. She did not bite in anger but did bite playfully and in demonstration of love.

Toni now imitated sounds. We heard her say "dada" in response to mother's "dada" and cluck in response to mother's cluck.

From these observations we could see a new progress which was probably facilitated by a number of factors. The change in mother's feelings toward Toni was seen clearly in response to the new achievements of the child and may also have been a vital factor in promoting progressive currents in the personality.

The child's new-found mobility probably played an important role in the changes that we saw. A decisive shift from passive to active was achieved, and the thrust toward activity became so powerful that the child made vigorous protests against the posture of passivity which, for her, was being put on the floor. Mobility brought her into a new relationship with the world of objects; she now actively explored and discriminated a widening range of objects. Toni's behavior toward objects that were removed from her field of perception told us that she had an emerging concept of the independent existence of objects. In the case of this blind child, mobility perhaps aided the evolution of the concept; and it would also be correct to say that the emerging concept afforded incentives to locomotion. Now, too, motor activity appeared to facilitate discharge of aggression (when she was mad she "scooted around the room"), and there may be a connection between this achievement and the newly reported goal-directed aggression against the frustrating person.

As we review this critical period in Toni's development we can identify some of the hazards in development that confront the blind child. This child with better-than-average endowment and adaptive capacity, living in a home that provided favorable opportunities for development, reached a point in development when absence of vision was an impediment to progress and the adaptive solutions could be found only through an elaborate detour.

We have mentioned earlier that the retrospective histories of the deviant blind children almost uniformly showed a delay in achieving locomotion that was even beyond the norms for blind children in general. We know that the normal, sighted child is given a tremendous impetus toward the achievement of separateness and individuation by the experience of independent locomotion. The blind child is to a far greater extent dependent upon locomotion to make the crucial distinctions between self and outer world and to construct a world of objects—and here, ironically, the absence of vision becomes an impediment to the establishment of locomotion. In a less than favorable environment, the blind child may not have strong incentives to find the complex adaptive solutions, and the failure to achieve locomotion within a critical period of time may be one of the factors that brings about a developmental arrest in the deviant children.

## The Mouth and the Hand

In his essay "The Primal Cavity" Spitz (1955) investigated the role of the oral cavity as interoceptor and exteroceptor; here all perception begins. The oral cavity, he said, fulfills the functions of a bridge from internal reception to external perception. Integrating the contributions of Hoffer, Lewin, Isakower, Linn, and Halverson with his own observations, Spitz examined the early alliance of hand and mouth. The participation of the hand in nursing (clutching, stroking, clawing, and scratching the breast) is in the nature of overflow at birth; the sensorium of the hand is not yet cathected. This activity of the hands becomes more and more organized in subsequent months, probably, Spitz suggests, as a function of the progressive cathexis of the hand's sensorium. The fusion in early infancy of oral, tactile, and visual perceptions into an undifferentiated unity is hypothesized by Spitz (later given experimental support through the work of M. Bender [1952] and L. Linn [1953]). Hoffer (1949) in his study "Mouth, Hand, and Ego-Integration" describes how in the second and third quarters of the first year the hands achieve a progressive independence from the oral zone and are more under the influence of the eyes, "playing the part of an intermediary between eyes and mouth. They have developed from instruments serving as a means for discharging tension into tools which control the outer world. They have at this stage become a most active extension of the growing ego." Gesell and Amatruda (1947), speaking of the blind infant and tactual experience, say, "The senses were made to function in synesthesia, two or more modalities blending. Even the primary tactual sense does not normally function in pure form. Tactual perceptions are visual-tactual perceptions for the normal mind. If this close reciprocal interacting relationship between vision and touch is not recognized it is impossible to appreciate the gravity of the handicap under which the blind or near-blind infant labors."

In our observations of Toni we were impressed to see that the mouth remained the primary organ of perception well into the middle of the second year. The hand was employed minimally for discrimination during the first year and did not achieve autonomy from the mouth until the second half of the second year. Since the hand, for the blind child, must achieve primacy as a perceptual organ, the progress from mouth to hand becomes an important area for study in the blind infant. We recall that one of the characteristics of the deviant blind children was mouth-centered perception and a failure to achieve hand autonomy.[3]

At nine months of age Toni had no interest in objects other than the bottle, a spoon, and a pacifier. There was transitory interest in rattles and bells. Each of the items in the first group has retained its oral cathexis, while for the sighted child of this age (and even much earlier) a large number of objects that are independent of need satis-

---

[3] Shortly after this paper was submitted for publication Anne-Marie Sandler's paper "Aspects of Passivity and Ego Development in the Blind Infant" appeared (1963). Mrs. Sandler's views and ours are strikingly similar in certain areas, particularly in her considerations regarding the role of the hand and the mouth in the early development of the blind child.

faction will attract and excite the child and invite his handling and exploration. If a novel object was presented to Toni at this age— and even much later in the second year, she brought it to her mouth. So will the sighted child, of course, during the first year. But there are these differences. The object, to be meaningful to Toni, had to stimulate the mouth in certain preferred ways. If it did not, it was immediately discarded. The sighted child of this age, in the act of exploring an object, will employ his mouth to acquire certain data about the object which are added to the group of data already acquired through the eyes, the hands, and other sense modalities. The qualities of the object itself are discovered in this way, and the attraction of the object has relative independence from mouth satisfaction.

During the period when Toni showed no interest in inanimate objects (and distressed her mother by appearing so dull) we saw, on the other hand, that her discrimination of human objects had achieved a high level. She discriminated her mother from a stranger; she recognized each of her siblings and responded selectively to them. Among sighted children we know that the interest in inanimate objects advances from the cathexis of human objects (Hartmann, 1952), and absence of interest in inanimate objects in a sighted child of Toni's age would indicate grave deficiencies in object ties. Evidently, for Toni, the path from human objects to inanimate objects was slow and circuitous compared to that of the sighted child, yet essentially the same path was followed.

To illustrate, we turn to a group of observations which tell us something about the way in which Toni recognized objects during the second half of the first year.

In our early film sequences we observed that Toni recognized the bottle only at the moment when her mouth or fingers made contact with the nipple, that is, the cathected portion of the bottle. At seven months Toni lost her bottle while lying on the floor. In random movements of arms and hands she came in contact with the glass bottle itself without showing signs of recognition. In a sequence at nine months when the bottle was presented to her inverted, she showed no signs of recognition although she took the bottom of the bottle in her mouth and sucked on it as she did with all objects at this time. When the bottle was righted for her and she made contact with the nipple, there was immediate recognition on her face. At eleven and a half months when the bottle was again presented to her inverted, she handled it familiarly, extended her fingers down the sides of the bottle until she reached the nipple, and slowly, quite unself-consciously reversed its position and brought the nipple to her mouth. From this behavior we inferred that she now had a concept of the whole bottle. Where vision would have conferred wholeness to the percept of bottle many months earlier, the blind baby had to achieve this through a laborious additive process.

In the behavior with the inverted bottle, we can also see that the perception of wholeness was achieved through the hand alone. The hand began to function as a discriminating sensory organ. This was a new behavior with regard to inanimate objects although it was not a new behavior with regard to human objects. As already indicated, at eight months when Toni was held experimentally by one of the investigators, she reacted with immediate anxiety to the stranger and followed this with anxious, exploratory fingering of the stranger's face; she was relying upon her hand for fine discrimination and for reality testing. At nine months we saw her hand exploring the faces of her brother and sisters as they played with her. The progression from human objects to inanimate objects in the behavior of the hand was first observed by us in connection with the bottle. It was not observed in connection with objects that were not libidinally cathected or were unfamiliar to her until many months later.

At seventeen months when Toni had already demonstrated very good tactile perception, we made this observation: Toni was playing a game with her bottle on the porch of her home. She repeatedly threw the bottle away and recovered it. Once, she lost the bottle and conducted a search for it. We then saw her crawling along the floor licking the floor with her tongue! In the emergency she fell back upon the mouth as the organ of perception.

For all blind persons the mouth retains its function as a leading discriminating perceptual organ throughout life. Villay (1930) describes how, even as an adult, he relied upon his mouth, and particularly his tongue, to make the finest perceptual distinctions. Our observations of Toni show the extent to which the mouth was required to serve as a substitute for vision from the third through the eighteenth month of life. The use of a highly cathected instinctual zone for perception has important implications for the study of ego formation. This line of inquiry, which was suggested to us by Dr. Joseph Michaels at an early stage of our work, is one that we consider central to this and subsequent studies.

The mouth, of course, dictates its own terms of perception. As we saw in Toni, in order for an object to be desirable, it must be need satisfying or associated with oral stimulation. When the mouth remains the primary organ of perception, it restricts the range of experience with objects and obstructs a crucial development that leads to the discovery of the nature of objects.

We have no analogy in the development of sighted children. The primary autonomy of vision guarantees the conflict-free development of perception. The prolonged mouth-centered perception of the blind infant promotes an alliance between drives and perception that can be a serious impediment to learning. The hand will later serve the development of a "conflict-free" perception, but the hand itself in the blind infant maintains its partnership with the mouth for an extended period that is not paralleled in the development of sighted children.

We are accustomed to speak of the hands of the blind as their "eyes." When we consider how the achievement of hand autonomy for sighted infants is facilitated by vision, the same achievement in the blind infant appears as a feat of extraordinary virtuosity. It may not be achieved at all—as we see in the deviant blind child. While we are not prepared to say how the adaptive failure of the hand should be weighed in the whole complex of factors that have led to developmental arrest in these cases, it is striking that this failure is consistently found in our own observations as well as all reported cases of deviant blind children.

As we followed Toni's development we saw that the hand very gradually took over perceptual functions that were centered in the mouth. The early partnership of mouth and hand facilitated a transfer of perceptual qualities and even oral-perceptive modes to the hand itself (Spitz, 1955) until, as we saw, near the end of Toni's second year the hand achieved autonomy from the mouth and was capable of increasingly complex discriminations.

As we traced the progress of the hand through the film record we saw that at seven months Toni recognized the nipple of her bottle when her fingers came in contact with it. At eight months when she

was held by one of the investigators, she cried in distress and anxiously fingered the stranger's face, verifying that this was a stranger.
At nine months we saw her playing with her brother, alternately
mouthing him and fingering his face. At ten months she demonstrated tactual recognition of her bottle when it was presented to
her inverted and, in a sequence where various stuffed animals and
dolls were presented to her, she used the mouth and her hands alternately for discriminating among them. Novel objects were still
brought first to the mouth as late as twenty-one months. The progress in tactual recognition evolved from human objects and the
cathected inanimate objects such as the bottle and gradually spread
to include a wide range of objects that were not, in themselves,
libidinally cathected. And this last achievement, which corresponds
to the autonomy of the hand from mouth, was seen only in the last
months of the second year.

We contrast this with the picture of the persistently mouth-
centered deviant blind child. The invariable picture of these children showed them lying on a bed or sitting on the floor absently
mouthing or sucking or tonguing or chewing a clothespin, a rubber
toy, or a metal ashtray. In the case of the deviant child, perception
could not free itself from the erotogenic overload of the mouth and
remained in a kind of morbid alliance with the drives. There was
no interest in objects other than those that were connected with
need satisfaction or self-stimulation (as we saw in Toni, too, during
the first year).

We do not know why the deviant children failed to develop hand
autonomy. As already indicated, however, we feel that this failure
is crucial and is one of the factors that maintains the personality on
the level of nondifferentiation. What we can see through the study
of Toni is that the adaptive use of the hand as a primary organ of
perception is an extraordinary feat which even under favorable circumstances evolved very slowly in this one blind child. We are
accustomed to take this adaptive achievement for granted in the case
of the blind child. The study of deviant blind children teaches us
that the route to hand autonomy for the sightless child is so complex
that it may never be found at all.

We hope that further developmental studies on blind children, including deviant blind infants, will illuminate this and other developmental failures.

BIBLIOGRAPHY

Bender, M. B. (1952), *Disorders in Perception*. Springfield: Thomas.
Blank, H. R. (1957), Psychoanalysis and Blindness. *Psychoanal. Quart.*, 26:1-24.
—— (1958), Dreams of the Blind. *Psa. Quart.*, 27:158-174.
Burlingham, D. (1961), Some Notes on the Development of the Blind. *This Annual*, 16:121-145.
Gesell, A. & Amatruda, C. (1947), *Developmental Diagnosis*, 2nd ed. New York: Hoeber.
Hartmann, H. (1952), The Mutual Influences in the Development of Ego and Id. *This Annual*, 7:9-30.
Hoffer, W. (1949), Mouth, Hand, and Ego-Integration. *This Annual*, 3/4:49-56.
Keeler, W. R. (1958), Autistic Patterns and Defective Communication in Blind Children with Retrolental Fibroplasia. *Psychopathology of Communication*, ed. P. H. Hoch & J. Zubin. New York: Grune & Stratton.
Klein, G. S. (1962), Blindness and Isolation. *This Annual*, 17:82-93.
Linn, L. (1953), Psychological Implications of the "Activating System." *Amer. J. Psychiat.*, 110:61-65.
Norris, M., Spaulding, P., & Brodie, F. (1957), *Blindness in Children*. Chicago: University of Chicago Press.
Omwake, E. G. & Solnit, A. J. (1961), "It Isn't Fair." The Treatment of a Blind Child. *This Annual*, 16:352-404.
Parmalee, A. H., Jr. (1955), Developmental Evaluation of the Blind Premature Infant. *A.M.A. Amer. J. Dis. Child.*, 90:135-140.
—— Cutsforth, M. D., & Jackson, C. L. (1958), The Mental Development of Children with Blindness Due to Retrolental Fibroplasia. *A.M.A. Amer. J. Dis. Child.*, 96: 641-648.
Piaget, J. (1937), *The Construction of Reality in the Child*. New York: Basic Books, 1954.
Provence, S. & Lipton, R. C. (1962), *Infants in Institutions*. New York: International Universities Press.
Sandler, A.-M. (1963), Aspects of Passivity and Ego Development in the Blind Infant. *This Annual*, 18:343-361.
Segal, A. & Stone, F. H. (1961), The Six-Year-Old Who Began to See: Emotional Sequelae of Operation for Congenital Bilateral Cataracts. *This Annual*, 16:481-509.
Spitz, R. A. (1945), Hospitalism: An Inquiry into the Genesis of Psychiatric Conditions in Early Childhood. *This Annual*, 1:53-74.
—— (1955), The Primal Cavity. *This Annual*, 10:215-240.
—— (1959), *A Genetic Field Theory of Ego Formation*. New York: International Universities Press.
—— (1963), Life and the Dialogue. In: *Counterpoint*, ed. H. S. Gaskill. New York: International Universities Press.
Villay, P. (1930), *World of the Blind*. New York: Macmillan.

# DYNAMIC DETERMINANTS IN
# ORAL FIXATION

AUGUSTA ALPERT, PH.D. and ISIDOR BERNSTEIN, M.D.

(New York)

Though much attention has been focused in analytic work with adults on the effect of oral fixation and regression on developmental disturbances, little systematic investigation has been devoted to oral fixation in early childhood.

Observations by one observer (Alpert) of the unusual intensity and persistence of thumb sucking in some of the children attending the nursery at the Child Development Center,[1] who would otherwise be described as "normal" in their development, raised questions about the role of variations in drive endowment in such cases. This was explored in a joint publication by Alpert, Neubauer, Weil (1956). This was followed by an investigation of the dynamic determinants of oral fixation by means of analytic treatment of the same case which had been studied by Alpert in the paper already referred to. The analysis was carried out by the co-author of this paper, Dr. Isidor Bernstein.[2]

## CASE REPORT

*Anamnesis*

Carl was the mother's second pregnancy, the first having terminated in stillbirth, due to delay in performing a Caesarean section. Carl was delivered by Caesarean section, at full term, condition nor-

[1] The Child Development Center is a research and treatment center for prelatency children and their families. The children attend a therapeutic nursery school daily, over a period of several years. The nursery school is an integral part of the Center program.

[2] This investigation was carried out with the help of a grant by the Psychoanalytic Research and Development Fund, Inc., Augusta Alpert, Chief Investigator, Isidor Bernstein, psychoanalyst.

mal, birth weight 6 pounds, 13 ounces, and was seen sucking his thumb "five minutes after birth" by his father. He was breast-fed for three months, each feeding lasting forty to forty-five minutes, after which Carl would cry. Breast feeding was discontinued because the mother could not stand these prolonged nursings. He accepted the bottle well but was finicky about solids. He gained and throve until twenty months, when he developed a diarrhea, diagnosed as celiac, which lasted until thirty months. He was on the usual strict diet for five months, the acute phase, during which he "assumed responsibility for his diet," that is, he would reject proscribed foods. Weaning from the bottle started at sixteen months, but was given up when the "celiac" started. In fact, the number of bottles was increased, a characteristic restitution by the mother for all deprivations, frustrations, and injuries. Thus, at twelve months, when Carl's thumb sucking had to be mechanically restrained because of a split lip from a fall, the mother offered more bottles; and again, when a sibling was born, Carl being then two and a half years old. At three Carl accepted milk from a cup for one week only and then demanded two bottles in a row, seemingly having already picked up mother's regressive cue! From then on, he became more dependent on his bottle than the sibling. Thumb sucking continued from birth, with peaks at the time of the "celiac" and the sibling's birth, and low points during summer vacations. In the nursery, it remained unchanged in intensity throughout his four years, with an increase in masturbation, noted in his fifth year. It acquired a more active concomitant of digging into his nose during the latter half of his fifth year. Perhaps it became more anal in character as a result of reactivating the anal phase in therapy.

Speech developed slowly, only a few words by one and a half, and a few more by two, and remained indistinct. Mild stuttering developed at about three, when he tried to make sentences, and lasted for about three months.

He began to walk at seven months, fell and interrupted walking until nine months. He was always wiry and vigorous, so active since seven months that he "wore us out," according to the father. (This comment reflects parental intolerance, according to later findings.) By the time he entered nursery at three, his use of the body was considered less than age-adequate, moving the total body "like a two-year-old."

Sleep was good until eighteen months, but at this time he began to insist on being rocked, and once rocked himself vigorously until the crib "walked." This lasted until two years. Toilet training was undertaken at one, and by two Carl was dry and clean, day and night. "He trained himself" during "celiac"! As an infant of three months, Carl woke up dry after a night's sleep and the parents were worried enough to call the pediatrician, who reassured them.

He always loved people, especially children, but was too devoted to the mother, and would not remain alone in his room or with his grandmother. He was inconsolable and refused to eat when his mother left for the hospital for the birth of his sibling, when he was two and a half.

Health, except for "celiac," was excellent.

The mother's memory for the child's developmental history and early events was exceptionally poor, and she would turn to the father; but his was, if anything, worse.

*Family*

The mother was twenty-seven years old when Carl was born. She experienced anxiety during the pregnancy with Carl because of the previous stillbirth. She herself was a persistent thumb sucker as a child, and various restraints were used for many years, which she still holds against her parents. She was always a finicky eater. She had had globus hystericus twice: first at the age of twenty, probably at the beginning of sex relations, and again about the age of twenty-six. She is a good organist, having studied with her father until eighteen, at which time she abruptly broke away. She may be described as a hysterical woman, with strong penis envy and unresolved conflict between oral dependency and masculine phallic assertiveness.

The father was thirty-two years old when Carl was born. He, too, was a thumb sucker and had his bottle until the age of five. Both he and Carl were described as gulping their milk and letting it "run down" their throats. He suffered from ejaculatio praecox which often seriously disturbed the marital relationship. He worked in his father's business with little job satisfaction. He was diagnosed as having an orally dependent character, with passive, feminine identification.

Though the younger sibling was held up as the child who did not suck her thumb and who could be weaned easily (she was not breast-fed for fear it would make Carl jealous!), she was seen in the nursery behind a blanket strip, her "transitional object," sucking her tongue. During rest periods, she made strong sucking movements and sounds. The "permissive" mores of the family were offered by the mother as a rationalization for absence of privacy in the home and for showering together with Carl, sitting down in the tub, followed by passionate caresses. These stimulating experiences took place between two and a half and three and were interrupted by the mother only as she gained fuller awareness in her own therapy. The mother's report that at this time Carl used to have erotic dreams about a nine-year-old girl in the same house is an interesting mechanism of displacement shared by mother and son. The use which the mother made of her son as an erotic object contrasts significantly with her habit of picking him up when he soiled, during the same period, like laundry, and washing him off under the faucet in the basin. Both must have been equally overwhelming, though uniquely different in their patterning effect on his personality development.

Carl was brought by his parents to the Child Development Center at the age of two years eleven months, because of persistent thumb sucking, inability to be weaned from the bottle, feeding difficulties, some stuttering, and aggression toward his younger sibling, then five months old. The first and last complaints were most troublesome to the parents. Observation in the outpatient nursery group showed Carl to be a normally developed boy, sturdy in build and bland of face. He was clinging to his mother, was passive, indecisive, for the most part keenly observant of surroundings, and at times withdrawn from them. He remained in this therapeutic nursery for three years, without noticeable reduction in his thumb sucking. Individual psychotherapy was introduced in his second year and continued for approximately one and a half years.[3] Learning difficulty was predicted, at the conclusion of his stay at the Child Development Center, at age six.

At this time Carl's family moved to a suburb, where he was en-

3 Dr. Marjorie Pfeffer was the therapist.

rolled in the public school. On subsequent follow-up contacts, the mother reported good progress in all areas except in the control of thumb sucking. Distressed though she professed to be by this symptom, she resisted continuation of treatment for herself or for Carl. The precipitating factor which motivated her to seek therapy for Carl, about two and a half years later, was an incident which revealed a sadistic break-through. Carl poured a lethal chemical on his cat and when "cross-examined" by his mother, confessed a seething resentment and destructive wishes against his father.[4] Arrangements were made for Carl's analysis, with the dual purpose of therapy and research.

## Abstract of Analytic Treatment

At the time the mother was first seen by the analyst, she declared that Carl had "normal difficulties" and was "basically a happy boy." She went on to say that he had shown great improvement in school but that he still had a tendency to daydream and not see things through. Furthermore, she reported that he lacked confidence in himself. Finally, she added that he still sucked his thumb although it had "practically stopped." Carl's mother is a short, stockily built woman who speaks in a rather loud and aggressive tone. Her manner covers a good deal of anxiety and tension. The mother's tendency to deny or at least to minimize her son's problems was quite marked.

In line with the mother's inclination to "normalize" Carl's behavior, she declared that he functioned well, was outgoing, made friends easily, and was independent. Actually he was quite dependent and demanding of the mother and was so passively resistant that she was "forced into the position of nagging him," e.g., to practice his music lessons. Also, he really had very few friends and tended to limit himself to a cousin and some girls. The unrealistic view of this boy the mother tended to take will be referred to later in conjunction with other problems relating to his self-image and impaired sense of reality. The mother also tended to glamorize and practically fictionalize her original family, particularly her father. She had inflated artistic (musical) and intellectual aspirations for Carl.

---

4 This occurred at the time of the sensational murder of parents, circumstantially ascribed to their six-year-old son, which may have brought both Carl's fantasies and those of his parents too close to consciousness, with an increase in their anxiety.

At the time of the initial interview, Carl was almost nine years old. He was chubby, soft-appearing, round-faced, with a large head. He spoke in a loud voice but did not articulate distinctly. He walked about frequently on tiptoe. Although he tried to appear casual and relaxed, this was easily seen to cover a great deal of anxiety. He told the analyst that he was coming to see a psychiatrist because of his problem, namely, sucking his thumb and picking his nose. Most of the time of that visit was spent examining the toys in the playroom, which he did in the manner of a younger child, going very quickly from one to the next.

Psychological tests were done by Dr. Miriam Siegel in April, 1959. She described him as a babyish, restless, excitable boy with a plump, immature appearance. He achieved an I.Q. of 106 on verbal, performance, and full-scale WISC tests. In regard to these, the examiner felt that he was probably brighter but was so confused and anxious that one could not accurately gauge his true potentialities. Projective tests presented an "indigestible combination of emotional infantilism and ineffectual pedantry." She found the Rorschach "overweighted with fantasy, with a severe inhibition of emotional spontaneity" and noted that he seemed quite anxious, with fears of personal injury. In the CAT stories, he conveyed "oral-dependency concerns." The over-all picture was one of immaturity in a depressed, emotionally inhibited boy who was bound up in fearful fantasies.

Because of recurrent mild throat infections, the parents decided to have Carl undergo a tonsillectomy. The operation was scheduled for early spring, just before the start of his analysis, an obvious resistance to treatment (see Lipton, 1962). Carl admitted to his mother that he was a little frightened and asked her if she thought he would die. This fear of death by various means was a persistent theme throughout his analysis.

Treatment was begun in April, 1959; he was seen four times a week. True to his compliant attitude, he came to his analysis at first without any outward show of resentment. However, he played out many fantasies of fights which were reflections of anxiety about the kind of struggle he was expecting to have with the analyst. What emerged after this were expressions of hostility toward his mother and sister. A major defense was massive regression to babyish behavior and passive dependence. Carl took a passive attitude toward the analyst-mother (wishing to be read to) and regressed to open thumb sucking. At this point, he confided that the trouble had started when his grandmother died—because he loved her. This could be understood to date the intensification of his passivity toward the mother when he became afraid of his hatred of her and his death wishes, and also related to his loss of her and her love. Carl had placed it forward to the time he was seven years old, but it would seem more likely to be temporally related to the birth of his sister. The anger at the mother's abandonment of him, fused with feelings of oral deprivation and actual deprivation due to the "celiac disease," was renewed when the mother was ill with hepatitis for about a year. This coincided with the terminal illness of the maternal grandmother. Carl inverted the time relationship and told the analyst that his mother had hepatitis when he was one and a half years old, thus betraying the real precipitating trauma to be the birth of his sister. It could also be seen that Carl was interpreting his being sent for analysis as another abandonment and oral deprivation (not having time to play and to cure him of his thumb sucking). Gratification of his passivity by reading to him was permitted for a while in the analysis and then gradually frustrated. He reacted first by increased passivity and withdrawal and then by the emergence of hostile fantasies and feelings toward the analyst-mother. Concurrently, there were fears of his own death by starvation and exhaustion which he attempted to defend himself against by fantasying himself as an engine that was refueled.[5] The boy oscillated between the regressive pull of strong oral-dependent wishes accompanied by a desire for fusion with the mother (dramatized by submersion, being drained down the sink) and the forward striving for assertive independence. This conflict was played out repetitively with sink, bathtub, and toilet. For instance, he would fill the sink with water and then submerge containers, figures, objects representing feces, in the water and then be occupied with the alternatives of their being lost, destroyed, drained down or recovered, emerging unharmed. He would fill the sink with water, submerge a man and then snatch the man out of the water, exclaiming that he was nearly dead because it was six minutes and the man would die if he could not get air. Carl hid

5 Cf. Mahler's reference (1963) to Furer's description of the symbiotic child refueling himself by contact with the mother.

in closets and the cabinets under the sink and then would have the analyst find him or come out on his own. The striving toward independence was expressed in more open defiance of the mother by messing, using anal language, and forgetting or ignoring her instructions. Ideas of strangling the mother, shooting her, or pushing her off a high place were followed by fears of retaliation and by self-directed aggression. A similar pattern was followed in a relationship with one of his peers. After Carl had expressed a fantasy of stabbing a boy who had taken something of Carl's, Carl reported that he himself had (in fantasy) died many times by being stabbed in the side or back, being strangled or pushed off a height. All of these masochistic fantasies were played out in subsequent hours. Intermingled with the defenses against dangers would be the unmistakable evidence of the underlying intra-uterine fantasies. Thus, he would use a breathing tube to overcome his fear of suffocation through strangulation or drowning. At a later stage in the analysis, the wish to be inside mother was expressed as a feeling of boredom whenever he felt imprisoned as in the analysis. Another facet of the fear of being imprisoned was a fear of being trapped or stuck and needing to get out as the reverse of the early diarrhea; in this he was equating himself with the constipated feces. This would be an anal derivative of the oral wish-fear to be incorporated by the mother and vice versa. The anal fantasy led to a fear of internal poisoning which was externalized as a fear of dying from bombs or atomic radiation. Another means of dealing with his impulses was by projection (e.g., the sadistic mother as reported in a "sick" joke: "Mother, I don't want to go to Europe." "Shut up and swim!" and "Mother, what's a vampire?" "Shut up and drink your tomato juice"). The conflict between his sucking, incorporative, dependent wishes and his fear-ridden desire to be active and aggressive and to free himself from the mother was repeatedly interpreted to him.

The mother reported that he was less demanding at home and that there had been a decided improvement in his schoolwork, particularly in his ability to read. Also, he was showing increased social aggressiveness, making his own arrangements to visit friends. Some of the aggressive feelings toward his mother were expressed directly to her. She expressed her conscious acceptance of this, telling him it was all right to be angry with her. Once he told her, "I wish I didn't have a mother and father." This death wish led to his questioning her about orphanages, i.e., his fears of being abandoned. He also verbalized fears of his father's getting angry and hitting him. In the analysis, the fear of punishment by the angry mother led to recollection of his defiant soiling in the bathtub and sink when his sister was born.

The material then became suffused with anality. This was heralded by an episode of diarrhea. It was followed by playing out bombings, shootings, and explosions, and was motorically expressed by whirling himself about and by nonsensical speech. The new material was interlarded with recrudescences of the familiar oral material. For instance, he spent most of an hour playing out an air-sea battle and then drew an oil tank with pipes leading to an engine. He then drew a measuring stick in the tank and a pipe where the tank would be filled. The pipe running to the engine had broken and the engine could not get oil for power. His hours would begin with a small orgy of candy eating and would end with borrowing money from the analyst or planning how to get money from a man by cheating him. On leaving, he would take a drink from the water in the sink and ask the analyst to help him button his sleeve. Gradually, some competitive feelings toward the analyst were expressed in the form of comparisons and by battles between respective armies played out with soldiers.

In a rather impressive forward thrust of the libido, he then began to build fires and give other evidence of his awareness of his penis (indicated by rising and falling rockets in his play and leaving his trouser fly open). The rocket play had overtones of orality in that he entered the rocket ship and journeyed to the center of the earth, thus returning to the intra-uterine fantasies. Likewise, his explorations of Mars ended up by his being shot but not killed—only put to sleep. Scoptophilic drives became apparent with memories of having seen other children undressed in nursery school; he denied having seen his mother nude. At the same time, definite castration anxiety emerged (concern about missing parts). He also began to react to the analyst as a person rather than some impersonal, inanimate feeding-reading machine. His concerns about illness and death were defended against by magic medicines and fantasies of omnipotence. The access of phallic drives was too threatening, it would seem, so he fell ill with a respiratory illness. This was exploited by the mother in the service of her own resistance and resulted in his being sent to Florida for ten days' convalescence. The description of his departure was remarkable. The mother reported it with pride, ignoring the complete absence of affect on his part, a performance which could be titled, "Have thumb—Will travel." That is to say, so long as he had his own part object, manifest reaction to object loss was not observable. We shall return to this point later. He resumed his analysis as if there had been no interruption. However, the material showed a reversion to his passivity and feelings of oral deprivation—a repetition of the earliest themes. He lay on the couch and asked the analyst to read to him, after which he sucked some candy and asked for a cup of water. He repeatedly climbed into closets, asking for a pillow and then a toy. He complained when things were not given to him or done for him (fetching water or reading comics) and having to interrupt his own reading of comics in the waiting room in order to begin his hour.

In a short time, however, renewed expressions of assertiveness and aggressiveness were reported by the mother; Carl himself isolated this from his analysis. In the analysis, there were indications of anal aggressiveness toward the analyst (spilling, messing, defiance), followed by reactions suggesting a masochistic attitude (dropping things, making himself wet, and hurting his finger). Here the fears of getting into a fight with the analyst-father led to the passive masochistic reaction. His increasing assertiveness produced marked progress in his studies, particularly reading. In the analysis, there were evidences of increasingly positive transference feelings, probably partly out of gratitude for the improvement. Carl could not bring himself to declare this openly; it came out in play with secret messages of manifest hostile content coupled with appeals for rescue and help. The dangers he wanted to be saved from were of being lost or abandoned and of starvation and thirst. One direct appeal to the analyst was to help him curb his appetite for candy. His mother was pressing him to cut down on his consumption of sweets, and this renewed the earlier hostility toward the mother and sister for the early oral deprivation. This was played out with dolls by having the sister doll fall off a height, having the leg of the mother fall off, having the sister commit suicide, and then the whole family dying only to be rescued

by the baby. The play was concluded the first time with the father
dying and "they all live happily"; the second time, the sister fell apart
and "everybody was happy." This brought Carl to his first summer
(1960) vacation. The gains he had made enabled him to enjoy a day-
camp experience where he was awarded a cup for the boy who showed
the most improvement. According to the mother, the thumb sucking
had diminished and he had stopped the rubbing of his nostril. His
relationship with the father was reported to be closer and more affectionate. He had actually looked for the analyst's home during the
vacation. When school started again, he felt inadequate and threatened by his accidental breaking of the teacher's ruler. In play, this
was expressed as getting into hot water; escaping into outer space
was a means of getting away from his earthly troubles. His anxiety
and fears of punishment caused him to behave in a provocative manner toward the analyst in an effort to convince himself that nothing
terrible would happen to him. It became clear that he feared the
loss of the teacher-mother's love which intensified feelings of rivalry
toward his sister and analyst-father. He brought out screen memories
of wishing to have a brother instead of a sister and having been told
eight months before his sister's birth that the mother was pregnant.
The real relationship with the father became closer and more intimate with their sharing of hobbies. It was expressed in the transference by a wish to visit the analyst at Halloween. The ambivalence
toward the analyst became more intense and more open. He tortured
and hung the father doll and enacted masochistic fantasies of being
shot in the stomach and needing the bullets removed. He described
specific fears which included anxiety at the beginning of any movie,
or hearing about the heart or the body, of someone yelling at him,
of someone bullying him, following him or stabbing him in the back.
It was plain that fear of rivalrous feelings led to a passive-masochistic
attitude toward the father with fears of castration. He became interested in the topic of Caesarean section (at the time of Mrs. Kennedy's
Caesarean); his mother explained it to Carl and informed him that
he had been born that way. This led him to remember seeing her
appendectomy scar which "looked horrible." He was then launched
into "memories" of his own operation (tonsillectomy) and the dec-
laration that he knew when his problem started: it was when he saw
some films about the heart when he was "two, three, four, or five

years old." From the way the material developed, the onset of his neurosis could be more directly related to the birth of the sister since the next few hours were concerned with intra-uterine fantasies and outwardly passive behavior. Despite vigorous denials and repudiation, hostile feelings toward the father became more directly expressed. He reacted to this by having a nightmare: "An insect had me around the foot and punctured it." In another part, he was "in a pond and there were all kinds of insects and a lobster." The pond reminded him of camp. In the dream, Carl had tried to crush the insect and it said, "I will get you for that." Associations were to an incapacitating illness and that night he actually did not feel well. He recovered by the next morning. Thus, hostility to the father led to fear of retaliation and resulted in a regression to thumb sucking and anxiety about an incapacitating illness in which there was identification with the ailing mother. A different conclusion to the sequence occurred a few sessions later when he reported the following "bad dream": "I had a valuable stamp worth a million dollars and my father and I were fighting over it. This was repeated with another stamp. There was a part about a maid shooting a girl cousin." In association, he related that his father had threatened that if Carl did not mount his stamps in his album, the father would take them away. He then was reminded of his grandfather visiting. Carl had heard from his mother that Carl's great-grandfather and grandmother had very much wanted to see Carl born, but both had died while Carl was still in his mother's stomach. Carl then enacted a "star-crusher" story: his arm was a "star-crusher" and, as the stars went by, his arm would catch one against the wall and crush it. This happened with a shooting star. Again the hostility to the father, expressed by the passive defiance of not putting away the stamps, led to a threat of castration. This time, however, Carl reacted by identifying with the aggressor and becoming the castrating star-crusher. Still struggling with his emerging phallic aggression, he had another dream: "There were millions of green-purple polka-dot houses. I was trying to get into my own house which was white with a red roof and they were trying to trick me into going into other houses. I was scared but went into my own house." He had been reading a book about the Secret Service which told about a swindler's money-making machine in which the trick was a secret drawer. Carl had been angry with his sister; she had hidden and observed him while he was undressing. The purple reminded him of a friend who had scared Carl by wearing a purple polka-dot sheet. A slip in which he said "yellow" reminded him of the song "Yellow polka-dot bikini." He had not eaten breakfast and was hungry. He asked the analyst to test his patellar reflex. This reminded him of a comic: a man was sleeping and his wife was cleaning; he was in a chair. When she accidentally touched his knee, he kicked her in the behind. She looked at him, but he was still sleeping. The dream and associations could be understood to describe the danger of expressing aggressive and active sexual wishes: he would be tricked into revealing his masculinity and then robbed. The defense is to retreat to the familiar, i.e., passive and dependent state. However, he then has to struggle against being submerged by his desire for fusion with mother. The thumb sucking is the narcissistic body substitute (related to the transitional object) which gratifies the oral need and yet avoids the threatening wish for oral incorporation and fusion with mother. In the transference, he attempted to conceal his aggressive feelings by playful hiding and then by playing outdoors when he was due to begin his hour. It did not completely avoid his anxiety, and he saw the analyst as a monster or as Mussolini ready to attack, strangle, and kill him.

A more competitive attitude then came out, expressed toward the analyst in relation to solving puzzles; with the father it was in the form of who could do better tricks with the yo-yo. This attitude alternated with the passive-dependent one. The aggression toward the father was displaced onto a taxi driver who, Carl claimed, had overcharged him. Carl played out his revenge by having the cab driver have accidents and by bombings which killed the old Emperor. Toward the analyst, these feelings were revealed by his throwing darts which chipped plaster from the walls. The aggressiveness provoked guilt in play (the murderous boy was punished) and in real life when Carl managed to hurt himself by falling down the stairs. Expressions of hostility toward the analyst continued to become more open, with disguised death wishes; these were intermingled with indications of positive feelings and attempts to placate the analyst and repair any damage done.

His relationship to the analyst became entirely different from his earlier one; previously he had regarded him as some inanimate

object there to fulfill Carl's needs. The perception of the analyst as
a person was accompanied by increased phallic drives expressed by
fire making and by competitive comparisons with the analyst. The
reason for the advance became clearer when it developed that he had
begun a stimulating relationship with the family's new maid. Then
began a gradual shift of his devotion to his mother over to the maid,
a twenty-four-year-old woman. In line with this, there emerged feelings of having been disappointed by the mother at times when he
had been displaced by his sister and father. A similar shift from
mother to another female (nine-year-old girl) had taken place when
Carl was four years old. Violent sadistic fantasies (hanging, etc.) were
played out in the analytic hours. His desire for the analyst's exclusive
interest revealed the earlier desire for mother's interest and, more
recently, the maid's. His rivalry toward siblings and father was covered by reactive defenses (wishing to make friends with other
patients); the inwardly turned aggression intensified masochistic
complaints of being bored, tired, and tortured in doing homework
and coming to treatment. Interpretations regarding the sadomasochistic character of torturing and boring experiences resulted in a
diminution of the complaints and a happier mood. Just at this time,
a maternal grandaunt living in Europe became seriously ill. The
mother was delegated by her family to journey there. Carl, who by
this time was enamored of the maid and had engaged in voyeuristic
experiences with her cooperation, denied any concern about the
mother's imminent departure. In fact, he declared, he would be
relieved of her bossy nagging. Despite these protestations, he became
depressed, the thumb sucking increased, and he finally fell ill with
the grippe. He made up a revealing jingle, "Over dirt, over grit,
what happened to my tit, as the caissons go rolling along."

The relationship with the maid stirred up memories of earlier intimacies with his mother in the bathroom. His partner in his revived
"oedipal" attachment attempted to stave off her admirer, but he
persisted. Her guilt over her involvement led to some petty thievery
on her part and culminated in her decision to leave when the mother
returned. The mother came back after ten days and Carl cried in-
consolably when informed of the maid's decision. He asked why they
had not waited to tell him until he was away in camp, which would
have been in a little more than a week. Whatever feelings Carl had

about the impending first sleep-away camp experience were displaced onto his blighted romance. He tried to avoid discussion of his loss in the analysis but was finally prevailed upon to talk with the analyst about it. Anger and fantasies of omnipotence and revenge came out briefly.

His camp experience went very well. While away, he was actually able to admit missing his mother. When he returned, he had given up sucking his thumb. His relinquishing this gratification renewed his feelings of having been deprived and of having been abandoned and reflected itself in expressions of anger at having to return to his analysis.

At this point in the treatment, it was decided to deal with his constant use of isolation as a defense. He reacted by more direct expressions of anger toward the analyst and then his mother. The inevitable concerns regarding disasters to the world and then himself (appearing as hypochondriacal symptoms) followed. A new symptom, anal pruritis, appeared for the first time when he was awakened at night by a loud noise from a TV program his mother had been watching. Then demands for greater interest from his mother and the analyst appeared, along with fears of losing control. Fears of radiation, cancer, and disease gradually shifted to more definite castration anxiety (amputation of finger and leg). Outside the analysis, his work and relationships improved markedly. Further expressions of anality involved flatulence, constipation, messing and smearing, and a verbalized request for a gift of money from the analyst. He was reminded of his jealousy of his sister at the time of her toilet training. Just as he had then challenged her position with his mother in terms of bowel care, he tried to take possession of the analyst's room and time (locking the door to keep others out). The introduction of the idea of terminating the analysis at the end of the year (June, 1962)[6] brought an access of homosexual feelings expressed by masochistic fantasies of being attacked, subjected to torture by Nazis, imprisonment, and castration. He defended against these by taking the role of the sadistic torturer and executioner. Another defense was the fantasy of being Superman; this not only served to deny the passivity but was to be a protection against retaliation for competitive feelings

6 The analysis had to be interrupted prematurely due to the mother's resistance and the simultaneous termination of the Foundation subsidy.

and hostile (death) wishes against the analyst-father. The aggression was projected onto Russians and enemies from outer space. The increased passivity and dependence on mother caused him to be demanding of her and to have magical expectations that were easily frustrated. Death wishes toward her as well as his father had to be isolated and found expression in an obsessional preoccupation with time.

A brief vacation by the analyst found Carl resorting to the same denial mechanism that had been utilized in relation to the mother's trip. Interpretations enabled him to express some positive feelings as well as envy and rivalry with mother and sister (the analyst's wife). The rivalry theme coincided with his sister's respiratory illness to which Carl reacted by falling ill himself. This revived memories of his "celiac disease" and references to his incontinence and dependence on his mother. Then followed material related to bathroom activities and the subject of privacy. There were distinct allusions to overhearing and possibly observing his parents during intercourse. This was dramatically "acted in" by his falling asleep during the analysis of this primal-scene material. His obsessional questioning could be understood to refer to his questions about the parental activities and also as a defense against the excitement and confusion he experienced in his half-awake state. His sexual drives, particularly the scoptophilic, had been powerfully stirred in the relationship with the maid and were reinforced by the pubertal physical maturation that was beginning. The struggle between activity and passivity became evident in his reactions to looking. He denied the desires and feared the consequences (going blind) and projected his scoptophilia onto others; as a result he was inhibited in the use of the school bathroom lest "everybody stare" and in a parapraxis broke a pair of his glasses. Nevertheless, he had become more active socially and in sports, and more effective in school. In his play, he symbolized the mother as Franken-girl, a demanding, dangerous woman who could not be disposed of. The resentment toward mother and analyst for interfering with his phallic freedom to exhibit was alluded to in jokes and play. Defiance was expressed in anal terms by obscene words and by smearing. The guilt and projected hostile feelings resulted in renewed fears of being attacked and imprisoned (jail, institution, and analytic room). This feeling of being imprisoned could also be understood to result from the mother's high ego ideals and strict superego demands. As a defense against the feeling of being imprisoned, he became preoccupied in his play with means of escape.

The anger at the mother for her dissatisfaction with him and because of her demands for him to accomplish more (in music and school) was brought into relation with the analysis as another of mother's nagging demands. His outward compliance and passive resistance were interpreted to him. So were the identification with the nagging mother and his provocation in nagging (about time) and feeling that he was being nagged by the analyst as by mother. The defensive aspect of his acting stupid and asking silly questions was revealed in this connection as magical protection (to hide aggression and avoid castration). As a result of the analysis of these defenses, he was able to become still more openly aggressive in the analysis and was much more assertive outside, especially in the classroom. He continued to center a great deal of anxiety about his body and showed fears of being annihilated, carved up, and swallowed.

As the material shifted to the impending termination, two affects were conspicuously absent: anger and sadness. As some glimmerings of feelings came through, he first indirectly expressed wishes for a present from the analyst and finally directly as a request for a comic. The door was left open for him to return; the invitation was barely acknowledged.

In May, 1962, three years after the initial examination, the same battery of psychological tests was administered by the same examiner. She reported significant changes in both his appearance and manner. "Traces of his tension and immaturity persist, but he has taken on more clear-cut psychological controls and he is no longer the amorphous baby, with such pronounced inappropriate reactions." The changes in his I.Q. scores (verbal 114, performance 107, full 112) were not so striking as the changes in the intellectual level of his Rorschach. On the WISC subtest pattern, certain basic modifications were noted: on the verbal scale, he showed his greatest gain in the Similarities, a measure of improved conceptualization and logical thinking. "His information responses were less silly. . . . His 'charity' response was more reality-geared without reference to disease. . . . The Rorschach reveals many significant changes. . . . He is more productive, more imaginative, and far better organized. . . . The major change appears in the growth of the integrative capacity. . . .

The intellectual level of the Rorschach is considerably improved, more so than the WISC ratings. . . . There is less diffusion in the current findings, a more clear-cut statement of his conflicts, with fewer ineffectual obsessive drives. Traces of immaturity, tension, and passivity are still evident, and his orality remains a dominant motif, but this too has jelled into a more cohesive pattern. He is less depressed, less inhibited, more responsive, with less panic about his impulses. Some of his patterns are deeply ingrained, but his gains do outstrip those anticipated in the normal maturational process."

*Summary*

At the beginning of treatment this boy had shown tremendous passivity and oral dependence with considerable immaturity to the point that it was clinically suggestive of an incipient psychosis. The analysis had enabled him to overcome his dependency to a large extent and to conquer his passivity to some degree. The analysis revealed the importance of several significant traumata, viz.: (1) the early mouth injury and intestinal disorder leading to the restriction of oral gratification; (2) the birth of the sister and the illness of the mother leading to feelings of maternal deprivation and real loss of mothering; and (3) the overstimulating physical intimacies with the mother in the bathroom. The relative absence of the father as an important figure for identification in the past was also evident throughout most of the material. What one gathered, then, was that this boy was struggling against a strong regressive pull toward fantasied union with the mother. For this purpose, the thumb and nasolabial junction (snout or perioral region as suggested by Rangell, 1954) acted as substitute part objects and anchored him firmly at the oral stage of libidinal development. His ego was concerned with defending itself against incorporative annihilation of his feeling of self, or identity, by these autoerotic and, at times, autistic defenses. Much of the early work of the analysis was directed toward overcoming his passivity, demonstrating the defensive aspect of it, and liberating enough aggression to enable him to resume the further progress in development. In the analysis, this could be seen in his more direct perception of the analyst as an object and in his expression of ambivalent feelings toward the analyst. Outside, Carl showed increasing social contact and assertiveness. From this point, he entered into an "oedipal" relationship with a cooperative maid, actively reliving the scoptophilic relationship with the mother and ending in similar disappointment. When last seen, Carl impressed the analyst as still rooted in early latency with slight awareness of genital interests, pointing to marked inhibition.

Brief reference was made earlier to the mother's unrealistic view of Carl. She was so determined to see him as some idealized product, a "normal, happy boy," that she denied his problems, became enraged at the unmistakable evidence of immaturity, i.e., the thumb sucking, and then alarmed at his sadistic treatment of a cat. Her wish was for him to be an intellectual and musical genius. This completely unrealizable goal (ego ideal) made Carl feel weighted down, nagged, and fearful of disappointing her. Since it bore so little resemblance to him as he really was, her goal for him led in turn to Carl's having an unrealistic view of his abilities and made reality seem unreasonably difficult and disappointing. For example, he would unconsciously expect to understand and finish schoolwork magically and would become frustrated, anxious, and discouraged when it required more. This unrealistic view of himself, then, led to an unrealistic view of the world as tremendously frustrating, disappointing, and threatening, since it did not conform to his beliefs and wishes for omnipotence.

The role of object relations is of special interest. As indicated before, the unconscious wish to merge with the mother led to many fears of drowning, being submerged, annihilated, etc., which could be understood as losing his sense of self or individual identity. He could have regressed to an autistic stage and, in the beginning, there were indications of this tendency, when he treated the analyst as though the latter were a stick of furniture (dehumanizing him). However, what prevailed was an intense cathexis of his own body, particularly his mouth, nasolabial junction, thumb and body musculature (the last evidenced by considerable bouncing, whirling, and other gross muscle movements). In the analysis, the shift to the perception of the analyst as an object was assisted by his special use of the couch. He would lie, slide, stand, jump, and roll about the couch, push and pull it, and drag it with him to the sink—in effect, holding on to it. One was struck by the similarity of this kind of attachment to a child's attachment to a transitional object. Lying on the couch at times was accompanied by thumb sucking and a fixed stare at the analyst's face, much as a nursing child stares at the mother's face (Spitz, 1955). This use and representation of the couch as a transitional object have also been suggested in analytic work with adults. One woman, who as a child had clung to her bottle until she was eight years old, would finger the towel on the couch, much as a child would finger a blanket. The couch has also appeared in dreams of patients concerning the analyst, suggesting an analogy with the dream screen (Lewin, 1946). From this point of view, one could see the progress toward separation and individuation via the use of the couch as a transitional object.

## THEORETICAL PROBLEMS

The writings of Greenacre, Hoffer, Lewin, Nunberg, and Winnicott provided many helpful theoretical formulations for integrating the patient's anamnesis with the findings in his analysis. The patient was born by a Caesarean section, with his thumb in his mouth. Thus, to quote Hoffer's (1949) clear statement, "from intra-uterine life onward it [hand] becomes closely allied to the mouth for the sake of relieving tension." In time the thumb-in-mouth satisfied other functions as well. Nunberg's formulation (1932), that the baby does not distinguish the breast as a foreign body but treats it as he does his own fingers—when he stuffs them into his mouth and gnaws them— still expresses the observations of research analysts studying the differentiation of mother and infant in the neonatal phase. This reference is cited by Lewin (1950) in his *Psychoanalysis of Elation*. But if thumb sucking had been established in *utero*, the breast may, indeed, be the *"foreign body"* which becomes *associated with the satisfaction of* hunger needs only. We do not know whether this infant showed the "competition between the feeding process and finger-sucking" which both Hoffer (1949) and Winnicott (1945) describe, but the mother reported that the breast feedings lasted forty to forty-five minutes ("they wore me out") and the infant gained well, but nevertheless cried and turned to his thumb after feedings, indicating unfulfilled sucking satisfaction. At any rate, the two basic needs, sucking and feeding, are differentiated from the beginning of life with respect to the satisfying object. We are not here and not yet differentiating the two kinds of sucking: nutritional and pleasurable, as

Freud did in *The Three Essays* (1905). David M. Levy presented experimental confirmation of this differentiation; but his finding, that finger sucking is more likely to become established with *short* nursing periods, seems to contradict the patient's experience; yet it actually confirms the importance of additional determinants. One can postulate that this long breast feeding failed to satisfy the infant's tension-reduction need and may even have increased it due to the mother's mounting tension during nursing. It is interesting to report the finding of two pediatricians, A. and T. Traisman (1958). Of the 2,650 infants they studied, 62.7 per cent of the slow feeders became thumb suckers; but those who sucked their thumbs the *least* belonged to the group who nursed for more than sixty minutes, 2.6 per cent of the total infant group, which suggests a natural satiety or exhaustion point. Greenacre (1941) expressed the belief that oral fixation may have a prebirth determinant. She wondered "whether some libidinal phase, probably most frequently the oral, might not be accentuated by being anticipated in fetal life, and a preliminary channelization for discharge established," whereas (still according to Greenacre) Carl's Caesarean birth may have been prejudicial against motor discharge of tension. *Both* determinants, the preference for oral discharge and the prejudice against motor discharge, are seen by the authors as interrelated and basic in the Greenacre sense.

Thus far our theoretical discussion has shown three early determinants of oral fixation: the thumb-in-mouth intra-uterine position (not fully validated); Caesarean birth; neonatal feeding experience. Lewin's oral psychology, which links the fantasies of the neonatal feeding experience with those of the intra-uterine period, which are then amalgamated with those of later development, provides the theoretical base for the reconstruction of the patient's psychoanalytic data in the light of his neonatal experience. Out of the "oral triad" —the wish to eat, to be eaten, and to fall asleep—the ingredients of a blissful nursing experience at a time when merging with the mother is complete and genetically determined, sucking develops as a defense, presumably regressively, when biting develops. In the case of this patient, the pre-existing thumb sucking not only made the defense readily available, but the defense was needed also for self-preservation, i.e., against biting the self, and may even have been stimulated by pain signals. Here we are reminded of Hoffer's (1949) surprising

discovery that infants do not bite their own fingers because of libidinal investment in the self. The assumption that thumb sucking was
utilized as a defense against oral aggression and cannibalistic fantasies is supported by the patient's strong preference for liquids and
avoidance of solid foods as an infant. It was a well-established defense
(together with overeating) against anger and aggression by the time
the patient came to analysis at the age of nine.[7]

The wish to be eaten, the complement of the wish to eat (and
thus to be reunited with mother), was expressed in an exaggerated
dependence on mother and a paralyzing fear of her disapproval,
which by the time of the analysis had become the basis of his object
relations. As the analytic content shows, intra-uterine and oral fantasies dominated the first two years of treatment, sometimes to an
orgastic degree. These fantasies of sucking or gnawing his way into
the mother's body may, for this patient, have had an unusually vivid
existence due to the mnemonic aid of his uninterrupted thumb
sucking. But the thumb sucking may also have served as a defense
against fantasies of fusion with the mother.[8]

Taking Lewin's hypothesis one step back, we see the thumb sucking as a compulsive repetition of the frustrated wish to recapture
intra-uterine bliss, which governs his response to frustration on all
levels. The pleasure of sucking ("It feels so good"), with the early
and persistent erotization of the lips and mouth cavity, is both a
primary and reactive determinant. Many experimental psychologists,
in addition to Freud, have noted that sucking acquires "habit
strength through reinforcement" (Davis et al., 1948).

So much for intra-uterine and neonatal determinants of the oral
fixation. Let us now turn to later environmental influences as gleaned
from the anamnesis and as reconstructed from the analysis. Both parents were late thumb suckers, especially the mother (twelve years).
This hints at the possibility of hypererotogenicity of oral mucosa as
a familial, constitutional factor, reflected also in the adhesiveness of
the patient's libido. This accords with Freud's discussion in "Analysis
Terminable and Interminable" (1937). Both parents were ambivalent
in the handling of their son's sucking. On the one hand, bottles were

---

[7] In a conversation with Dr. Margaret Mahler, she made the stimulating remark that
there is no reaction formation to sucking—only substitute gratification.

[8] See discussion of object relations above.

increased at every crisis—the "celiac disease" (twenty to thirty months), the birth of the sibling (two and a half years)—and on the other, he was scolded and guiltily restrained. The patient's sucking may thus have represented the unconscious sucking wishes of the parents (Johnson, et al., 1942).

The anal phase, normally marked by an increase in the aggressive drive component, is in this patient's case most difficult to assess in these terms. "Celiac disease," which lasted from twenty to thirty months, must have significantly influenced drive distribution. One must assume that sphincteric retention was altered as a subjective experience, and may not only have reinforced oral retention, but even blurred differentiation between oral and anal zones and sphincters. The sense of mastery associated with the anal phase may not subjectively have been experienced as such, despite mother's reports that he "trained himself"—more likely an act of compliance out of fear. Fusion of orifices was expressed in the analysis by the play of submerging objects in water and sucking of water, interrupted by rushing off to urinate or defecate. This continued for months.

It was perhaps during the anal phase that thumb sucking took on the additional feature of defiance against the mother, clearly seen throughout the analysis. Perhaps it was also during this phase that an anal component was added to the thumb sucking, i.e., simultaneous nose boring, in full bloom when the patient came to analysis (Rangell, 1954).

As the anamnesis has shown, during the anal phase, the patient experienced considerable out-of-phase stimulation by the mother in the form of nude embraces and showering together. This introduces two additional determinants of the oral fixation: (1) phase-specific tension reduction; (2) regressive defense against castration anxiety. The analysis furnished us with firsthand evidence of both. During the second year of analysis, when he began to express rivalry with the therapist or aggressive fantasies against the father, this would be followed invariably by fantasies of self-punishment, acting out, and thumb sucking.

The "love affair": In the second year of analysis when Carl was approaching his eleventh year, he was precipitated into the "oedipal" phase by "falling in love" with the family maid, aged twenty-four. In view of our hypothesis that the earlier, out-of-phase stimulation by the mother reinforced the already overdetermined thumb sucking as a defense, it is of interest to study the patient's behavior in this "oedipal" conflict experienced in the course of the analysis. It should be noted that his psychosexual development as seen in the analysis at this time was that of a barely phallic boy with strong oral and anal components. He showed a marked preference for the passive-receptive position, though the balance of passive-active had already begun to shift toward active during this phase of the analysis.

Carl's role in this affair was nevertheless more active than we would have predicted, but was foreshadowed by the earlier shift to the nine-year-old girl, shortly after the out-of-phase "love affair" with his mother. In fact, one may see it as an active voyeuristic revival of the previously passive visual confrontation with the mother's nudity. During the analytic sessions he would hum sentimental tunes, play "sealing in games," lie down and suck more often, finally admitting his sadness. Thus, the archaic intra-uterine fantasies and the regressive oral impulse were intermingled with voyeuristic (oral-derivative) and phallic impulses.

His "love affair" was first sensed in the analysis by his repetitious complaints of boredom, as though he could not wait to get back, as though he were "trapped," an archaic intra-uterine image which reflects his anxiety on all levels. Phallic games, such as fire-play: "burning holes," "scars of war," "smoke screen," and some genital stroking came into analysis for the first time, but also an increase of thumb sucking and lying around, with complaints of aches and pains. This conflict between phallic assertiveness and regressive passivity barely reached genital primacy when he became ill with an upper respiratory infection.

The "affair" with the maid suffered another setback when she insisted on more privacy, which Carl interpreted as a rejection; he became angry and then fell sick with a relapse of the infection.[9]

The rest of the analysis is marked by a sadomasochistic struggle against boredom and "having to come." It is consistent with the regressive pull implicit in Lewin's "oral psychology," which we have used as the theoretical framework for this patient's developmental pattern, that he turned this period of the analysis into the acting out

---

[9] Respiratory phenomena are prominently connected with fantasies of being a fetus, according to Lewin (1935).

of an intra-uterine-tinged sadomasochistic fantasy, dominated by the following features: he is forced to come, is trapped, has no escape into the world outside where he can play, have fun, be free! It is as though he felt himself trapped in this strange, inner world, which exerted an ineluctible regressive pull, from which the only way out was by gnawing and nagging. The patient remains with a consistent distaste bordering on anxiety, for strong physical activity, and an equally strong preference for "peace." This is so marked and persistent that we feel it cannot be explained only as a reactive or defensive phenomenon. As stated in the paper already referred to (Alpert et al., 1956), it appears to be an expression of an "unusual variation in drive endowment." But psychoanalysis is perhaps neither the tool nor the method of choice for investigating variations in drive endowment. We feel somewhat the same frustration that Freud must have felt when he complained that instincts are superb in their indefiniteness, and that we are never certain we are seeing them clearly.

Nevertheless, we shall attempt a theoretical formulation for the vicissitudes of the oral drive in this patient in the course of his analysis. As we indicated, the original oral fixation in the form of thumb sucking was gradually given up. But the oral fixation persisted in his demandingness, in overeating of sweets, in garrulousness (jokes, etc.). In the "love affair," longing for a kiss, eager listening to the maid's tales of her life, and voyeurism were the main "ingredients." The latter we see as a phallicized expression of the oral drive. The higher integration of the ego, as reported in the second psychological test, and in his improved ability to learn may be seen as sublimations of the oral drive. The limitations of the analytic content, especially masturbation fantasies, do not permit us to go further in our speculations.

## FOLLOW-UP AND PROGNOSIS

The patient is being seen by his analyst about twice a year, on the analyst's initiative. Recently Carl himself called to request an appointment. When the patient's and parents' motivation is more favorable for a continuation of the analysis, we should like to resume the treatment. This is indicated both scientifically and therapeutically. At this time our prognostic expectations, based on theoretical implications of the vicissitudes of the oral drive and on our clinical evidence, include the possibility of addiction, hypochondriasis, and depression. Hypochondriasis, passivity, and depressive features make up the father's personality structure.

## BIBLIOGRAPHY

Alpert, A., Neubauer, P., & Weil, A. P. (1956), Unusual Variations in Drive Endowment. *This Annual*, 11.
Davis, H. V., Sears, R. R., Miller, H. C., & Brodbeck, A. S. (1948), Effects of Cup, Bottle and Breast Feeding on Oral Activities of Newborn Infants. *Pediatrics*, 2.
Freud, S. (1905), Three Essays on the Theory of Sexuality. *Standard Edition*, 7. London: Hogarth Press, 1953.
—— (1932), *New Introductory Lectures on Psychoanalysis*. New York: Norton, 1933.
—— (1937), Analysis Terminable and Interminable. *Collected Papers*, 5. London: Hogarth Press, 1950.
Greenacre, P. (1941), The Predisposition to Anxiety. In: *Trauma, Growth and Personality*. New York: Norton, 1952.
—— (1952), Pregenital Patterning. *Int. J. Psa.*, 33.
Hoffer, W. (1949), Mouth, Hand and Ego Integration. *This Annual*, 3/4.
Johnson, A., Szurek, S., & Falstein, E. (1942), Collaborative Psychiatric Therapy of Parent-Child Problems. *Amer. J. Orthopsychiat.*, 12.
Levy, D. M. (1928), Finger Sucking and Accessory Movements in Early Infancy. *Amer. J. Psychiat.*, 7.
—— (1934), Experiments in the Sucking Reflex and Social Behavior in Dogs. *Amer. J. Orthopsychiat.*, 4.
Lewin, B. D. (1935), Claustrophobia. *Psa. Quart.*, 4.
—— (1946), Sleep, the Mouth and the Dream Screen. *Psa. Quart.*, 15.
—— (1948), Inferences from the Dream Screen. *Int. J. Psa.*, 29.
—— (1950), *Psychoanalysis of Elation*. New York: Norton.
Lipton, S. D. (1962), On the Psychology of Childhood Tonsillectomy. *This Annual*, 17.
Mahler, M. S. (1963), Thoughts about Development and Individuation. *This Annual*, 18.
Nunberg, H. (1932), Principles of Psychoanalysis. New York: International Universities Press, 1955.
Rangell, L. (1954), The Psychology of Poise. *Int. J. Psa.*, 35.
Spitz, R. A. (1955), The Primal Cavity: A Contribution to the Genesis of Perception and Its Role for Psychoanalytic Theory. *This Annual*, 10.
Traisman, A. & Traisman, H. (1958), Thumb and Fingersucking. *J. Pediatrics*, 52.
Winnicott, D. W. (1945), Primitive Emotional Development. *Int. J. Psa.*, 26.

# EGO IDEAL AND PSEUDO EGO IDEAL IN ADOLESCENCE

## M. LAUFER, M.SC. (London)

The material which forms the basis of this paper comes from the work I am doing at the Hampstead Child-Therapy Clinic and the Young People's Consultation Centre. Some of the problems discussed in this paper, such as (a) the content and structure of the ego ideal, and (b) problems encountered in the treatment of adolescents, are also being investigated by two research groups at the Hampstead Clinic, i.e., the Index Group and the Adolescent Research Group. In the course of this paper I shall refer to the work of these research groups and compare my views with theirs.

The analytic literature dealing with adolescence puts great emphasis on the vulnerability of the ego and the various demands made upon it at this time—from the drives, from the superego, and from the external world. This paper focuses on one aspect of the superego, the ego ideal, and examines the factors which, coming together in adolescence, may affect its content and determine its function during this period. I shall follow Hartmann and Loewenstein (1962), who suggest that the superego should be studied from the functional and genetic approaches—points of view which have already proved very fruitful in the study of the ego.

I shall show the relation of the ego ideal precursors in the pre-oedipal and oedipal periods to the ego ideal as it appears in adoles-

The author is a member of the Hampstead Child-Therapy Clinic where much of the material used in this study has been collected. The Hampstead Child-Therapy Clinic is maintained at present by The Field Foundation, Inc., New York; The Anna Freud Foundation, New York; The Grant Foundation, Inc., New York; The Estate of Flora Haas, New York; The National Institute of Mental Health, Bethesda, Maryland; The Old Dominion Foundation, New York; The Psychoanalytic Research and Development Fund, Inc., New York; The Taconic Foundation, Inc., New York.

Director, Young People's Consultation Centre, which is financed by the Youth Studies and Research Foundation of the Bernard Van Leer Trust.

cence. Comparison of these precursors with the later ego ideal can contribute to an explanation of the special functions of the ego ideal during adolescence—that is, to aid in changing the internal relationship to the original objects, to help in controlling ego regression, and to assist in social adaptation. I shall also show how the ego ideal in adolescence may become involved in conflict and may then act as a hindrance, rather than a help, to the ego in its effort to move toward greater internal freedom and adult functioning.

I

Various authors differ with regard to the place in the psychic structure to which the ego ideal should be assigned—that is, whether the ego ideal should be considered to be a part of the ego or the superego, or whether it constitutes a separate structure on its own (Jacobson, 1954b; Blos, 1962; Erikson, 1959; Lampl-de Groot, 1962). I believe that the ego ideal can be referred to as such only when it has become one of the functions of the superego—that is, after the resolution of the oedipal conflict (Hartmann and Loewenstein, 1962). Before this time, we can observe ego-ideal precursors which are governed by laws different from those which apply to the superego. For example, in the preoedipal period ideals are still much more dependent on the presence of, and quality of the relationship to, the object. Similarly, in the preoedipal period, conflicting standards can exist side by side without necessarily arousing anxiety or requiring defensive maneuvers. This is not true after the formation of the superego. These precursors will affect the quality and structure of the superego which is internalized, but this is not the same as viewing the ego ideal as a separate structure. It is also my belief that the ego ideal in adolescence is made up of several constituents—including the content which has been internalized as part of the superego and which remains unchanged throughout life, together with temporary additions which reflect the demands and expectations of contemporaries. I shall return to this point later in the paper.

In examining the history of the concept "ego ideal" in Freud's writings, most authors have emphasized one of the following two points—that Freud used the terms "superego" and "ego ideal" synonymously, or that he changed the meaning of the term "ego ideal" as he developed his metapsychology. It is necessary to note that in whatever way Freud used the term "ego ideal" it always meant one special thing to him—an agency in the mind which continues to try to recapture the narcissistic perfection of childhood. This meaning Freud never changed. In the *New Introductory Lectures* (1932), Freud states, "I hope you will by now feel that in postulating the existence of a super-ego I have been describing a genuine structural entity, and have not been merely personifying an abstraction, such as conscience. We have now to mention another important activity[1] which is to be ascribed to the super-ego. It is also the vehicle of the ego-ideal, by which the ego measures itself, towards which it strives, and whose demands for ever-increasing perfection it is always striving to fulfill. No doubt this ego-ideal is a precipitation of the old idea of the parents, an expression of the admiration which the child felt for the perfection which it at that time ascribed to them . . ." (p. 92f.).

A recent paper from the Hampstead Index (Sandler, Holder, and Meers, 1963) expresses the view that the concept of "ego ideal" had different meanings for Freud at different times. Also, these authors distinguish between the objects as figures of authority and introjects, and various ideals created by the child both before and after the formation of the superego. These ideals are referred to as the "ideal self." The ideal self, they state, is "far more fluid and flexible than the ideals held up to the child by his introjects, although it will contain a solid core of identifications with the admired parents of his earliest years. In the well-adapted individual the content of the ideal self will undergo continuous modification in the light of the person's experiences of reality" (p. 154). My view is that, although identifications will be used by the postoedipal child in a variety of ways, it is the ego ideal as part of the superego which continues to set the ideal standard of behavior for the child, and it is only in adolescence that certain ego identifications are temporarily felt as being equivalent to superego expectations and demands.

In the behavior of adolescents we commonly observe the effort to acquire specific attributes either of one person or of a group. These sought-after attributes often become the basis on which contemporaries are judged. Thus, contemporaries who seek to acquire the same attributes and value them in other persons feel that they

---

[1] *Funktion* in the German original.

have a common bond. The internal use which each of these persons may make of the attribute may vary greatly, but this does not change their feeling that they are striving toward similar perfection. What is seldom asked are the questions: what is the internal function of a given attribute or form of behavior which one strives to acquire? What is the adolescent confronted with and by what means does he find a solution to problems which he must solve before he can move toward adult emotional functioning? The ego strives to establish narcissistic equilibrium at every stage of life. The means vary in different periods of development, and depend on a number of factors: the source of the demand, the defenses available to the ego, and the dependence of the ego on either internal or external sources of satisfaction. In adolescence, there are new internal and external factors which threaten both the previously established means of coping with anxiety and the earlier ways of obtaining narcissistic supplies. This means that the task of the ego now is to find new ways of living up to an old internal standard as well as to meet the demands of a new external standard. The extent to which the adolescent reacts to the external expectations of his contemporaries and the way in which he experiences them as a demand vary a great deal in different persons, but these expectations nevertheless represent a new demand upon the ego.

We know that an internal standard exists only after the resolution of the oedipal conflict and the establishment of the superego as a structure. Before the internalization of standards takes place, the child behaves in accordance with what he thinks are the demands and wishes of the parents. Two recent papers (Ritvo and Solnit, 1960; Hartmann and Loewenstein, 1962) describe the factors which affect ego-ideal development, and how ego-ideal precursors participate in determining the kind of superego standards which are internalized. Ritvo and Solnit (1960) state, "The ego ideal can be considered to arise from three main sources: the idealization of the parents; the idealization of the child by the parents; and the idealization of the self by the child. . . . Such an ego ideal can influence superego formation by increasing the child's capacity to recognize and follow the limits of socially acceptable behaviour" (p. 299). Hartmann and Loewenstein (1962) state that one can speak of the ego ideal as a function of the superego only after the superego as a system has become established. Before this time, that is, before internalization has taken place, ego-ideal precursors are still relatively unstable, are partly dependent on external sources, and have a different relation to other aspects which make up the superego.

Before going further, I would like to define the meaning of the terms *internalization* and *identification*. I single out these two terms for definition because they seem to me to be the two most important ego mechanisms which affect structural development, and which can help to explain the structural changes occurring from the oedipal period through to the end of adolescence. Again I quote from the paper by Hartmann and Loewenstein (1962):

> We would speak of *internalization* when regulations that have taken place in interaction with the outside world are replaced by inner regulations (Hartmann, 1939). The development through which trial activities in the outside world are gradually replaced by thought processes is an example of what we have in mind. . . . Not all analysts assign exactly the same meaning to the term *identification;* and we have already stated that there are certainly different kinds of identification. Some questions as to its meta-psychology are under discussion. But we all agree that the result of identification is that the identifying person behaves in some way like the person with whom he has identified himself. The likeness may refer to the characteristics, features, attitudes of the object, or to the role the object plays in reality (or to the role it plays in reality according to the fantasy of the person who makes the identification); it may mean to "take the place" of the other person. Freud (1921) describes it also as "moulding oneself" after the fashion of the object that has been taken as a model. We use the term both for the process and for the result [p. 48f.].

I would now define *ego ideal* as that part of the superego which contains images and attributes the ego strives to acquire in order to re-establish narcissistic equilibrium. Depending on the use made of preoedipal and oedipal idealizations of the self or of the object, the ego ideal can later participate in either normal or pathological forms of social adaptation. I say this because idealization always carries with it overvaluation, and therefore distortion, of that which is idealized. The amount of distortion involved will affect the way the child sees himself in relation to the environment. Nevertheless, the ego ideal continues to define perfection to the ego (and that perfection may be determined either by fantasy or reality). In this sense, the ego ideal participates in the task of setting aims for the ego. The extent to which the image of perfection is felt by the ego as an aid or as a demand will depend upon the interrelation of the three functions of the superego, that is, upon conscience, self-criticism, and ego ideal.

Although identifications will affect the manifestations of ideals after the oedipal period, the content of the ego ideal as part of the superego structure is determined at the stage of internalization, and remains unaltered thereafter.

Freud has emphasized just this point in his references to the superego; namely, although modifications may take place throughout life, the contents of the superego are determined at the stage of internalization. In the following quotation from *New Introductory Lectures* (1932), Freud shows how important it is, in understanding the development of the structures, not to confuse changes in the ego with what takes place in the superego. He states:

> Normally the super-ego is constantly becoming more and more remote from the original parents, becoming, as it were, more impersonal. Another thing that we must not forget is that the child values its parents differently at different periods of its life. At the time at which the Oedipus complex makes way for the super-ego, they seem to be splendid figures, but later on they lose a good deal of their prestige. Identifications take place with these later editions of the parents as well, and regularly provide important contributions to the formation of character; but these only affect the ego, they have no influence on the super-ego, which has been determined by the earliest parental imagos [p. 92].

Even though the content of the ego ideal does not change throughout life, the adolescent encounters new expectations from the outside world (primarily from contemporaries) and he identifies with them. These are now ego identifications, but they will be felt as having the same quality as the earlier internalized demands, and in this sense I refer to them as part of the *ego ideal in adolescence*. The commonly held belief that adolescents easily give up old standards and earlier identifications and readily adopt new criteria upon which to base their present behavior refers to these ego identifications. But it is not correct to equate this behavior with an ability to change the content of the superego. In my opinion, it is precisely this inability to give up old standards which creates some of the typical behavior in adolescents. Instead, what occurs is that identifications, whether they are transient or defensive, are the only means available to the ego to help it in its effort to alter its relationship to the superego as a structure; moreover, identifications can help change the interrelation of the superego functions to each other. We know, for example, that one superego function may be more highly cathected than the others —it may be of special importance to "do a good turn every day," or to "meditate for an hour," or to "ask for forgiveness." The adolescent may be bound by these superego expectations, but they may also represent continued attachment to the oedipal objects, and he may then try to change their relative strength by the use he now makes of identifications.

These factors, I think, are often overlooked in attempts to understand what one observes during adolescence. Although the content of the superego does not change, the relationship of the various superego functions to each other can change. What is often generalized under the heading of "adolescent turmoil" may partly be explained in terms of the ego's need to alter its own relation to the superego as a structure, and the changing importance of each of the superego functions.

## II

The major problems confronting the ego in adolescence are related to: (a) the reaction to the physical primacy of the genitals; (b) the changing relationship to the original objects; (c) the finding of a heterosexual love object; and (d) the integrating of preoedipal identifications, oedipal identifications, and present internal and external expectations of behavior.

The ego will seek both internal and external allies to assist it in controlling regression, in overcoming guilt and shame, and in giving up its earlier guaranteed means of narcissistic supply. While this would be the optimum result, we frequently observe the unsuccessful efforts to move to adult functioning. A satisfactory solution to the problems which have been stated must satisfy the internalized standards as well as the new ego identifications arising mainly from the expectations of contemporaries. Friends take on a special mean-ing—they may act as an auxiliary ego or auxiliary superego (or, more specifically, as an auxiliary to one or more of the superego functions); they may temporarily take on the role of assisting in defense or in sanctioning otherwise usually unacceptable behavior.

Although these two kinds of expectations are related and affect behavior, they nevertheless can be kept separate in the adolescent's life. The gap between the ideal of the external world and that of the inner world can often tell us what use is now being made of iden-tifications—that is, whether some of the adolescent's present stand-ards of behavior and manifest solutions to the problems confronting the ego are used primarily in the service of defense or in an effort to establish internal signs of maturity. It is as if the adolescent were saying, "To feel wanted by my contemporaries, and to avoid ostracism, I must perform in a prescribed way, and I must be interested in certain accepted things. But at the same time there are things I do and think which are contrary to this picture. I must fight against these manifestations."

A boy of fourteen arrived for his analytic session wearing Chelsea boots, drain-pipe trousers, and a new pullover. He got these after weeks of convincing his father and stepmother that this was what all his friends were wearing. Some days later, when we discussed his jealousy of his younger half sister, he complained, "I don't want to talk of the past. That's in the past, and now I'm different."

A nineteen-year-old young man, whom I saw in consultation, said of his feelings of attraction for younger boys, "It's terrible. I may like it if I got to know them. But it's terrible. People of my age go out with girls. All I do is dress up like all the others of my age."

These examples illustrate situations in which the inner wish and the external expectation are at variance; in which the behavior has been chosen mainly as a defense, rather than in pursuit of one's own wishes. It is a means of dealing with anxiety.

During adolescence the preoedipal and oedipal identifications have a special bearing on the choice of solutions to problems. The expectations set by the superego can now be a help or a hindrance. While in general the more critical aspects of the superego are em-phasized, Schafer (1960) and Sandler (1960) stressed the point that the superego can be an important source of approval and well-being.

The adolescent may be satisfied to act in accordance with the earlier inner expectations because in this way he achieves a temporary narcissistic gain. At the same time, however, he may be confronted with the fact that his ego ideal is different from that which is presented and valued by his contemporaries. For the first time, the ego ideal which has made valuable contributions to his mental economy and until now has been a source of satisfaction may prove to be insufficient. The external expectations of his contemporaries (or what he believes these expectations to be) may now be experienced as a further demand on the ego. The adolescent may withdraw from these demands and seek more predictable but, at the same time, more infantile ways of narcissistic satisfaction, or he may try in whichever way is open to him to adopt this new external ideal. In this case, however, the advocation of the new ideal serves primarily as a defense against the anxiety aroused by the awareness of the inner insufficiency and does not constitute part of an effort to establish inner signs of maturity.

## III

I have said that the ego ideal in adolescence derives from two sources—the superego and the external expectations of one's contemporaries with which the adolescent has identified. I would like to choose two problems with which every adolescent is confronted, and show the part played by the ego ideal in solving them. Having reached physical genital primacy, the adolescent is faced with (a) the need to find a new love object and to take on the role of sexual partner; and (b) the need to find a means of coping with the masturbation conflict.

### Finding a New Love Object

In "On Narcissism: an Introduction" (1914) Freud lists what he sees as the paths leading to the choice of an object. He says:

A person may love:—
(1) According to the narcissistic type:
    (a) what he himself is (i.e. himself),

(b) what he himself was,
(c) what he himself would like to be,
(d) someone who was once part of himself.
(2) According to the anaclitic (attachment) type:
(a) the woman who feeds him,
(b) the man who protects him,
and the succession of substitutes who take their place [p. 90].

If we apply these remarks by Freud to what takes place in adolescence, we see that the choice of a love object must simultaneously answer a number of inner demands and expectations. That is, the factors determining the adolescent's choice of an object are related to:—

(a) what he actually is (the image of himself),
(b) what he would like to be (present ego ideal),
(c) what he ought to be (self-criticism),
(d) what he must not be (conscience).

For the first time in life, there is a demand made upon earlier identifications within the context of physical genitality. Until adolescence, the various identifications could be used for structure building and for the purposes of defense, and were the means by which the child was able to resolve the oedipal conflict. But in adolescence, genitality makes a new and additional demand. Because of it the identifications which once were adequate may prove to be insufficient in helping the person to assume his role as a sexual partner. For example, the male child who during the oedipal period identified with a passive father may well find in adolescence that this oedipal model not only is insufficient but may be a hindrance in his relation to a new love object. The behavior which he now strives to adopt may then be in the main determined by external factors (or factors which he experiences as externally determined), and will be used as a means of overcoming the inadequacy of the earlier identifications and of strengthening the repression of the ambivalence toward the oedipal object.

In whichever way the oedipal conflict has been solved, however, the combination of the newly acquired genital ability and the presence of the original objects is felt by the ego as a danger. A further important point is stated by Anna Freud (1958): "The libidinal cathexis to them [the love objects of the individual's oedipal and preoedipal past] has been carried forward from the infantile phases, merely toned down or inhibited in aim during latency. Therefore the reawakened pregenital urges, or—worse still—the newly acquired genital ones, are in danger of making contact with them, lending a new and threatening reality to fantasies which had seemed extinct but are, in fact, merely under repression. The anxieties which arise on these grounds are directed toward eliminating the infantile objects, i.e, toward breaking the tie with them" (p. 268).

The ego is now confronted with demands from each of the structures—the id seeks gratification; the superego says what the person ought to be like but at the same time no longer permits gratifications as readily as previously. While the ego must find a way of satisfying these demands, there now is the additional demand from one's contemporaries to behave in a prescribed way—even though the internal structure may not be prepared for this.

Choice of an object can have a number of meanings. It can be a normal progressive move toward adult functioning; this implies that the object choice is removed from the original oedipal determinants and is not primarily a replacement of the oedipal object. The new object may also have been chosen to meet superego demands, or to live up to the demands of one's contemporaries, or to keep ego-dystonic thoughts and wishes from becoming conscious. The choice of the object can be a form of flight from the original objects, or it can be a means of avoiding id and ego regression to preoedipal forms of satisfaction and to preoedipal levels of object relationship. In the more normal process, the object choice is removed from the direct oedipal determinants, and id satisfaction is not primarily dependent on preoedipal factors.

If one examines the present content of the adolescent's ego ideal, one can determine whether he uses identifications mainly to meet an inner wish or to avoid conflict. The frantic effort to find replacements for the parents and to adopt the mannerisms and dress of different persons is clearly a way of denying the continued relationship to the parents; the contemporary idols are more a reflection of the perfect self, with the narcissistic supply coming from the fantasied admiration by others. Or there is the overmasculine young man, who may be fighting the manifestations of a feminine identification; his ego ideal then becomes an ally in the defense against something which he would now experience as ego dystonic. What we observe in him is a pseudo ego ideal. In such instances, the earlier identifications may become a source of anxiety because they suddenly prove to be insufficient in assisting the ego to meet the new demands made upon it.

Choosing an object can then be simply a perpetuation of the earlier relationship to the oedipal objects. It is as if the individual can still have a guaranteed level and source of narcissistic supply and at the same time can feel that his overt behavior is in accordance with external expectations. Yet the tie to the oedipal objects has in fact not been qualitatively changed by the choice of a new object. This is a kind of prolonged oedipal relationship (Blos, 1954), within the context of pseudo normality. This type of object choice represents the ego's compromise due to its inability to cope with the ambivalence toward the oedipal objects and its inability to risk replacing the original sources of narcissistic supply. The ego has found a means of fooling itself.

I have worked with adolescents who yearn for a relationship to another person, but who are in reality quite unable to allow this to take place. Unconsciously they are aware of their wish for a relationship on an earlier level but which is now in conflict with the expectations set up by their contemporaries. For example, a passive boy described his wish for and inability to date a girl: "My friends talk of going out with girls. I like hearing it, but it worries me. I want to be like them, but I just know that I can't. Maybe it would be easier to be the girl."

*Masturbation Conflict*

The struggle against masturbation is directed against the autoerotic activity itself as well as against the content of the fantasies (Anna Freud, 1949). In adolescence this struggle becomes especially meaningful and intense. The adolescent may experience masturbation as a regressive form of behavior, which is contrary to the image he wishes to preserve of himself. Autoerotic manifestations and fantasies of a regressed nature can constitute a threat to the ego in its effort to integrate the various images the adolescent has of himself, and can act as a hindrance in overcoming the barrier between fantasy and actual behavior.

Masturbation can almost simultaneously represent a regressive and progressive phenomenon. The regressive aspect is related to the autoerotic activity and to the danger of allowing ego-dystonic fantasies to become conscious. The progressive aspect lies in the fact that masturbation and the accompanying fantasies can be experienced as a trial action—as a preparation on the part of the ego for assuming the role of the sexual partner in the reality situation.

The ego ideal in adolescence can be directly related to the current masturbation conflict. The threat from the superego is as strong as ever, but in addition the earlier masturbation conflict is now experienced within the context of physical genitality. Identifications may be used in the attempt to alter the content of the ego ideal to rid it of all but the fantasied perfect figures, free of sexual demands or completely in control of their actions and thoughts. While this endeavor may temporarily assist the ego in its fight against masturbation, it also contains the core of the person's pathology, e.g., the ascetic adolescent. In fact, what we see in such cases is a pseudo ego ideal, aimed at avoiding anxiety and assisting in the defense against instinctual demands.

Such a pseudo ego ideal was shown by a patient, now in late adolescence, who presented a picture of stupidity although he had an I.Q. of over 120. He arrived each Monday for his analytic hour and described how he succumbed to the "urge to masturbate." He felt terrible, he said, because he knew his parents disapproved of such dirty activity. The guilt, which had been sexualized and was used for masochistic purposes, was seen as proof that masturbation was harmful.

He also complained that he must wash his hair every morning to avoid any itch and that he must eat all the food which his mother prepared for him. In addition, homosexual manifestations were completely defended against because of their link to the oedipal father. Close relationships to male contemporaries were possible because they represented part of himself rather than the oedipal parent. The people whom he now idealized were those who could "say they have had enough to eat, and can leave some food."

In this patient, we can discern an awareness of the ego's helplessness in relation to the instinctual demands; he needs an external prop to assist him. At the same time, there is an implied criticism of the oedipal father who is described as "a man who can't even stand up to my mother or my uncle, and they always succeed in making him look like a little boy." The adolescent's inevitable disappointment in the oedipal parent includes in this case the awareness that the oedipal ideal has failed him. The ideal he now seeks to attain represents complete control over instinctual demands which he equates with these demands being nonexistent.

Freud (1905) has remarked that, in masturbation, the person is both the active and passive partner at the same time. Most often this fantasied double role can remain completely unconscious. The predominating fantasy may be ego syntonic, and in this sense will safeguard the ego by preventing the unacceptable preoedipal and oedipal wishes from becoming conscious. However, when the fantasy is ego dystonic, the ego experiences the wish for instinctual gratification as a demand and is further threatened by the danger of ego regression.

A seventeen-year-old patient, in describing his masturbation thoughts, said, "When I think of older women I like it and it also frightens me. It disgusts me, and yet I go on thinking about them, but only when I masturbate." In describing his reaction after masturbation, he said, "At the time I feel as if I'm crazy or something, but when I come back to normal I just feel ashamed."

The guilt in this case is related to the direct incestuous representations in the fantasy, and therefore to the superego-ego conflict. The shame, which is also present, is more a reaction to behaving in a way which is contrary to the picture of himself which he must now uphold. But, at the same time, there is an awareness that some of his wish, which may now be ego dystonic, is for satisfaction on a preoedipal level. However pleasurable masturbation and the accompanying fantasies may be at the time, he subsequently feels as if he has let himself down—that is, he has allowed into consciousness a part of himself which represents a regression and which at the same time produces anxiety.

The adolescent fights against any signs of regression. The ego struggles to preserve the image which the person is striving to acquire and attempts to deny any dependence on the original objects. The present ego ideal can now become a critic of the ego and temporarily act as a full superego equivalent, adding to the guilt reaction. The latter will be most extreme when the present expectations toward which one strives are in opposition to the content of the masturbation fantasies.

Sometimes adolescents refer to their fear of regression as a feeling that they will lose control or become disorganized. Fear of loss of control is, I think, related to fear of id regression; fear of becoming disorganized is related to fear of ego regression. Regressive manifestations bring about temporary narcissistic injury. If the ego ideal is more closely related to reality and contains attributes or goals which are attainable, then it can have an important economic function in re-establishing narcissistic equilibrium.

## IV

Every period of development carries with it an ideal form of behavior toward which one strives. The ideal forms of behavior until adolescence are aimed at assuring the love from the original objects or their equivalents in the superego. In adolescence, the ideal toward which one strives has the additional important roles of helping the person to free himself from the original sources of narcissistic supply and of paving the way to emotional maturity. This in turn means that the earlier identifications must now be used in a different way —though they may previously have assisted the person in development, they may prove to be ineffective in adolescence.

For example, the child's ideal in the preoedipal and oedipal periods can comprise a combination of factors and serve several functions including identification, control of drive manifestations, a means of dealing with intrasystemic conflicts in the ego. Ordinarily, in the preoedipal period, the male child will not see the father as a rival for the love of the mother, but will identify with him. When, in the phallic-oedipal period, the father is seen as an obstacle toward the satisfaction of the sexual wishes toward the mother, the boy's relationship to the father becomes ambivalent. Freud (1923) states, ". . . it seems as if the ambivalence inherent in the identification from the beginning had become manifest" (p. 32). For the oedipal child, the most important thing in his life is to safeguard the continued love of his parents. By identifying with the oedipal parent of the same sex the child feels that he is like that parent, and this in turn acts as an assurance of a continued object relationship to the other parent. The identification assuages the castration fear and acts as an ally in keeping the oedipal wishes and the ambivalence under repression. The child adopts an ideal which allows him to feel more certain of the love of the oedipal parent. In the postoedipal period, the ego ideal still contains remnants of the negative oedipal relationship and thereby can be the means of retaining the relationship to the parent of the same sex.

Though some of the conflicts involving the ego ideal may have their origin in the oedipal period, they may manifest themselves only when the person has reached adolescence. Such conflicts may arise when the parents' expectations of the child during the oedipal period contradict what the child observes to be the relationship between the parents. For example, a girl may see her mother as a dirty, loud woman, but the demand on the child will be to be clean and different from the mother. Yet, being dirty and loud may mean, for the girl, an assurance of the love from the oedipal father. When such a girl reaches adolescence, the oedipal ideal may become manifest: we may then have a seemingly unkempt, uncontrolled adolescent. But unconsciously, the living out of this oedipal ideal could mean a continuation of the relationship to the oedipal father and may be the only way in which the adolescent can handle the original ambivalence to the object. A rejection of this ideal in adolescence could be experienced as an aggressive act against the oedipal objects. In addition, it might create conflict with the current standards that have been adopted; that is, the oedipal ideal may be at odds with the expectations of one's contemporaries. In this case, the ego is faced with a demand to choose between the oedipal parent and one's contemporaries. The fate of the oedipal ambivalence will partly determine the choice made in adolescence. The ambivalence can tie the person to the oedipal objects; on the other hand, in perpetuating the tie to the oedipal objects, the need to cope with the ambivalence is avoided.

As I said earlier, identifications in adolescence do not basically influence the content of the superego, but affect the ego's relation to the superego, and in this way they help in changing the interrelation of the superego functions to each other. These identifications can then be used as a means of bribing the conscience or of bypassing the strictures imposed by it. While this process is often referred to as a change in the content of the superego, it is more correctly described as an ability on the part of the ego to cope with the demands and expectations of the superego.

I believe that in clinical assessments it is important to determine whether the attributes the adolescent strives to acquire at this period of development are used mainly to fight the demands of the superego, or whether they aid the adolescent in achieving inner independence from the oedipal objects. What we often observe is the adolescent's unsuccessful effort to fight superego demands, though in his behavior he gives the appearance of having succeeded in becoming independent of these demands. That is, the present standards according to which he acts may be used to create the illusion that the adolescent has freed himself of earlier demands. He is behaving as if the internalized expectations can be ignored, which is his means of dealing with the disappointment in the oedipal objects. But this solution, instead of assisting the ego in its struggle to change the internal relationship to the oedipal objects, becomes a way of preserving the infantile relationship.

It is mainly these adolescents who seem to be experiencing much mental pain. They are engaged in a struggle in relation to both inner and outer expectations and toward re-establishing narcissistic equilibrium. The problem for all adolescents is the need to satisfy superego demands and the demands which are made upon the ego by external sources. The adolescent can feel pleased with himself only when both demands have been met—when he has satisfied the demands of the superego, and when he feels that his contemporaries approve of him. The mental pain is experienced when the external demands of one's contemporaries (or what they are felt to be) are in conflict with the superego demands. In this case, meeting an external expectation also becomes a superego-ego conflict. One can sometimes observe the existence of this double conflict; it is as if there were a conflict in relation to both the superego and to the standards which are felt to be determined by contemporaries. The affects can tell us what is involved: guilt is always a sign of superego-ego conflict; shame is, in adolescence, a conflict between the ego and the present standards which the adolescent is trying to meet. An example of these simultaneous conflicts can be seen in a young woman of nineteen who was seeking help for a symptom of hair pulling. She described her reaction to this activity as follows: "When I do it, I feel I am doing something wrong. My mother gets furious, but more than that I feel as if I can't stop doing something which I know I shouldn't be doing. At the same time, I will never do it when I am with my friends. Can you imagine what they would think?" Consciously, this person of course had no idea of the link between her hair pulling and masturbation, but she experienced feelings of both guilt and shame in relation to the activity. At one point she talked of wanting help with this symptom "partly for cosmetic reasons," namely, the bald patch might distort the picture of an otherwise attractive-looking person. At the same time she clearly knew that hair pulling was a type of regressive behavior which her contemporaries would not accept. This fact was as important as the guilt she felt.

There is another area which is in need of clarification, namely, superego regression, and the role played by the ego ideal when superego regression occurs in adolescence. Hartmann and Loewenstein (1962) state:

The superego "has not been there from the beginning" (Freud), while the instinctual drives and the ego have. This is one reason why regression is harder to conceptualize with respect to the superego than with respect to the drives and the ego. Sometimes "superego regression" is caused by a regression of the instinctual drives as is probably the case in obsessional neurosis. As a result of "superego regression" we see early identifications and early object relationships taking the place of the contents and the functions of the superego. . . . It is commonly accepted that the severe or punitive character of the demands and the expected punishments which we find in at least some forms of "superego regression" is to be considered a consequence of early object relations taking the place of the later ones. Of course, this does not mean that the real objects of those earliest stages of development have been as cruel as the regressed superego is. It reflects also the child's fantasies and fears and the ways in which he is dealing with his own aggression [p. 73f.].

I think that, in adolescence, superego regression takes place when the oedipal identifications are expected to perform their task within the context of genitality and are no longer adequate for this task. Genitality does not mean that pregenital wishes and fantasies have ceased to exist; rather it describes the stage when the primacy of the genitals has been reached, when genital strivings have become the dominant means of sexual satisfaction. There is a lapse of time between the period when physical genital primacy has been reached and the time when it is possible to develop object relationships on a genital level. It is during this intervening period, I believe, that we see a change in the relationship between the mental structures; and during the same period temporary superego regressions are apt to occur.

This whole area requires much more detailed work, but I believe the answers to the problems will help us to explain some of the behavior we observe in adolescence and contribute to our understanding of the dynamic and structural differences between pathology and variations in normality in adolescence.

## V

The preceding remarks can be of help in the understanding of the special problems encountered in the treatment of adolescents. Some aspects of the treatment process counteract, even if only temporarily, the adolescent's effort to integrate the various images he has of himself. Recovery of past events, experiences, and affects can be a threat to the adolescent's endeavor to free himself of the past. Treatment temporarily encourages a more infantile relationship to the analyst. The adolescent may want it and yet feel that he must fight it. There is no doubt, though, that many adolescents are in need of treatment, some urgent and others less so. In discussing some of the problems repeatedly encountered in the treatment of adolescents, Anna Freud (1958) states:

> Experience has taught us to take a serious view of such major and repeated inadequacies of the analytic technique. They cannot be explained away by individual characteristics of the patients under treatment nor by any accidental or environmental factors which run counter to it. Nor can they be overcome simply by increased effort, skill and tact on the part of the analyst. They have to be taken as indications that something in the inner structure of the disturbances themselves differs markedly from the pattern of those illnesses for which the analytic technique has

been devised originally and to which it is most frequently applied. . . . To my mind the libidinal position of the adolescent has much in common with the two states described above [unhappy love affairs and periods of mourning]. The adolescent too is engaged in an emotional struggle, and moreover in one of extreme urgency and immediacy. His libido is on the point of detaching itself from the parents and of cathecting new objects. Some mourning for the objects of the past is inevitable; so are the "crushes." i.e., the happy or unhappy love affairs with adults outside the family, or with other adolescents, whether of the opposite or of the same sex; so is, further, a certain amount of narcissistic withdrawal which bridges the gap during periods when no external object is cathected. Whatever the libidinal solution at a given moment may be, it will always be a preoccupation with the present time and . . . with little or no libido left available for investment either in the past or in the analyst [p. 261ff.].

I think that this statement can be used to pose several questions: What should the analyst expect to accomplish in treatment, and how do the results of the treatment of adolescents differ from those one expects from the treatment of children and adults? What technical considerations can help the analyst to assist the adolescent to create a treatment alliance? Some of these problems are now being studied by the Adolescent Research Group at the Hampstead Clinic by following the progress of a number of adolescents now in analytic treatment, and by follow-up studies of adolescents who have been in treatment. The material being collected by this group, and recently described in three papers (Frankl and Hellman, 1962, 1963; Hellman, 1963) focuses on the following issues—the adolescent's ability to participate in a treatment alliance; how one can judge this at the early stage of treatment; what are the criteria for predicting analyzability? The work of this group shows that some of the factors which must be taken into account in treatment are: the ego's relation to both the inner and outer world; the ego's changing capacity at various stages of development; the quality of the relationship to the oedipal objects; the person's ability to give up or risk giving up earlier forms of gratification. The work of this group also shows the importance of differentiating between the therapeutic alliance and transference phenomena. My view coincides with the points made by this group, but I would place more emphasis on the role of the analyst in developing a treatment alliance.

Most of the factors comprising the adolescent process add up to being an obstacle to progress in treatment. The most important single factor on the side of the treatment is the patient's anxiety. How then can the anxiety which the patient experiences be used to help create a treatment alliance? And once we have established this, in what areas of the patient's life should we help to create insight?

The meaning of the past, the role of fantasy, the use of reconstruction, the part played by the analyst in creating a treatment alliance—each of these aspects of the treatment will be different with the adolescent, with the child, or with the adult (Geleerd, 1957). Every analysis, if it is able to deal with the period of negative transference reaction or of temporary narcissistic injury, must also carry with it some level of narcissistic satisfaction. Without this, I do not think that any analysis can overcome the more difficult periods which are invariably encountered in treatment. In the treatment of adolescents this narcissistic satisfaction must be of a special nature, offered by the analyst in doses, and being determined by the immediate identificatory needs of the patient.

To create a treatment alliance, the adolescent must be aware of the fact that he needs help; he must have the feeling that the analyst can help him with his inner conflicts and also is a person who can be counted upon to assist in important reality situations. Day-to-day events in the life of the adolescent can often assume crucial significance and call for important decisions which will affect his relation to his friends, his work, his attitude to the oedipal objects, and so on. However unsuccessfully these aspects may have been handled in the lives of adult patients, there nevertheless has usually been some kind of compromise solution, and in analysis it becomes both possible and necessary to link the patient's disturbance with the manner in which he has found an answer to important life situations. Usually this cannot be done in the case of the adolescent. He is still very much involved in trying to detach himself from the original objects, to meet external demands of contemporaries, and to find a new balance between the superego and ego demands. In fact, however much he wishes to be part of the world of his contemporaries, he is at the same time very much alone in the struggle toward adult maturity. In treatment, therefore, great care must be taken neither to increase the susceptibility to narcissistic injury nor to provide satisfactions which would encourage the sexualization of the treatment situation. The manner in which the adolescent patient uses identification with the analyst will be one clue indicating to us in which way and when we should temporarily become more active in the treatment and in his daily life. To help in establishing a treatment alliance, the analyst may find it necessary to offer himself as an object for identification, and to encourage the patient temporarily to adopt attributes which are a reflection of the analyst. It is as if the analyst had changing roles during the treatment of the adolescent—he may be an auxiliary ego, an ego ideal, an auxiliary conscience, sometimes all at the same time. I do not think that what I am saying is contrary to classical analysis, but the treatment of adolescents does require some temporary adaptations. The adaptations mentioned are simply a reflection of what we assume to be temporary inadequacies of the ego, temporary strivings toward new ideals, ongoing struggles against manifestations of regression, and especially intense efforts to eliminate the past. When the adolescent sees the analyst as someone quite different from the oedipal objects, and realizes that a relationship to the analyst does not imply a perpetuation of his state of childish dependence, then it becomes possible to use the classical analytic method.

In papers dealing with treatment of adolescents (Anna Freud, 1958; Eissler, 1958; Geleerd, 1957, 1961; Gitelson, 1948; Spiegel, 1958) the problems mentioned above are referred to and are recognized as requiring special measures. When I was confronted with these technical problems, I found that I had to consider the special role of the ego ideal in adolescence. Further theoretical understanding of the content and function of the ego ideal and of the various ways it is used in adolescence could, I felt, help answer some important technical problems.

## Summary

The ego ideal is considered to be one of the functions of the superego; it must be viewed in relation to the two other superego functions, i.e., self-criticism and conscience. As one of the superego functions the ego ideal can be a means of utilizing and perpetuating the negative oedipal attachment.

Identifications in adolescence can be used to change the interrelation of the superego functions, and can also be a means of changing the relationship between the ego and the superego. The content of the superego, however, does not change in adolescence.

The most crucial problems confronting the ego in adolescence are related to (a) the reaction to the physical primacy of the genitals; (b) the changing relationship to the original objects; (c) finding a new love object; and (d) integrating preoedipal identifications, oedipal identifications, and present expectations (both internal and external) of behavior.

The part played by the ego ideal in adolescence is determined by the quality and the uses made of the preoedipal and oedipal identifications, and the fate of the ambivalence toward the original objects during these developmental periods.

The ego ideal in adolescence either can serve the purpose of strengthening the effort to be like the parent of the same sex, or it may be used to maintain the repression of ego-dystonic thoughts, behavior, and wishes. In the optimum case, the ego ideal can help the adolescent toward maturity if the demands of the superego and the standards of the present ego ideal are closely linked. If, however, identifications at this time are used primarily in a defensive way, e.g., to disprove the existence of a negative oedipal attachment, then one will observe what is here called a pseudo ego ideal. In such cases, the effort to attain certain goals serves the function of protecting the ego from anxiety, rather than assisting in the development toward maturity. It may also be that the ideals toward which such persons strive remain unattainable.

When the ego ideal in adolescence is close to the demands and expectations of the superego, it is relatively easier to attain narcissistic equilibrium. If identifications are used in a defensive way, resulting in a pseudo ego ideal, then the attainment of narcissistic equilibrium is much harder, and the ego will require constant maneuvers to keep it free of anxiety.

An understanding of the role of the ego ideal in adolescence also enables us to add to our understanding of the special technical problems encountered in the treatment of adolescents.

## BIBLIOGRAPHY

Abraham, K. (1924), A Short Study of the Development of the Libido; Viewed in the Light of Mental Disorders. In: *Selected Papers on Psycho-Analysis*. London: Hogarth Press, 1949.

Aichhorn, A. (1925), *Wayward Youth*. New York: Viking Press, 1931.

Arlow, J. A. (1953), Masturbation and Symptom Formation. *J. Amer. Psa. Assn.*, 1.

Beres, D. (1958), Vicissitudes of Superego Functions and Superego Precursors in Childhood. *This Annual*, 13.

Bernfeld, S. (1938), Types of Adolescence. *Psa. Quart.*, 7.

Bing, J. F., McLaughlin, F., & Marburg, R. (1959). The Metapsychology of Narcissism. *This Annual*, 14.

Blos, P. (1954), Prolonged Adolescence. *Amer. J. Orthopsychiat.*, 24.

—— (1962), *On Adolescence*. New York: Free Press of Glencoe.

Buxbaum, E. (1958), Panel Report: The Psychology of Adolescence. *J. Amer. Psa. Assn.*, 6.

Deutsch, H. (1942), Some Forms of Emotional Disturbance and Their Relationship to Schizophrenia. *Psa. Quart.*, 11.

Eissler, K. R. (1958), Notes on Problems of Technique in the Psychoanalytic Treatment of Adolescents; With Some Remarks on Perversions. *This Annual*, 13.

Erikson, E. H. (1959), *Identity and the Life Cycle* [*Psychological Issues*, Monogr. 1]. New York: International Universities Press.

Feldman, S. S. (1962), Blushing, Fear of Blushing and Shame. *J. Amer. Psa. Assn.*, 10.

Fenichel, O. (1945), *The Psychoanalytic Theory of Neurosis*. New York: Norton.

Fraiberg, S. (1955), Some Considerations in the Introduction to Therapy in Puberty. *This Annual*, 10.

—— (1961), Homosexual Conflicts. In: *Adolescents*, ed. S. Lorand & H. I. Schneer. New York: Hoeber.

Frankl, L. & Hellman, I. (1962), The Ego's Participation in the Therapeutic Alliance. *Int. J. Psa.*, 43.

—— —— (1963), A Specific Problem in Adolescent Boys: Difficulties in Loosening the Infantile Tie to the Mother. *Bull. Philadelphia Assn. Psychoanal.*, 13.

Freud, A. (1936), *The Ego and the Mechanisms of Defense*. New York: International Universities Press, 1946.

—— (1949), Certain Types and Stages of Social Maladjustment. In: *Searchlights on Delinquency*, ed. K. R. Eissler. New York: International Universities Press.

—— (1952a), A Connection Between the States of Negativism and of Emotional Surrender. Abstract in: *Int. J. Psa.*, 33:265.

—— (1952b), The Mutual Influences in the Development of Ego and Id. *This Annual*, 7.

—— (1958), Adolescence. *This Annual*, 13.

Freud, S. (1905), Three Essays on the Theory of Sexuality. *Standard Edition*, 7. London: Hogarth Press, 1953.

—— (1909), Family Romances. *Standard Edition*, 9. London: Hogarth Press, 1959.

—— (1914), On Narcissism: An Introduction. *Standard Edition*, 14. London: Hogarth Press, 1957.

—— (1917), Mourning and Melancholia. *Standard Edition*, 14. London: Hogarth Press, 1957.

—— (1921), Group Psychology and the Analysis of the Ego. *Standard Edition*, 18. London: Hogarth Press, 1955.

—— (1923), The Ego and the Id. *Standard Edition*, 19. London: Hogarth Press, 1961.

—— (1930), Civilization and Its Discontents. *Standard Edition*, 21. London: Hogarth Press, 1961.

—— (1932), *New Introductory Lectures on Psychoanalysis*. New York: Norton, 1933.
Geleerd, E. R. (1957), Some Aspects of Psychoanalytic Technique in Adolescence. *This Annual*, 12.
—— (1961), Some Aspects of Ego Vicissitudes in Adolescence. *J. Amer. Psa. Assn.*, 4.
Gitelson, M. (1948), Character Synthesis: The Psychotherapeutic Problem of Adolescence. *Amer. J. Orthopsychiat.*, 18.
Greenacre, P. (1952), Some Factors Producing Different Types of Genital and Pregenital Organization. In: *Trauma, Growth and Personality*. New York: Norton.
—— (1958), Early Physical Determinants in the Development of the Sense of Identity. *J. Amer. Psa. Assn.*, 6.
Greenson, R. R. (1954), The Struggle against Identification. *J. Amer. Psa. Assn.*, 2.
Harley, M. (1961a), Masturbation Conflicts. In: *Adolescents*, ed. S. Lorand & H. I. Schneer. New York: Hoeber.
—— (1961b), Some Observations on the Relationship between Genitality and Structural Development at Adolescence. *J. Amer. Psa. Assn.*, 9.
Hartmann, H. (1939), *Ego Psychology and the Problem of Adaptation*. New York: International Universities Press, 1958.
—— (1950), Comments on the Psychoanalytic Theory of the Ego. *This Annual*, 5.
—— (1953), Contribution to the Metapsychology of Schizophrenia. *This Annual*, 8.
—— Kris, E., & Loewenstein, R. M. (1946), Comments on the Formation of Psychic Structure. *This Annual*, 2.
—— & Loewenstein, R. M. (1962), Notes on the Superego. *This Annual*, 17.
Hellman, I. (1963), Assessment of Analyzability Illustrated by the Case of an Adolescent Patient. Unpublished paper.
Jacobson, E. (1954a), Contribution to the Metapsychology of Psychotic Identifications. *J. Amer. Psa. Assn.*, 2.
—— (1954b), The Self and the Object World. *This Annual*, 9.
—— (1961), Adolescent Moods and the Remodeling of Psychic Structure in Adolescence. *This Annual*, 16.
Kris, E. (1951), Some Comments and Observations on Early Autoerotic Activities. *This Annual*, 6.
—— (1956a), The Recovery of Childhood Memories in Psychoanalysis. *This Annual*, 11.
—— (1956b), The Personal Myth. *J. Amer. Psa. Assn.*, 4.
Lampl-de Groot, J (1947), On the Development of the Ego and the Superego. *Int. J. Psa.*, 28.
—— (1960), On Adolescence. *This Annual*, 15.
—— (1962), Ego Ideal and Superego. *This Annual*, 17.
Mack-Brunswick, R. (1940), The Preoedipal Phase of Libido Development. *Psa. Quart.*, 9.
Novey, S. (1955), The Role of the Superego and Ego Ideal in Character Formation. *Int. J. Psa.*, 36.
Piers, G. & Singer, M. B. (1953), *Shame and Guilt*. Springfield, Ill.: Charles C Thomas.
Rapaport, D. (1955), Seminars on Psychoanalytic Ego Psychology. Western New England Institute for Psychoanalysis (mimeographed).
Reich, A. (1951), The Discussion of 1912 on Masturbation and Our Present-day Views. *This Annual*, 6.
—— (1954), Early Identification as Archaic Elements in the Superego. *J. Amer. Psa. Assn.*, 2.
—— (1960), Pathologic Forms of Self-Esteem Regulation. *This Annual*, 15.
Ritvo, S. (1962), Panel Report: Object Relations. *J. Amer. Psa. Assn.*, 10.
—— & Solnit, A. J. (1960), The Relationship of Early Ego Identifications to Superego Formation. *Int. J. Psa.*, 41.
Root, N. N. (1957), A Neurosis in Adolescence. *This Annual*, 12.
Sandler, J. (1960), On the Concept of Superego. *This Annual*, 15.

—— Holder, A., & Meers, D. (1963), The Ego Ideal and the Ideal Self. *This Annual*, 18.
Schafer, R. (1960), The Loving and Beloved Superego in Freud's Structural Theory. *This Annual*, 15.
Spiegel, L. A. (1958), Comments on the Psychoanalytic Psychology of Adolescence. *This Annual*, 13.
Tausk, V. (1912), On Masturbation. *This Annual*, 6, 1951.
Wittenberg, R. (1955), On the Superego in Adolescence. *Psa. Rev.*, 42.

# ON ARREST IN DEVELOPMENT, FIXATION, AND REGRESSION

HUMBERTO NAGERA, M.D. (London)

While fixation and regression are essential concepts of psycho-analytic theory, especially the theory of the neurosis,[1] they have not always been clearly separated in practice when one is confronted with actual clinical pictures. In this paper I shall try to demonstrate that it is frequently possible, at the diagnostic stage, to ascertain how much, in certain neurotic developments or disorders of children, is the result of regression and how much can be ascribed to fixation. I shall discuss some aspects of the clinical and prognostic value of this distinction; describe the different types of fixation and regression that can be observed (but only in so far as this is required by the central theme of this paper[2]); and, finally, refer briefly to some of the clinical problems inherent in the effort to distinguish what, in the disorders of children, is due to fixation and what to regression.

A similar evaluation of the psychopathology in the adult is some-what more complicated, though not impossible. However, an under-standing of the problems posed by what one observes in the adult presupposes some clarification and at least a limited discussion of the forms in which fixations manifest themselves in children and of

---

The present paper is the result of the work of a study group on the problem of "Fixation and Regression."

In this paper only a limited number of aspects have been selected for discussion. The "Clinical Concept Research Group" is nevertheless continuing this and other related studies and future publications will deal with the problem from different angles.

The need to study these questions more closely arose with the application of Anna Freud's Developmental Profile to our clinical material. The latter work is supported by funds from the National Institute of Mental Health in Washington.

1 For a historical review of the concepts of fixation and regression as postulated by Freud throughout his life, I have consulted the drafts on "Fixation," by Miss Elsa First, and on "Regression," by Mrs. A. Gavshon, prepared at the Hampstead Clinic by the Concept Research Group. The Concept Research Group is presently engaged in scholastic research work on basic psychoanalytic concepts.

2 For a fuller account of other aspects, see Anna Freud (1963).

the possible vicissitudes they undergo in the development from childhood through to adulthood.

We know that the term fixation may have several referants. We speak of fixation to a given component instinct, to a phase of libidinal and aggressive development, to a type of object choice, to a type of object relationship, and to a traumatic experience. We further know that all these different forms of fixations are expressions of similar and somewhat equivalent phenomena. For example, the controlling, domineering, obstinate, stubborn, sadistic type of object relationship of the anal phase is only the form in which certain drives express themselves in behavioral terms. This behavior is, of course, largely determined by the activity and predominance of the group of component instincts characteristic of this phase.

Nevertheless, our clinical experience shows that there are differences among our cases with respect to where it is that the emphasis is placed in terms of fixation. We may feel obliged to speak of a fixation to a component instinct as in some perversions; while in other cases we have to talk rather in terms of fixation to a given phase, because there seems to be a more extended type of disturbance related to the phase as a whole and not to a single component instinct. Similarly, in certain cases we may observe that the fixation at the anal level manifests itself in a peculiar type of relationship, which is the only one possible for such children, while in other cases the marked activity of the well-known anal component instincts may be in the foreground. The fact that anality expresses itself in a type of object relationship which is the only one the patient is capable of nevertheless implies that a step has been taken away from the direct gratification of the anal component instincts. Such differences make it incumbent upon us to study what precisely determines the different types of emphasis, modes or levels of expression, and outcomes.

In children we establish the existence of fixation points at any given level by several means. We observe their behavior, games, play, attitudes, interests, fantasies whenever available, or symptoms where present. These will indicate at what level or levels of development the child is functioning. One takes into account the age of the child and the wide range of variations in normal development. A child's environmental circumstances, state of health, tiredness, etc., may indicate, as Anna Freud (1963) has pointed out, the existence of temporary regressions due partly to the above-mentioned circumstances and states rather than to permanent ones. One similarly tries to evaluate whatever is observed in relative quantitative terms. In the end, and after the necessary corrections have been made, one is in a good position to estimate whether or not a fixation exists and what its importance is.

To illustrate briefly, we may observe an unusual and extensive activity of a given component instinct at a time when it is no longer age adequate; that is, when it is no longer normal for such an activity to be an important and permanent area of discharge and gratification.

## FIXATION VERSUS REGRESSION

In a previous paper (1963) I advanced the hypothesis, already referred to, that it is possible to determine how much of the drive (libido and aggression) manifestations seen at a particular pregenital stage is present owing to the existence of a fixation point at that level and how much to regressive processes. Fixation points indicate a certain degree of arrest in drive development. In regressive phenomena, on the other hand, the drives have at one point or another reached a higher level of development but were, as a result of conflicts at these higher levels, forced back to earlier developmental positions. The majority of cases lie between these two extremes, showing arrested development (fixation points) which receives regressive reinforcement resulting from later conflicts. I claimed that even in these cases it is possible for the clinician to determine how much can be attributed to regression and how much to fixation. It is clear that since we have no direct and concrete method of assessing either fixations or regressions, this evaluation can be made only in relative quantitative terms, on the basis of a number of clinical facts and observations.

I shall discuss here primarily the cases where a combination of fixation and regressive processes is or has been in operation at some point. The two possible theoretical extremes in this series are represented by cases of massive arrest in drive development and by cases where extremely unusual, severe, or traumatic circumstances have created such intense conflicts that regression ensued even when no obvious or important fixation points existed. (I will shortly discuss the latter type of case.)

To start with, these assessments are in most instances easier in children than in adults. In the child the forms of expression of drive gratification, on which we base our judgment, remain quite direct or at least close enough to the original drive to permit a relatively ready identification. In the adult a series of displacements and transformations of the original drive expression has taken place complicating their elucidation, as will be seen later in the section on the "Vicissitudes of the Form of Expression of Fixations." I believe that when a fixation point exists in a child, it betrays itself by the excessive activity of the component instinct or instincts involved in the fixation. In normal development, when a given phase is reached, the characteristic activity of the phase-specific component instincts is clearly in the foreground, while the activity of those component instincts belonging to the previous phases tends to recede somewhat into the background, more and more so as development progresses and the normally expected overlapping between phases is slowly left behind. When a fixation has taken place, this recession into the background does not occur to the same degree.[3] On the contrary, we

[3] In "Analysis Terminable and Interminable" (1937) Freud states that his first account of libidinal development assumed an original oral phase succeeded by a sadistic-anal and in turn by a phallic-genital one. He goes on: "Later investigation has not contradicted this view, but we must now qualify our statement by saying that the one phase does not succeed the other suddenly but gradually, so that part of the earlier organization always persists side by side with the later, and that even in normal development the transformation is never complete, the final structure often containing vestiges of earlier libidinal fixations. . . . All that has once lived clings tenaciously to life" (p. 330f.).

Earlier (1913) he had said: "Another and far more surprising discovery has been that, in spite of all the later development that occurs in the adult, none of the infantile mental formations perish. All the wishes, instinctual impulses, modes of reaction and attitudes of childhood are still demonstrably present in maturity and in appropriate circumstances can emerge once more. They are not destroyed but merely overlaid . . ." (p. 184).

I am grateful to Dr. Hartmann for calling my attention to a statement by Freud which highlights how the problems I am concerned with here relate in a broader sense to the question of the immutability of the id contents. In this passage Freud refers to his previous assumptions, according to which the repressed instinctual impulses themselves remain unchanged indefinitely; however, because of the differentiation of the ego and the id, the whole question receives a fresh impetus and is in need of re-examination. Freud says (1926): "But now our interest is turned to the vicissitudes of the repressed and we begin to suspect that it is not self-evident, perhaps not even

then observe an "unusual degree" of activity belonging to the earlier phase side by side with that of the later ones; moreover, in some cases this persisting activity shapes and modifies the form of expression and activity of the component instincts belonging to the later developmental phases.

Clinically such a situation shows itself openly in the child through symptoms, inhibitions, behavior, interests, play, games, fantasies, etc. Thus, though certain portions of the drives (more or less according to the importance of the fixations) may have reached the phallic-oedipal phase and quite clearly express themselves in phallic-oedipal activity, the manifest signs of fixation to the earlier levels will at no point have disappeared from the developmental picture. Unusual oral activity remains present in one form or another, side by side with the anal component instincts, when the nonarrested libido has been moved into the anal stage of drive development. If no further major arrest occurs during the anal phase, and the move to the phallic-oedipal stage takes place, side by side with the signs of the phallic components will be those of the oral fixation. However, if a fixation point has been established at the anal phase, then by the time the phallic stage is reached a combination of oral, anal, and phallic components will be present in the clinical picture. The new intensity and relative importance of the oral, anal, and phallic-oedipal manifestations are in some way proportionate to the amount of libido and aggression that has remained arrested at the anal and

---

usual, that those impulses should remain unaltered and unalterable in this way. There is no doubt that the original impulses have been inhibited and deflected from their aim through repression. But has the portion of them in the unconscious maintained itself and been proof against the influences of life that tend to alter and depreciate them? In other words, do the old wishes, about whose former existence analysis tells us, still exist? The answer seems ready to hand and certain. It is that the old, repressed wishes must still be present in the unconscious since we still find their derivatives, the symptoms, in operation. But this answer is not sufficient. It does not enable us to decide between two possibilities: either that the old wish is now operating only through its derivatives, having transferred the whole of its cathectic energy to them, or that it is itself still in existence too. If its fate has been to exhaust itself in cathecting its derivatives, there is yet a third possibility. In the course of the neurosis, it may have become re-animated by regression, anachronistic though it may now be. These are no idle speculations. There are many things about mental life, both normal and pathological, which seem to call for the raising of such questions. In my paper, "The Dissolution of the Oedipus Complex" (1924d), I had occasion to notice the difference between the mere repression and the real removal of an old wishful impulse" (p. 142, n.).

oral levels,[4] and to whatever amount was left free to reach the phallic phase. It is clear that there is an infinite number of possible variations in terms of the relative strength and importance of each one of these elements, in its own right and in combination with others.

As Freud's formulations indicated, the stronger the pregenital fixations, the stronger is the pull exerted from such points on whatever has reached a higher development. Even slight difficulties at the higher levels will quickly lead to regressions when important fixation points are present and exert their strong pull.

Once the phallic-oedipal stage is reached, conflicts at that level (with marked castration anxiety) may or may not induce regression. If regression from the phallic phase takes place, we can observe two results, their relative importance and manifestation being dependent on how much of the libido that has advanced to the phallic-oedipal stage takes the regressive path. If all or most of it does so, the previous behavior and fantasies of an obviously phallic-oedipal nature will tend to disappear from the foreground. In some cases of massive regression from the phallic to earlier levels, one is forced to ask oneself whether a particular child has ever reached the phallic-oedipal stage, since no signs of it are any longer observable by the time the child comes for assessment. This is by no means a rare diagnostic situation. Yet the problem may be solved by a good "developmental history" of the child. This will make it possible to show that a few weeks, months, or even years ago, that is, just before the massive regression took place, there were in the child's behavior, play, interests, fantasies, etc., signs of his having reached the oedipal stage. In this way the differential diagnosis is made, and regressive processes are distinguished from an arrest in drive development.

The second result of a massive regression from the phallic-oedipal stage to the fixation points consists in an intensification, a sudden reinforcement, of the libido that has remained arrested all the time. The outcome of the further regression is thus an intensification of

4 Freud (1913) stated: "The strength in which the residues of infancy are still present in the mind shows us the amount of disposition to illness; that disposition may accordingly be regarded as an expression of an inhibition in development" (p. 184). This statement highlights the importance of quantitative considerations in the analysis and study of this type of phenomena. Between normal and abnormal phenomena there are mainly quantitative differences. Certainly quantitative considerations are one of the factors on the basis of which one will establish the presence or absence of fixation points.

whatever earlier manifestations of symptoms, fantasies, behavior, etc., were representative of the fixation point or points.

It is understandable that if the regression is not a massive but only a partial one, it will still be possible to observe a child's phallic-oedipal activities, though they will be present to a lesser degree; similarly, the reinforcement of the activities betraying a fixation will be less dramatic. In any case, any previous manifestation of fixations such as thumb sucking, overeating, biting, clinging, demandingness, dirtiness, stubbornness, etc., becomes much more apparent and obvious.

To summarize, the existence of fixation points is indicated by the ever-present manifestations of the earlier phases at the later stages, far beyond the age at which such behavior corresponds to specific stages in development and is accepted as normal. Their intensity and activity will be *proportionate to the amounts of libido and aggression arrested*. The reinforcements and intensifications described above correspond and are *proportionate to the regression* that has taken place.[5] Hence the extreme importance of taking a very careful "developmental history" of the child, in which one tries to follow as closely as possible the vicissitudes of his drive development and even of the specific component instincts operative in the various phases, especially when there are indications of any kind of interference with normal development.

In some analytic circles the view is held that no such distinction between fixation and regression is possible at the diagnostic stage. As a result no effort is made in this direction, leaving to the analysis the task of sorting out what belongs where.

Still, this distinction is of great prognostic importance, because it is unquestionably easier to help the forward movement of libido which has at some point in development reached the higher stages and then regressed than that of libido which has always been arrested at the earlier stages. Furthermore, I believe, this approach might throw some light on such clinical questions as the choice of neurosis,

---

5 It is not infrequent that the diagnostician sees the patient long after the regression has taken place and when the whole situation of conflict has settled down. In some of these cases, the attempt to trace back when it was that the regressive move took place (betraying itself by the increase in the symptoms, etc.) enables us to recover the accidental factors, the environmental triggering circumstances that started or contributed to the situation of conflict, the very nature of which may thus become clearer.

problems relating to symptom formation, and especially the whole field of the relationship of infantile disturbances to adulthood psychopathology. At the same time the problems involved in the theory of fixation and regression might well be further elucidated.

I shall now illustrate, with a very simple example, how regression and fixation manifest themselves in the clinical material of the diagnostic interview of one of our cases, where no special effort was made to sort out what belongs to fixation or regression. I shall single out, from the clinical picture presented by this four-and-a-half-year-old boy, the elements pointing to his oral fixation, and how they show all through his development up to the present day. In this case it is further possible to point out the regressive reinforcement of the oral manifestations that seem to be due to the unhappy confluence of a number of events in his life, one of them at least of a traumatic character.

J. was described by his mother as a hungry baby who had to be given supplementary bottle feedings. He was breast fed for about six weeks, at which point the mother developed a breast abscess. When the mother tried to reintroduce breast feeding later on, J. seemed to prefer the bottle. He was weaned from it with no apparent difficulty at about nine months. At sixteen or seventeen months he showed a marked dislike of chewing and would spit out his food. His mother claims that he always tended to dislike new foods and that he has had different food fads. She recalled a week's visit to Holland when J. was twenty-two months; during that time he could eat nothing but cornflakes and toast. At present (four and a half) he still sucks his thumb when he is tired.

It is of interest to observe how the child spontaneously introduced the subject of food in his diagnostic interview with the psychiatrist by referring to his brother Simon: "My brother Simon was really a rascal because he said that you mustn't eat more than three Easter eggs, but Simon ate thirteen of them." At another point during the same interview he started to make a square cage for hens and sang: "Will you lay me an egg for my tea. . . ." (All the above clearly shows the ever-present fixation.)

When he was about three, a number of events succeeded each other: his entry into nursery school, a hospitalization for tonsillectomy, and the birth of a sibling. *Since that time his feeding difficulties increased.* The social history says: "The mother made it quite clear that since his operation the feeding difficulties have seemed worse. He is finicky, but the mother sees to it that he gets a balanced diet by preparing meals which she knows he likes." (Here the mother's account clearly points to the regressive reinforcement.)

Finally, psychoanalytic theory assumes that massive conflicts at higher levels of development may force a regressive movement of the libido even in cases where it is not possible to demonstrate the existence of relevant fixation points in the previous developmental phases. Clearly when such fixation points exist they favor regression by the constant pull they impose on the libido that has moved forward. Furthermore, the existence of such clear fixations is an obvious indication to the diagnostician where the libido that is regressing will finally stop and settle.

For these very reasons the diagnostician finds himself in a more helpless position when he attempts a similar assessment in cases where development has proceeded close to the ideal of normality and no clear-cut or outstanding fixation points can be noted, and a later traumatic episode has forced a regressive movement. Nevertheless, I believe that in such cases the backward movement of the libido will lead to those component instincts which have proved to be particularly strong in any given personality. That this is so is due not to the existence of fixation points proper but to the normal tendency to revert, when it is impossible to obtain gratification at the higher levels, to these primitive and intense forms of gratification that had previously been experienced. What seems to happen during the backward movement of the libido is a recathexis of those old channels of discharge which in the past have rendered intense satisfaction, while the simultaneous constant attraction of the libido, assumed to exist in cases of well-established fixation points, is here absent.

Clinically, one will observe a clean sheet as far as evidence of fixation is concerned. A careful developmental history will show only slight signs, if any, of fixations at the earlier levels. Nevertheless, at a certain point in the development of the child, for example, at four or five years of age, and perhaps as the result of massive traumatic castration anxiety, regression may start; we can then observe manifestations appropriate to the oral and anal phases, either as symptoms or pieces of behavior *that were previously absent, or that were only present at the age-appropriate stage* and disappeared as soon as the next step in development was taken or the next phase reached.

## Vicissitudes of the Form of Expression of Fixations

I have been able to study a few children whose development from babyhood or early infancy till adulthood was well known to the Hampstead Clinic. It was partly this study which highlighted and made clear how many of the indicators of fixation points at the earlier stages of development disappear from the surface, that is, from the overt behavior of the child. Having gone underground, they then hide behind what are considered to be normally acceptable forms of gratification and discharge. In this way valuable pointers and indicators of diagnostic and prognostic significance are either hidden from or lost to the unaware diagnostician.

What I am calling the vicissitudes of fixations is in many ways comparable and similar to the vicissitudes of the component instincts in general. The "fixation point" is, after all, the result of the same activities on the instinctual side, only to an abnormal degree and with incorrect timing.

For the sake of simplicity I shall confine myself to the oral phase and to oral fixations, taking as a hypothetical example excessive or constant thumb sucking, in children well past the age and stage at which thumb sucking can be considered to be within normal limits.

In such children thumb sucking may sometimes tend to persist until somewhere around what ought to be the latency period. This happens especially in cases where this tendency is a very marked one. Yet even those children who have so excessively and for so long engaged in this type of gratification seem to give it up at some point in their development. At least, thumb sucking seems to disappear from the foreground and is no longer observable in the overt behavior of the child.

A closer scrutiny may show that this abandonment, this giving up of the "habit," conceals a substitution for another socially acceptable form of oral gratification.[6] Such a change releases the ego from a

[6] In the *Introductory Lectures* (1916-1917), Freud says that "we must bear in mind that the sexual instinctual impulses in particular are extraordinarily *plastic*, if I may so express it. One of them can take the place of another, one of them can take over another's intensity; if the satisfaction of one of them is frustrated by reality, the satisfaction of another can afford complete compensation. They are related to one another like a network of inter-communicating channels filled with liquid . . ." (p. 345).

situation of growing conflict between the instinctual demand in the form of thumb sucking and the environment that has turned more and more intransigent to the "habit" as the child has aged.

It is a confluence of several factors that makes it possible for the child to exchange thumb sucking for another form of gratification at a certain point in his development, perhaps long before latency or at the beginning of it. His ego growth implies not only that the child disposes over a stronger and more capable structure, which can put forward more acceptable alternative solutions, and perhaps even enforce them; there is also a growing awareness of the environmental demands, particularly of the persons looking after him, and of the need to preserve their love. This is coupled with an increasing concern for these persons' feelings as well as a greater readiness to comply, partly because more and more superego precursors (in the form of environmental demands) have become internalized.

Thumb sucking, which has thus become involved in a major conflict, may now be exchanged for a craving for sweets or for any other form of gratification of oral needs more acceptable to the environment of a child of four or five years of age. Later on some of these intermediate forms of oral gratification will be exchanged for more age-adequate and socially acceptable ones, like smoking, certain types of overeating, somewhat excessive drinking, etc.

In still other cases the exchange takes place within the sphere of the subject's sexual life, where it anchors itself especially at the fore-pleasure stage of the sexual activity. Kissing, licking, sucking, biting the sexual partner, or specific parts of his body, etc., are highly cathected and by far the most exciting elements of the person's sexual life. Behind some preferences, peculiarities, and pieces of sexual behavior of the above-mentioned type and other similar ones may lie hidden some fixation points which are now secret and become active only in certain sets of circumstances. Though "fellatio," for example, is a highly overdetermined sexual practice, the importance of the role it plays in the sexual life of some patients is probably closely connected with significant oral fixations and perhaps especially with the sucking component instinct of the oral stage.

What I have described here for the oral phase and sucking as a specific component of that phase applies to the other phases and the other component instincts. There are socially acceptable and age-adequate equivalents for each, though on the whole there is greater tolerance for the oral and phallic strivings than for the anal ones.

In normal development some component instincts regularly make a contribution to normal sexual life and a person's character structure. This circumstance introduces an added complication into diagnostic problems. Nevertheless it is the assessment of the economic and quantitative aspects which must decide whether we are dealing with normal or pathological manifestations.

The fact that many forms of gratification of the oral component instincts can be quite normal and socially acceptable complicates diagnostic assessments, because marked oral fixations may be hidden under this cover of normal oral activity and discharge. In this way valuable pointers and indicators for the study of characters, personality structure, and the nature of the conflicts are concealed, and elements of great prognostic significance are obscured. The diagnostician will do well, during the assessment of adults, to examine in minute detail all those areas where, behind manifestations which are usually normal, potential pathology may be hidden. He will no doubt do so in the extreme cases of eating leading to obesity, or chain smoking, or habitual drunkenness, but he should not neglect those cases that are far from these extremes. Whenever the existence of oral fixations is suspected or needs to be taken into account, it is desirable to inquire closely into the patient's smoking, eating, and drinking patterns in order to avoid overlooking pointers in these areas.

The diagnostic and prognostic value of such findings can prove especially important when the more or less original and direct forms of expression of childhood orality are no longer observable. It is well known, for example, that many cases diagnosed as hysteria are offered to candidates in psychoanalytic training as relatively easy first cases for analysis; not infrequently, however, as treatment progresses, such cases turn out to be severe depressions; the oral fixations then become manifest and more evident and alarming as the depressive episode develops.[7]

A careful diagnostic examination of such patients, and especially

---

[7] In his discussion of the Schreber case (1911). Freud pointed out: "For it is possible for several fixations to be left behind in the course of development, and each of these in succession may allow an irruption of the libido that has been pushed off—beginning, perhaps, with the later acquired fixations, and going on, as the illness develops, to the original ones that lie nearer the starting-point" (p. 78).

the recognition of the existence of earlier fixation points now under cover, would have acted as a warning that behind the observable hysteric-type conflicts at the phallic-oedipal level lie deeper and stronger roots at the oral level. As the result of these fixations, more serious disturbances may develop as soon as the precariously maintained conflict equilibrium (of a hysterical type) at the phallic-oedipal phase is upset by internal or external circumstances.

## FIXATION POINTS: SOME CLINICAL PROBLEMS

Some children reach the phallic-oedipal stage after rather troublesome oral or anal conflicts. One can then frequently observe a marked contamination of the later phase by the fixation at the previous ones. A contamination of the phallic-oedipal stage and its fantasies by the oral one and its fantasies will betray itself, for example, in the circumstance that the child's phallic fantasies are expressed in oral terms; intercourse, pregnancy, making babies, etc., are conceived as being the result of activities involving both the phallus and the mouth. Babies are thus made by eating or drinking certain substances; they may come out of the genitals or because the genitals themselves are eaten. In these cases the child's castration anxiety is frequently expressed through fears of having his penis bitten off or eaten up, as can be observed in his fantasies and games, e.g., when animals are constantly biting off or eating up other animals' tails, legs, heads, etc.

Similarly, an important fixation at the anal level will tend to contaminate the child's phallic-oedipal wishes, leading him to conceive of sexuality as an aggressive sadistic fight and attack on the sexual partner.

Sexual fantasies of an oral or anal nature may to some extent be present in normal development since the oral and anal phases even in ideal conditions leave behind some remnant or other. Here again the diagnostic problem will be solved by the quantitative factor which perhaps points to a predominance or even exclusiveness of one or another form of expression.

That phallic-oedipal fantasies are expressed, e.g., in oral terms is not accidental. Such an apparent preference for one or another form of expression of the conflict or conflicts is not a matter of chance. On the contrary, I believe it is determined by the relatively greater strength of the oral component instincts and by the particular fixation points which in comparison with those of other phases are of far greater importance. Consequently they ought to be taken as indicators of the special strength of the oral component instincts and of important fixations that have led to a contamination of the later phases. Similar considerations apply if anal fantasies are predominant.

Regressive processes, especially in their first stages, will intensify this form of expression of the conflict. To my mind, this circumstance affords an indication of where the important fixations have been established and of the points to which the libido will retreat if a more or less complete withdrawal from the phallic phase is going to take place. When such a development occurs, the phallic elements of the previous fantasies tend to disappear and are no longer easily observable. The fantasy then becomes less of a contamination of oral and phallic elements and turns more into a purely oral type.

Clinically, one must distinguish between true regression to earlier levels and those cases where the conflict, though it is on the whole at the phallic-oedipal level, is expressed in oral and anal terms on account of previous fixations. These forms of expression can be observed the moment the libido moves into the phallic-oedipal phase. If, on the contrary, the oral or anal expression of the phallic-oedipal conflict is due to a partial regression or to a beginning regressive move, there would be a previous period at which the oral contamination of the phallic-oedipal phase was not so evident or not observable at all in the clinical material.

Perhaps the more frequent case is a mixed one, consisting of a reinforcement and accentuation of the oral or anal contamination of phallic fantasies that were present all the way through. The sudden accentuation or reinforcement indicates the sudden regressive movement, while the previous, not so intense, but clearly present contaminated fantasies indicate the fixation point.

So far analysts have concentrated their attention mainly on the role played by the fixation points in the choice of neurosis and in the mechanism of symptom formation. I believe that no less useful results will be achieved by studying the role played by the presence of fixation points of a very diverse nature in the development of the ego. It is important to know, as I have pointed out elsewhere (1963), that at some time (ideally at the proper time) the right amount of libido[8] has moved forward and thus made its contributions to the development of the ego and to the personality as a whole; in contrast, where excessive fixations exist, large amounts of libido have remained arrested and were unable to contribute to normal development at the time when that contribution was required.

It is not far-fetched to assume that arrests in the drive development of the child will in turn influence in some ways his ego development. Psychoanalysis assumes a very close developmental interaction between the drives and the ego. The how, when, where, and why the drives make their contribution to ego development is still a rather obscure area; but we work with the assumption that any development move on the drive side acts as a trigger for a number of chain reactions of developmental processes on the ego side. These in turn will feed back to the drives, which again will further stimulate ego development in certain specific directions. A similar situation of interaction and influence on the drives can be assumed to have its origin in certain developmental processes (maturational and otherwise) that take place in the ego.

In this context it may be useful to refer to the clear influence which any fixation points have on the sexual theories of children and on their understanding of the world. It is well known that a child at the oral phase of development understands the world around him largely in oral terms and through oral imagery, just as the child in the anal or phallic stages does so mainly in anal and phallic terms, more markedly so as more of his libido has moved freely forward to cathect the corresponding body zones. It is due to this later factor that the world is interpreted in oral, anal, and phallic terms, since through the massive cathexis of the zone all other mental activities, interests, etc., become to a certain extent subordinated to it, especially so in early childhood.

The child who has reached the phallic-oedipal phase, though preferring to relate to and understand the world and its objects in the terms dictated by that phase of development, has nevertheless complete freedom to use oral and anal imagery when necessary. He

---

[8] Throughout this paper whenever I refer to libido, similar arguments of course apply to the aggressive drives.

has reached a very high and complex level of integration and function on the drive and ego sides. On the other hand, a child whose fixations impose upon him an oral imagery, for example, is dealing with similar phenomena with very different means when he reaches the phallic stage. I do not want to imply that the one form of development leads to a better ability on the side of the ego, since observation of oral or anal characters and their ego performance makes it clear that this is not necessarily the case. Nevertheless, in these unexplored areas of differences in human development, and in the differences in basic personality structures resulting from it, lie the answers to many intriguing and obscure problems of psychopathology in general, and especially to those of symptom formation, choice of neurosis, intrinsic differences among basically hysteric or obsessional patients,[9] as well as answers to problems relating to so-called health and normality, character structure, etc.

In certain types of character organization, for example, in obsessional characters and especially in adults, one frequently observes an extraordinary increase in the defensive system or defensive attitude of the ego against certain component instincts that have received a reinforcement through the regressive process. During the first stages of the regressive process one generally cannot demonstrate any direct manifestations of the regressively reinforced component instincts; in this case the regressive move betrays itself by the increase in the defense activity. Thus, in some "anal characters" the desirable tendencies to orderliness, thoroughness, and meticulousness (which are well-known precipitates of the reaction formations against some of the anal component instincts in the character structure) can increase to such an extent that the performance of daily tasks becomes impossible. Then tendency to orderliness and meticulousness transforms itself, for example, into a compulsion to check and recheck every step so many times that productive work is completely paralyzed.

We have occasionally observed children who relate to a given object, e.g., the mother, at a level that seems to point to a fixation to the anal stage, when chronologically and otherwise one would expect such a child to have left behind that phase. Further observation of the same child discloses that he relates to other objects at a higher

---

[9] It is well known that there are very marked differences between two hysterics or two obsessional patients.

and normal level. Clearly, if this difference in his relationships is to be attributed to a fixation at the anal-sadistic level, the fixation is restricted to the relationship with the mother and is not as severe as it would be if this were the child's only possible way of relating to all persons.

Furthermore, I believe that an important and by no means easy differential diagnosis is required here. The study of the role played by the object in this type of relationship is most important. In some of these cases, one gains the impression that the child's ego is adapting to the environment, that he complies with the demands made by such an important object as the mother by forming the only type of relationship that is possible in view of the mother's own psychopathology. This situation can be very different from one in which the ego is forced to an anal-sadistic type of relationship and is itself incapable of forming any other types of relationships. In the one case the ego chooses a type of relationship that it knows to be the only form of communication possible with a given object, or perhaps the only way to get a response from that object, while in the other the ego is helpless, having to endure its limitations and having no choice or possible alternative.

Finally, throughout this study of the problems involved in fixation and regression, attention has been called to the necessity of a more precise and accurate description of the specific points to which the regression has taken place. Thus it really is not sufficient to say that regression has taken place to the anal phase; a specification of the proper subphase within the anal phase is of clinical relevance. Even within the subphase one needs to know which are the really relevant component instincts or their equivalents in any given case. Certain qualitative differences—in some cases of prognostic value— between neuroses of the same type in different individuals lie hidden behind such details.[10]

BIBLIOGRAPHY

Freud, A. (1963), Regression as a Principle in Mental Development. *Bull. Menninger Clin.*, 27.
Freud, S. (1911), Psycho-Analytic Notes on an Autobiographical Account of a Case of

[10] These and similar problems are at present being studied at the Hampstead Clinic in the "Clinical Research Group" under a project known as "Studies on the Psychoanalytic Theory of the Neuroses."

Paranoia (Dementia Paranoides). *Standard Edition*, 12. London: Hogarth Press, 1958.
—— (1913), The Claims of Psycho-Analysis to Scientific Interest. *Standard Edition*, 13. London: Hogarth Press, 1955.
—— (1916-1917), Introductory Lectures on Psycho-Analysis. *Standard Edition*, 15 & 16. London: Hogarth Press, 1963.
—— (1926), Inhibitions, Symptoms and Anxiety. *Standard Edition*, 20. London: Hogarth Press, 1959.
—— (1937), Analysis Terminable and Interminable. *Collected Papers*, 5. London: Hogarth Press, 1950.
Nagera, H. (1963), The Developmental Profile: Notes on Some Practical Considerations Regarding Its Use. *This Annual*, 18.

# AUTOEROTISM, AUTOEROTIC ACTIVITIES, AND EGO DEVELOPMENT

## HUMBERTO NAGERA, M.D. (London)

During the course of a research project concerned with the concept of narcissism in Freud's works it became clear that a preliminary and unavoidable step was a revision of the concept of autoerotism, erotogenic zones, and component instincts.[1]

Many of Freud's formulations on autoerotism are of course to be found in his *Three Essays on a Theory of Sexuality* (1905). The sexual theory has become one of the corner stones on which the whole structure of psychoanalytic theory has been built and safely rests. Autoerotism and autoerotic activities lie at the base of the sexual theory, both as important elements in the discharge of tension aroused by the sexual drives (component instincts) all through development, and as the very first manifestations of sexual activity out of which adult sexuality will develop.

This being the case, it is puzzling that not enough attention has been paid to the concept of autoerotism. As a result of this relative neglect, there is a great deal of confusion and misunderstanding and sometimes even a failure to grasp many of its implications. In turn this misunderstanding has led to reformulations, new theoretical propositions, and ever more confusion.

A revision of some aspects of the concept of autoerotism inevitably leads us into other areas of confusion among analysts, but I believe

---

This paper forms part of a study entitled "Assessment of Pathology in Childhood" which is conducted at the Hampstead Child-Therapy Clinic, London. It has been financed by the National Institute of Mental Health, Washington, D. C.

[1] The need to study these questions arose when we applied the Developmental Profile (developed by Anna Freud, 1962) to our clinical material. This was specially required in those cases where important elements of the child's disturbance were related to certain types of narcissistic injuries, disturbed cathexes of the self and the objects, and inappropriate self-esteem regulation. Similarly, we frequently saw cases where the presence of specific forms of autoerotic gratification demanded some judgment as to the level and severity of the type of autoerotic manifestation observed.

some light is thrown on them once the phenomenon of autoerotism is clearly defined and properly placed among Freud's other theoretical formulations. One such area of enormous confusion relates to the term *object* and the use Freud made of it.

Though many factors are responsible for some of the misunderstandings, two of them are perhaps of particular relevance and deserve to be mentioned here.

First, not enough distinction is made between autoerotic activities viewed within the frame of the "phase of autoerotism" (in Freud's timetable), and autoerotic activities considered in the broader frame of sexual development, long after autoerotism as a phase in libidinal development has been left behind. Secondly, not enough attention is paid to the fact that some aspects of the sexual theory were developed after 1905. Freud made many additions to the original *Three Essays,* in some cases many years later, that is, when further work in other areas had thrown new light on certain aspects of the original formulations. It should not be forgotten then that different portions of the *Three Essays,* though closely related to each other, are sometimes found on close analysis to belong to very different levels of concept formation and of development in psychoanalytic theory. This makes it necessary when quoting from such material to take into account the context and background against which they first appear, in order not to distort their significance.

The implications of autoerotic phenomena for the understanding and for the development of theoretical formulations in relation to the early stages of ego development are obvious. A clarification of the meaning of autoerotic phenomena will also throw some light on the theory of narcissism. I am inclined to think that it is not possible to deal with the questions inherent in this theory until the ground has been cleared of these misunderstandings of Freud's assumptions in relation to autoerotism and the use of the term "object," both in relation to autoerotic phenomena and in a more general sense. Very many of the alleged contradictions in the area of narcissism either disappear or fall into proper perspective and place, once the difficulties due to misconceptions in relation to autoerotism and autoerotic activities are overcome.

Finally, I want to call attention to, and will try to distinguish, three different types or levels of autoerotism and autoerotic phe-

nomena which can be seen at three different stages in the development of the personality. They are, of course, closely connected with
each other. Although the phenomena remain basically the same,
there are important differences among these three types or levels of
autoerotic manifestations.

I think that it was these differences that were implicit in Freud's
mind when he established the timetable: autoerotism, primary narcissism, object relationships.[2] I hope to show that he explicitly distinguished the "phase of autoerotism" and the autoerotic activities
then present; further, these first autoerotic activities do not have
quite the same organization and complexity as those present in the
next stage of his timetable, that is, primary narcissism.

## THE CONCEPT OF AUTOEROTISM AND AUTOEROTIC ACTIVITIES

"Autoerotism" is a term used by Freud to describe a phase in
libidinal development, while "autoerotic" is a term used to describe
a specific type of sexual activity and gratification.

"Autoerotic" sexual activity and "autoerotic" forms of gratification can be observed during the phases of "autoerotism" and "narcissism" (primary) and not infrequently side by side with other forms
of sexual gratification characteristic of more advanced phases of
development such as that of "object love."

I believe an autoerotic activity can best be described by saying
that it is an objectless instinctual activity seeking for a particular
kind of pleasure. This pleasure is normally brought about by a
special handling, stroking, or other type of manipulation necessary
to produce the gratification. In this way the excitation in the corresponding erotogenic zone or the excitation of a particular component instinct (expressing itself through an appropriate erotogenic
zone) is reduced.

Autoerotic activities are observable during early sexual development in all erotogenic zones—mouth, anus, and genitalia.

Freud's first mention of the term appears in a letter to Fliess
(December 9, 1899) in which he says: "The lowest of the sexual
strata is auto-erotism, which renounces any psychosexual aim and

[2] A historical revision of the concept of narcissism will be the subject of another
publication. The problems involved are too complex to be dealt with in this paper.

seeks only local gratification. This is superseded by allo-erotism (homo- and hetero-), but undoubtedly survives as an independent tendency" (Freud, 1887-1902, p. 303f.).

Though Freud borrowed the term from Havelock Ellis who introduced it in 1898, he used it in a different sense. He insisted frequently that autoerotism is an objectless condition. In the *Three Essays* he says: "It must be insisted that the most striking feature of this sexual activity is that *the instinct is not directed towards other people, but obtains satisfaction from the subject's own body. It is auto-erotic . . .*" (1905, p. 181; my italics).

In 1920 Freud added a very significant footnote to this sentence: "Havelock Ellis, it is true, uses the word 'auto-erotic' in a somewhat different sense, to describe an excitation which is not provoked from outside [whether directly or indirectly] but arises internally. *What psycho-analysis regards as the essential point is not the genesis of the excitation, but the question of its relation to an object*" (my italics).

It is now necessary to determine how far this "objectlessness"—the main characteristic of autoerotic activities—is carried in Freud's formulation. This is by no means an easy task. Careful consideration in this respect seems to indicate that neither the cases in which there is a physical biological dependence of a component instinct on an object in the external world, nor the cases in which there is an object choice through the agency of the ego (though mainly operative in fantasy) are truly autoerotic manifestations. That seems to be the reason for such statements as: "At a time at which the first beginnings of sexual satisfaction are still linked with the taking of nourishment, the sexual instinct has a sexual object outside the infant's own body in the shape of his mother's breast. It is only later that the instinct loses that object. . . . *As a rule the sexual instinct then becomes auto-erotic . . .*" (1905, p. 222; my italics).

It is clear that the object referred to in this statement is the biological object of the oral component instinct. It must be noted that Freud is quite specific in pointing out that the relation here is one between the *sexual instinct* and its *sexual object* and not between the child's ego and its object: "the sexual instinct has a sexual object outside the infant's own body." He further stated that it is only later *when the instinct loses that object* that the sexual instinct becomes autoerotic.

From this and many other similar statements one is forced to conclude the following: Freud thought that the relationship to an object determines whether a given sexual activity is autoerotic or not; this excludes from autoerotic phenomena all cases in which the physical-biological relationship of a component instinct to an object still exists and in which gratification is dependent on this relationship. Sucking at the mother's breast is consequently not an autoerotic activity, in contrast to sucking one's own finger, which is an autoerotic activity.

Similarly, when there already exists a relationship to an object on the ego side (even in fantasy, as, for example, in masturbation during the phallic phase), we cannot speak of pure autoerotic activity but must consider the phenomenon a composite in which a fantasy has inserted itself into the previously pure "autoerotic" activity.

Freud (1908) linked fantasies with autoerotism when referring to masturbation. He mentioned that during a period of masturbation the fantasy was evoked in conjunction with some active behavior for obtaining self-gratification at the height of the fantasy (p. 161). A very clear example can be taken from Little Hans's own comments when he said: "I put my finger to my widdler just a very little. I saw Mummy quite naked in her chemise, and she let me see her widdler" (1909, p. 32).

In current usage one would refer to this type of masturbation as an autoerotic activity. Strictly speaking, however, one could not call this autoerotic, since by now the activity is a highly complex composite of which the relationship to an object in fantasy is an important part. Thus the cases in which there is a relationship through the agency of the ego with an object are not truly autoerotic manifestations either. Strictly speaking, a true autoerotic activity is taking place only in those cases in which the object of the component instinct is the subject's own body or a part of it.

During this early period in the development of psychoanalytic theory Freud had not yet asked the question whether the child had any psychological awareness of his own body. This question of self-awareness was taken into account a few years later, starting in about

1909 with the introduction of "narcissism" as an intermediary libidinal position on the way from autoerotism (as the first libidinal position) to that of object love. The autoerotic activities are now seen
in a new and psychologically more meaningful context: "Recent
investigations [e.g., Freud, 1910, p. 100] have directed our attention
to a stage in the development of the libido which it passes through
on the way from auto-erotism to object-love. This stage has been
given the name of narcissism. What happens is this. There comes a
time in the development of the individual at which he unifies his
sexual instincts (which have hitherto been engaged in auto-erotic
activities) in order to obtain a love-object; and he begins by taking
himself, his own body, as his love-object, and only subsequently
proceeds from this to the choice of some person other than himself
as an object" (1911, p. 60f.).[3]

During the phase of autoerotism each component instinct that
is aroused is seeking gratification quite independently of any other.
According to Freud, in the next stage of libidinal development (narcissism), the different component instincts somehow become unified
and take the self as a love object. Consequently the type of sexual
gratification during the phase of primary narcissism is autoerotic as
well, the object being one's own body and not an external one as
in the following phase of object love. "One's own body" as an object
is now a psychologically meaningful experience, owing to the degree
of development we assume to have been reached at the stage of the
narcissistic libidinal position.

The difference between the autoerotic activities of the phase of
primary narcissism and those of autoerotism, as I see it, is that those
corresponding to primary narcissism are less close to the biological
realm of phenomena than those belonging to the phase of autoerotism in which there is no awareness of the self as is the case in
primary narcissism. As Freud said, ". . . the ego cannot exist in the
individual from the start; the ego has to be developed. The autoerotic instincts, however, are there from the very first, so there must
be something added to auto-erotism—a new psychical action—in order to bring about narcissism" (1914, p. 77).

Furthermore, it must be noted that Freud considered it important clinically that the regression in dementia praecox extends

3 This sentence was also added as a footnote to the *Three Essays* in 1910.

not merely to narcissism (as in paranoia) but to a complete abandonment of object love and a return to infantile autoerotism. The dis-
positional fixation point must therefore be situated further back
than in paranoia, and must lie somewhere at the beginning of the
course of development from autoerotism to object love (1911, p. 77).

It may have become clear by now that the first accounts of the
phenomena we are concerned with here were mostly of a descriptive
nature and given by Freud against the background of his theory
of infantile sexuality as formulated in his *Three Essays* (1905). Considerations pertinent to ego development, its possible relationship
to, and mutual influence on, autoerotic phenomena were not so explicitly in the foreground at this stage. Ego psychology as we know
it today was not developed until many years later.

In any case, with the introduction of the theory of narcissism the
first such links were established, but unfortunately, as with some
other aspects of psychoanalytic theory, this formulation was never
integrated with the later, more advanced conceptualizations of ego
developmental psychology. A modest attempt in that direction is
made in the last section of this paper.

It may be worth while at this point to remark on how some
analysts after Freud have added to the confusion by what, in my
opinion, is a misinterpretation of some aspects of Freud's formulations. The statement that "the sexual instinct has a sexual object
outside the infant's own body in the shape of the mother's breast"
has not infrequently been taken to imply a psychological relationship of the type that only the developed ego is capable of. It seems
obvious that what Freud had in mind here is that *the sexual instinct*
and *not the child's ego finds an object*. Furthermore, this is a ready-
made biological object for the particular instinct, characteristic of
the species. This will be the biological prototype of the finding of
an object later on in development by the ego.[4]

In the same type of statement, Kleinian theory assumes that object relationships are mediated through an agency which would

[4]These biological prototypes should not surprise anybody who has noticed similar
statements made by Freud in the *Three Essays*. For example, in two footnotes added
in 1924, he mentions Abraham's paper of 1924, pointing out how the anus is developed from the embryonic blastopore—a fact which seems like a biological prototype of psychosexual development. Another one refers to the phallic phase having,
according to Abraham, its biological prototype in the embryo's undifferentiated genital
disposition which is the same for both sexes.

have to be a highly developed ego structure present "from the beginning."

Freud's final point of view in this question can be clearly seen in the following statement from the *Outline:* "A child's *first erotic object* is the mother's breast that feeds him, and love in its beginnings attaches itself to the satisfaction of the need for food. To start with, *the child certainly makes no distinction between the breast and his own body;* when the breast has to be separated from his body and shifted to the 'outside' because he so often finds it absent, it carries with it, *now that it is an 'object,'* part of the original narcissistic cathexis" (1940, p. 89f., my italics).[5] Kleinian theory can consequently dispose—and in fact does so implicitly—of the whole range of manifestations covered under autoerotism and autoerotic activities.

Lastly, another important source of confusion is due to the fact that at the time of the *Three Essays* Freud postulated that infantile sexual life "exhibits components which from the very first involve other people as sexual objects. Such are the instincts of scopophilia, exhibitionism and cruelty, which appear in a sense independently of erotogenic zones; these instincts do not enter into intimate relations with genital life until later, but are already to be observed in childhood as independent impulses, distinct in the first instance from erotogenic sexual activity" (1905, p. 192). It is not always realized that later on, partly as the result of the introduction of the narcissism theory, Freud modified the formulation given above. He said: "For the beginning of its activity the scopophilic instinct is autoerotic; it has indeed an object, but that object is part of the subject's own body. It is only later that the instinct is led, by a process of comparison, to exchange this object for an analogous part of someone else's body" (1915, p. 130).

## AUTOEROTISM AND EGO DEVELOPMENT

The autoerotic activities proper to the phase of autoerotism and those autoerotic activities that supersede this phase must be considered against the background given by the stage of ego development reached.

[5] This very argument and other similar ones are to be found in several places in Freud's writings. Compare, for example, *The Introductory Lectures* (1916-1917, p. 314).

In accordance with my introductory premises, I shall describe three different types or levels of autoerotism and autoerotic phenomena which can be observed at three different stages in the development of the personality.

## First Type

The phenomena described under this heading correspond in Freud's timetable of libidinal development to the phase of autoerotism. At the very beginning the ego as an organized system is not yet present, though some of the functions that will later be taken over by the ego and form an integral part of its organization are already present. Yet at this point they occur as isolated manifestations, with little or no correlation between them. Among these are perception and perceptive processes both of external and internal stimuli, memory impressions that are constantly being formed, feelings of the pleasure-unpleasure series, etc.

Similarly the picture on the side of the drives during this phase of autoerotism resembles that of the ego side. Each component instinct that has already appeared on the scene with each erotogenic zone is on its own, as isolated nuclei of libidinal activity, as disconnected points of excitation and discharge; in brief, as zones independent of one another. This implies of course the total lack of organization and integration on the side of the ego that we assume to be the state of affairs at birth.

Again at this stage all one can postulate is the existence of the mental apparatus, whose basic endeavor is to recover homeostatic equilibrium whenever it is lost by tension arising in the organism itself or coming from outside. The increase of tension, as is well known, is felt as unpleasure and vice versa. At the same time this mental apparatus is still unable to differentiate the source from which the stimuli of an unpleasurable or pleasurable nature arise.

Later on the organism—or rather, this mental apparatus—will be able to differentiate between external and internal stimuli by different means; for example, it will have learned that one can escape from external stimuli by taking flight, but not from internal ones. It may not be too far reaching to postulate that at this very primitive stage every feeling of unpleasure that comes to disturb the mind—whose only aim at this point is homeostasis—is felt like a disturbance coming from the outside (outside here means outside the mental apparatus, including the body that may well be, in fact, the source of the unpleasurable feeling).

There is no awareness of any objects in the psychological sense, neither external nor internal (the body or part of it). There exists only the capacity to feel pleasure and unpleasure and gradually also memory traces of these experiences. Yet even these memories must be acquired through experiencing: they are not there from the beginning.

At a given point during this phase it will become possible for the mental apparatus of the child to identify certain patterns with which he has been confronted, and which already have created representations associated with pleasure or unpleasure in the mnemic systems.

The identification of these patterns comes about through perception (not only through the ordinary senses, but also through proprioceptive perceptions, like the position of the body when held at the breast, etc., as well as the recognition of tactile experiences, sounds, warmth of the mother's body, etc.). The recognition of this pattern can now be associated with the oncoming experience of pleasure. Recent experiments have made it clear that there is no recognition of individual objects (e.g., the mother); the child will react similarly to any object that repeats the pattern he is familiar with. Similarly, the child will react to a mask that contains the pattern he can recognize (Spitz and Wolf, 1946).

At this stage the child's reaction, functions and mode of response are closer to the animal being, and of the nature of conditioned reflexes. Yet one can see the beginnings of what will later be a response through highly complex psychological ways. At this point they are still primitive and not based on his ability to recognize "objects" (in the psychological sense) either outside his body or in his own body, which later in development will become an object.

This mode of response is closer to the reflex phenomena, to typical biological responses. The pause introduced by the activity of the mind is not yet developed, with the exception—presumably after some experiences of satisfaction—of the possibility of dealing with certain types of tension by means of hallucinatory wish fulfillment.

*Second Type*

This second type of autoerotic activity belongs no longer to the phase of autoerotism that I have described above but to that of primary narcissism. The changes that now have occurred on the ego side make the autoerotic activities appear in a different light.

The autoerotic activities remain basically the same, since by autoerotic we understand the capacity to satisfy certain component instincts in one's own body. Yet one must distinguish this second phase (primary narcissism) from the phase of autoerotism, just as one must distinguish autoerotism as a phase in libidinal development characterized by the absolute dominance of autoerotic activities of a particular kind (due to the stage of development of the child) from autoerotic activities which occur later on when the development of the child has proceeded further; these autoerotic activities now take place in a different setting, and by virtue of this fact have acquired certain qualitative differences which distinguish them from activities occurring during other phases.

During this phase the autoerotic activities no longer occur as isolated manifestations of tension and discharge phenomena, taking place anywhere in the body and totally independent of each other. The lack of awareness and organization typical of the previous phase (autoerotism) is now modified. A certain degree of differentiation and structuralization has taken place, through the first steps in the formation of the body image. This constitutes the beginnings of what we acknowledge to be one of the functions of the ego, the establishment of the self; in fact, the development of the body image is the very beginning of the ego as an organized system.[6] With this beginning of structuralization the autoerotic activities now occur in the frame of reference of the body image.

The impingement of the tension caused by the drives or component instincts looking for gratification in an autoerotic manner can no longer be viewed or felt as the same attack from outside as they were in the previous phase, against the homeostatic equilibrium of the mental apparatus.

During the first stage the child can cathect only the experiences of pleasure and unpleasure and the memory traces that go with

[6] "The ego is first and foremost a bodily ego" (Freud, 1923, p. 26).

them, or rather, that are formed out of these experiences. The degree of organization of the mind and the lack of a body image, of a concept of the self, make it impossible at that stage to cathect the body, at least that part of the body that brings about the pleasurable sensation; the cathexis goes to the experience itself. A little later, when the beginning of the concept of the self is present, the part of the body involved in the experience of pleasure can be cathected, since it can now be identified by the mental apparatus as part of itself.

I believe Freud had this type of phenomena in mind when he said: "that a unity comparable to the ego cannot exist in the individual from the very start; the ego has to be developed. The autoerotic instincts, however, are there from the very first; so there must be something added to auto-erotism—a new psychical action—in order to bring about narcissism" (1914, p. 77). Considerations of that kind may have led him to the original formulation of the timetable: autoerotism, primary narcissism, object relationship.

Furthermore, now that these tensions and consequently the pleasurable sensations that accompany their relief through a given autoerotic activity are identified with one's own body, the body is recognized as the "me" and as that which yields the pleasure, thus making it possible for the child to cathect it, and bringing about primary narcissism.

The development of the self takes a long time and phenomena related to it must be viewed according to the stage of its development. In fact, it could be said that the self is constantly being modified all through life, even though its basic structure remains more or less permanent after a certain point.

It will be clear that the libidinal gratifications at this stage of primary narcissism are autoerotic in character, just as they were in the previous phase of autoerotism. Nevertheless there are certain differences due to the level of organization that the mental apparatus has reached. The nature of their impingement on the mental apparatus differs from that of the previous phase of autoerotism, and so does their whole relationship to it. They have become psychologically significant in a way that they were not before.

Yet, in order to maintain this stage of primary narcissism the child is extremely dependent on the external environment. During these early phases of autoerotism and primary narcissism, the mother as the child's biological object performs for him a number of essential functions. She acts as a barrier against undesirable or excessive stimuli for the child and is the provider for all of his essential physical needs. She is the most important regulating factor in the constant struggle for the recovery, at least to a tolerable degree, of the homeostatic equilibrium which is forever disturbed by external and internal stimulation.

Furthermore, she provides for certain types of stimulation and forms of body contact which are required as an important contribution for the normal development of the child. They are essential elements, for example, in the development of the body image and of a healthy self at the appropriate time. Her role as the triggering and releasing agency of many other processes furthering drive and ego development must never be underestimated. With the increasing delineation and awareness of the child's "self," that has developed during the stage of primary narcissism, the mother becomes distinct from the self. From then onward an ever-growing psychological awareness of the existence of the mother and her essential functions develops, drawing to her larger and larger amounts of cathexis and interest.

Yet even in the best environments and with the very best mothering, the child inevitably must suffer frustrations. It is the frustrations which, according to Freud, force the next step in development and away from the phase of primary narcissism. Though frustrations are inherent in this phase, further development and maturation cannot proceed without the many ministrations of the mother.

*Third Type*

Gradually we have moved into the next phase in ego development which already allows for true object relationships. A relationship to an object though starting with the beginning of life is at the very first established on a "need-satisfying basis." Out of this primarily biological link with the external object will slowly develop a psychological relationship through the agency of the "ego." "Need satisfying" thus gives way in due time to "object constancy," the relationship to the object growing more and more complex and acquiring new facets and forms of expression as development proceeds further (Hartmann, 1952; Hoffer, 1952; Anna Freud, 1952).

In any case at some point in the development of the mental apparatus the role played by the autoerotic activities is again modified and made more complex by the addition of a new dimension provided by the development of the ego. This new dimension is marked by the appearance of an object-related fantasy life which now attaches itself to the autoerotic activities.

For the special purposes of this presentation I shall choose an example belonging to a state in development long after "psychological object relatedness" has been firmly established. The example is masturbation as it occurs in the phallic-oedipal phase or later. When Freud speaks of the "choice of an object" during this stage, he is of course referring to the choice of an object for the satisfaction of the child's phallic strivings, coming to the foreground anywhere between two or three and five years of age. But now the satisfaction takes place in fantasy. This can be considered the forerunner of later stages in sexual development, where gratification of the sexual impulses in normal conditions requires a partner to produce the release of tension.

Thus Freud said in the *Three Essays:* "It is in the world of ideas, however, that the choice of an object is accomplished at first; and the sexual life of maturing youth is almost entirely restricted to indulging in phantasies, that is, in ideas that are not destined to be carried into effect." In a footnote added in 1920, he continues: "The phantasies of the pubertal period have as their starting-point the infantile sexual researches that were abandoned in childhood. No doubt, too, they are also present before the end of the latency period" (p. 225f.).

A regression to the stage in development in which the object is still in the world of ideas Freud considered important for the differential diagnosis between paraphrenic affections and the transference neurosis. ". . . in the former, the libido that is liberated by frustration does not remain attached to objects in phantasy, but withdraws on to the ego" (1914, p. 86).

At the stage in development "in which the object is still in the world of ideas," the activities remain fundamentally autoerotic; they do not require the active participation of the object or its body (physically speaking), the gratification coming from one's own body. Yet in fantasy this autoerotic activity is object-directed. Masturbation at the phallic phase is generally still referred to as an autoerotic form of gratification which, on the one hand, is accompanied by fantasies that are object-directed, and on the other does not require the presence of the body of the object. In "Hysterical Phantasies and Their Relation to Bisexuality" (1908), Freud said: "At that time the masturbatory act (in the widest sense of the term) was compounded of two parts. One was the evocation of a phantasy and the other some active behaviour for obtaining self-gratification at the height of the phantasy. This compound, as we know, was itself merely soldered together. Originally the action was a purely auto-erotic procedure for the purpose of obtaining pleasure from some particular part of the body, which could be described as erotogenic. Later, this action became merged with a wishful idea from the sphere of object-love and served as a partial realization of the situation in which the phantasy culminated" (p. 161).

The transition from the second to the third stage is no doubt a very slow and gradual one and at this point can be referred to only in the vague terms I have so far used.

## SUMMARY

Each one of the stages in the development of the ego and the self makes some contribution to the nature of the autoerotic phenomena, and they in turn play an important role in the development of the ego and self.

In the evaluation of autoerotic phenomena careful consideration should be given to the contribution of these different levels of integration and complexity and to the use made of them, first by the organism (biological being) and afterward by the ego (at the stage of the psychological being).

Though an autoerotic type of gratification can be forced into the ego in certain situations of conflict or frustration at any time in life, it is also possible that in other cases the ego makes use of this type of phenomena for very constructive purposes. One is reminded here of persons who seem to be better able to concentrate, study, or work when at the same time they engage themselves in some kind of autoerotic activity like curling of the hair, sucking their tongues, handling of the penis, etc.[7]

## BIBLIOGRAPHY

Abraham, K. (1924), A Short Study of the Development of the Libido. *Selected Papers.* London: Hogarth Press, 1927.

Freud, A. (1952), The Mutual Influences in the Development of Ego and Id: Introduction to the Discussion. *This Annual, 7.*

—— (1962), Assessment of Childhood Disturbances. *This Annual, 17.*

Freud, S. (1887-1902), *The Origins of Psychoanalysis: Letters, to Wilhelm Fliess, Drafts and Notes: 1887-1902.* New York: Basic Books, 1954.

—— (1905), Three Essays on the Theory of Sexuality. *Standard Edition, 7.* London: Hogarth Press, 1953.

—— (1908), Hysterical Phantasies and Their Relation to Bisexuality. *Standard Edition, 9.* London: Hogarth Press, 1959.

—— (1909), Analysis of a Phobia in a Five-Year-Old Boy. *Standard Edition, 10.* London: Hogarth Press, 1955.

—— (1910), Leonardo da Vinci and a Memory of His Childhood. *Standard Edition, 11.* London: Hogarth Press, 1957.

—— (1911), Psycho-Analytic Notes on an Autobiographical Account of a Case of Paranoia (Dementia Paranoides). *Standard Edition, 12.* London: Hogarth Press, 1958.

—— (1914), On Narcissism: An Introduction. *Standard Edition, 14.* London: Hogarth Press, 1957.

—— (1915), Instincts and Their Vicissitudes. *Standard Edition, 14.* London: Hogarth Press, 1957.

—— (1916-1917), Introductory Lectures on Psycho-Analysis. *Standard Edition, 15 & 16.* London: Hogarth Press, 1963.

—— (1923), The Ego and the Id. *Standard Edition, 19.* London: Hogarth Press, 1961.

—— (1940), *An Outline of Psychoanalysis.* New York: Norton, 1949.

Hartmann, H. (1952), The Mutual Influences in the Development of Ego and Id. *This Annual, 7.*

Hoffer, W. (1952), The Mutual Influences in the Development of Ego and Id: Earliest Stages. *This Annual, 7.*

Spitz, R. A. & Wolf, K. M. (1946), The Smiling Response. *Genet. Psychol. Monogr., 34.*

—— —— (1949), Autoerotism: Some Empirical Findings and Hypotheses on Three of Its Manifestations in the First Year of Life. *This Annual, 3/4.*

---

[7] Spitz and Wolf (1949) described observations of children in whom some specific autoerotic activities served the purpose of object relationship with their abnormal mothers.

# DEVELOPMENT OF ARTISTIC STYLIZATION
## A Two-Year Evolution in the Drawings of a Normal Child

JOSE BARCHILON, M.D. (New York)

This is a comparative study of some drawings spontaneously made by a little girl over a period of two years, starting when she was four and a half years old. The drawings express a frankly sexualized reaction to a specific erotic threat and temptation, and illustrate at least two types of defenses used by this child against her conflicts. One is a wish to return to the womb and the other her invention of a form of vagina dentata as a protective mechanism. Her reaction to a threat of death, loss of love, and annihilation, awakened by President Kennedy's assassination, revived, in a different symbolic form, the "return to the womb" drawings and led to a pictorial and probably realistic solution of her mourning reaction by an aesthetic affirmation of the love and life forces in her. The drawings of this little girl reveal a transformation of the initial sexualized elements into personal, artistic symbols, which became less and less clearly sexual, until she developed a truly idiosyncratic artistic stylization of the human face. This was accompanied by a definite lessening of tension in the child and an increased effervescence and richness of color and forms in her paintings in general. These observations are discussed from several points of view, but because they highlight a specific artistic problem, stylization in painting, the final discussion is limited to this subject.

## OBSERVATIONS

The child whose drawings are shown in this paper is the daughter of a psychoanalytically sophisticated friend, who lives in a town close

Paper read at the Annual Meeting of the American Psychoanalytic Association, Los Angeles, May, 1964.

From Albert Einstein College of Medicine, Yeshiva University, New York.

to where I sometimes go for a vacation and sometimes spend a long week end. On those occasions my wife and myself are frequent visitors to his house, and I believe that we are favorites with his children. Under those circumstances, permission to publish this material was requested from the parents, and minor distortions introduced in the data to avoid accidental identification. This child will somewhat arbitrarily be named Alice, after Alice in Wonderland. She is the youngest of several brothers and sisters, and her house, like many homes with children, is a beehive of activity. Several boys and girls between the ages of four and sixteen are always playing in, out, around, and sometimes—or so it seems—on top of the house. For some reason, drawing and painting are quite often among the activities of the younger children in this group.

About two years ago, in February of 1962, I was watching with amused interest a group of four or five little girls drawing and coloring Valentine Day cards. Alice and another four-and-a-half-year-old girl, her closest friend at that time, seemed intensely involved in what they were painting.

These two little girls were always together and Alice usually initiated most activities, while her more passive friend copied her innovations, be they in play or paintings. No grownup was supposed to peek while they were painting, but later on, when they were showing me their productions, I saw the colored drawing which little Alice made (Fig. 1). This drawing intrigued me, it was so different from all of the others. It consisted of a series of concentric hearts, each of a different color, and suggested to me a symbolic representation of pregnancy. This was confirmed by the young artist when I asked her to tell me what this "nice Valentine" represented. She replied without hesitation: "Can't you see, it's a baby heart inside its mother's heart, inside its grandmother's heart, inside its grand, grand, grand, grand, grandmother's!" That seemed a reasonable explanation! Because I was intrigued by some of the blue, curly type of hair on the top of the drawing, I asked about it; she said that it was: "DECORATION!" Obviously I had encountered a resistance. When I pointed to the green, bowlike ribbons on each side of the largest heart, asking, "Is this decoration too?" (by this time I felt that the whole drawing seemed also to represent a face and that these two green bows might have been ears), the child who had something else in mind, without hesitation, blasted my theory: "Can't you see those are teeth" and she made a gesture with her thumb and fingers —a gesture which suggested the opening and closing of two jaws or dentures. The bows are unmistakable, yet they have a kind of distant resemblance to the dentures often seen in cartoons and comic strips. I pursued our dialogue, telling the young artist that I did not understand why she had put two sets of teeth on the sides of her drawing, and again she answered directly by saying: "It is in case someone pokes his finger at the little baby heart inside. The teeth will bite any finger that is poked at the baby."

I now understood the meaning of this interesting drawing. About two months previously these two little girls had witnessed something which had made a deep impression on them. The older brother of the little friend of the artist, a boy who was just starting puberty, had exposed himself to them and asked his sister and little friend to touch his penis. The two little girls had not seemed frightened by this experience. In fact, they had told their parents this story at the time with much giggling and making funny faces, and I had discussed the subject with all four parents, by correspondence at first, and directly afterward as a friend and supposed expert. The young artist had shown at various times some preoccupation of a more anxious nature about this event, which she acted out in play and with her female dog.[1] Now the drawing revealed that she had fully understood the sexual, and in fact genital, nature of the seduction. She had understood that the penis was aimed at her genitals including the uterus, that this could result in pregnancy, and had defensively placed herself, in the form of a baby heart through many protective layers of mother wombs; in addition she had placed on the sides of the uteri the two sets of teeth as guardians against danger. The curly "decorations" were no doubt pubic hair, since the girls mentioned that he "was having hair like a grownup." There is some reasonable doubt about this fact. It is not impossible either that the boy bragged or that the two girls "invented" the pubic hair by identifying the boy with either their parents or some

[1] The young boy in question had been in treatment previous and subsequent to the events reported here with a child psychiatrist who told me, a few months later, without knowledge of Alice's reactions or drawings, that the boy had a phobia about this particular dog biting his genitals. Interestingly enough, little Alice curled herself between the legs of her dog, ordering her to bite anyone who might disturb her sleep.

older brother or sister. This drawing, which I kept as an interesting memento, seemed to disprove the idea that the vagina dentata is a purely aggressive construct, motivated by penis envy in the little girl. This construct has another important reactive function: it is also a defense against the fear of being penetrated; in all probability a combination of penis envy and fear of being penetrated is necessary to give rise to a vagina dentata complex. Alice's first drawing also showed that the desire to return to the womb can be precipitated by sexual excitement and threat, and can thus be used unconsciously later on as a substitute for sexual intercourse. One can also safely assume that in the child's mind, the mother needed teeth to protect her babies. In the following year or so there was no reappearance of this type of drawing, nor did anyone pay any close attention to the productions of these two little girls.

A year later when Valentine's Day came around again, Alice's father mentioned incidentally that they were drawing Valentines again, but these were conventional drawings of hearts pierced by arrows, copies of cards they had seen. Sometime around spring or early summer, I chanced to look at the drawing I had kept and found that the colors had rubbed off and faded considerably. Since I wanted a good copy, I sent it to the father with the request that he ask Alice to copy it for me. When he showed the drawing to Alice and her friend, they recognized it at once, giggled a great deal, thought it a little silly, but were not interested in reproducing it. He insisted, mentioned my name, and asked our artist if she would not copy it for my benefit. As a great favor to me, she accepted and very rapidly made a new drawing (Fig. 2). When she finished, she decided to embellish it, with a red heart transfixed by an arrow at the right bottom of the page and by signing her name within a heart on top of the page. (The name is hidden in this reproduction.) Clearly one can assume that of these two additions, made over a year later, the lower one might indicate a return of the repressed in the form of a transfixed red heart. This idea is reinforced by the three crosses, a symbol for kisses familiar to these two girls. The upper addition shows without question an increase in individuation and a transformation of the symbolic identification of the little girl with the littlest heart within the womb: it is now expressed by using her own name rather than a pictorial symbol, while the fact that the little heart is added to the side rather than inside the larger mother heart indicates again more self-awareness and individuation.

In June 1963, Alice made a self-portrait (Fig. 4) as a gift to her father for Father's Day. This drawing was unusual and not quite in keeping with the rest of her drawings because her face was so obviously shaped like an egg. She had previously made only four or five drawings with faces shaped in this fashion. The shape of her own face might have justified the small end of the egg representing her chin, but she invariably placed the small end of the egg at the top of her faces. I can only speculate that the egg was a substitute for the heart and womb, a defense needed against her wish to accept penetration, and a regression to an even more passive union with the mother instead of the father.

The drawing reproduced in Figure 3 belongs to an earlier period. I cannot tell its date with any certainty. It is interesting because it is a portrait of her little friend, the one whose brother exposed himself, and it is shown here for two reasons: first, to show her usual style of drawing faces; and second, she has placed a little bow in the hair which is now definitely there for decorative purpose, yet must have some links to the previous bow-teeth condensation.

Thereafter nothing unusual appeared in her drawings until November 1963 when President Kennedy was assassinated. Alice, like many of her friends, was very impressed, saddened, and disturbed by the President's death. She mentioned to her mother that this was one of the saddest things that she had ever heard of, and that she was very glad it had not happened in her own family. She was a bit subdued, not her vivacious self for a few days, developed a cold, and ate rather poorly. In the few days following the President's death she made drawings 5 and 6. The interesting fact is that she suddenly revived, after a lapse of almost two years, the heart form to enclose inside it the face of Mr. Kennedy and the sad, tearful face of his wife, Jacqueline Kennedy.

The identification with Mrs. Kennedy and her children was carried so far that Alice asked not to be called by a nickname which was identified with the Kennedy family; she wanted her friends, brothers, sisters, and parents to call her by her real name. Yet, since everyone persisted in using her nickname, she resigned herself or gave up this attempt at denial after a few weeks. However, she did not want to watch TV for the few days when most stations were showing the funeral ceremonies. For two or three days she did not even watch her favorite cartoons, preferring to play out of doors, but even then she was subdued and possibly somewhat depressed.

Alice's drawings represented in the center of a heart the coffin covered with the American flag. She might have drawn four or five such pictures; when I visited at her home the following vacation, I asked her if she would give me one or two of them. She decided to give me drawing 5, but she thought that she had "made" the face of the President "too smiley," so she drew it again as it should look when dead, above the coffin in the middle of the heart, and then gave it to me. She hesitated about offering me drawing 6 because, she said, it was not very well drawn; nevertheless, she decided to sign it, interestingly enough by her nickname rather than her real name—but then she did a curious thing: she enclosed her signature within a heart as she had done in Figure 2, but put two eyes where she had previously drawn the President's and the First Lady's face. (The signatures are hidden in the reproductions.) She had thus converted the heart into a full face. This was an interesting development, which alerted me and her parents to the next phase of her artistic expressions. In the next few weeks, among many paintings which Alice had executed with considerable skill around the theme of Santa Claus, reindeer, varicolored forests and houses, Christmas trees glittering with decorations, etc., we found a few drawings similar to drawings 7 and 8. In these she had now created a new style in drawing faces: a face stylized to be completely heart-shaped. There were no obvious remnants of the older sexualized or return-to-the-womb elements. The deep indentation in the heart was even skillfully handled to look somewhat like a natural part in the hairdo in Figure 7. The markedly pointed chin was the only possibly jarring element. As she described these drawings, they were "pretty ladies, that's all." Why were these faces heart-shaped? Because they were "nice and pretty."

In a way that cannot be communicated by words alone, this sensitive little girl conveyed to me that you feel, in or with your face if you are pretty and nice, and that when you have been sad, a heart means that someone loves you and "makes you feel good, that's why you give a heart for Valentine." Unmistakably, she told me that her face was what she felt with, since "You are sad if you look at someone crying." Thus inside the womb became inside the heart, and then *inside* or *in* the face. Hence, to her, this heart-shaped drawing was a transformation (magical?) of something which had made her sad into something to make her feel good, pretty and nice, which were all related.

This raises, to my mind, important issues about affects. Alice seems to be saying that affects are felt and communicated by facial expressions and that it is through those expressions that we perceive affects. Yet she must have felt the usual concomitants of affects: the visceral awareness of changes in blood vessels, organs, and hemo-dynamics inside the chest or in the gut. Is it farfetched to assume that her pictorial condensation of heart and face is predicated on those two different factors, the subjective and the expressive facets of affects? Some artists and cultural anthropologists may feel that the proximity of Valentine Day and its ritual played the most im-portant role, but analysts will point out that the heart as a symbol for the site of feelings, in certain cultures, is no doubt preceded by equations similar to those seen in this little girl. Adolescent school-boys often laugh at drawings of a woman's torso, in which the breasts can be ambiguously perceived as eyes in a face or breasts on a chest. Among countless examples of this equation one may remember Peter Arno's famous *New Yorker* cartoon in which two breasts look cross-eyed, and the Belgian painter Magritte who drew a well-known sur-realistic woman's torso for an illustration to Isidore Ducasse's "Chants de Maldoror" (1938). Was little Alice reaching in that direction when (in Figs. 5 and 6) she made two circles (breasts?) to enclose the faces of the President and his wife? To try and prove this point she was asked to draw a naked woman and a naked man (Figs. 9 and 11). We can see that her picture of a naked woman is not incom-patible with such an equation of eyes and breasts.

It seems, then, that when Alice was exposed to a sexual tempta-tion two years ago she felt some mixture of excitement and fear and this was felt inside the body, chest, genitals, and gut. The Valen-tine Day coincidence gave her a chance to express this "inside-the-body sensation" through her own distortion of a suitable, ritualized symbol: the heart. But she was already aware of the expressive ele-ments in the mixture of pleasurable excitement and fear even though she felt unequal to accepting their full awareness. This is why the first drawing represses the expressive aspects and why the potential face is hidden in Figures 1 and 2. Later as she somehow integrated her experience, she started to accentuate and exhibit more and more the expressive, communicative aspects of her affective experience (Darwin, 1872), so that now the full face took precedence over the more visceral aspects of her feelings. Yet the two elements were condensed and she combined the heart form with the outline of the human face.

In these new heart-shaped faces, the hair is smooth, there are no remnants of the kinky pubiclike hair (which never reappeared after the initial drawings), the teeth-bow condensation is replaced by a flower naturally placed in the smooth hairdo. Were it not for the previous drawings and our knowledge of their sexual antecedents, it would be impossible to see here any specific signs of their past sexual origin. It is "art" of a creative and inventive nature, original for a child of six and a half years. This gradual desexualization and purification (neutralization) of the drawings, from vagina-womb to heart to face, raises many interesting questions about the genesis and function of stylizations (Hartmann, 1939, 1955).[2] For example, in some recent paintings of a landscape with a horse Alice drew a flower, which was exactly like the one placed in the hair of Figure 7. Are we to think that this type of flower, because it now appears in such a normal context, does not retain its unconscious roots and is not derived from them? Is it not also highly probable that under certain stressful conditions, regressive mechanisms and defenses might revive the hidden sexual elements?

An interesting detail, which seems at first sight very simple, illus-

---

[2] These observations fit remarkably well with Hartmann's theoretical considerations in "Notes on Sublimation." For example, he says, "That changes in the degrees of neutralization do not without exception coincide with a change of the aims. . . . aside from primary autonomous ego functions, and before the ego has been established as an organization, primordial aims and functions come under the influence of libidinal and aggressive displacements and symbolizations. In the course of development, their cathexes will be neutralized, and they will gain a certain degree of autonomy vis-à-vis the instinctual drives, which happens in constant interdependence with processes of maturation. Secondary autonomy is certainly dependent on neutralization. . . . Once the ego has accumulated a reservoir of neutralized energy of its own, it will—in interaction with the outer and the inner world—develop aims and functions whose cathexis can be derived from this reservoir. . . . This gives the ego a comparative independence from immediate outside or inside pressure. . . ."

trates the complexity of symbolic condensation: Why did Alice in Figures 5 and 6 draw a rather heavy line across the American flag covering President Kennedy's coffin? She did see a belt tied around the coffin to hold the flag while it was transported outdoors, but this was a very small detail; most of the time and in impressive close-ups the coffin had no belt around it. Yet the little artist chose that one insignificant detail, in preference to many others, to be represented in her highly simplified drawings. Our knowledge of her symbolism authorizes us, after seeing drawing 9, to wonder whether this unimportant detail was not picked like a day residue in a dream (Freud, 1900) because it was suitable to represent, through a safe symbolic derivative, part of the girl's sexual conflicts and regression (Kris, 1950). The realistic rendering of the female genitalia in drawing 9 makes this quite plausible. Obviously, this little girl knows from self-observation exactly how her genitalia are constructed, since she represented them masterfully, unerringly, and in the fewest possible lines. The belt could thus become a condensation of the slit in her genitalia as well as a means of making sure that the body remained securely tied inside the flag (secure inside its mother like the baby heart). An answer which she gave her father when he questioned her about drawing 9 is also noteworthy. Looking at the breasts on this figure, he asked why the nipples were drawn at the bottom. First he drew a blank, but then she said, "That is how the breasts look on a dog." When he mentioned that she must have seen breasts with nipples in the center, she laughed at him, adding, "Do you want it to look like eyes?"

As mentioned above, Figures 9 and 11 were requested drawings, she was asked to draw a naked man and a naked woman. She did this rapidly and without hesitation. As far as I know, she never drew nudes spontaneously even though paintings and reproductions of nudes abound in her home. Figures 10 and 12 are reproduced to demonstrate her easy and spontaneous versatility; an analysis of some of their interesting features would take us too far afield.

## DISCUSSION

If we can witness this rapid, changing symbolization and creation occurring in a child, over a two-year period, what could happen

Fig. 1   Feb. 1962

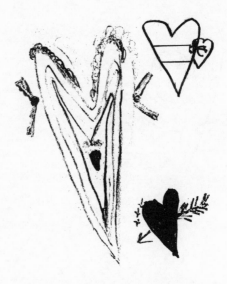

Fig. 2   Spring 1963   (Requested Drawing)

Fig. 3   Spring 1963

Fig. 4   June 1963

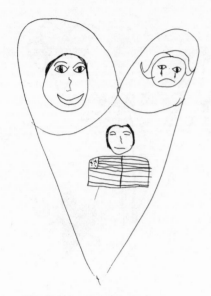

Fig. 5 Nov. 1963

Fig. 6 Nov. 1963

Fig. 7 Dec. 1963

Fig. 8 Dec. 1963

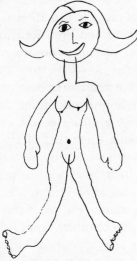

(Requested Drawing)
Fig. 9 Feb. 1964

Fig. 10 Feb. 1964

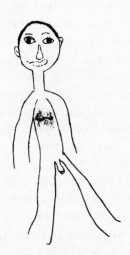

(Requested Drawing)
Fig. 11 Feb. 1964

Fig. 12 Feb. 1964

when a mature artist uses all his skill and art to express some of his archaic conflicts, repressed, transformed, yet seeking expression? As in dream work, the process of secondary elaboration can then use all the symbolic arsenal, accumulated by culture and cross-fertilization of cultures upon cultures. In addition, the personal endowment of an artist can be piled upon the achievement of artists from the past and remove the symbols even further from their origin.

The study of some of Alice's drawings highlights how some unconscious conflicts can mobilize the integrative abilities of the ego (French, 1952, 1954) in several directions, among them that of artistic mastery. It is felicitous that Alice had this specific ability because serial drawings are so eminently suited to illustrate as well as permanently preserve the fluctuations and variations of integration. But since human behavior always occurs on a continuum and since there was no sharp demarcation between the various mechanisms employed by this child, many persons may question my assumption that what occurred in her drawings parallels and illustrates what took place in other areas of her psyche. They may well have a point, but imitating my numerous predecessors in this field (Freud, 1910; Kris, 1950, 1955), I can only hope that the process illustrated by these drawings is a valid indicator which affords us a glimpse into the obscure and difficult problem of integrative functions.

We can probably tell why instead of a neurosis or symptom formation (essentially private types of solution) Alice used other human activities more open to consensual validation, more compatible with further growth and acceptance of social reality (a solution essentially public). Moreover, one would like to say that she mastered her conflicts at a pictorial level and that this was concomitant with and facilitated mastery in other areas of her psyche, but things are really more complicated. We know only too well that the freest creators in art and science are just as riddled with neurotic problems as the rest of us. It is true that she seems free in life and in her drawings and does not have a compulsion to draw heart-shaped faces. In all probability she will remain reasonably free from unconscious compulsions to repeat in this one area. We can only speculate here, and it is far beyond the scope of this paper even to touch upon the compatibilities and incompatibilities of creative art and neuroses (Kubie, 1958); in fact, it is quite irrelevant to our main thesis. What I would like to do is raise a hypothetical question: let us assume that twenty years hence this little girl now a young woman of twenty-seven were to seek analysis. How would her future analyst reconstruct the links which we have recognized in this study? I very much doubt that she will become an artist and paint or draw. Too many children lose this kind of artistic spontaneity before the age of ten, under the combined impact of further growth, the development of more complex associative patterns,[3] inhibitions, and what we call education, which unhappily is all too often a renunciation of spontaneous learning and "invention of knowledge" in favor of a passive acceptance of the knowledge which parents, educators, and society impose upon the child (Barchilon, 1963, 1964).

In all likelihood Alice's conflicts would be expressed verbally since our culture and the technique of analysis emphasize that mode of expression above the others. In the course of her development her conflict will involve or find other avenues of expression, but I believe on the basis of what we often see in the analyses of adults and children that these pictorial symbols are much more likely to appear in her dreams.[4] A close scrutiny of her dream imagery would show, in its full pristine freshness but in an evanescent changing form, most of the elements and symbols arrested for us, in time, by the paper on which they were drawn. By this I mean that while words can express almost anything human, other very human avenues of expression, especially in music and the plastic arts, cannot be grasped by words alone. Freud (1900) recognized this clearly and he demonstrated how many of the elements appearing in the dream images come from infancy and childhood. These drawings, paintings, integrations, and plastic solutions of childhood are more likely to express themselves through the very imagery and style of the dream, an element often neglected in favor of the more easily translatable content of the dream into thoughts, words, or actions.

3 H. Birch demonstrates that memory, which in childhood is organized in patterns around sensory modalities, changes markedly between ages eight and ten. Complex associative paths between these patterns develop and a real integration of most sensory modalities takes place. I believe, and he agrees, that this may be an important factor in explaining the seeming loss of spontaneity and freedom in children's drawings. (Personal communication, 1963, work in progress.)

4 Many patients and children feel the need to complement their dreams by drawing some parts of them. (Since I am not a child analyst I am speaking from hearsay only when I mention child analysis.).

There are quite a few reasons for calling attention to these pictorial expressions. First and foremost, they are valid human expressions eminently suited and culturally acceptable for conveying much unconscious meaning; in addition, they might further our understanding of dreams. Second, from the point of view of analytic technique, it may be important to become more aware of these nonverbal aspects of human communication. Any trained clinical psychologists looking at the last heart-shaped faces of little Alice would be able to guess their bisexual origin and tell us that the deep notch has something to do with acceptance of penetration, while the pointed chin reveals phallic envy, but this is hardly enough.

If an interpretation is to be given in a meaningful way, so that it carries its full affective and intellectual impact, we know that it must reconstruct for the analysand the complex, complete, and exquisite relatedness of all the elements in his neurosis or character traits. When the gleanings from free association become sparse, I have often turned my attention, with fair results, to the style and pictorial elements of the dreams, looking at them much as I would at a painting or other visual art work.

And this brings me to my conclusion: a full understanding of the hidden meaning of artistic stylization may require more than free association with words. At this point one may ask: if not words, then what kind of free associations? I hope, in a subsequent paper, to describe in detail how Picasso, that creator *par excellence*, uses, and even has published many times, a kind of pictorial free association in which he seems to follow in reverse the path which children, such as little Alice, take. One such example, and a very striking one, can be seen in a book by and about Picasso, *Les Déjeuners* (1962).

Picasso takes as his starting point Manet's masterpiece "Le Déjeuner sur l'herbe," a painting which raised such storms and controversies in its day, but which today most people would consider a sedate, even conventional, bucolic scene. Instead of simply presenting us with a new version of that old theme, Picasso offers us close to 200 drawings, studies, sketches, and paintings. These, in my opinion, are much more than studies in preparation for a new painting; or if they are, then these preparatory sketches probe as deep into the unconscious of human beings as does any psychoanalytic process. I would like to highlight here one of their aspects. These studies are like pictorial associations, now to the whole theme, now to some of its elements, and quite often they are seemingly unrelated to any facet of the painting. These free associations are unmistakably a pictorial dissection and analysis which uncovers graphically the hidden psychological sources in Manet's theme. Little by little the relationship of those *two men and two women* having a peaceful time in the country is shown to be full of currents and undercurrents of ambivalence, narcissism, homosexuality, desires for motherhood, masculine aggression and passivity, and the pointed finger of one of the male protagonists reveals itself for what it is: an erect penis. The woman facing him defends herself through a variety of reactions so numerous that they can only be matched by the principle of multiple causality in symptom formation. One of these reactions involves the feet of the woman which, by means of laced espadrilles, turn themselves into all kinds of autoerotic and defensive instruments (much in the manner in which the ribbon bows of little Alice became teeth). We are reminded of Freud's early method in the *Interpretation of Dreams,* when, for example, he would associate to the whole dream and then systematically to its various elements, as he did in the Irma or the Botanical Monograph dreams. The similarity is more than skin deep. Moreover, we must remember that all creative artists free-associate, for long periods of time, in the process of creating, be it with brush, sounds, clay, pen, or ideas. This may be another instance in which the Father of Analysis has resorted to an age-old method from the world of the artist to further our scientific knowledge of the unconscious.

Nor does the similarity stop here. When Freud dissected the dreams into their elements, he was not tearing down and destroying or reducing that complex psychological phenomenon to some simplistic common denominator. He was demonstrating a fact that no one had really suspected before: the complexity and fabric of that neglected, nay despised aspect of our whole self. As he was analyzing, he was continuously synthesizing and creating something new. Finding common denominators does not mean that one is a reductionist, especially since in the process Freud found unknown, unsuspected elements, and added a whole dimension to our psychological awareness. If his discoveries reduced or simplified anything, it was only the amorphous mass of previously held beliefs and errors.

In reality he demonstrated the complexity of the synthesizing functions of the ego even during sleep. This is a fact which detractors of psychoanalytic incursions into art continuously forget when they accuse efforts such as this one of being reductionistic.

I hope to show in my next paper on the subject that Picasso—and for that matter any great creative artist—did for himself, either with thoughts or by weaving thought into the fabric of his art, precisely what Freud did in the analysis of dreams. When Picasso felt that he had reached the rock bottom of Manet's theme, he did not simply paint a satyr having an erection; a woman defending herself against him, while her own man was trying to detach himself from the whole business; and a pregnant nymph in the center background who was involved only with herself and the life within her. Rather, he resynthesized those elements in different relationships and offered us new versions of "Le Déjeuner" in which the basic components are either hidden, transformed, or reveal their presence indirectly.

Art resides somewhere in that metamorphosis and there only, and the workings of what is called Art appear as the resultant of innumerable forces. A few of them, powerful and simple, supply most of the energy and come from the depth of our mind and body. These are unconscious on the whole, and related in their mode of operation to the primary process. In contrast, other forces, almost fully conscious in nature, operating with neutral and neutralized types of energy and more or less under the control of secondary-process thinking, reveal themselves as much the more complex and numerous ones. What we have learned or forgotten through experience plays the more important role in their interaction. While none of the latter reaches any great intensity, by combining themselves they gain more than enough energy to modify and transform some instincts common to all animals into something singularly human. Art in fact is so humanly new and different that one is tempted to assume that it is fully autonomous, obeying and making its own laws and even transcending its human substrate.[5] But we cannot forget that Art is an interplay between those two sets of forces; and its autonomy, power, and complexity, which are real enough, have always collapsed when they were separated from their more base but

[5] New and recent in the scale of evolution, assuming that man has existed for at least 500,000 to 1,000,000 years.

no less basic elements, like Anteus whenever he lost contact with mother Earth.

Interestingly enough, what Picasso did with Manet's "Déjeuner" was really what Manet had done to Raphael's "Gods of Rivers," who in turn might have been retelling us what Giorgione had attempted to put in his "Concert Champêtre,"[6] who in turn was. . . .

In each succeeding attempt these artists have brought us closer to a pictorial expression of psychological reality, conscious and unconscious. They have added something which was missing in the preceding versions. They have marched on, on the path of artistic progress, just as surely as in science Newton and Einstein advanced further than most of their predecessors.

Picasso, in his book, has shown us how a symbolic representation which had lost some of its impact with the natural evolution of our culture was revitalized by being brought into a closer or different contact with the springs and affects of human nature.

Many readers will probably disagree, but it seems to me that the insights of a Picasso and the infantile attempts of the little girl described in this paper have one deep human element in common: Alice has followed the path of "nature," whereas the artist and man of science in order to understand or to "create nature" must retrace that very path in reverse—a painstaking process for which not many men are really suited.

BIBLIOGRAPHY

Barchilon, J. (1963), Some Unconscious Aspects of the Different Teaching Methods. *Proceedings of the 3rd Onchiota Conference*. New York: Albert Einstein College of Medicine Press, pp. 27-44.
—— (1964), Some Conscious and Unconscious Factors in Teaching Psychotherapy with One-Way Screens, Closed-Circuit TV or Movie Films. Paper read at the Annual Meeting of the American Psychiatric Association, Los Angeles, California, May, 1964.
Darwin, C. (1872), *The Expression of the Emotions in Man and Animals*. London: John Murray, 1899.
Ducasse, I. (1938), Chants de Maldoror. *Oeuvres Complètes* [d'Isidore Ducasse Comte de Lautreaumont]. Paris: G.L.M., p. 53.
French, T. (1952, 1954), *The Integration of Behavior*, 1 & 2. Chicago: University of Chicago Press.

6 Raphael's "Gods of Rivers" is only part of a larger painting, "The Judgment of Paris," now lost but known through an engraving by Marcantonio. Giorgione's "Concert Champêtre" at the Louvre Museum has recently been reattributed to Titian.

Freud, S. (1900), The Interpretation of Dreams. *Standard Edition*, 4 & 5. London: Hogarth Press, 1953.

—— (1910), Leonardo da Vinci and a Memory of His Childhood. *Standard Edition*, 11. London: Hogarth Press, 1957.

Hartmann, H. (1939), *Ego Psychology and the Problem of Adaptation*. New York: International Universities Press, 1958.

—— (1955), Notes on the Theory of Sublimation. *This Annual*, 10.

Kris, E. (1950), On Preconscious Mental Processes. In: *Psychoanalytic Explorations in Art*. New York: International Universities Press, 1952.

—— (1955), Neutralization and Sublimating: Observations on Young Children. *This Annual*, 10.

Kubie, L. S. (1958), *Neurotic Distortion of the Creative Process*. Lawrence: University of Kansas Press.

Picasso, P. (1962), *Les Déjeuners*. Text by Douglas Cooper. Paris: Editions Cercle d'Art.

# SOME OBSERVATIONS OF MATURATIONAL FACTORS IN YOUNG CHILDREN AND ADOLESCENTS

MARY E. BERGEN (Cleveland)

The young child and the adolescent share a common problem. Each of them, beset by the tensions of rapid growth, must learn control of impulse. Ernest Jones (1922) commented on this similarity in his paper, "Some Problems of Adolescence," in which he discussed the recapitulation of infancy that occurs during adolescence. During the first five years, he stated, the child learns control over volitional motor outflow; in adolescence he gains control over emotional outflow. In both age periods maturation creates conflict and also, in normal individuals, new capacities with which to resolve it.

The maturational force has special interest for child analysts. We try to safeguard and promote the curative forces of growth in the young patient as we help him understand the problems which have prevented the development of normal outlets and controls. We are equally concerned with the ways in which the patient attains eventual mastery, for, paradoxically, constructive steps toward mastery may jeopardize his treatment. This is particularly true of adolescents whose healthy need to rebel causes them to turn against everything which they regard as external restraint. They feel compelled to relinquish help which they still require and want. The adolescents who act on such a wish are often the ones most in need of help. With these patients it is especially important to find ways to protect them against impulsive action. This paper is based on observations of young children who are learning to master impulse and of adolescent patients with severe regressions who must re-establish their ability to synthesize experience and to control their actions as well as their

From the Child Rearing Study at Western Reserve University Medical School, Cleveland, Ohio. This study is supported by the Grant Foundation.

emotions. Work with these patients suggests that the therapist has a strong ally in certain forces in the individual which strive for mastery of impulse, for order, and for the acceptance of limitations.

## THE ADOLESCENT

The adolescent seems to have a realistic appraisal of his need. Even when in active conflict with authority he may tell parents or other adults exactly what controls he believes should be imposed. When caught up in violent acts he may reveal pathetic attempts to enlist outside aid in curbing his impulses. The adult then is surprised by the vigor with which he struggles against the limitations he has asked for. His apparent sense of reality disappears; he is truly angry and hurt by the fancied narcissistic blow inflicted by outside control. If the adult relinquishes his authority, many of these children resent the lack of control and feel let down, although they may protect themselves and make sensible decisions.

The majority of adolescents and their parents protect their relationship in this period of growth. Parent and child, despite frequent antagonisms, seem to have a tacit agreement to refrain from taking the rigors of the age too seriously. The rebellion ordinarily is worked out within recognized limits.

Psychoanalytic investigations have given us a better understanding of the factors which can disturb the normal ability to protect one's self. Anna Freud (1936) has discussed the primitive nature of the anxiety which threatens to flood the organism as an adolescent attempts to free himself from infantile attachments. We have learned that it is often fruitless and sometimes disturbing to explain dynamic conflicts to certain adolescent patients. In the retreat into narcissism the ego is unable to integrate recognition of the need for self-protection. An adolescent in this disturbed state may seek external help but fear it. One part of him acknowledges the need for limitation so he will not be swept into action by instinctual drives. Another part acts as if protection is dangerous—it may submerge him in regressive love relations which leave no sense of identity.

We have sought clues to the breakdown of self-preservation in the early experiences and object relations which affect the individual's sense of worth. Ordinarily the mother's protection of the infant allows him to experience the impact of the world without unbearable tension—she provides the "good enough" environment which Winnicott (1941) defined. Hoffer (1949) discussed the importance of the mother's role in the libidinization of the body. Other writers have traced the influence of preoedipal and oedipal experiences which may result in strongly ambivalent object relations, and have commented on factors that predispose an individual to acting out. Hartmann (1939) emphasized the need to consider the various elements which affect an individual's adjustment in life—the congenital, maturational, and environmental determinants.

The struggle to preserve life if one is in danger is such a natural reaction that Freud (1917) commented on our tendency to take the immense self-love of the ego for granted and on our difficulty in comprehending self-destruction. This normal tendency to preserve life is not lost in acting-out adolescents. The behavior is a cry for help. The capacity for self-protection continues to operate even when identifications with protecting parents break down and ego functions which help the individual to judge reality and to control action are lost. These children persistently seek help from unheeding parents. The delinquent may reach out for protection through courts and institutions. Some frantic individuals use suicide attempts to gain the control from authorities which they cannot find in themselves or their parents. In these panicky states the patient's search for control seems to have a more primitive aim than the desire to find objects of the past (the forbidding parent or the ego ideal once incorporated in the superego)—he simply wants to protect himself from stimulation which he fears will completely disorganize him.

The adolescent balances the actions which might lead to self-destruction by using them to seek the conditions he needs for survival and growth. He seems impelled to find a safe place for his necessary rebellion. Then he can test new ideas and attitudes against established limits. The purpose of the revolt is not to win or to fail, but to gain the freedom to choose—to learn the limits of authority and to find ways to synthesize the expectations of parents and of society with his own desires. He can also maintain his right to a choice by rejecting the teachings of authority and remaining in rebellion.

## The Young Child

The adolescent employs a process with which he is very familiar. His maturation has always depended on the mastery and integration of new experiences. He has always tested the strength of his instinctual wishes and solved conflicts by identification at other crucial points in his life. In a study of child rearing at Western Reserve University we were interested in observing this maturational process in normal young children. We have been impressed by how active children just over a year of age can be in securing for themselves the controlled, supportive atmosphere they need for growth.

Twenty-one young families, beginning with their first child, have participated in this study. The parents were referred by private obstetricians and joined the study in the last trimester of the mother's pregnancy. We began with a group of twelve families; another group of nine was added the following year. With siblings born subsequently there are now thirty-five children, the oldest of whom are five years old. The parents were offered counseling around the problems of physical and emotional development. The eleven counselors, members of the Departments of Pediatrics and Psychiatry, regularly discuss the data which are obtained from every two-weekly interview with the parents, from observations of the children, and from nursery school sessions. The counselors share experiences and try to balance pediatric and psychiatric contributions in considering various phenomena.

Spock (1964) has pointed out the early age at which self-restraint, unrelated to the mother's specific teaching, becomes evident in the child. At seven or eight months when the child learns to crawl and in every way shows his intense curiosity and eagerness to explore the world, he nevertheless controls the impulse to grab an object presented by a stranger. Some children hesitate only for a moment, draw back slightly, then reach out again impulsively. Others completely inhibit any motion while the stranger offers the object, and will accept it only if it is offered by the mother. This is the stage when children sharply differentiate their safe parents from outsiders and may react to the latter with "stranger anxiety." He also pointed out that babies show particular caution in handling their oral aggression. In the middle part of the first year when a breast-fed baby's first teeth are nearing eruption and he will chew constantly on almost any object, he will only rarely make the mistake of biting his mother's nipple. And then her sharp cry or abrupt jerk will usually reimpose an inhibition that will last for days or weeks. Later in the first year a breast- or bottle-fed baby may deliberately experiment with biting his mother's cheek or hand when he has become overstimulated or tired after a period of play with her. But he goes at this bite with great caution, being very slow to bring his mouth to her flesh and watching her eyes intently as if he expected disapproval. She can stop him with a firm prohibition or encourage him with a sado-masochistic byplay.

When children later show inhibitions against biting, these appear to be related completely to the mother's teaching. One mother described her two-year-old boy's efforts to refrain from biting his younger brother. He carefully held the baby's arm in his teeth, released him, and said to the mother, "You will spank me if I bite him." He was relieved by the mother's firm direction to find another way to express his feelings.

Around the beginning of the second year the child seems interested and ready to use this restraint in social relations of a more complicated nature. The mother usually begins to teach social conformity through cleanliness demands. Toilet training can enlist the child's delight in mastery, his interest in order, and his increasing ability to bring together different ideas, feelings, and demands. In fact, when some of the mothers in this study hesitated in beginning the training, some of the children took the initiative. In a number of ways they demonstrated to their mothers that they were ready. They had the wish to replace instinctual gratification with the pleasure of expanding control of body and impulse.

Several mothers in the first group of twelve families showed uncertainty in training their children. They were conscientious women whose previous exposure to popular lectures, articles, and courses in child psychology had made them unduly anxious about "forcing" a child to do anything against his will. They lacked conviction that training represented an important social achievement for the child. Their indifference or vacillation, however, did not result in uncontrolled messing in all these children.

The mother of an intelligent fifteen-month-old boy was reluctant to begin training because of her concern about his earlier problem of constipation. She had purchased a potty, but had only explained its use to him and had not suggested that he sit on it. She believed he was too young to signal, although he had developed early speech. During her conversation with the counselor the child showed discomfort. He finally approached the mother and tried to pull her out of the chair in the direction of the bathroom. When she made no response, he said, "Potty," in a clear voice. The mother remained oblivious and continued an anxious discussion of his constipation. Two months later the mother announced to the counselor with pleasure that he had signaled for the first time that day. The boy evidently had persisted in his efforts to attract her attention.

Another child whose mother made no attempt to train him found a special place for his bowel movements and carried out a ritual every day. The mother was convinced that the child gave no warning. She told the counselor that he wrapped himself in the drapes at these times. By the time she became aware of this it was always too late to take him to the toilet. The counselor at this point in the conversation noted that the child was wandering toward the window. He slowly wound himself in the office curtains with a far-off look on his face. The counselor asked the mother if the child was now doing what she had described. The mother absently agreed, but when the counselor asked what she thought the boy was doing, she had no idea. The counselor urged her to take him to the toilet. The mother was surprised at her son's willingness to cooperate and at his delight in using the toilet.

Some of the children whose mothers began toilet training reacted to any interruption of their training with indignation.

One mother had good initial success when she began her son's training at fifteen months. This boy had early speech and could say "potty" or "wet." Despite excellent progress between fifteen and eighteen months, the mother was frightened by an outbreak of hives which she believed was the result of emotional conflict, caused by her "forcing," and she abruptly discontinued the training. Actually the boy had had similar skin reactions earlier, and this mother was distressed by all maturational steps which reduced the need for her to participate in his body care. The child took over when the mother could no longer encourage his progress in training and tried to preserve his independence. He signaled when he wished to use the toilet and verbally protested when she put him back in diapers. He insisted in words that he did not want to be a baby.

An exaggerated concern about messing prevented one mother from really supporting the training of her child. But when he was twenty months old she told him that he could have training pants when he learned to use the pot. The boy immediately told her of his need and used the toilet. He fought angrily when she tried to keep him in diapers after this.

But the other side of the child's wish also appeared—his desire to do what he pleased when and where it suited him. Several mothers complained of the subtle child, who quietly shifted his bowel movements to naptime, and of the openly defiant child. The conflict was not limited to toilet training, and the mothers described many situations in which the children ignored the mothers' demands. It was apparent, however, that the child needed to feel that limits existed.

A working mother postponed her son's toilet training until her vacation. A baby sitter had shown him how to use the pot at fourteen months, and the boy persistently signaled to all adults who would respond. He showed resistance to training only after the mother took over some months later and the child felt sure that she would insist on his cooperation.

Another child with an inconsistent mother finally forced her into finding her limits and taking a stand by smearing his feces at age two and a half. He responded to her evident anger by acquiring the sphincter control which he had undoubtedly been capable of achieving for many months.

When the mothers supported the training of their children with more consistency, the emotional intensity of the learning experience was most evident. Usually the children tried hard to please their mothers, but they could be provocative or antagonistic, and they aroused strong feelings in their mothers. When some mothers failed to carry out training, on the other hand, the strength of the child's independent wish to acquire mastery of his sphincters and to learn a socially acceptable method of control was revealed.

Increased autonomy seems to demand not only mastery but synthesis of the new experience. The child tries to fit every accomplishment into the pattern of his life in a way which will please him and those whom he loves. Through this synthesis his more autonomous existence remains in harmony with his environment. The mother's training supports the child's wish to develop further autonomy. His

rebellious moods are not motivated solely by a wish to cling to more
infantile instinctual gratifications. In them he seeks a more realistic
concept of himself by testing the extent of his own power against the
firmness of his mother's restrictions.

A young child creates many situations in which he must repeatedly test reality in spite of frustration. The psychologist who tested
all the children in the study described the increasing rage of a couple
of the two-year-olds. During the test they insisted on trying to string
beads on the knotted end of a cord. They refused advice or help in
accomplishing this task. They seemed determined to learn from
experience how reality limited their efforts. They learned it was not
influenced by their rage. The young child deals with his object
relations in the same way. He perseveres in testing parental limits
as he has persisted in all learning—as if he must overlearn everything to make it a part of himself. He zealously practices maturational
steps—sitting, standing, walking—long after he has acquired adequate motor skill. This repetition may be important in the development of permanent identifications. They too may depend on opportunities in human relations for repeated testing which leads to
assimilation.

## Adolescent Treatment

In the treatment of adolescents one sees the maturational need
for a sustaining emotional relationship which can establish limits
and allow testing of controls. The use of limits, however, is sometimes viewed as a necessary but unfortunate adjunct to treatment
and the positive therapeutic value is minimized. Hacker and Geleerd
(1945) pointed out that the adolescent who acts out regards even
severe restrictions as an indication of a basically friendly approach.
These authors stressed the need for the adolescent's conflict with
authority to be dealt with in treatment. Otherwise this crucial problem of adolescence is acted out in the environment and cannot be
worked through therapeutically.

Restrictions may be regarded as a means of supporting the conflict-
free part of the ego which, in acting-out patients, may be the only
part of their personality that can participate in treatment. These
patients are asking for the necessary environment for growth. Responsibility for control of the patient, therefore, should not be rele-

gated entirely to outside sources. To insist that such an adolescent maintain his own controls puts too great a burden on the weakened ego. Support of the patient's wish for inner organization gives him a sense of mastery. This approach can further analytic therapy, for the feeling of greater autonomy and the more integrated ego which result enable the patient to progress to deeper understanding of his unconscious motivations.

One adolescent patient used uncontrolled, self-destructive behavior to secure help with her severe disturbance. But consciously she was unable to accept responsibility for the treatment. She sought protection against a need to destroy the analysis by acting out her mother's unconscious wish to have her fail. The patient gave ample warning that she felt under this compulsion. She said, "I am never going to come again, but you won't let me stop." She then fought vigorously against the restriction she had asked for with no knowledge of her actual cooperation. When she was not permitted to destroy the opportunity to obtain help, she was protected against a frightening introject as well as from real consequences.

This girl made an important step when she indicated that she wanted the prohibition against acting out her problems extended to her hostile verbal attacks which she was unable to control. The patient was terrified of her fantasies of omnipotence. To think was tantamount to the commission of an act. Whatever she said immediately seemed to come true. No discussion of conflict or explanation of reality reassured her, for the analyst's words also had magical meaning and were regarded as attacks. The girl, troubled by an imminent break in the contact during the week end, began the interview with biting, angry remarks. She tried to be silent, but soon began another attack. She was relieved at the suggestion that the analyst help her control by not permitting the abusive language. The girl nodded an emphatic agreement, but started at once to argue that the restriction was unfair and took away her freedom of speech. She tried a few expletives in tentative fashion, but desisted as soon as she was told to stop. The next day the patient repeated the angry outburst at the beginning of the session, but stopped herself by coughing. After she obtained a drink of water, she remarked that she felt better and could make a new start. For the first time she described a troubling event at school without being overwhelmed by fantasy. When this patient was finally convinced that she could protect herself and others, words were gradually divested of their magic significance, and the many problems connected with her oral aggression could be considered on a verbal level in the analysis.

As she moved into the problems of anal aggression, this patient sensed that her mounting tension would force her again into uncontrolled action. She was not consciously afraid of losing control, but mentioned that if she ever ran away she would be easy to find. She always wore a red coat and she planned to take her kitten with her. "There isn't likely to be another sixteen-year-old girl on the bus to Chicago with a kitten." This announcement was no idle threat, for the girl had run away frequently. Nevertheless, she was indignant when her poor control was pointed out, and she was told that restriction of her actions was necessary to protect her. At first she denied any thoughts of running away, but then she recalled her statements. At this stage of ego organization the girl could accept responsibility for her thoughts, and was able to respond to a verbal prohibition of impulsive action. She was pleased at her success in controlling herself in spite of complaints about being forced to conform. Her next step was to become aware of thought content in periods of stress and to exert her own control over action. She was secure enough now to test authority in less drastic ways and could learn from these experiences. She then began to experience the feelings—usually in isolation —which formerly had propelled her into action. Eventually she developed the capacity to associate thought and feeling.

Early in treatment a second patient was distressed at the suggestion that unconscious feelings could exist and influence her actions. She reacted with panic to the comment that she seemed annoyed because she had had to wait a few minutes. She had discussed the unreasonable reactions of her senile grandfather. Now she burst out that if she resembled him in his unreasonable attitudes, she must be completely uncontrolled and therefore psychotic. Even as she rejected the idea that she might be like him and declared that she would never come again, she tried to preserve the help. "It does no good to come, but I know you will keep on insisting that I do." At this stage she was unable to judge the appropriateness of her reactions, and she could not accept her wish to maintain treatment. She was reassured only by "insistence" that she continue.

Another patient alternated between severe attacks of asthma and impulsive acting out. She had learned to aggravate her illness to protect herself against the consequences of impulsive acts, although the state of helplessness which ensued aroused more anxiety and conflict. The patient was finally convinced that other protection was possible by the analyst's provision of controls, including psychiatric hospital care. She used this opportunity to acquire a maturational experience which her long-standing illness and disturbed home environment had denied her. She carefully outlined how she thought her infringements of rules in the hospital should be dealt with, but was quite indignant when some of her suggestions were carried out. At times she was well aware of her wish to find sufficient controls and told the analyst not to be misled by her impulsive wishes. After prolonged testing of the analyst's limits the girl reported that she first learned to control an impulse by telling herself firmly that she must not act; then when she was able to stop, she carefully explained to herself why this was not a wise action. She was delighted with her self-mastery. This gave her better control over her serious illness.

The internalization of controls follows the infantile pattern with these patients. First they seek help by their behavior, if not by conscious decision. The therapist's respect for their wish to cooperate is essential. Equally necessary are restrictions because they enable these children to reveal their basic problems—how to acquire the control which will result in integration of character. The rebellion then has the element of cooperation. It is not desirable, however, to dilute the rebellious feelings of an adolescent by constantly reminding him of this fact. He needs to feel his struggle.

## CONCLUSION

Maturational forces in the individual strive for mastery of impulse and synthesis of new experience. The young child and the adolescent, who share the task of gaining control over impulse, both try to set up a safe environment for growth. They repeatedly test impulse against protecting limits. In therapy with adolescents such limits provide a counterbalance for self-destructive tendencies. The establishment of inner controls which results from the testing of limits makes it possible for the patients to progress to a deeper understanding of unconscious conflicts.

BIBLIOGRAPHY

Eissler, K. R. (1958), Notes on Problems of Technique in the Psychoanalytic Treatment of Adolescents: With Some Remarks on Perversions. *This Annual*, 13.
Fenichel, O. (1945), *The Psychoanalytic Theory of Neurosis*. New York: Norton, pp. 367-386.
Freud, A. (1936), *The Ego and the Mechanisms of Defense*. New York: International Universities Press, 1946.
——— (1958), Adolescence. *This Annual*, 13.
Freud, S. (1905), Three Essays on the Theory of Sexuality. *Standard Edition*, 7. London: Hogarth Press, 1953.
——— (1917), Mourning and Melancholia. *Standard Edition*, 14. London: Hogarth Press, 1957.
Geleerd, E. R. (1957), Some Aspects of Psychoanalytic Technique in Adolescents. *This Annual*, 12.
Greenacre, P. (1950), General Problems of Acting Out. *Trauma, Growth, and Personality*. New York: Norton, 1952.
Hacker, F. J. & Geleerd, E. R. (1945), Freedom and Authority in Adolescence. *Amer. J. Orthopsychiat.*, 15.
Hartmann, H. (1939), *Ego Psychology and the Problem of Adaptation*. New York: International Universities Press, 1958.
Hoffer, W. (1949), Mouth, Hand and Ego-Integration. *This Annual*, 3/4.
Jones, E. (1922), Some Problems of Adolescence. *Papers on Psycho-Analysis*. London: Ballière & Cox, 1950.
Spock, B. (1964), Personal communication.
Winnicott, D. W. (1941), The Observation of Infants in a Set Situation. *Collected Papers*. New York: Basic Books, 1958.

# A GENETIC VIEW OF AFFECTS

## With Special Reference to the Genesis of Helplessness and Hopelessness

ARTHUR H. SCHMALE, JR., M.D. (Rochester)

Much has been written about affects and their significance for psychic functioning. This paper is primarily concerned with the earliest evidences of affective differentiation. Such a perspective has been of special interest in our attempt to understand the role affects may play in the psychosocial setting of psychiatric or somatic disease onset.

Our group at the University of Rochester Medical Center has been interested in the affective reactions which either accompany or precede the apparent onset of a wide variety of somatic or psychological dysfunctions (Greene, 1954, 1958; Greene and Miller, 1958; Engel, 1955, 1962a,b; Engel and Reichsman, 1956; Schmale, 1958, 1962). The affective reactions of what are being called helplessness and hopelessness have been found to be the most frequently experienced and reported antecedents of disease onset. These affects are considered to represent two different types of ego "giving up," i.e., the ego's awareness of its inability to defend against a loss of autonomy. Helplessness reflects a loss of ego autonomy with a feeling of deprivation resulting from the loss of gratification which is desired from an other-than-self object. Hopelessness, on the other hand, is a loss of autonomy with a feeling of despair coming from the individual's awareness of his own inability to provide himself with

From the Departments of Psychiatry and Medicine, University of Rochester School of Medicine and Dentistry, Strong Memorial and Rochester Municipal Hospitals, Rochester, N.Y.

This investigation was supported in part by a grant from the Foundations' Fund for Research in Psychiatry.

gratification. Thus, in our clinical work, it became important to understand at what point in time these affects might first be experienced and what significance they might have for the growth of intrapsychic object relationships and for the development of ego controls.

Rapaport and Gill (1959) have indicated that a complete metapsychological theory of affects must include consideration of the dynamic, economic, structural, genetic, and adaptive points of view. The genetic or developmental perspective of affects will be the major focus of this presentation.

Rapaport (1960) emphasized that all behavior is part of a genetic series and is viewed "as the product of an epigenetic course which is regulated both by the inherent laws of the organism and by cumulative experience." Among the inherited laws to be stressed here will be the concept of the autonomous functioning of the ego as conceptualized by Hartmann (1939): "A state of adaptedness exists before the intentional processes of adaptation begin . . . we cannot assume that the regulating factors and their relation to the external world begin to function only when the ego is fully developed." The cumulative experience, which is considered an inherent part of the epigenetic perspective, will be conceptualized in terms of acquired intrapsychic self and object representations. A detailed developmental concept of psychic self and object representations has been presented elsewhere (Schmale, 1962).

Affects, as described in this paper, represent the conscious awareness by the individual of his over-all psychic functioning at any point in time. Affects, which begin as a psychic awareness of mostly biological activity, become differentiated as the psychic system differentiates, integrates, and reacts to internal (instinctual) and external world (bodily and other-than-self) experiences and activities. The importance of affects as indicators of the stage or state of the differentiation and integration of the intrapsychic self and the objects with which it has related and is relating will be emphasized.

## EARLY DEVELOPMENTAL STAGES

### Awareness of the Newborn—Anxiety

If one postulates an undifferentiated ego-id phase of psychic organization at the beginning, it is also reasonable to assume that affects have an undifferentiated form during the earliest period of intrapsychic functioning.

Anxiety is postulated to reflect the earliest psychic awareness of biological disequilibrium and is herein considered to be the undifferentiated primal prototype from which all the other affects are derived. Anxiety, then, is the first psychic awareness of discomfort and probably remains throughout life the first and immediate reaction to the perception of psychic tension in any situation.

Although there is probably no psychic perception of the birth experience, Freud in 1926 postulated that "In man, birth provides a prototypic experience of this kind, and we are therefore inclined to regard anxiety-states as a reproduction of the trauma of birth." He also, some nine years earlier, stressed that this reaction was a biological prototype or Anlage which "has been so thoroughly incorporated into the organism through a countless series of generations that a single individual cannot escape the affect of anxiety" (1916-1917). Later in the same lecture he stated that "Anxiety is therefore the universally current coinage for which *any* affective impulse is or can be exchanged if the ideational content attached to it is subjected to repression." Developmentally the duration and degree of preoccupation with the feeling of undifferentiated tension indicate the diffuseness of the ego perception of danger and the unavailability of an activity or a specific defense to control the tension.

As Freud postulated in 1900, "All our psychical activity starts from stimuli (whether internal or external) and ends in innervations. Accordingly, we shall ascribe a sensory and a motor end to the apparatus. . . . Reflex processes remain the model of every psychical function." From birth to the end of the first month of life, the infant responds with global and relatively fixed reflex patterns to a limited set of stimuli. Toward the end of this period, the responses are more specific to various stimuli, but the reflexes themselves remain essentially unchanged. The primary autonomous ego, being at first biological in its orientation and related to instinctive behavior patterns, gives rise to affects which are mostly representative of physiological or somatic processes. In these early weeks of life, it is difficult for the observer to distinguish the affect experienced. In fact, there may be no differentiation or so little psychic awareness that for all practical purposes this awareness does not exist. The psychic process by which the passive taking in of gratification leads to intrapsychic representation is referred to as incorporation.[1]

## Awareness of Approach Gratification—Differentiation of Fascination and Anger

During the third and fourth month, somatomotor organization allows the infant to follow objects with his head and eyes, to grasp with his hand, and to bring things he sees to his mouth. Piaget (1937) calls this the period of first acquired adaptations; Spitz (1951) refers to this as the period of purposive grasping, while Hoffer (1949) considers this alliance as the first achievement of the primitive ego and Hartmann (1939) speaks of this as the first signs of intentionality. This repeated reaching out with eyes, hands, and mouth in an attempt to extend and hold on to activities enlarges the range of perceptual experience. At this stage there is probably no psychic differentiation of the discharge action of the drives from the affective awareness related to this action. There is a perception of pleasure when the action achieves gratification and unpleasure when it does not. It may also be added that at this time there is probably only one representation developing in the mental apparatus and this is one of an undifferentiated object-world-self gratification.

The memory traces of such gratification increase the perceptual awareness of the environment's characteristics which are similar and potentially gratifying. The somatomotor organization in turn facilitates this discrimination. The feelings of what could be called eagerness or fascination are probably first experienced when there is an awareness that gratification is associated with activity. The feeling of fascination continues to have throughout life the quality of gratification through exploratory activity and discovery. (Affects of satisfaction are probably important for the maintenance of specific representations of gratification. Feelings of deprivation or discomfort are probably the stimuli for the further differentiation of object representations, mechanisms of control, and the avoidance of unpleasure [Schmale, 1962].[2])

----

[1] Incorporation is used in an object-relationship perspective as defined by Engel and Reichsman (1959).

[2] Freud (1900) discussed these differences in terms of a tension-reducing experience of satisfaction, which produces memory traces and a perceptual identity, and a tension-

When gratification is not forthcoming as expected, there may be the feeling of what later will be more clearly felt as anger, which may lead to activity (reinforcement of activity) with greater searching or reaching out to re-establish or find again specific gratification previously experienced. Thus anger reflects an intrapsychic awareness of the unavailability of gratification from a previously experienced or fantasied object-activity. The affect of anger may reappear whenever an object-directed activity does not produce the expected results. In effect, it indicates a desire to force an object to provide what is wanted. (Such affective reactions of fascination and anger indicate that an intrapsychic process of actively taking in specific forms of gratification has been established. This process of actively taking in gratification intrapsychically is referred to as introjection.[3])

*Awareness of Need Avoidance—Differentiation of Bliss and Fear*

By the sixth to the tenth month of age, the child has acquired the capacity to differentiate features of mother from other objects on the basis of more specific memory traces of mother, which have been laid down by the repeated experiences of the body-mother interaction. In addition, the child has acquired the capacity through psychic control over his somatomotor apparatus to approach or to withdraw. Another parameter is thus added to the intrapsychic awareness of achieving pleasure and avoiding or minimizing unpleasure. Perception of object-action experiences (including bodily object experiences) in which moving away from or stopping an activity are experienced as pleasure will give rise to feelings of bliss and contentment. The Anlage of this affect of bliss or contentment is to be found in the infant's pleasurable withdrawal from and decrease of interest in the external world after being fed.

On the other hand, the feeling of fear ensues if unpleasure persists or increases at a time when the individual is moving away from or reducing activity. The affect of fear will recur whenever object-

increasing experience of external fright, which leads the mental apparatus to find a way of avoiding a distressing memory of the same experience.

Kris, in an unpublished statement paraphrased by Provence and Ritvo (1961), stated that in an infant comfort serves to build object relations while discomfort stimulates differentiation and structure formation of the psychic apparatus.

3 For a more elaborate description of introjection as it is used here see Engel and Reichsman (1959).

activity is perceived as producing discomfort and cannot be avoided. Intrapsychic representations at this stage of development include an object representation of unfamiliar objects and activities upon which discomfort is projected. A body-mother-activities representation is associated with pleasure and comfort. Thus we see the beginning differentiation of the intrapsychic representations in the memory traces of body-mother-self as pleasurable and other objects as unpleasurable.

The affect of fear, as defined in this conceptualization, corresponds to Spitz's (1950) eight-month anxiety or anxiety at the sight of the stranger. "The reaction can go from 'bashful' averting of the eye to a hiding of the face in the blankets and to screaming and weeping." The turning away or attempting to avoid an unfamiliar object, which results from the affective reaction of fear, is the first attempt of the infant to redirect and detour action in an anticipation of discomfort. This is the first manifestation of an intrapsychic attempt at defense in response to an awareness of discomfort (Schur, 1960). Such feelings may be re-experienced throughout life whenever an activity or object relationship is perceived as potentially providing unpleasure. (The process of actively displacing the source of unpleasure onto an object representation of the external world is called projection.) Specific fears develop as bodily pain or psychic unpleasure is actually experienced, learned about, remembered or fantasied through object-relationship experiences.

As can be seen in the differentiation of each affect, there are elements of the former affects in the subsequent ones. Take fear, for example; there are elements of anxiety and anger in what is described as feeling tense with a desire to find gratification and to avoid or overcome unpleasure. There is also evidence that any new, unexpected, or sudden change in bodily or external world activities may lead to a series of intrapsychic activities in an attempt to adapt to or to overcome the resultant disequilibrium. During such efforts at adjusting, the affects of anxiety, anger, and fear may be experienced in a sequential pattern indicating that incorporation, introjection, and projection have been used in an attempt to achieve equilibrium or to avoid disequilibrium. With further growth and psychic maturation, the choice of any one or all of these mental mechanisms will be determined by the success or failure of past individual experiences in their use.

## Awareness of Mother-Self Symbiosis—Differentiation of Help and Helplessness

As observed by Piaget (1937) in terms of sensorimotor development from the age of twelve to sixteen months of life, "the child ceases to place his own activity in the center of the world and instead conceives of it as maintaining relations of mutual dependence with objects . . . [the child also] considers himself dependent on laws external to himself." The ego of the child at this stage is probably aware of a dependence on the external world for gratification and experiences helplessness when it is not available. The need for help and the feeling of helplessness, when help is not forthcoming, are reflections of the first psychic awareness that the self is separate from the rest of the world. The beginning realization that external and bodily objects are not just for the immediate gratification of the psychic self is referred to by Hartmann, Kris, and Loewenstein (1946) as a change from primary narcissistic cathexis (primary narcissism) to object cathexis.

Helplessness, as an affect, may thereafter be experienced whenever active pursuit or active avoidance of external objects does not bring gratification or relieve unpleasure. The child from this stage on perceives that specific types of mother gratification do not always result from his activities, and he is aware of an absence of gratification for longer periods of his waking time.

There is then a recognition of having to depend on external objects and their activities for help in achieving gratification and overcoming danger. With the assurance of available protecting external objects, there is an extension of activities to explore new territory—to perceive and react to the external world with greater specificity. If undue or prolonged loss of gratification occurs, however, the child will experience a feeling of helplessness.

Feelings of helplessness may recur at any time during life whenever there is a loss or threat of loss of an object which is a supplier of immediate gratification and there is no way found for avoiding or overcoming the loss. This means the object or its activity has been and remains, or has become an active part of the self representation.

Benedek (1956) describes this as the stage of recognized mother-child emotional symbiosis. In terms of psychic representation, loss of mother means a loss to the differentiating mother-body representation. Benedek (1956) refers to this as the stage when confidence is acquired, while Erikson (1950) refers to this as the stage of development when basic trust is acquired. (Thus undue deprivation in Benedek's and Erikson's terms leads to lack of confidence and mistrust.)

To emphasize the need for help and the feeling of helplessness at this stage of development, however, highlights the infant's awareness of dependence on the activities of the mother-body objects. Helplessness, which reflects psychic immobilization, is an expression of the infant's inability actively to pursue gratification along with the awareness of a need to be taken care of by an external other-than-self object.

Although Freud (1926) used the term helplessness to represent the state in which the infant experienced anxiety, he did indicate that developmentally anxiety and helplessness were experienced in two different ways. One was the passive helplessness in the face of tension experienced during the birth process, and the second was the active helplessness which occurs "When the infant has found out by experience that an external, perceptible object can put an end to the dangerous situation which is reminiscent of birth, the content of the danger it fears is displaced from the economic situation on to the condition which determined that situation, viz., the loss of object. It is the absence of the mother that is now the danger, and as soon as that danger arises, the infant gives the signal of anxiety, before the dreaded economic situation has set in. This change constitutes a first great step forward in the provision made by the infant for its self-preservation, and at the same time represents a transition from the automatic and involuntary fresh appearance of anxiety to the intentional reproduction of anxiety as a signal of danger." The affect I am calling helplessness is the second variety of active helplessness which is related to the anticipated loss of the mothering object. This form of anxiety has been referred to by Freud and others as separation anxiety, and as such it is differentiated from free-floating anxiety which is objectless. Thus it seems metapsychologically appropriate to limit the use of the term helplessness to the form of anxiety which appears as a reaction to the felt loss of the mothering object.

Jones's concept of temporary aphanisis probably also applies to this level of affect differentiation. Jones (1929) proposed "the danger against which it [the infant] feels so helpless is the loss of control in respect of libidinal excitation, its capacity to relieve it and enjoy the relief of it. . . . With fear there is first the primal aphanistic dread arising from the intolerable tension of unrelieved excitation, and, secondly, when this privation has become identified with external frustration, the 'signal' dread of this danger."

Spitz (1946) observed a phenomenon correlated with total deprivation of mother-object gratification which took place between the sixth and eighth month of life and extended for an unbroken period of three months. He has called the phenomenon "anaclitic depression." The observed behavior included restlessness, weepiness, rejection of environment, withdrawal from all activities, and finally stupor. Spitz postulated, "Its [anaclitic depression] etiology is related to a loss of love object, combined with a total inhibition of attempts at restitution through the help of the body ego acting on anaclitic lines."

E. Bibring (1953) refers to helplessness as a basic ego response to danger, diametrically opposed to anxiety—anxiety indicating a desire to survive and helplessness indicating a paralysis of the ego because it finds itself unable to overcome or avoid danger.

Rapaport's (1953a) remarks about passivity are of relevance to the concept of helplessness proposed in this formulation: "in the absence of the drive object the organism is helplessly passive in relation to the mounting drive tension and can rid itself of it only by building a complex psychic apparatus by which on the one hand finding of the drive object becomes possible." However, during the period of helplessness, and here Schur (1960) has formulated the possible consequences more clearly, "The result may be passivity towards the instinctual drives and towards the instinctive 'avoidance and fright responses' resulting in the phenomenon of repetition compulsion."

Engel and Reichsman (1956) reported instantaneous "depression withdrawal" with accompanying gastric achlorhydria in an infant, Monica, studied between the ages of fifteen and twenty-four months. They repeatedly reproduced this behavioral response experimentally by having a stranger enter her room alone.[4] From their observations and from the general observation that all biological organisms go through phases of irritability and withdrawal, they speculated that in the psychic system of man awareness of such changes will be reflected in its functioning. In their formulation, anxiety and "depression withdrawal" have existence as biological or pre-ego processes, which constitute two separate primary Anlage for the later differentiation of all other affects. Engel, in a later paper (1962b) postulated that "depression withdrawal" begins as a biological discharge phenomenon and proceeds to the level of a psychological experience (ego affect) when self and other have been differentiated intrapsychically.

Bowlby's (1960a,b, 1961) observations of infants and his writings on separation anxiety and grief and mourning fit best with the helplessness stage of affective development, although his nomenclature, the ages of the child at which various observations have been made, and the theoretical formulations derived from such observations have changed somewhat from paper to paper. He postulates three phases of reactions to the loss of a mothering object: protest, despair, and detachment. The initial phase of protest includes the child's crying, throwing himself about, and rejecting all substitute figures. This is followed by a phase of despair, wherein physical movements are diminished or come to an end and the child is withdrawn, inactive, and makes no demands on the environment. Finally, there is a phase of detachment in which the child shows no feeling, becomes increasingly self-centered, and appears no longer to care for anyone.

Spitz (1959) considers the oral stage of libidinal development to be concluded by the appearance of the eighth-month anxiety (the affective indicator of what he calls "the second organizer of the psyche"). I think that a natural extension to this differentiation of affects in the oral stage of development is that of help and helplessness. Here objects are recognized for the first time as other-than-self, and there is the awareness that the rudimentary ego is unable to

---

[4] "Depression withdrawal" is a description of a specific behavior observed by Engel and Reichsman. It included prompt loss of muscle tone, profound immobility, eyes staring away from or past the stranger and then closing, face sagging with the corners of mouth down and the inner corners of the brows elevated. Sleep would ensue if the stranger remained and was not too active.

adapt without the help of the mothering object. The experiencing of the affect of helplessness indicates developmentally the beginning of the transition from the part-object representation in the mental apparatus to what will be differentiated as body-self and other-object representations. With the new level of intrapsychic organization which potentially also provides a greater chance for security, there is at the same time a greater awareness of danger. At this stage, affects which have previously reflected more of the discharge component of the early need-gratification interaction now begin to be expressive of the limits, delays, and detours which are imposed through continuing experiences of the relationship between body-self and external objects. The alerting aspect of the affects serves as part of the ego's warning system and thus may be important for the initiation of alternate or delayed action.

### AWARENESS OF DIFFERENTIATION OF OBJECT AND SELF

The increasing somatic sensory and motor coordination of the body is also important in the continued differentiation of the bodily self and its psychic representation from that of the external world. The activities of walking, defecation, and talking in an object-relationship context become most important in this next stage of psychic differentiation and assimilation. The acquisition of speech as an organizer of thought processes is called "the third organizer of the psyche" by Spitz (1959); now verbal action (communication) replaces bodily action.

### Awareness of Prohibitions—Differentiation of Goodness and Guilt

During the second year of life, objects which gain intrapsychic representation are related to the child's activities and the gratification achieved in being a part of such activities. There is a recognition that gratification is conditional and dependent in part on whether the external object permits the activity or punishes the child for having engaged in the activity. The affective quality resulting from the gaining of gratification from a self-initiated object-activity which also has the approval and acceptance of the external object is referred to as a feeling of being virtuous or feeling good. In this situation, activity has allowed both drive gratification and object satisfaction.

If the activity meets with the object's disapproval and punishment, there may be initial drive gratification but then object dissatisfaction and no further gratification. In this situation there is an awareness that anger is experienced by the object and aggression may be directed toward the body-self by the external object. The awareness that the danger from the outside was provoked by the way in which the object was related to leads to an affective reaction called guilt. These demands and restrictions on the body-self become consolidated into a special object representation which with the later repression of the oedipus complex will become the superego. Whenever in thought or deed there is a gratification sought which does not gratify this introjected object representation, the feeling of guilt will occur since the desire is perceived as a self-initiated transgression against the external object world. In addition, as expressed by Freud (1923), "the more a man controls his aggressiveness, the more intense becomes his ideal's inclination to aggressiveness against his ego. It is like a displacement, a turning round upon his own ego."[5] Likewise, the greater the gratification found through object-relationship activity, the less intense are the aggressive tendencies and the greater is the chance of the introjected representations becoming more related to the self and its representation.

### Awareness of Self-Control—Differentiation of Pride and Shame

With the awareness of limits on activities set by the external world come not only the restrictions on drive gratification but a greater awareness in general of self activity and accomplishment. (Piers and Singer [1953] and Erikson [1956] postulate that the evidences of shame occur before those of guilt while in Jacobson's [1954] formulation those for guilt come first.) The individual's expectations for himself, which include what he believes his objects expect him to achieve, make up another special representation which also will be important in the repression of the oedipus complex and will become known as the ego ideal. When his goals are achieved, there is a feeling of pride, and ultimately a sense of autonomy will result. When he is unable to live up to these expectations, he feels afraid.

---

[5] Ego ideal and superego were used synonymously by Freud in 1923. Many still consider a differentiation of these concepts unnecessary. Piers and Singer (1953), however, point up their major differences.

These feelings of fear directed onto the self are referred to as shame. The feeling of shame may be augmented by an external object's turning away or avoiding the individual. Thus the ego-ideal aspect of the self representation will become and remain the standard by which the ego measures the worth or success of the self. Here again, success has to include the gratification of drives as well as satisfaction of external object expectations. The feeling of shame will result whenever, in thought or action, the self is unable to accomplish or achieve the standard set by the previously internalized objects. With repeated achievement of goals through object-relationship activity the ideal becomes more closely related to other aspects of the self and its representations.

*Awareness of Sexual Identification—Differentiation of Hope and Hopelessness*

By four to six years of age the child has an increased awareness of his instinctual drive for which he finds gratification in genital identification and manipulation (masturbation). This then marks the beginning awareness of sexual identification and its place in the self and other relationships. The presence or absence of a penis and its size plus the privileges and obligations of various roles become the focus for the child's identification with parents and siblings. The psychic self now seeks additional gratification from objects which are specifically chosen for their genital sexual characteristics and roles. The relationship with objects and the degree to which the objects limit or accept the child's sexual fantasies and activities will be of great importance in the differentiation of the individual's sexual identity. Through the controls and restrictions, which began in the previous maturational period, the child experiences fantasies of being injured (castrated). The intensity of these fantasies will reflect the amount of guilt that the child experiences in his intrapsychic awareness of the object world's acceptance or rejection of his sexual activity and interest. Also of great importance, but more subtle and difficult to recognize at this stage, is the struggle between instinctual wishes and the beginning self expectations.

The child's pleasure in making a sexual identification and in being accepted by the parental objects as having an identity similar to that of the parent of the same sex gives rise to a feeling of hope—

a hope that he is an individual recognized for his own characteristics and accomplishments and that he can choose the objects with which he wishes to relate. A feeling of hopelessness occurs, however, when the child is unable to achieve the wished-for sexual role and in turn the wished-for gratification. No matter how hard he struggles to prove his competence, he is not able to achieve the gratification he desires and in addition he is threatened by castration if he persists in his struggle. The affective reaction of hopelessness indicates giving up the struggle to achieve sexual gratification. The child may experience the range of affective reactions which have been acquired by this stage. There may be feelings of anger, fear, and helplessness toward the depriving object; feelings of guilt and shame toward himself for wanting the incestuous object; and finally, a feeling of hopelessness because his wishes cannot be gratified.

The intensity of the feeling of hopelessness will depend on the degree of guilt and shame experienced in the previous stages of development. If the child has been able to meet the expectations of the parents and still maintain a growing autonomy of self, the wish for sexual gratification will be repressed. The child may then go on to partial gratifications and sublimations which highlight the latency period of development. In any case, hopelessness expresses the ego's giving up in its attempts to maintain the fantasied omnipotence or importance of the self. The experiencing of hopelessness is thus a part of normal development and is necessary for the attainment of a more reality-oriented sense of psychic self. Hopelessness will be re-experienced whenever the self is perceived as too inadequate or too bad to achieve a desired gratification. The only resolution lies in accepting demands made on the self as being hopelessly unrealistic and unobtainable. If the feeling of hopelessness is not too threatening and is not too completely defended against, other more modest and achievable goals may replace the earlier ones. Such a change in psychic self means giving up a part of what has been fantasied and wished for the self. One would expect that those individuals who do not experience a fairly complete resolution of the oedipus conflict during adolescence would have a high hopelessness potential during their adult years. Such individuals would experience feelings of hopelessness whenever life events reawaken their unresolved oedipus conflict.

The affect of hopelessness was mentioned by Freud in "The Dissolution of the Oedipus Complex" (1924). Here Freud describes the painful disappointments expressed in giving up the choice of the libidinally desired parental object, "Even when no special events occur, . . . the absence of the satisfaction hoped for, the continued denial of the desired baby, must in the end lead the small lover to turn away from his hopeless longing." Freud went on to say that the painful disappointments experienced at this stage of development, which are the result of biological inheritance and over-all maturation, have to be overcome or put aside in order to go on to the next level of development.

Thus the more independent and flexible the self representation, the less is the chance that any one change or series of changes in object-relationship activity will lead to the threat of loss and feelings of hopelessness. As discussed by Freud (1924), those who have had completely to repress the unresolved oedipus complex will have a confused self identity with an undue but tenuous attachment to objects. This occurs because of the ambivalent way in which the oedipal objects are introjected as well as projected in an attempt to provide gratification and avoid danger. The longing for complete satisfaction of the self in a relationship with such objects is recognized by the child as a hopeless one and such longing is thus repressed.

As referred to by Abraham (1924), hopelessness is an expression of the ego's inability to achieve a complete love or an unyielding hatred as the result of unresolved ambivalence. Abraham assumed there was some fixation at the anal level of libidinal development along with regression to the earliest level of oral development. (As can be seen in this presentation, the reaction to feelings of hopelessness first experienced at the phallic phase may lead to a return to earlier forms of adaptation.)

Freud (1926) called the transformation of anxiety which takes place during the phallic phase of development castration anxiety. He related fear of object loss at this stage of development to the danger of being separated from one's genitals.

Jones's (1927) formulation of the threat of total extinction as permanent aphanisis, in which there is an intrapsychic giving up along with the total extinction of the capacity and opportunity for sexual enjoyment, fits with the conceptualization of hopelessness presented in this paper. "The nearest approach to the idea of aphanisis, that we meet with clinically, is that of castration and of death thoughts (conscious dread of death and unconscious death wishes)." Erikson (1950) included in his description of the stage of infantile genital sexual curiosity (the stage of guilt versus initiative) the idea that, "The child must regress or forget many of his fondest hopes and most energetic wishes, while his exuberant imagination is tamed and he learns the necessary self-restraint and the necessary interest in impersonal things—even the three R's."

Similarly, as described by French (1952), "Frustration is the realization that a goal to which one is committed is unattainable. If one has been pursuing a goal with confidence and realizes that it is unattainable, hope is destroyed."

I have previously described the relevance of Rapaport's (1953a, 1958) ideas about passivity to the developmental level at which the all-self-oriented world has to be given up. Rapaport's ideas are equally relevant to the level characterized by the need to give up objects with whom one has identified. Such giving up means relinquishing part of the psychic self representation. The ego, which still needs external stimulation to maintain the self and other differentiation, will become passive if its autonomy over the environment is threatened or lost.

One could apply and extend Schur's formulation mentioned earlier in relation to the passivity toward instinctual drives to this stage of development. Here repetition-compulsion phenomena may result from passivity toward the instinctual drives and toward the internalized sources of self esteem and control.

The relationship of the affects of helplessness and hopelessness to normal or pathological mourning and depression is beyond the scope of this paper and will be discussed elsewhere.

Several other conceptualizations in the psychoanalytic literature appear to be related to the same developmental stages as the affects of helplessness and hopelessness. Eidelberg (1957, 1959), in advancing the concept of narcissistic mortification, postulates that the emotion of terror is experienced whenever an external or internal agent has succeeded in, or is in the process of, overwhelming the total personality. It is the sudden recognition of the loss of control over the external world or over the self which produces these feelings. Eidelberg (1959) called these agents, which are perceived as overwhelming, aggressors. One of these aggressors is external, personified, and often perceived animistically. The other is an internal aggressor and represents the power of part of the personality to force the total personality to do what it resents. It is the sense of being overwhelmed with a loss of control over the external world which fits the conceptualization of helplessness. The overwhelming defeat or loss of control over the self is related to what I have described as the feeling of hopelessness.

Two other related states are those of apathy and boredom. Greenson (1949) described apathy as seen in inmates of a Japanese prison camp. He found their interest in sexual activity diminished and restricted; they had completely lost interest in genitality. They were concerned only with food and eating and showed no overt signs of guilt or self-reproach. Authority seemed to be vested in the external world and was no longer internalized. Greenson postulated that apathy represented a regression to a passive, oral, narcissistic libidinal level. "Psychologically, the lack of food is felt as loss of love. This loss of love then diminishes the feeling of self-esteem which results in the feelings of being abandoned." It is this feeling of being abandoned by the external world that I have conceptualized as the affect of helplessness. Apathy may represent the reaction to prolonged, continuing helplessness. Although Greenson has formulated boredom less clearly (1949, 1953), he speaks of it as a feeling of self-administered deprivation and emptiness: "There is a restriction of perception for external and internal stimuli which might remobilize these forbidden strivings." Boredom, which reflects the ego process of repression of sexual aims or object, may be a reactive state which results from a continuing feeling of hopelessness.

The focus of this paper does not permit further differentiation of affects and the fate of the self representation, which is still incomplete at the beginning of latency. Many further important changes must still take place before the self identity can be called complete. A further differentiation of affects will accompany perceptual gratification and frustration as new ideas, relationships, and responsibilities are experienced. Freud (1926) expressed this by emphasizing that every period of an individual's life has its determinants of anxiety. "Thus the danger of psychical helplessness is appropriate to the period of life when his [the individual's] ego is immature; the danger of loss of object, to early childhood when he is still dependent on others; the danger of castration, to the phallic phase; and the fear of his super-ego, to the latency period. Nevertheless, all these danger-situations and determinants of anxiety can persist side by side and cause the ego to react to them with anxiety at a period later than the appropriate one; or, again, several of them can come into operation at the same time."

## OTHER METAPSYCHOLOGICAL CONSIDERATIONS

Rapaport (1953b) and others have considered affects as drive derivatives which in early infancy have a discharge quality and later on develop ego-taming and signal-scanning qualities. Affects in this presentation have been considered as reflecting the total psychic awareness of the individual's psychobiological state at any moment in time. Thus what begins as an awareness of somatic and objectless instinctual-drive tension and is called anxiety is differentiated through relationship activity to include feelings indicating psychic awareness of needs and gratifications and then a psychic self in relationship to psychic representations of objects. Finally, in the adult, affects reflect the adequacy of the self and the differentiation of the ego. Such differentiation reflects the capacity to deal with abstract concepts of ideals and goals for the self in an object world. The specific affect perceived at any moment in time may include a psychic awareness of the composite of sensations, ideas, thoughts, and actions and will indicate the degree to which these forces are integrated or opposi-tional. In this paper I have said little about the specific role of affects as motivational forces for ego differentiation although much could be inferred. The role of various affects in the differentiation and in-tegration of various ego processes must be systematically studied. It is yet to be determined whether affects should be conceptualized primarily in terms of quantitative energy forces or qualitative per-ceptions of the ego's adaptive autonomy. However, it can be said that irrespective of whether affects are endowed with psychic energy or not, they are indicators of the level of ego functioning and are representative of the ego's activities and attempts to maintain the self representation in an interaction with the object representations.

No specific mention has been made of the topographic model in this formulation of affects; however, following through on the theme of affects representing the intrapsychic awareness of the individual's psychophysiobiological state at any moment in time, it is assumed that affects are conscious phenomena. Freud's formulation of affects as presented in his paper on "The Unconscious" (1915) is relevant here. He said, "In every instance where repression has succeeded in inhibiting the development of affects, we term those affects (which we restore when we undo the work of repression) 'unconscious'. Thus it cannot be denied that the use of the terms in question is consistent; but in comparison with unconscious ideas there is the important difference that unconscious ideas continue to exist after repression as actual structures in the system *Ucs.*, whereas all that corresponds in that system to unconscious affects is a potential beginning which is prevented from developing. Strictly speaking, then, and although no fault can be found with the linguistic usage, there are no unconscious affects as there are unconscious ideas. But there may very well be in the system *Ucs.* affective structures which, like others, become conscious. The whole difference arises from the fact that ideas are cathexes—basically of memory-traces—whilst affects and emotions correspond to processes of discharge, the final manifestations of which are perceived as feelings." The formulation proposed in this paper separates the discharge from the perceptual process, and only perceptual awareness is considered appropriate to be labeled affect or feeling. Nevertheless, it is accepted that early in development, and in threatening or traumatic situations, differentiation of perceptual awareness of tension and the discharge which follows are more theoretical than real and observable. Likewise, early in development, it is difficult to distinguish between conscious and unconscious levels of psychic activity.

Another important question is whether affects can be utilized as a means of defense as suggested by many investigators, including Jones (1929), who postulated a layering of affects with one defending against the perception of another. In view of Freud's (1915) theoretical formulation of affects, this is difficult to accept. "In the first place, it may happen that an affective or emotional impulse is perceived, but misconstrued. Owing to the repression of its proper representative it has been forced to become connected with another idea, and is now regarded by consciousness as the manifestation of that idea." The inborn apparatuses of the ego, which include thresholds and inhibiting mechanisms, are the sources for defense, and it is the perception of how well these ego mechanisms or defenses are working that gives rise to what is called affects. Indeed, the affects themselves may be important for the development and differentiation of the mental mechanisms which in turn may become ego defenses. Affects, which express the summation of intrapsychic awareness of object-relationship activity, also may indicate which defensive pattern is in use and how effective or ineffective it is. Affects may also presage a change in defenses by indicating to the ego a need for a change in defense. In this regard, affects are signals indicating which pleasures or dangers are anticipated. The ideational content of the affects relates to the recall of previous experiences and may in turn give rise to an affect for which an action or a defense is sought. Some authors consider the awareness of danger or disequilibrium as the beginning of, or a part of, the ensuing defense, but there is some utility in considering the perceptual alerting and the action which follows as separate processes.

## Conclusion

Anxiety is conceptualized as the most primal of the affects, and represents an awareness of disequilibrium during the earliest and most undifferentiated psychic state. Over the first year of life, a series of intrapsychic mechanisms are acquired epigenetically which have their prototype in sensory and motor experiences. When these sensory and motor activities lead to gratification, the affects of fascination, bliss, and trust are differentiated from anxiety, and there is an increasing tendency to form mental representations of the gratifying activities. When the sensory and motor activities do not provide gratification, the affects of anger, fear, and helplessness are differentiated from anxiety, and there is a further differentiation of intrapsychic mechanisms for displacing, tolerating, and overcoming the awareness of a need for gratification.

Biological growth and sensorimotor experiences continue to play an important role in facilitating the intrapsychic differentiation of self and other from the second to the fourth year of life. When activities are successful in achieving gratification, the affects of goodness, pride, and hope are differentiated. When these activities are unsuccessful in achieving gratification, the affects of guilt, shame, and hopelessness are differentiated, and the mechanisms of introjection and projection are further differentiated in order to create a means of defending against feelings of frustration.

The affects of helplessness and hopelessness are recognized as affects of intrapsychic "giving up" which highlight two critical periods in the differentiation of ego processes and the crystallization of the self representation.

The affect of helplessness is postulated to occur first at the end of the oral phase of psychosexual development when there is a dawning awareness of a separate identity from mother. Along with this goes a recognition that a relationship with mother is necessary, although she is no longer perceived as the automatically all-providing object. If objects are inconsistently gratifying at this level of development, the child may not develop the trust and confidence necessary for the further intrapsychic differentiation of self and objects; he may remain sensitive to all shifts or changes in his gratification coming from the external world; thus relative autonomy from the external environment may not occur. At times of actual loss or even threat of loss of gratification, the feeling of being deprived by the external environment and being powerless to do anything about the needs which remain ungratified will recur.

If in the course of psychic development the feeling of helplessness is not too overwhelming or is not too quickly defended against or overcome by an overprotective object, the feeling will lead to an acceptance of or trust in a relationship with objects for the re-experiencing of gratification.

The affect of hopelessness is postulated to occur first during the phallic phase when on the one hand there is an increased awareness of sexual wishes and on the other hand incestuous gratification is not permitted. If objects are overseductive or inconsistently gratifying at this stage of development, it may be difficult to repress the oedipal wishes and thus a fantasied hope for sexual gratification and a weak ego autonomy in relation to the external world may develop. If objects are too restrictive and controlling, there may be a more complete repression and excessive ego control over the unresolved oedipal complex. With any actual loss or threat of loss of gratification, a feeling of hopelessness may be re-experienced which will be perceived as resulting from an inability to overcome a feeling of personal failure.

The experiencing of the feeling of hopelessness in relation to unfulfilled aspirations may, if not too overwhelming or too quickly defended against, lead to a giving up of fantasied wishes. Such giving up is basic to the acceptance of a more realistic sense of self as well as to a more appropriate and realistic awareness of the object world.

The experiencing of the affects of helplessness and hopelessness indicates that an actual, threatened, fantasied, or reawakened unresolved loss for the psychic self has occurred—a loss for which there is at the moment the affect is experienced no available recompense. A change in psychic self may be necessary to meet and maintain ego autonomy over the ever-pressing instinctual drives and the bodily and external objects. In order to remain reality oriented and psychically as well as somatically healthy, such changes in self representation are repeatedly required as man grows, explores, achieves, ages, and declines. Freud (1914) expressed this same idea in somewhat different terms: "A strong egoism is a protection against falling ill, but in the last resort we must begin to love in order not to fall ill, and we are bound to fall ill if, in consequence of frustration, we are unable to love."

### BIBLIOGRAPHY

Abraham, K. (1924), A Short Study of the Development of the Libido, Viewed in the Light of Mental Disorders. *Selected Papers on Psycho-Analysis*. London: Hogarth Press, 1948, p. 418.
Benedek, T. (1956), Toward the Biology of the Depressive Constellation. *J. Amer. Psa. Assn.*, 4:389.
Bibring, E. (1953), The Mechanism of Depression. In: *Affective Disorders*, ed. P. Greenacre. New York: International Universities Press, p. 13.
Bowlby, J. (1960a), Grief and Mourning in Infancy and Early Childhood. *This Annual*, 15:9.
—— (1960b), Separation Anxiety. *Int. J. Psa.*, 41:14.
—— (1961), Process of Mourning. *Int. J. Psa.*, 43:317.
Eidelberg, L. (1957), Narcissistic Mortification. *Psa. Quart.*, 31:657.
—— (1959), The Concept of Narcissistic Mortification. *Int. J. Psa.*, 40:163.
Engel, G. L. (1955), Studies of Ulcerative Colitis: III. The Nature of the Psychologic Processes. *Amer. J. Med.*, 19:213.
—— (1962a), *Psychological Development in Health and Disease*. Philadelphia: Saunders.

—— (1962b), Anxiety and Depression-Withdrawal: The Primary Affects of Unpleasure. *Int. J. Psa.*, 43:89.

—— & Reichsman, F. (1956), Spontaneous and Experimentally Induced Depression in an Infant with Gastric Fistula: A Contribution to the Problem of Depression. *J. Amer. Psa. Assn.*, 4:428.

—— (1959), On Identification. Letter to the Editor. *Int. J. Psa.*, 40:60.

Erikson, E. H. (1950), *Childhood and Society.* New York: Norton.

—— (1956), The Problem of Ego Identity. *J. Amer. Psa. Assn.*, 4:56.

French, T. (1952), *The Integration of Behavior,* Vol. 1. Chicago: University of Chicago Press.

Freud, A. (1960), Discussion of Dr. John Bowlby's Paper. *This Annual,* 15:58.

Freud, S. (1900), The Interpretation of Dreams. *Standard Edition,* 4 & 5. London: Hogarth Press, 1953.

—— (1914), On Narcissism: An Introduction, *Standard Edition,* 14:67. London: Hogarth Press, 1957.

—— (1915), The Unconscious. *Standard Edition,* 14:159. London: Hogarth Press, 1957.

—— (1916-1917), Introductory Lectures on Psycho-Analysis. *Standard Edition,* 15 & 16. London: Hogarth Press, 1963.

—— (1920), Beyond the Pleasure Principle. *Standard Edition,* 18:7. London: Hogarth Press, 1955.

—— (1923), The Ego and the Id. *Standard Edition,* 19:3. London: Hogarth Press, 1961.

—— (1924), The Dissolution of the Oedipus Complex. *Standard Edition,* 19:173. London: Hogarth Press, 1961.

—— (1926), Inhibitions, Symptoms and Anxiety. *Standard Edition,* 20:77. London: Hogarth Press, 1959.

Greene, W. (1954), Psychological Factors and Reticuloendothelial Disease: I. Preliminary Observations on a Group of Males with Lymphomas and Leukemias. *Psychosom. Med.,* 16:220.

—— (1958), Early Object Relations, Somatic Affective, and Personal: An Inquiry into the Psychology of the Mother-Child Unit. *J. Nerv. Ment. Dis.,* 26:225.

—— & Miller, G. (1958), Psychological Factors and Reticuloendothelial Disease: IV. Observations on a Group of Children and Adolescents with Leukemia: An Interpretation of Disease Development in Terms of the Mother-Child Unit. *Psychosom. Med.,* 20:124.

Greenson, R. R. (1949), The Psychology of Apathy. *Psa. Quart.,* 18:290.

—— (1953), On Boredom. *J. Amer. Psa. Assn.,* 1:7.

Hartmann, H. (1939), *Ego Psychology and the Problem of Adaptation.* New York: International Universities Press, 1958.

—— Kris, E., & Loewenstein, R. M. (1946), Comments on the Formation of Psychic Structure. *This Annual,* 2:11.

Hoffer, W. (1949), Mouth, Hand and Ego-Integration. *This Annual,* 3/4:50.

Jacobson, E. (1954), The Self and the Object World. *This Annual,* 9:75.

Jones, E. (1927), The Early Development of Female Sexuality. *Int. J. Psa.,* 8:1.

—— (1929), Fear, Guilt and Hate. *Int. J. Psa.,* 10:383.

Kanner, L. (1942), Autistic Disturbances of Affective Contact. *Nerv. Child,* 2:217.

Mahler, M. S. (1952), On Child Psychosis and Schizophrenia: Autistic and Symbiotic Infantile Psychoses. *This Annual,* 7:386.

Piaget, J. (1937), *The Construction of Reality in the Child.* New York: Basic Books, 1954.

Piers, G. & Singer, M. B. (1953), *Shame and Guilt.* Springfield: Thomas.

Provence, S. & Ritvo, S. (1961), Effects of Deprivation on Institutionalized Infants: Disturbances in Development and of Relationships to Inanimate Objects. *This Annual,* 16:189.

Rapaport, D. (1953a), Metapsychological Considerations Concerning Activity and Passivity (unpublished MS.).
—— (1953b), On the Psychoanalytic Theory of Affects. *Int. J. Psa.*, 34:177.
—— (1958), The Theory of Ego Autonomy: A Generalization. *Bull. Menninger Clin.*, 22:13.
—— (1960), *The Structure of Psychoanalytic Theory* [*Psychological Issues*, Monogr. 6]. New York: International Universities Press.
—— & Gill, M. M. (1959), The Points of View and Assumptions of Metapsychology. *Int. J. Psa.*, 40:153.
Schmale, A. (1958), Relationship of Separation and Depression to Disease. *Psychosom. Med.*, 20:259.
—— (1962), Needs, Gratifications and the Vicissitudes of the Self Representation: A Developmental Concept of Psychic Object Relationships. *The Psychoanalytic Study of Society*, 2:9. New York: International Universities Press.
Schur, M. (1960), Phylogenesis and Ontogenesis of Affect- and Structure-Formation and the Phenomenon of Repetition Compulsion. *Int. J. Psa.*, 41:275.
Spitz, R. A. (1946), Anaclitic Depression: An Inquiry into the Genesis of Psychiatric Conditions in Early Childhood. *This Annual*, 2:313.
—— (1950), Relevancy of Direct Infant Observation. *This Annual*, 5:66.
—— (1951), Purposive Grasping. *J. Personal.*, 1:141.
—— (1953), Aggression: Its Role in the Establishment of Object Relations. In: *Drives, Affects, Behavior*, ed. R. M. Loewenstein. New York: International Universities Press, p. 126.
—— (1959), *A Genetic Field Theory of Ego Formation*. New York: International Universities Press, p. 38.
—— & Wolf, K. M. (1949), Autoerotism: Some Empirical Findings and Hypotheses on Three of Its Manifestations in the First Year of Life. *This Annual*, 3/4:85.
Wolff, P. (1959), Observations on Newborn Infants. *Psychosom. Med.*, 21:110.

# CLINICAL CONTRIBUTIONS

# A BRIEF COMMUNICATION ON CHILDREN'S REACTIONS TO THE ASSASSINATION OF THE PRESIDENT

AUGUSTA ALPERT, PH.D. (New York)

These notes are based on excerpts from therapeutic sessions as reported in supervision, and cover one boy aged four and a half, twin boys aged five and a half, and another boy aged six and a half.[1] On the basis of age one would expect at least three of these boys to be in the oedipal phase and one in early latency, but their psychosexual development shows them to be at various substages in the phallic-oedipal phase.

The double tragedy of the killing of President Kennedy, the "father-of-his country," and of his assassin was a concrete and dramatic demonstration of the law of talion which characterizes the superego of this development stage. We should expect, therefore, that the anxiety and guilt of these boys would be heavily reinforced by this event. On the other hand, the fact that they became aware of the event, with one exception, in their home and in the presence of mother (and father), would tend to have an attenuating effect on their anxiety. The parents of the exception, the four-and-a-half-year-old, were out of town attending a wedding. A further fact to keep in mind is that the first therapeutic sessions with these children were held after a long week end of viewing, in the midst of the family, the full pageantry of the event, with ample time in which to assimilate, elaborate, and repress what they had seen and heard. Notwithstanding all this, the marked shift in defenses seen in the therapeutic sessions leaves no doubt as to the anxiety-arousing effect of the event.

---

These notes were presented at a Panel on "Children's Reactions to the Death of the President," Albert Einstein College of Medicine, April 3, 1964.

[1] These children attend the Nursery and are in individual treatment at the Child Development Center, New York City.

*Freddy,* four and a half years old is deeply attached to his father and ambivalent toward his mother. Before the assassination, in analysis and out, he was obsessed with games of "get-the-enemy." But this externalization of his aggressive feelings was coupled with a turning of the aggression against himself in the form of accident proneness and depression. He is the little boy whose parents were out of town attending a wedding during the week end of the assassination.

Freddy's therapist[2] reported that in his first therapeutic hour after the events, "Freddy did not mention Kennedy's death. However, there was a change in his behavior. Whereas he had been playing shooting games, he now was subdued and depressed. He requested we have a party and began to drink from the doll bottle, something he had never done in previous periods of depression. For the next two weeks there were no shooting games. Instead, he began to impersonate a bull, confined in a fenced-off area. He developed a ticlike clearing of the throat, which proved to be 'angry noises' of the otherwise gentle bull."

His defense shifted from identification with the aggressor, which had never adequately bound his anxiety, to *avoidance,* a primitive protection against pain, and *regression,* i.e., drinking from the bottle. The latter may also represent a regressive attempt to repair the damage of the early relationship with the mother and to establish a more positive, less ambivalent one (in transference). A further attempt is made to control his aggression in identifying with a gentle, confined bull, i.e., by *restriction* of his own aggression as expressed previously in the shooting games. The ticlike throat clearing is an interesting symptom condensing a reaction against the self-imposed restraint, with aggression in miniature.

Though not strictly on the subject of defenses, another example of condensation in Freddy's analytic hours following the assassination suggests that a climate of anxiety is favorable to such distortion of the thought process. He described Kennedy as having been "the most important man" and referred to Mrs. Kennedy's putting the wedding ring on his finger; Freddy then talked of his own father, who was the "best man" and had the ring at the wedding. Thus the two fathers lent themselves readily to a fusion of images and some confusion as to who the dead hero was, especially in the absence of Freddy's father.

[2] Mrs. Charlotte Kearney.

One can speculate on the accretions which such a condensation would acquire over the years and its implication for the analytic work.

Saul, a five-and-a-half-year-old twin, was the first-born of the two boys. Typically, he was from the beginning taken over as the mother's boy, whereas the second twin, Roy, was related to the father, as his boy. This continued over the years and of necessity placed an indelible stamp on their personality development.[3] Saul is the passive member of the twinship, with an already clearly masochistic orientation. Both in therapy and in the Nursery, his libidinal development at the time preceding the event was that of a barely phallic boy, with a rich fantasy life dealing mainly with sadomasochistic themes. These were often interrupted by welling up of anxiety for which *projection*, turning *aggression against self*, and *regression* were his main defenses. The therapeutic period immediately preceding Kennedy's assassination was full of overdetermined fire play, with better sustained phallic behavior in the Nursery and at home. He started his first therapy session after the event by jumping into his therapist's[4] lap and kissing her on both cheeks, taking her by surprise. His mood was euphoric and his first words on meeting the therapist were, "I wasn't sure you would come today." Still in a euphoric mood, and out of context, with a note of uncertainty he said, "My mother loves me—she really loves me." He showed very little interest in the fire games and was furtive in what lukewarm approaches he made. He made no reference to President Kennedy until the therapist made some comment on the long week end, to which Saul replied in a *flat* voice, "Kennedy was shot." "For the rest of the hour," Miss Tejessy reports, "he tried to be a terribly good boy, carefully cleaning up what messes he made. When I said he was trying to be so good, his answer was, 'It isn't fair that you should have to clean it up.' "

In terms of defenses, this boy's behavior seems to say: it is safest

---

3 This confirms my observations of a number of twins treated over the years at the Child Development Center. The mother reacts to the first twin as the expected child. The second one is either an extra "gift" or more often an extra burden. The extent to which the second twin is rejected or neglected or overprotected varies with the mother's health or pathology. Similarly, the role of the father in the emotional vacuum between the mother and the second twin also varies in accordance with observable variables. But the broad pattern I speak of here, i.e., mother—first twin and father—second twin, is a verifiable phenomenon, which has been insufficiently studied in its effect on the personality development of twins.

4 Miss Charlotte Tejessy.

to be mommy's and therapist's good little boy, i.e., via *regression* and *identification* with her, away from hostile fantasies and phallic mastery which he had only so recently permitted himself with the help of the therapist. The accompanying mood of *euphoria* is appropriate for the reunion with the primary love object, i.e., mother, as it is for the renunciation of hostile, rivalrous feelings toward father (and twin), a triumph of the barely nascent superego. It also represents a *reversal of the affect* of sadness. The euphoria disappeared soon enough, and in the next sessions he remained regressed: wanting to be picked up, passive, enuretic, sickish, sleepy, in fact, just as he had appeared before therapy.

In the Nursery, his teachers'[5] diary notes state that Saul, looking at the picture of Mrs. Kennedy, said, "She's a widow now. I have some good advice for her and she'd better listen: she should marry President Kennedy's brother and make some more babies." It is consistent with this boy's feminine identification that his chief interest should be with the widowed wife-mother. It also confirmed what we have already glimpsed in therapy, i.e., that Saul's oedipal fantasies are fused with his twin rivalry. Thus the surviving brother, he, will marry the wife of his dead brother, Roy.

*Roy,* the second twin, was forced, as we saw, into an early identification with the father, who is given to emphatic statements of how much *he* resembles his son. It is not surprising that Roy's most available defense before therapy and in therapy has been *identification with the aggressor.* This took on phallic rivalry with the father whom he vastly admired and envied. Dressed in his defensive armor, he was something of a caricature, what with his bombast and managerial manner. But barely beneath the surface lurked the hopelessly frustrated and anxious little boy. He was a one-defense boy.

In his first therapeutic session after the event, he came down *sucking his thumb,* by no means typical for him. "On the way down," according to his therapist,[6] "he asked, 'Did you hear the President was killed? There is a new President Johnson. The man who killed the President was shot by a man named Ruby, who is now in the county jail . . . I feel sad.' In the room he drew a picture of a donkey and three tails and said he was going to play Pin-the-Tail-on-the-

---

[5] Mrs. Harriet Cuffaro and Miss Paige Epps.
[6] Mrs. Harriet Berchenko.

Donkey. He peeked in order to pin the tail precisely. (He had not played this game over the week end, nor ever before in therapy.) Roy then played briefly with puppets: the boy puppet says, 'I'm so angry, I could bust,' then he strikes the other boy puppet who complains to mother who calls the doctor. He then lines up some plastic policemen, blows them over, saying: 'I'm like a bad giant and they are good.' He cuts off the hands and head of one policeman and then decapitates another. He interrupts this and then selects a book to be read to: about a little girl who grows bigger and bigger and can do many things, again sucking his thumb while listening; asks to leave because he'd like to tell his brother what he did to the policemen."

*Regression* is seen in the thumb sucking. This is followed by an attempt at *mastery* by a detailed verbal account. Then comes the *undoing* of castration death by means of the donkey game, which incidentally fits in with the dismemberment fantasies, shared with his twin, only to be followed by a frank expression of his hostile fantasies vented on his twin brother (puppet) and the policemen. It is after this break-through that he *regresses* again in the choice of story, "The Little Girl Who Grew Bigger," as well as in the *passive receptive* attitude, so untypical of him. But apparently his defensive shifts have failed to subdue his guilt-laden anxiety and he asks to leave so he can tell his brother what he did to the policemen, presumably to share the guilt.

By Christmas, Roy recovered and returned to his old defense. The teachers report that he came to the Nursery after the holidays announcing that he was President Lyndon Johnson and insisting on being called Lyndon. In the sessions, his most reliable defense, identification with the aggressor, appeared less protective. As late as January 23, he interrupted the reading of "Bunny Book" at the point when Bunny becomes the Mayor, with, "Oh, no, there may be a shot!"

The family, a closely knit unit, often behaves in a *folie-à-quatre* style, which does not help these boys to differentiate between fantasy and reality. Thus during the recovery period, the father was elected President of his professional organization, but the parents had decided to keep these happy tidings from the boys lest they worry that their father may be shot. I was reminded by Roy's teacher, Mrs. Cuffaro, that in October both twins had received from their parents miniature pistols of the type used in the assassination of Lincoln, and had acted out for the group the shooting of Lincoln (Roy), by his brother, Saul. The father's name is very like Abraham. Thus the twins' oedipal fantasy is intimately associated with the fate of presidents! The group play in the Nursery, following the assassination, as reported by the teachers, indicates the typical defense of mastery-through-play, and consists of re-enacting the funeral pageantry, and of undoing the assassination: a "funny play" was put on about killing the President who then gets up and makes funny faces (clearly indicating the wish: Ha, ha—he's not really dead!). One child, not in my report, looked at the picture of Kennedy and passionately called him "Stupid," thus expressing his contempt and anger at the father who dies. The outburst was followed by a kiss of undoing.

*Martin,* six and a half years old, now in first grade in public school, is chronologically in latency, but in his psychosexual development he is deeply involved in his phallic-oedipal conflict. He came into therapy about one and a half years ago with severe narcissistic anxiety against which he defended himself with *strong omnipotent fantasies,* and when these failed, with *deep regression* into immobility. But these ego weaknesses in reality testing and in identity were beginning to be compensated for in therapy by the time of this report. *Denial* of painful reality and *identification with the aggressor* against castration anxiety became the established defenses. The central conflict was between rivalry with the father over size, power, omnipotence and a preoedipal longing for handling and fondling by the mother overlaid with a passive orientation to the father. In the course of therapy, this shifted to a phallic orientation toward the father and therapist, and he was in the process of moving toward a more normal oedipal conflict in the period preceding the assassination.

In the session on Friday, before the event, his therapist[7] reports that Martin, concerned with the absence of his father, elaborated fantasies of his Father's death in the midst of catastrophies. His mother reported that he watched TV with his family (the father had returned) over the fateful week end, and saw Oswald shot. He did not seem overly disturbed but protested whenever the President's death was discussed. In the first session (Tuesday) after the event, he talked of the assassination in a relatively realistic fashion. By Friday

7 Dr. Norman Frankel.

there was a resurgence of his phallic competitiveness with the therapist which had been in the foreground before the event. The following Monday, Martin's mother phoned to report that Martin had behaved in a frightened and violent manner over the week end: he would prowl around and make stabbing gestures with a pencil at his younger sister, with an alternation of roles; he would throw himself on the floor in an exuberant manner, roll around and get up, and continue doing this over and over.

In his Monday session, he reported two dreams he had had during the week end. In the first dream, "A funny dream, my glasses needed to be fixed, so you came to school and gave me new glasses." In the second dream an elephant was chasing him and he cut the elephant's trunk off. He then turned his attention to some play money which in the past he had greatly coveted, especially when the therapist held it. Now he said as he was lying on the floor, "I'm better, I don't want it any more. I hardly even want your tie pin!" The rest of the session was spent drawing two happy faces representing himself and his sister, "because we both have appointments." For the next few sessions, according to Dr. Frankel, he was a "model boy," i.e., compliant and more communicative, accepting interpretations and demanding no direct gratification, in contrast to the past.

In terms of defenses, Martin starts out trying to *avoid* the painful topic when it comes up at home. In his first therapeutic session when questioned, he gives a detailed, factual account, with *repression* of affect. This was followed by a quiescent period and by Friday there is an upsurge in the phallic competitiveness with his therapist, in the foreground before the event. The mother's report on Monday indicates that *avoidance* and *denial* failed to accomplish their defensive work. What we saw was an attempt at *active mastery* of anxiety through the repetitive game of stabbing and falling. In this game he characteristically identified himself with the victim and the aggressor. His identification with the killer, Oswald, brought the inevitable punishment of death, by his *own* hand, accompanied by exuberance, indicative of the return of his earlier *masochistic* position, as a defense against castration from outside. His dream of the glasses, reported in the Monday session, expressed a strong positive reliance on the therapist as the fixer of his defective eyes (strabismus), which contributed to his damaged narcissism. In his next dream, he did to the charging elephant exactly what he expected from the elephant (father), i.e., he cut off his trunk. In other words, he *identified with the aggressor* under the influence of his positive alliance with the therapist. Under the pressure of oedipal guilt and anxiety and to insure the alliance of his therapist, he made a remarkable *renunciation of phallic envy,* disclaiming any interest in his money, his tie pin, or other possessions. He was only grateful for his appointments and was too ready to be a compliant patient, incidentally demonstrating that a positive transference can be a source of serious resistance to treatment!

In summary, all four little boys reacted to the assassination of President Kennedy as though they felt implicated and were out to prove their innocence. They all renounced their phallic strivings, and each in his own unique way moved back to earlier libidinal positions. It is an interesting developmental confirmation of the structural hypothesis that the only child to show clear signs of superego anxiety (guilt) is the oldest boy, Martin, six and a half years of age.

# DEATH AND THE YOUNG CHILD

## Some Preliminary Considerations

ROBERT A. FURMAN, M.D. (Cleveland)

During one recent year the Hanna Perkins School witnessed the tragic deaths of two mothers: the mother of a four-year-old nursery school girl in January; the mother of a six-year-old kindergarten boy in June.

The children's responses to these deaths were studied from three different perspectives, as described in the reports which follow this one. In the first Marion Barnes has drawn on her work with the family of the little girl to describe the reactions of both the four-year-old and her two-and-a-half-year-old sister. In the second, Marjorie McDonald has utilized the observations of teachers and therapists alike to report the reactions of the thirteen other nursery school children. In the third report, I describe the little boy's responses as observed during his analysis. He had started his analytic work four months prior to his mother's death.

As an introduction to these papers, I would like to present some theoretical considerations about death and the young child.

### INTRODUCTION

In 1937 Helene Deutsch drew attention to the importance of "mourning as a reaction to the real loss of a loved one that must be

I am indebted to Dr. Anny Katan for originally suggesting a paper describing a developmental line about death. Most particularly I am indebted to my wife, Mrs. Erna Furman. I have discussed all aspects of this paper so thoroughly with her that it is no longer possible to delineate my own thoughts from hers. In addition, any clarity of presentation results in large measure from her editorial assistance. The responsibility for the paper, however, must rest with me.

From the Department of Psychiatry, Western Reserve University School of Medicine, Cleveland, Ohio.

carried through to completion." She delineated some unfortunate vicissitudes of development observable in adult analysands who as children had been unable to complete a mourning task. Despite an almost universal acceptance of Deutsch's observation, there is little agreement about the crucial questions concerning the age at which a child is capable of mourning and the factors which are responsible for the child's apparent difficulty in mourning.

In her 1960 discussion of Bowlby's paper Anna Freud pointed the way to clarity. First, she stressed the twofold aspect of mourning: the acceptance of "a fact in the external world (the loss of the cathected object)" and the effecting of the "corresponding changes in the inner world (withdrawal of libido from the lost object, identification with the lost object)." Then she began to outline some of the capabilities of the mental apparatus required for mastery of the two tasks.

For the purposes of this report it would seem helpful not only to approach mourning as a twofold task, but, in addition, to consider the first task, the acceptance of death in the outside world, as it applies to an object not intensely cathected by the child. If the death involves a person deeply loved or vitally needed by the child, his ability to comprehend the death will immediately become clouded and complicated by the many other stresses to which the loss will expose him.

Death and the young child will be approached, then, by considering three questions: When is a child capable of understanding the external reality of death? When is he capable of the painful internal decathexis of the lost object that is the essence of mourning? Which are the factors responsible for the child's inability to mourn or, phrased in a different way, which factors interfere with the utilization of his capacity to mourn?

In the first section of this paper I will consider these questions by reviewing the literature to demonstrate the wide divergence of opinion currently available. In the second section, following Anna Freud's lead, I will try to describe the mental capacities necessary to comprehend death and to deal affectively with the loss of a loved one. Here also I will try to enumerate the factors that can interfere with a child's utilization of these capacities. In the third and final section, the insights accruing from this developmental approach will be used to attempt to clarify the views prevalent in the literature and to suggest ways of assisting young children with the vital task of mourning.

## REVIEW OF LITERATURE

Excerpts from three authors may suffice to indicate some of the various views about a child's ability to understand death. In one of her most recent papers Lilli Peller (1963) states, "It is hard and almost impossible for a young child to understand adult sexuality. It is outright impossible for him to understand death." In 1958 Anna M. W. Wolf wrote that between five and nine "children may grasp the finality of death" but not until ten or eleven is "found the beginning of something like adult comprehension of death." But in 1943 Anna Freud and Dorothy Burlingham had written: "It can be safely said that all the children who were over two years at the time of the London 'blitz' . . . realise that the house will fall down when bombed and that people are often killed or get hurt in falling houses" (p. 15f.). They also described four-and-a-half-year-old Bertie acknowledging his father's death: "My father has been killed . . . he will not return" (p. 69). Further on they discussed a five-year-old whose mother wished the children to deny their father's death. But the child insisted, "I know all about my father. He has been killed and he will never come back" (p. 141).

Regarding the mourning process itself there is also a wide range of opinion about a child's capabilities. At one extreme are Rochlin (1953, 1959) and Shambaugh (1961) who stress the child's inability to grieve or mourn. In describing a seven-year-old whom he observed before and after his mother's death, Shambaugh wrote, "Rather than coping with the burden of grief work, his ego had to deal with the burden of regression and anxiety. . . . He did not mourn as an adult might mourn but reacted in ways consistent with his childish condition" (p. 522). At the other extreme is Bowlby (1960) who feels that mourning may occur at six months of age. It was this paper which prompted Anna Freud's discussion, in which she expressed her conviction that six months was too early an age for what she considered to be mourning.

Somewhere between these extremes are a few reports of children under five dealing most feelingfully with the loss of loved ones, although the descriptions are perhaps too brief to convey the full picture of mourning. Meiss (1952) reported the reactions of a boy aged three years three months whose father had died suddenly. The mother described the child's fear of nightmares of seeing his father, his playing with a doll called Daddy, caring for it as if it were a baby. He told his mother that when Daddy (a violinist) was alive, the house was "full of music" but "there's no music in our house now." In a recent article in one of the popular magazines a parent recounts the reactions of a three- and a five-year-old to the loss of the three-year-old's twin sister. Although the focus is on the children's anxieties and their management, the author, Len Chaloner (1962), conveys a picture of the children mourning. "For all of us it was a long, winding road of adjusting to loss" but "in sharing our grief with them, we may be able, in time, to diminish their bewilderment and distress" (p. 102).

Less has been written regarding the child's difficulty with mourning, but here again there seems to be no consensus of opinion. Reference has been made and will be made again to Anna Freud's 1960 paper. Deutsch (1937) called attention to the inability to comprehend death and the inadequate formation of object relationship. But she stressed the defense mechanism of omission of affect to protect the integrity of the ego when its development was insufficient to the task of mourning. She mentioned the threat of anxiety, not just as a reaction to the immediate loss, but rather as a derivative of early separations that were responded to with anxiety.

Rochlin (1953, 1959) stressed the absence of depression in the child: he seemed to feel that the painful affects were replaced by fixations, regressions, identifications, and a narcissistic position, which then become the characteristics of a child's response to the loss of a loved one. Shambaugh seemed inclined toward a similar view, stressing the regressive phenomena in his case.

## MENTAL CAPACITIES FOR MOURNING

In 1960 Anna Freud stated that "the individual's effort to accept a fact in the external world (the loss of the cathected object) . . . presupposes certain capacities of the mental apparatus such as reality testing, the acceptance of the reality principle, partial control of id tendencies by the ego," and, lastly, a tantalizing "etc." (p. 58). Applied to the ability to master the concept of death, the necessary levels of reality-principle acceptance and of reality testing would require: (1) sufficiently stable and differentiated self and object representations in the inner world so that the integrity of the self representation can withstand the threat implicit in the death of someone else; (2) sufficient ego mastery over the id so that the concept of death can be relatively more integrated within the ego's expanding pool of knowledge rather than utilized for the arousal of instinctual derivatives; (3) the ability to distinguish animate from inanimate and thus have a concept of the living as opposed to the nonliving; (4) some ability to understand time in terms of the past, present, and future; and (5) sufficient secondary-process causal thinking to understand that since something is dead, it can no longer do certain things.

It is apparent that there is a quantitative element involved with each of these five factors that is difficult to delineate precisely. For example, a two-year-old may understand that the dead bird will never fly or sing again, while at the same time he may not always be certain after awakening from his nap whether the happenings of the morning occurred that day or the day before. Or he may understand the dead bird no longer has life, but at the same time report his teddy bear's new feelings, thoughts, and accomplishments. Nevertheless one can expect that between two and three years these ego functions will have matured sufficiently so that the child can comprehend the meaning of death. This would be consistent with Anna Freud and Burlingham's observations about the understanding of the blitz in children after two.

The mourning task is initially dependent on the ability to have a concept of death. But further maturations of the mental apparatus must have transpired, foremost among them being the achievement of a phallic level of object relationships. This would mean the child would essentially have mastered the high degree of ambivalence of the anal-sadistic phase of relationships, referring here to the phases of object relationships described by Anna Freud in 1963.[1] Unless

---

[1] This significance of the phallic level of relationships evolves from a personal communication Anna Freud sent the Cleveland group in which she further clarified for us the concept of object constancy.

326 ROBERT A. FURMAN

the phallic level of relationship had been reached, the anxiety engendered by the fear of the destructive component of the ambivalence could force a denial of the external perception of the object's loss. Or the unmodified aggressive component could obliterate the internal representation of the lost object. If the representation of the object cannot be maintained in the object's absence, the decathexis cannot occur.[2]

This level of object relationship, and the stability of the inner-world representations which accompanies it, requires further maturation of reality testing, further ego mastery of the drives, and further ascendancy of the reality principle than was needed to master the concept of death. The increased reality testing endows the representations with the stability only objective attributes and characteristics can bring. The increased mastery of the drives helps to bring about their fusion as well as a neutralization of aggression, thus assuring the continued libidinal cathexis of the object's representation essential for its maintenance. The increased ascendancy of the reality principle brings the necessary concomitant diminution of the power of magical thinking.

Apart from the question of object relationships, the pain associated with the decathexis further requires increased ascendancy of the reality principle over the pleasure-pain axis. For mastery of this pain the ego would, in addition, need the ability to identify and verbalize affects. Again quantitative elements are involved, but adequate level of attainment of these ego functions should be anticipated in the three-and-a-half- or four-year-old.[3]

[2] A complete decathexis clearly does not occur. A discussion of the characteristics of the energy removed from the inner world representation during mourning and the energy remaining invested after mourning is beyond the scope of this paper.

[3] By the time the phallic level of object relationships has been reached, it is reasonable to assume that the ego has at its service the other attributes necessary for mourning. Although the ages of three and one half or four are given above for this achievement, sufficient mastery of the anal-sadistic relationships may occur in some three-year-olds. The younger of the two girls described by Miss Barnes (1964) seems such a child.

In a personal communication Dr. M. Katan (1963) has drawn attention to the situation existing when a loss occurs before the acquisition of phallic-level object relationships. The child's relationships prior to this stage of his development are intense and vital but are primarily based on the fulfillment of needs. Interruption of such a relationship, as with the death of the mother of a child under three, places the child in great difficulty. His needs will persist, and, if they are not fulfilled by a person to whom he is sufficiently attached, he will experience tremendous anxiety. The measures the ego

It is clear, however, that there are many situations in which a young child would be unable to utilize his capacity either to understand death or to mourn. Three in particular are worthy of mention regarding the comprehension of death. If the child's first contact with death involves a deeply loved or vitally needed person, then, as mentioned earlier, the affectual pain and the fear of unmet reality needs could, under the sway of the pleasure-pain axis, drive the perception from conscious awareness as unbearable. Second, because of the two- and three-year-old's emotional closeness to the one who tends him, he would be apt to ignore and keep from awareness those things his mother treated in this fashion. This would obtain not just with deeply cathected objects but also with those less dramatic, more frequent contacts with death, such as with dead animals or insects, which parents so often prefer to ignore. Third, any organic or emotional factors which have interfered with normal ego maturation could inhibit or prevent the development of those functions needed for the comprehension.

With mourning also the young child's capacity can easily be placed in jeopardy. The child must be relatively free of the fear of reality needs going unmet, lest his anxiety force a denial of his loss. In these circumstances a vital factor is the attitude shown by those who tend the child toward his painful feelings. All children would need the full acceptance of these feelings, but many children might initially need the support afforded by seeing the adults endure their pain and by having the opportunity to share this experience with them.[4]

There is one aspect of the fulfillment of reality needs that merits special mention. The person or persons who replace the lost one in fulfilling needs should be consistent and unchanging. As the child

---

adopts to protect against this anxiety may be crippling for the child's future development.

The young child may show feelings of depression, but these would not be a sign of mourning. At this stage the child would be identifying with the sadness of the surrounding objects and by this means clinging to them.

[4] I am indebted to Dr. M. Katan for the following thoughts on the relationship between sadness and object loss. After a child has acquired stable internal representations, his sadness in response to loss may not necessarily be indicative of his mourning for the lost object. It may represent an identification with the mourning relatives instituted for any number of reasons. Or it may represent his reaction to what he feels as a loss of the love of his relatives who might be withdrawn from him in their own grief.

proceeds with the decathexis of the representation of the lost object, he should have a new object that can be invested with some of this energy. Without such an object he is in danger of developing degrees of identification with the lost object or hypercathexis of the self representation that would impede his future development. Formation of a new inner-world representation of the need-fulfilling object or objects would require the relatively consistent availability of the person or small group of persons who are assuming this responsibility.

Regarding the child's own development, once more mention must be made of any organic or psychological factors which could interfere with normal ego development. Of central significance, however, is the child's relationships to his own affects. Any factors which impede his ability to endure sadness or mental pain would make his mourning most difficult. The important relationship between mourning and ambivalence to the lost object is well known, holds for children as well as adults, and has been stressed above in the emphasis on the necessity for a phallic level of object relationships. The degree of mastery of the anal-sadistic phase will, of course, be crucial. Conflicts which keep a child's aggression from the degree of control and consciousness appropriate to the phallic level will threaten the fusion of instincts so vital to the maintenance of the object representations. It would seem so often that what appears as a child's difficulty with mourning may primarily be a manifestation of difficulty in mastery of aggression.

Reviewing the literature calls attention to another factor that can complicate or interfere with the child's mourning. The child described by Bergen (1958) was practically the witness of one parent's murder of another. The five- and eight-year-old girls described by Scharl (1961) had witnessed their father's decapitation. The little boy whose analysis is described in the third of the following reports had seen the operative site of his mother's radical mastectomy. All of these children were forced to cope with something far different from what was faced by the little boy Meiss (1952) described whose father died of a heart attack when the child was not present. In many instances where young children prematurely lose an important person, the circumstances of the loss may so invest the loss with castration anxiety as to make its continued acceptance untenable for them.

## Application of the Developmental Approach

If mourning and the young child are considered in terms of the child's capacity and the factors inhibiting the utilization of this capacity, then it is possible to understand some of the apparent discrepancies in the literature. Some two-year-olds will have a concept of death, while some five-year-olds will not. Some three-and-a-half- or four-year-olds will truly mourn, while some latency children will not. There is no reason to question the apparently conflicting observations of different authors. It is fundamental, however, to make a sharp distinction between a child's not mourning and his incapability of mourning. When Lindemann's (1944) observations revealed the total inability of some adults to grieve and the professional assistance required by others to initiate the process, there was no suggestion that adults were incapable of grief. And so it should be with a child.

There may be further explanations for the discrepancies found in the literature. Shambaugh describes his seven-year-old patient returning to him following the mother's death in a mood of pressured happiness that evoked the term euphoria in his report. He describes the boy's regression and concludes that this burden prevented his ego from assuming the burden of mourning. No mention is made of any interpretation of the gaiety as a reversal of affect, the pressure as a response to anxiety about the amount of sadness, and the regression as a retreat to the time when the mother was alive. Unless these interpretations are given and the responses to them dynamically studied, it seems premature to view the child's reactions as evidence of an inability to mourn. Interpretation of defenses against affects are too much a cornerstone of child analytic understanding to be omitted here.

The last factor that may account for the discrepancy in views about the age of mourning ability is the almost universal pain evoked in all adults when they are exposed to the poignancy of a child's mourning, particularly for a parent. Each one of us who has presented our reports has been struck with how emotionally trying it has been for every audience; how often it is wished that the child should not know the pain of mourning, and then how difficult it becomes to acknowledge evidence of this pain. Certainly anyone who has tried to support a child with his mourning becomes keenly aware of the stress involved. Only if there is a full understanding of the vital importance to the child of completing this task, is it possible to persevere.

The developmental approach reported here may be of assistance in understanding some of the factors that have been held responsible for a child's apparent inability to mourn. Deutsch spoke of an anxiety that would not be a direct consequence of the immediate loss and was referring, I believe, to what might be described in the context of this report as anxiety engendered by a fear of needs going unfulfilled. Other possible sources of anxiety beyond that immediately springing from the loss could be seen as related to aggression, when there is deviation from normal development in the mastery of this drive, and to castration anxiety either from developmental deviation or from the circumstances directly associated with the death, as described above.

Rochlin observed fixations, regressions, identifications, and heightened narcissism. The first three may be understood in part as defenses against anxiety from any of the sources previously described and also as defensive attempts to retreat from the painful decathexis of the object representation. The heightened narcissism would raise the question, however, whether some decathexis of the object representation might not have already transpired and been the source of the hypercathexis of the self representation. But here again, as in Shambaugh's material, the important point would be to distinguish clearly between a reaction to a difficult mental task in a given child and an inability to undertake that task in all children.

The developmental approach outlined here may serve as a guideline for considering some of the ways in which the young child can best be supported and sustained in his mourning. The three papers which follow stress the assistance afforded by verbalization, judicious interpretation of defenses, and, in the specialized situation of analysis, the efforts to keep the child's neurosis from interfering with his ability to mourn.

Two other points are implicit in these papers that might well be explicitly stated here. It has been stressed earlier that the under-standing of death is a prerequisite to mourning. Our experience indicates that children who have not been capable of affectively dealing with death in their first contact with it have been able to do so a short time later with a second experience. They apparently utilized the first experience to master the concept of death. With the concept then at the disposal of the ego, they were able, on the second occasion, to devote their full energies to the more difficult affective task.

The question arises of when and how a child should be helped to understand death. Our thinking suggests that the two- or three-year-old is capable of understanding this concept if his mother can realis-tically discuss it with him as it involves the loss of life in objects that are minimally cathected by him. Few parents, perhaps, will approach this task unless encouraged to do so, by nursery school teachers, for example, or forced to do so, as in the wartime conditions such as Freud and Burlingham described at the time of the blitz.

This educational task is often delayed until the child is about to be faced by a meaningful loss, e.g., that of a grandparent. This may suffice if the child is mature enough and the anticipated loss is not a great one, so that it is possible to master the two tasks practi-cally simultaneously. With the little boy whose analysis I describe in the third report, the period of gradual demise that preceded his mother's death evoked in him an attempt to surrender the object prematurely, a reaction that would have greatly intensified his guilt after her death. The chances of such a reaction would seem increased if a young child is asked to master the concept of death while a loved one is dying.

The second point to be stated explicitly concerns the advantages of professional guidance and support for parents of a child facing a mourning reaction. Without such outside help, few parents, in the midst of their own grief, are capable of the empathic understanding Chaloner describes, which initially can only heighten their pain. In our daily analytic work we are all too familiar with the instances when a child is reassured about his reality needs in the hope that he will not grieve, when his feelings are denied or discouraged, his questions unheard or unrecognized. In our experience, however, professional guidance for the parents and those responsible for the child has been effective in enabling them to support the child in his mourning. These parents have come to know the gratification and assistance with their own mourning that Chaloner describes.

## SUMMARY

If Helene Deutsch's thoughts on the importance of completing the mourning task are accepted, then it is important to stress certain considerations: that a two- to three-year-old can master the concept of death; that a three-and-a-half- to four-year-old can mourn; that these precious abilities can be made unavailable to a child by unfavorable circumstances but can be supported and sustained to be at his service in favorable circumstances.

These considerations suggest the validity of encouraging and supporting parents to convey the essence of death as a part of life to two-, three-, and four-year-old children and the validity of trying to make professional guidance and support available to the parent or parents of small children who have suffered an important loss.

### BIBLIOGRAPHY

Barnes, M. (1964), Reactions to the Death of a Mother. *This Annual*, 19.
Bergen, M. (1958), The Effect of Severe Trauma on a Four-Year-Old Child. *This Annual*, 13.
Bowlby, J. (1960), Grief and Mourning in Infancy and Early Childhood. *This Annual*, 15.
Chaloner, L. (1962), How to Answer the Questions Children Ask about Death. *Parents' Mag.*, 37.
Deutsch, H. (1937), Absence of Grief. *Psa. Quart.*, 6.
Freud, A. (1960), Discussion of Dr. Bowlby's Paper. *This Annual*, 15.
—— (1963a), The Concept of Developmental Lines. *This Annual*, 18.
—— (1963b), Personal Communication to the Cleveland Child Analytic Group.
—— & Burlingham, D. (1943), *War and Children*. New York: International Universities Press.
Furman, R. (1964), Death of a Six-Year-Old's Mother during His Analysis. *This Annual*, 19.
Katan, M. (1963), Personal Communication.
Lindemann, E. (1944), Symptomatology and Management of Acute Grief. *Amer. J. Psychiat.*, 101.
McDonald, M. (1964), A Study of the Reactions of Nursery School Children to the Death of a Child's Mother. *This Annual*, 19.
Meiss, M. L. (1952), The Oedipal Problem of a Fatherless Child. *This Annual*, 7.
Peller, L. (1963), Further Comments on Adoption. *Bull. Phila. Assn. Psa.*, 13.

Rochlin, G. (1953), Loss and Restitution. *This Annual*, 8.
—— (1959), The Loss Complex. *J. Amer. Psa. Assn.*, 7.
Scharl, A. E. (1961), Regression and Restitution in Object Loss: Clinical Observations. *This Annual*, 16.
Shambaugh, B. (1961), A Study of Loss Reactions in a Seven-Year-Old. *This Annual*, 16.
Wolf, A. M. W. (1958), Helping Your Child to Understand Death. *Child Study*.

# REACTIONS TO THE DEATH OF A MOTHER

MARION J. BARNES, M.S.S. (Cleveland)

How children react to their own mother's death will depend upon their age and the stages of drive and ego development already achieved at the time the crisis is experienced.[1] Just as important in shaping their reactions to such serious loss will be the kind and amount of emotional help available to them from the bereaved members of their family. The opportunity to observe the reactions of two small sisters to the death of their mother, and also to help the family with the subsequent management of the children, came to me when a mother died suddenly during my mother-guidance work with her. At the time of her death her daughters, Wendy and Winnie, were four and two and a half years old. The mother-guidance work was being conducted in connection with Wendy's attendance at the Hanna Perkins Nursery School.[2]

In giving guidance to the three main persons—father, maternal grandmother, and maid—who cared for these two little girls, my first objective was to assist them intellectually and emotionally in allowing a period of mourning. This entailed helping them with their own feelings and defenses so they would then be able to give emotional

---

From the Department of Psychiatry, University Hospitals, Western Reserve University School of Medicine, and the Hanna Perkins Nursery School, Cleveland, Ohio.

[1] Robert A. Furman (1964) has reported the case of a kindergarten boy whose mother died during his analysis. Marjorie McDonald (1964) has reported reactions of nursery school children to the death of a classmate's mother. (Wendy, the nursery school child who lost her mother, is one of the subjects of the present paper.)

[2] A therapist gives weekly mother guidance or parent guidance to the family of each child in the nursery school (see E. Furman, 1957; A. Katan, 1959). She also meets weekly with the teachers so that the work and observations of school and home may be integrated into a meaningful whole. In this particular case, after the mother's death, three consultation hours weekly were made available for the grandmother, maid, and father, as they were the three constant caring parental figures. The purpose was to prevent, if possible, the development of pathological defenses and to permit the maximum forward emotional development. This preventive service had continued, at the time of writing, for a year after the death of the mother.

support to the children. I anticipated that they would have little difficulty in recognizing the children's overt reactions to the death but that they would need help in recognizing the defensive adaptations such as denial, reversal of affect, displacement, and transformation of passive into active. To help them to recognize these manifestations, I encouraged all three of these people to bring to both individual and group guidance sessions a detailed report of the daily happenings in the children's lives. Then, as our work progressed, I was able at times to give them simple explanations of the meaning of the behavior they observed. At times I could counsel the adults to verbalize the children's feelings when emotional reactions were too painful to tolerate or unrecognizable without external assistance. Help was needed most frequently when the anxiety about death was displaced to common illnesses and separations, and those occasions when the denial of the finality of death was founded upon misconceptions of reality and magical thinking. To be avoided were an overintellectualization and interpretation of feelings at the expense of allowing a full affective response. I stressed that a long period of time would be needed for the children to adjust to the loss of the mother and that much of our work would consist of careful observation to determine the extent of the inherent natural capacity of each child to cope with the trauma. Only then would we be able to determine what extra assistance each child needed and how best to give it. There would be discreet use of verbalization and interpretation for the children, and we would resort to these techniques only when defensive adaptations were leading to unhealthy resolutions. My aim was to avoid as far as possible regressions or fixations which would prevent progress in personality growth along normal developmental lines.

## GUIDANCE BEFORE THE DEATH OF THE MOTHER

Wendy entered the Hanna Perkins Nursery School when she was three and a half years old. I had been giving mother guidance intermittently since the child was two and a half years old. The educational advice focused on developmental problems—night wetting, attachment to a blanket, some typical fantasies around penis envy, and an inability to express aggression verbally, particularly toward her sister, Winnie, eighteen months younger. Over the months the mother was able to work through many of these difficulties with the child, so that there was forward movement. By the age of three, the mother's main concern was Wendy's overattachment to her blanket, thumb sucking, and a reluctance to separate.

We did not consider that these problems warranted admission to our nursery school for special help, because Wendy was just three, still in the process of change, and functioned very adequately in other areas. She attended another nursery school for a four-month period, although I continued my work with the mother.

Admission to our nursery school was deemed advisable only when we discovered that this young mother of twenty-five had multiple sclerosis which had been in remission since the age of eighteen. For the child there were no outward signs of the mother's illness other than the unusual two-hour daily rest periods.

I then learned that Wendy often showed anxiety around naptime in her own home and was sometimes resentful that she had to be quiet because her mother had a longer rest period and was still sleeping. Both parents had a strong need to deny the illness. As a preventive measure, it was felt advisable to enroll Wendy in our nursery school so that we could work through both the parents' and the child's unverbalized feeling about the illness, and Wendy's negative attitude toward sleep and rest. No one anticipated any incapacity of the mother within the near future, and the possibility of death did not even occur to us. However, in the fourth month after Wendy entered nursery school, the mother had an acute and fulminating flare-up of multiple sclerosis, was hospitalized suddenly, and died within two weeks.

The development of the younger child, Winnie, had been extremely smooth. She was a happy, outgoing little girl well ahead of her age on all levels. The only guidance the mother asked for was around toilet training when Winnie was two years old. The child had already given many signs of readiness and, when the mother responded to the cues, was completely trained in two days for both day and night. Most of our work at that time had been focused on Wendy, but after the mother's death we also followed the development of Winnie very closely.

Just a month before her mother's death, when Wendy was three years eleven months old, she was verbally expressing some oedipal material. She did not regard her mother as too attractive, although in reality the mother was a beautiful young woman. Wendy was very critical of her mother's clothes and wished that her mother might be as well groomed as some of the other mothers—again not a realistic appraisal. She had suggested to her mother that they take turns going separately with daddy for a winter vacation, her one concession being that her mother could go first. On two occasions she expressed a worry that her mother would die. The mother told this story to another mother in the nursery school, who laughingly said, "Oh, my, you are just experiencing a phase that I've been through. Wendy is not afraid you will die; she unconsciously wishes you would die."

Also during this period the mother reported that Wendy had been asking a number of questions about death because the paternal grandfather, whom they were visiting almost daily, was suffering from a serious heart ailment, and death was imminent. Wendy on one occasion said, "It would be okay if you died, Mommy, because I would still have a daddy to take care of me." The mother assured her that she would not die for a long time.

During a week when the mother felt fatigued—in retrospect a forewarning sign of the illness—Wendy's father brought her to the nursery school. Wendy objected to leaving her mother at home and cried in the car. I spoke with the mother about this normal negative phase and suggested she tell Wendy that although Wendy might have angry thoughts and wishes, these would not come true. This explanation was helpful in easing the separation.

Just three weeks before her death, the mother had a pain in her shoulder. Wendy was very much worried and showed unusual reluctance to come to the nursery school. I suggested the mother talk with Wendy about her angry feelings as well as her anxiety about the mother's illness. The mother told her, "My shoulder aches and I don't feel very well, but it is not because you are sometimes angry with me and sometimes even want me to go away. I had this pain a long time ago, even before you were born. The doctors say it will be better soon." She commented further that often little girls felt displeased with their mothers, but that she was not angry with Wendy and that Wendy's sometimes angry thoughts would not affect the mother's well-being. Wendy seemed relieved and left for nursery school. Two days later the mother was hospitalized.

The focus of the nursery school and my daily conferences with the father shifted to preparing the two children for the seriousness of the illness. They were given an explanation of multiple sclerosis— a very serious disease of the muscles. Mommy was so sick she could not lift her head or raise her arms. She was so sick she could not even talk. (Wendy had asked, "Why can't I talk to her on the phone?") The children were told that many doctors were trying to help her but that she was very, very sick. In an effort to minimize Wendy's guilt after such direct expressions of aggression toward her mother, an explanation was given by the father that this illness had occurred long before Wendy was born, even before he married mother. Father said he sometimes felt bad, too, because he had been cross with mother, but neither his nor Wendy's once-in-a-while angry feelings had caused her sickness. He loved Mommy very much, and Mommy loved all of them. During this critical time I suggested he not hide completely his sadness, concern, and anxiety from the children, which he had felt he must do.

### THE PERIOD IMMEDIATELY FOLLOWING THE DEATH

On the afternoon when the mother's death occurred, the father took both children for an automobile ride.

In talking over details of the funeral arrangements, we were all in agreement that the children were too young to attend the funeral and that the family should not sit *Shivah* in the children's home but that this custom should be honored in the maternal grandmother's household. The father was not religious and wished the children to be told that the mother would be buried in the ground and this was the end. Other family members, however, felt that this concept was too harsh for such young children and wanted the belief in heavenly angels and a hereafter to be adhered to. The father realized he would have to spend much time in clarifying his point of view with the children, because many people, both adults and children, would use the concept of angels and heaven, not only out of a feeling of spiritual conviction but also out of a need to deny the painful finality of death. The father thought he should miraculously pull himself together and with the children, at least, be very matter-of-fact. I advised that this would not be therapeutic—that he should avoid hysteria, but on the other hand he should not deny his tremendous sorrow; that it was necessary for the children as well as for him to have a period of mourning. I emphasized the importance of the sorrow being openly expressed and not repressed.

On this automobile ride, therefore, the father told the two children about the mother's death. She had stopped breathing; she was not alive any more; she could not feel anything; she was gone forever and would never come back. She would be buried in the ground, protected in a box with a cover on it, and nothing would hurt her— not the rain, or the snow, or the cold. Wendy asked, "How will she breathe and who will feed her?" The father explained that when one is dead, one does not breathe any more and does not need food. It was snowing when he showed the children from a distance the burial ground where the mother would be placed the following afternoon. The cemetery was about a mile from their home, and adjacent to it was a water tower. The water tower could be seen from their living room window.

On the evening of the mother's death, even after the visit to the cemetery, the children seemed relatively unaffected. They were both quite active, however, and for quite some time were described as "happily" playing "London Bridge Is Falling Down." Relatives in the home, in an effort to deny the painfulness of this tragedy for the children as well as for themselves, tried gaily to enter into the game, and when this subsided, bravely suggested many other cheerful projects. They stalwartly made every effort to show no sorrow. I advised a more natural response on the part of the adults. The children could not and should not be protected from experiencing some sorrow.

## REACTIONS OF WENDY TO THE DEATH OF HER MOTHER

For several days following the mother's death, two games that Wendy played revealed the efforts of her ego to cope with the trauma.

One game, played with the father, was called the John-Joan game (the parents' first names). This was a twirling game, in which Wendy would twirl until either she or the father called "John." Then she would lie down. At the command "Joan," she was supposed to get up. However, when Wendy delegated the calling role to her father and he called the name "Joan," which was to signal rising, she remained down. In making a game of the mother's inability to rise, Wendy was employing the defense of reversal of affect. In being in control of the mother's falling and not rising, Wendy was employing the defense of transformation of passive into active. This game was not interpreted to Wendy because of its usefulness in helping the ego to cope with the death. She played it for several days.

A second game which Wendy played concurrently was another twirling game in which she became very dizzy, fell down on the floor, and then quickly demonstrated how she could get up. She would laugh in getting up and would comment, "You thought I was dead, didn't you?"

I encouraged the relatives to tolerate these games in spite of the anxiety this play aroused in them, because it meant that Wendy was trying to master her fear and the painfulness of death by actively reversing the process. They were able to do this when they saw the therapeutic implications of the play.

Certain of Wendy's expressions and behavior as she drove back and forth to nursery school with her grandmother were enlightening and revealed some of the processes that went into adapting to the loss of the mother. These processes incorporated certain elements then current in a developmental phase—her ambivalence toward her mother in the oedipal period.

On the day after the funeral Wendy sang a song while driving to nursery school. The made-up song was, "Snowflakes come and they disappear. I love my mommy and she is dead. I hate my mommy and I hope she doesn't come back. I love my mommy and I want her." On the third day she sang her song again, much as before, except that now she left out "I hate my mommy." On the sixth day she sang the same song but now changed it to the past tense, "I loved my mommy and want her to come back."

The maid reported that in some ways Wendy acted almost happy that the mother was gone. She described Wendy as behaving like a little matron, particularly at the dinner table when she talked to her father: "Daddy, this is such a pretty tie. Where did you get it?"

"What did you have for lunch today?" "Anything interesting happen at the office?"

A week after the mother's death Wendy and her grandmother gave a ride to the grandmother of another child, Victor, when they were leaving the nursery school. Victor's grandmother became very emotional when talking about the mother's death. Wendy paled and fell over on the seat but did not cry. Her own grandmother comforted her, held her, and finally they both cried.

During this first week Wendy went to visit her relatives. The little cousins, in an effort to be comforting, told Wendy that her mother was an angel in heaven with their maternal grandfather. Then they showed Wendy her mother's picture, indicating that she really was not dead. Wendy cried hysterically and said her mother was in the ground.

In the third week after the mother's death, as Wendy was being dressed by the maid to come to nursery school, she had what the maid felt was an unreasonable temper tantrum about the clothes she was to wear that morning. Not only did she refuse to get dressed, but she was adamant about not coming to the nursery school. The maid, feeling that Wendy was acting like a spoiled child, slapped her. As we talked over this incident, the family recalled what was no doubt behind the expression of this anxiety. Three weeks before Christmas the mother had taken both little girls shopping, to look at the toy window displays. In one decorative scheme, along with Santa Claus, were little angels dressed in black leotards with a little white overdress. These were commercially known as angel costumes. The mother bought one of these dresses for each of the girls, and they were delighted with them. Their pictures in this outfit had even appeared in the Christmas holiday supplement of the newspaper. It was this dress that Wendy objected to wearing. She was unable to verbalize the reason why. I suggested the family talk with her about the associations that this evoked—an older memory of a pleasant shopping trip with the mother, and its new association with the anxiety aroused by an angel's synonymity with death.

It was during this third week that the grandmother took Wendy to the beauty parlor for a haircut. Wendy cried, saying, "Don't take me in there. That is my mommy's beauty parlor." The grandmother cried, too, and told Wendy it was all right to be sad. She then took her home and trimmed her hair herself.

Also in the third week there began to emerge indications of a secret fantasy wish that the mother would return. Wendy was observed sitting on the floor with Winnie, the two-and-a-half-year-old. Wendy said, "My mommy is coming back, my mommy is coming back. I know she is coming back." Winnie said loudly in an adultish monotone, "Mommy is dead and is not coming back. She is in the ground by the 'tower water.'" Wendy said, "Tsh, don't say that."

In the fourth week Wendy was sad and said that no one loved her. Her father enumerated a long list of people who loved her. Wendy commented sadly, "But when my mommy wasn't dead I didn't need so many people—I needed just one."[3]

On the fourth week end after the mother's death, Wendy said several times that she did not want to grow up or to be a big lady; if she had to grow up, she wanted to be a boy and to be a daddy. The father estimated that about fifty times Wendy asked the question, "Daddy, am I this big [very big] or this big [rather small]?" He replied that she was a good-sized four-year-old. Wendy said, "I don't want to ever grow up." She also asked how old one is when one dies, and how one gets sick. After this talk, Wendy wet the bed on three consecutive nights. It seemed clear that she was struggling against identification with the female who dies so young. I suggested that the father talk with Wendy about the uniqueness of the mother's illness and Wendy's fear of being a girl and dying young. With this explanation, the night wetting disappeared. However, three days later Wendy had her grandmother carry her into a department store. She said, "Grandma, are you strong?" The grandmother replied that she was very strong. Wendy said, "I'm only a baby." Again she was testing the strength of a woman and feeling that there was a danger in growing up and dying. Upon my advice the grandmother talked with Wendy about her underlying fears concerning the

3 To take the mother's place, a considerable readjustment in family living was necessary. The maid, who had been in the household since the children were infants, now stayed the whole night through for five days of the week. The maternal grandmother came in the morning to bring Wendy to nursery school and picked her up in the afternoon. The grandmother also spent several hours with both children until the father returned from work. Over the week end another maid and the paternal grandmother gave relief. No one person could give full-time care without disrupting her own family life.

strength and longevity of girls, and how hard it was to believe that girls do not die young when one's own mother had died so young.

Again for several days Wendy played a twirling game, would become dizzy, fall to the floor, pretend to be dead, and then spring up.

In driving to nursery school with her grandmother, Wendy had almost daily conversations about the ducks on the pond. "Are they cold? Will they freeze? Who feeds them?" From our discussions, the grandmother recognized the displacement in these questions but answered in terms of the ducks. I suggested handling the affect only in the displacement, to guard against stunting spontaneity in conversation or play. At other times there were direct discussions that revealed Wendy's concern about her mother buried in the cold. "Do dead people have to be fed? Do they have any feelings?"

Wendy again began singing her snowflake song on the way to school. She was whispering so low that her grandmother could hardly hear her when she said, "My mommy is coming back." The grandmother smothered this with a realistic interpretation instead of asking Wendy why she thought her mother was coming back. However, this incident gave me an opportunity to discuss with the grandmother the power of magical thinking and the strength of the wishful fantasy for the mother's return.

Wendy then suggested that she would pretend her grandmother was her mother—she would call her Mommy, and the grandmother should pretend in return that Wendy was her own little girl. I suggested the grandmother tell Wendy that she was in part trying to take the mother's place but could not really be her mother, and that she, too, felt very sad about the loss. Wendy was further helped to a more realistic resolution by another child. At nursery school Wendy told Mary that she had a mother for pretend—her grandmother. Mary said, "Oh, it really isn't the same, is it?" Wendy said sadly, "No, it isn't."

Wendy then showed another reaction, this time not verbalized. When nursery school closed for the day, she would watch eagerly for her grandmother. However, when the grandmother arrived, Wendy would look in the direction petulantly and then quickly run away and play. I advised that the grandmother talk with Wendy about her disappointment that her mother was not there to pick her up.

Three days later Wendy again repeated the fantasied wish for her mother's return, and the denial of the finality of death. The incident was as follows: Wendy needed a new pair of shoes. Always in the past the mother had taken her shopping. Now the grandmother was taking her. Wendy behaved in a very quiet, sad way and showed no enthusiasm for the project, although buying shoes in the past had been quite a joy. Suddenly she sat bolt upright in her chair and said, "Grandmother, I just saw my dentist. He went down the street." She was most insistent, although the grandmother knew that the dentist lived and worked in another section of the city. Wendy then complained of having a toothache and wanted to go to the dentist's. When she got home, she told her grandmother that she had only been fooling about her tooth hurting but that she really had seen the dentist. The grandmother phoned me, feeling that this was a fantasy, and I was able to confirm her suspicion. Several weeks earlier Wendy had been reluctant to go back to the dentist after her first visit because of his insistence that the mother sit in the waiting room while Wendy was in the dental chair in his office. I had advised the mother that it would have been better if she could have stayed in the same room with Wendy on her first visit until Wendy became less fearful and had established a relationship with the dentist. The mother afterwards explained to Wendy that she and the dentist had made a mistake in trying to have Wendy separate and that this would not happen in the future—the mother would stay with Wendy.

Another incident which showed the strength of the fantasied expectation of the mother's return was the following. Wendy was at her grandmother's. A boy cousin about twenty-two years old, of whom they were both very fond, came to call. The grandmother was glad to see him and, without thinking, commented, "Wendy, look who is here!" Wendy immediately turned very pale, and the grandmother instantly knew what her wish was. The grandmother then talked to Wendy about how difficult it was to have one's mother die, and how one could wish it were not so.

I have already referred to the fact that Wendy's concern for the ducks on the pond in freezing weather was a displacement of her anxieties and questions about the mother buried in the ground. Her conversations about the pond also revealed the strength of the denial of the finality of death. In a very subtle way Wendy would secure a confirmation from her grandmother about freezing temperature and its relation to the thickness of the ice. Then, having established this scientific principle, she would shatter its veracity with the following comment: "But, Grandma, I see a little part that is not frozen, even though it is so cold." Sure enough, upon closer observation, about a square yard of the pond over a bubbly spring never froze. I suggested the grandmother talk over with Wendy how very hard it was to believe that a person was dead forever and would never return.

Five weeks after the mother's death the paternal grandfather died. Both children had been close to him and visited him frequently. This second trauma revealed Wendy's ego capacity to deal with the tragedy. When told of the death, Wendy said, "I can hardly believe it, I was just talking to him yesterday." Friends and relatives were amazed at her ability to discuss details of the funeral and to comprehend the finality of death. At nursery school she was sad, immediately showed an appropriate affect, and sat on the teacher's lap. As she told about the death, she cried a little and then said she was just yawning. Later she commented, "It's all right to cry if your mother and grandfather died." This second death reactivated memories of the mother's death, and Wendy spoke of how, when she first came to nursery school, her mother was not sick and would bring her to the nursery school and wait in the reception room for her. Wendy picked out "Little Bear's Visit" (a story about visiting grandparents) to be read that day. She had picked out the same story just after her mother died.

There was one detail connected with the grandfather's death that disturbed Wendy very much. She heard someone mention that the grandfather's house would be sold. Until we could clarify what meaning this had for her, she acted out her anxiety by again refusing to come to nursery school. At home she checked on the dishes, chairs, etc. When it was explained to her that their house would not be sold, that this was not a necessary contingency of death, her anxiety subsided and once more she willingly returned to nursery school.

Under the impact of this second trauma, Wendy again resorted to the fantasy of believing that her mother would come back, and again she pretended that her grandmother was her mother.

Four months after the mother's death the memory of a very meaningful experience with the mother reactivated in Wendy the powerful magical wish for her mother's return. Wendy, Winnie, the father, and the grandmother were going to Florida for the spring vacation. The previous year they had all made the same trip together with the mother. All had had a particularly delightful time and had been reluctant to return to the city. The mother had promised that they would go back again during other vacation periods. Now they were returning without the mother. Wendy was very enthusiastic about this second Florida trip, and from the time they got into a taxi and boarded the plane until their arrival in Florida she was very elated and kept up a steady stream of conversation. Her recall of the previous trip had a photographic quality and accuracy for detailed material that was startling—the doll she carried, the color of her mother's suit, the side of the plane on which she sat, having tomato soup for lunch, the decor of the motel, what her daddy said when Winnie spilled milk, walks on the beach, arguments over nap-time, etc. So vivid was Wendy's elucidation that her grandmother and father were moved to tears.

Upon the family's arrival in Florida, however, a disenchantment set in. Wendy was whiny, none of her clothes suited her, she complained about the food, and all in all was quite petulant. The one activity she thoroughly enjoyed was swimming—an activity that her mother had spent much time encouraging.

The father talked with Wendy about the sad and happy memories that this trip evoked and how very tragic it was for all of them that Mommy would never return. Wendy asked, "Can't Mommy move in the grave just a little bit?" She was given a realistic interpretation. Winnie, on the other hand, showed only a happy reaction during the vacation, but did ask her father, "When are we going to get a new mommy?" To this Wendy replied, "Never, 'cause I'm going to be the mommy." Throughout the remainder of the vacation Wendy showed the positive side of the oedipal attachment. She was very fussy about dressing up for dinner and wanted her father with her most of the time. One evening, while waiting for him to return, she played a little fantasy game, enacting the parts of both mother and father. "John, you know I get lonesome when you play golf all day. . . . Okay, Joan, I won't play golf, but if I do I'll be home for dinner."

In this paper I have described Wendy's reactions to her mother's death during the first year. She showed specific vulnerabilities which expressed themselves in certain emotionally significant areas. In other respects Wendy showed adequate development both at home and at school. The following brief excerpts from nursery school notes further illustrate some of Wendy's emotional responses as her ego coped with the trauma.

*Reaction to Naps:* For two months after the mother's death there was sadness and a reluctance to go to sleep at naptime. On several occasions Wendy just sat on the teacher's lap. Finally she was able to talk about her anxiety connected with sleep: "You cannot get up when you want to." When her sadness about separation from a loved one was worked through, and her association to fear of death and sleep was clarified, this difficulty receded. There was a sleep disturbance at home for only two days after the death, probably because Wendy was able to get out of bed when she chose to.

*Reaction to Illness:* When Winnie had a cold and went to the doctor's, Wendy talked about it every day at school until Winnie recovered. During this time Wendy was insistent that she would not go out for the play period. One morning she would not agree to come to school until her grandmother promised to tell the teachers it would not "be good" for her to go outside. Later that same day, when the teacher was writing on pictures, Wendy asked her to write, "I miss my mommy."

On another occasion Wendy became very anxious when Eddy got sick and went home. She took her blanket and sat by the teacher.

Janet asked a visiting mother why she smoked and said the mother would die sooner if she continued. Wendy looked up quickly and wanted to know what had been said.

Joe announced one morning that he had gotten a bump on his head the night before and did not know how it happened. Wendy stiffened up and looked frozen.

One morning Wendy was uninterested in group play, which was quite unlike her. At lunch she talked about her grandmother having a cold and not coming to their house. Wendy's anxiety about her grandmother's health no doubt affected her freedom to play.

When Wendy had a measles shot, she expressed concern about the probable reaction—how sick would she feel? That day she did not eat lunch.

*Reaction to Separation:* For the first few months after the mother's death Wendy was often upset and ornery at nursery school on Monday mornings. When asked what troubled her, she replied that she was angry because her maternal grandmother and the maid had not been at her home over the week end. She said she did not want them to leave—ever.

On two occasions it was necessary for the father to be away overnight on business trips. During his absence the teacher commented that when Wendy first came in she seemed sad, but snapped out of it when she started painting. The teacher was writing on pictures for some of the children, and Wendy asked her to write on hers, "I miss my mommy." Wendy said she was sad because the father had been away on a business trip. On the second occasion of the father's absence, it was very hard for Wendy to leave her grandmother upon arriving at nursery school. She went to her cubby, got her quilt, and sat close to the teacher. She had not used her quilt except at stories and at naps for a long time. At naptime she cried and admitted she missed her father and was worried about his return.

When two new little girls who were to begin nursery school came accompanied by their mothers, Wendy looked very sad and could not get started at anything. The teacher talked with her about how hard it was for her and offered to stay if she needed a teacher with her.

On another occasion Wendy looked sad as she watched a new little girl and her mother for quite a long time. That day, in the bathroom, she said, "My mommy will wash my face because Lena [the maid] has forgotten to." The teacher said that her mother used to do it, but now she (the teacher) would do it for her.

When her teacher was out ill, Wendy missed her. She was sad and sat close to another teacher.

The teachers changed Wendy's lunch table for the first time since she had been in the nursery school. She had been prepared in advance for what was supposed to be a promotion. However, that afternoon at naptime she urinated on the floor by her cot.

When the maid was not able to be at work for five weeks because of a leg injury from an automobile accident, Wendy was understandably perturbed.[4] She immediately reacted by being sick over the week end and developed the symptom of frequent urination, which persisted for a week. (Pediatric examination revealed no organic basis for this.) The teacher talked with Wendy about her anxiety and sadness, as the temporary absence of the maid reactivated the painful feelings associated with her mother's death. In school everybody sent cards and pictures to the maid frequently; there were visits back and forth and daily phone calls. After a week Wendy's symptoms subsided. When the maid returned to work, Wendy came to school looking very sad, and with her quilt, which she had not been using for some time. She had cried and had not wanted to come to school because she wished to stay home with Lena.

At the end of nine months the maternal grandmother took a week-end vacation out of town for the first time since the mother's death. For three successive week ends Wendy wet the bed until we discussed with her the anxiety she must feel about a loved one going away and, like her mother, not returning. Concurrent with this, she showed anger when her grandmother came to pick her up at the nursery school in the afternoon. Her father talked with her about fantasies related to anger—anger that could make a person disappear, anger toward a loved one who has left, and the fear of anger in retaliation. Wendy then offered an explanation of why she was often freer and more aggressive at home, and more restrained at the nursery school. She said, "I don't want the teachers to become angry with me." Once again these reactions receded when talked about, and she became her usual self.

*Reaction to Death:* The following examples illustrate Wendy's ego capacity to adjust to loss and to differentiate fantasy from reality.

Four months after the mother's death, there was this notation: "The children were playing a game today in which they lay on the ground and said they were dead. Wendy sat in the middle of the play area picking up stones. The teacher called Wendy's attention

4 During this period the maternal and paternal grandmothers divided the week, each remaining full-time with the children for half the week.

to the game they were playing and asked if Wendy thought she could answer questions about death if she were asked. Wendy said yes, she thought she could. The teacher added that if Wendy was sad and it was too hard, she could ask for help. At lunch George played dead, and the teacher commented that it looked as though he had some questions. Wendy commented, 'I think I know why. Because my mommy died.' She then added that George should ask questions 'instead of showing it.' Shortly afterwards she left the table and looked out of the window."

Six months after the mother's death, there was this report: "Steven found a dead bird, and when it was talked about at stories, the teacher was struck by how little affected Wendy seemed to be by it. Wendy did say that once she had found a dead bird and then it came alive again. The teacher commented that it could not have been dead, then, because dead things don't come alive. When George said that dead birds could look as though they were sleeping, Wendy referred to how late it had been the night before when she and her cousins went to sleep, and how Susie wasn't really asleep although her eyes were closed. In the afternoon Wendy and Carol just sat and looked at the dead bird for a long time, talking about touching it and wondering if it were alive. Finally Wendy said the bird was dead, and wanted to help 'bury it.' "

A year after the mother's death, a distant relative died. When the father was talking about the death with Wendy, a discussion followed about the burial in the ground. The father, anticipating some pain on Wendy's part, added that the deceased would be comfortable in the ground because he would be protected by a box. Wendy's response to this was, "But if he is really dead, why does he have to be comfortable?"

## REACTIONS OF WINNIE TO THE DEATH OF HER MOTHER

It is striking to contrast the reactions of the younger child, Winnie, with those of sister, Wendy, who was eighteen months older. Winnie was a great conversationalist and talked constantly from the time she arose until she went to sleep. However, after the mother's death, she did not once mention her mother. For the first three weeks she continued to be her usual cheerful self. When natural and spontaneous remarks came up about the mother in the course of the day, she would run off and play. From time to time she would make one very blunt and matter-of-fact statement: "My mommy is dead. She is never coming back." She sang a song, too, in competition with Wendy's snowflake song, but said only, "I love my daddy." She would see her mother's car and comment, "My daddy's car," although previously she had been very definite about the specific ownership. She observed her mother's books on the stairs but quickly looked away. One evening three weeks after the mother's death, the grandmother was wearing the mother's apron. Winnie said angrily, "Take off that apron." Wendy commented, "It's all right, Grandma, if you wear our mommy's apron." Six weeks after the death, the children were making Valentines. Winnie said, "I'm making mine for Mommy." Wendy said, "You can't do that. She is dead." Winnie replied, "Tsh, don't say that."

Winnie was very frequently in the car driving back and forth to the nursery school with Wendy. She imitated almost all of Wendy's behavior and always participated in and added to any of her sister's conversation. It was all the more significant, then, that she completely ignored and in no way identified with Wendy's grief reactions and never entered into any of the discussions about death. She showed only the strongest denial.

Although there was an inability to express sadness or to talk about her mother, Winnie's feelings came out in the form of a symptom. Three weeks after the death Winnie began pulling her right ear so that it became red and swollen. She also sought comfort in her blanket more frequently. Just at this time, too, she wet her bed one night, after being completely dry for four months, and called out for her mother. In the daytime, however, she acted as though the mother were not dead and never mentioned her name. In the fourth week the family reported a little loss of weight and the fact that Winnie was not eating as well. Another reaction to the death was expressed in behavior—she became an excessively good child. Both the maid and the grandmother reported how amused they had been by her negativism before the mother's death. She had an engaging manner of putting her hand on her hip, tapping her foot on the floor and saying, "No, I will not do that." Now she became very compliant. With this very good behavior, there was a tendency on the part of the maid to let her play quietly by herself. On one occasion Winnie was observed trying for approximately an hour to lace her shoe. This episode had about it a quality of sadness and not the delight of a two-and-a-half-year-old who is mastering a skill. At this early age it was not enough to show Winnie an understanding attitude and to verbalize feelings and thoughts about death for her. She clearly needed more—she needed a great deal of physical mothering care, to replace what she could not get from her mother.

This aspect of her problem was discussed at length with the father, grandmother, and maid. I advised them to hold Winnie and to talk to her as her mother had done, and to follow the mother's routines as much as possible. I also suggested that at these times they make appropriate references to the mother. For example, "You and Mommy used to go to the store. Now she is gone and I will take you." "Mommy read you a story every afternoon. Now I will do it." I suggested that the father talk to Winnie about how some little girls think their mothers get sick or even die if the children are naughty, but that this is not really so. With these few changes in handling, Winnie became her usual self again and the symptoms disappeared. She still made no spontaneous mention of her mother. The main characteristic of her behavior was that she sought out mother substitutes—her grandmother, the maid, the father, and sometimes her sister Wendy. She seemed happy and contented and showed no signs of disturbance as long as she was taken care of and loved, which she was.

At the time of the grandfather's death, just five weeks after the mother's death, Winnie showed exactly the same response as she had when her mother died. There was a complete denial. Her comment was, "He is not dead. I talked to him." (In contrast, Wendy could talk about the death and showed an extensive emotional reaction.) There was one brief expression of sadness. Winnie came into the nursery school with Wendy and stayed about ten minutes. The sisters just stood there for quite a while with their arms around each other. Wendy was very motherly. However, three months after this second loss, Winnie and her grandmother were visiting a tailor (a perfect stranger to the child) who was an elderly man. Winnie immediately ran to him, hugged him affectionately, and insisted on being held for about an hour. Her grandmother, recognizing the intensity of the feeling, told her that this old gentleman must remind her of her grandpa whom she missed very much.

As far as we could ascertain, Winnie's emotional development progressed satisfactorily. It was not until she was three years one month old that she began to talk about her mother and to pose some of the questions that Wendy had been expressing for over a nine-month period. Now, suddenly, Winnie was able to verbalize her sadness with the remark, "Daddy, I am so sad. I miss my mommy very much." During the days and weeks that followed this remark, Winnie talked voluminously about her mother, asked questions about the meaning of death, and wondered about her own health and the welfare of the immediate members of her family. She showed that she was trying to arrive at some adjustment based upon a more realistic understanding of death.

The incapacity of an immature ego to comprehend death—which is certainly a factor—did not seem to be sufficient reason to explain the strength of Winnie's previous denial. We looked to influences in the environment for a more comprehensive explanation. A significant clue emerged when Winnie entered Hanna Perkins Nursery School at three years of age. Her entry into nursery school coincided with the Jewish New Year. At this time the maternal grandmother, who had shown some grief all along, went into a delayed deep mourning. She left town for several days in order to permit herself to give in to her sadness. Until then her preoccupation with the children several hours a day had, as she put it, "kept me going." We observed many times when grandmother and children were reunited after any brief separation that she would hold them to her tightly as though never to let them go. Winnie especially resembled her mother and was very close to her grandmother. Thus for the grandmother the coincidence of the holiday and the separation process associated with Winnie's entering nursery school emphasized the reality of the loss of her own daughter. I believe the grandmother's ability to allow her sadness to emerge was immediately reflected in Winnie's capacity to verbalize her thoughts and feelings about the death and to accept it.

Another factor which had to be taken into consideration was the mother's very prominent denial of her illness. Winnie's strongest object tie was to her mother, and, after her mother's death, to her grandmother. With both of them Winnie had in common the defense of strong denial. In contrast, Wendy's main object attachment at the time of the mother's death was to her father, and she identified with him in his greater capacity to mourn and gradually to accept the finality of death.

Certain observations in the nursery school notes revealed some of the ways in which Winnie coped with the trauma of her mother's death. The importance of the sister as a mother substitute was clear. During the first days at school, Winnie asked for Wendy whenever she disappeared from sight. Wendy took Winnie's hand, put her blanket into it, even put Winnie's thumb into her mouth, and took her to her grandmother in the mothers' waiting room. On one morning Winnie was observed watching Amy's mother hugging her. Winnie went to her cubby and stayed there. Immediately afterwards she went outside and played house. She announced to her playmates, "There cannot be any house without a big sister." A few months later Winnie made a reclining figure of clay and told the teacher she had to finish her dead man. Then she played with three boys and said she would cook for them. First she announced she was the big sister, but then said, "Well, I could be the mother also." She cooked and baked, set the table, and called the boys for dinner.

At lunch one day in the second month of nursery school, Winnie said she did not think that Janet "knows where my mother is." Winnie told Janet, "My mother is under the ground."

When one of the children remarked that she would be picked up by her mother, Winnie said, "Me, too—but not really, because my mother is dead."

On another occasion a child said to Winnie, "When your mother comes for you." Winnie corrected her, saying, "My mother is dead. She is not coming." At the time of a holiday the teacher was writing a message for Amy on her greeting card. Winnie said with feeling, "I wish my mother would come back." At another holiday time when the children were working at the table, Winnie said, "We are looking for a mommy but cannot find one." (This may have referred to the possibility that the father might one day remarry.) Wendy added, "At least we know where she is." Winnie said, "She is dead, you know." She then went to the book corner, sat on the rocking chair, cried for just a second, and returned to the table.

Another time several children were coloring, and Winnie was talking about a cousin of hers who said that her mother was in the clouds. The teacher asked Winnie what she thought. Winnie said her cousin meant in heaven, but Winnie did not believe in heaven. She knew her mother was in the ground. Wendy chimed in, saying, "A person has to be in an airplane or a rocket to stay in the sky."

Separations from immediate members of the family caused more than the ordinary amount of anxiety even when Winnie was well settled in the nursery school and secure with her teacher. One morning Wendy did not feel well and had to be taken home from school. At lunch Winnie talked about Wendy's place being empty, and then was quiet. The next day Winnie was again at the nursery school without Wendy. Winnie did not eat any lunch and could not say why. On another day Winnie's nursery teacher was absent because of illness. All day Winnie stayed close to Wendy and was quite subdued. She sat next to another teacher at lunch and said she could not pour her milk very well. A sad, solemn attitude permeated her behavior during the whole day.

For Winnie, as for Wendy, arguments in the family were especially traumatic, because they seemed to evoke fears of a permanent separation. One morning, for example, the maid and the father exchanged sharp words over a trivial detail. When Winnie arrived at school, she cried, could not separate from her grandmother, and had to go home. When asked about her anxiety, she said she was afraid she might go home and not find the maid there. Another time the grandmother went away on a vacation, and although Winnie was prepared well in advance, she came down with a heavy cold just before the grandmother's departure. For over a week Winnie resorted to nose picking and produced a sore. (A child can have a cold independent of emotional reactions. However, this was the first instance of persistent nose picking associated with a cold.) When the maid was in an auto accident and could not come to work for several weeks because of a leg injury, both children reacted with understandable anxiety. Winnie clutched her blanket to her and sucked her thumb for longer periods of the day. After the maid returned to work, Winnie only occasionally held the blanket or sucked her thumb. Any reference to the death of a person, rather than to death as an abstraction, caused anxiety. One day at school

Winnie was telling her table mates how frightened she had been
when she saw Peter Pan. When they asked her what had made her
so frightened, she replied, "When Tinker Bell almost died."

### ADJUSTMENT OF WENDY AND WINNIE ONE YEAR AFTER THEIR MOTHER'S DEATH

During the year following their mother's death, both Wendy and
Winnie have gone forward in their development. Both children have
been able to achieve an understanding of death and to mourn the
loss of their mother. They have been able to verbalize to others their
feelings in connection with death. Wendy has completely resolved
her conflict around sleep, has worked through the magical qualities
of the wish for her mother's return, and has corrected fantasies about
her own role in her mother's death through an understanding of the
real facts about the death. Winnie has been able to give up her
initial strong denial of her mother's death and to go through an
appropriate mourning for her mother. That she has done so be-
latedly seems related to her very young age (two and a half years)
at the time of the death and to her initial identification with the
strong denial shown by her maternal grandmother. Later, when the
grandmother could give up her denial of her own reaction to the
death, Winnie, too, could go through the process of mourning. It
seems unlikely, however, that either child could have accomplished
this without the extensive educational enlightenment and management by father, mother substitutes, and teachers. If this help had not
been given, defensive adaptations, temporary regressions, and symptom formations at the time of conflict might have resulted in the
development of an infantile neurosis.

In such young children the loss of a mother will have long-lasting
effects. We anticipate that Wendy will probably have difficulties in
resolving the oedipus complex, since the need for its resolution will
lack the constant reality reinforcement in the absence of her mother.
In Winnie's case, we are mainly concerned about her easy regression
to somatic symptoms in stressful situations, particularly those involving long separations.

We anticipate that for a long period of time certain life situations, memories, and events will reactivate feelings of loss. As demon-

strated in the past year, separations, illness either in the children themselves or in others, quarrels, and the deaths of both animals and people, will continue to produce a surplus of anxiety, sorrow, and at times some temporary regressions. The working-through process, we believe, will go on for a prolonged period of time.

## BIBLIOGRAPHY

Furman, E. (1957), Treatment of Under-Fives by Way of Their Parents. *This Annual*, 12.
Furman, R. (1964), Death of a Six-Year-Old's Mother during His Analysis. *This Annual*, 19.
Katan, A. (1959), The Nursery School as a Diagnostic Help to the Child Guidance Clinic. *This Annual*, 14.
McDonald, M. (1964), A Study of the Reactions of Nursery School Children to the Death of a Child's Mother. *This Annual*, 19.

# A STUDY OF THE REACTIONS OF
# NURSERY SCHOOL CHILDREN
# TO THE DEATH OF A CHILD'S MOTHER

## MARJORIE McDONALD, M.D. (Cleveland)

When Wendy's mother died[1] the teachers and mother-guidance therapists on our nursery school staff anticipated that all of Wendy's classmates—eleven four-year-old boys and girls and two five-year-old boys—would be profoundly affected by the tragedy. Shortly after the death occurred we decided to make a systematic effort to collect observations on the reactions of the children to it in order to learn whatever we could from them. Our original plan was to have one person (one of the mother-guidance therapists) review all of the teachers' daily recorded observations on the children. But once the project was under way, it became obvious that such a review was both a tedious and an unproductive procedure. Even though the teachers made a special effort to record in their usual daily notes every happening in the school which seemed to have any bearing upon the death, the information obtained from their records was meager. Consequently, in addition to reviewing the records, I began to hold weekly meetings with the teachers, still with the plan of acting solely as a collector of observations. The teachers, however, immediately made use of these meetings to discuss the death and to seek help in identifying and coping with the children's reactions to it. In turn these discussions stimulated an outcropping of pertinent observa-

---

From the Department of Psychiatry, University Hospitals, Western Reserve University School of Medicine, and the Hanna Perkins Nursery School, Cleveland, Ohio. This nursery school and the mother guidance practiced in it, under the direction of Dr. Anny Katan, have been described by A. Katan (1959) and E. Furman (1957). This study benefited from Dr. Katan's help and especially from the insights presented in her paper, "Some Thoughts about the Role of Verbalization in Early Childhood" (1961).

[1] Wendy was a four-year-old girl whose mother died during her first year at our nursery school. Marion Barnes (1964) has reported Wendy's reactions to the loss of her mother.

358

tions. Thus the teachers effectively introduced a much-needed change in our project. They made it clear to us that our original goal of collecting observations without intruding in any way upon the school scene under observation was unrealistic. Before the teachers (particularly those who were young and inexperienced) could be expected to function as reporters of observations, they first needed a considerable amount of help in order to acquire and to act appropriately upon insight into the children's reactions. Otherwise they risked the danger of succumbing to a denial of reactions to the death. Then they would be ineffective not only as observers but also in their primary role as teachers in helping their young pupils to cope with facts and feelings about death.[2]

Our findings about Wendy's classmates, as presented here, are based upon the teachers' recorded observations, the weekly meetings with the teachers (which continued for about four months, until the end of the school year), and specially prepared reports from the child therapists who held individual weekly guidance sessions with the mothers of each of the children. Unfortunately none of these nursery school children were in analysis at the time of the death, so that we lack the added insight into the reactions which psychoanalytic findings could provide.[3]

### REACTIONS IN THE GROUP AS OBSERVED IN THE NURSERY SCHOOL

Although all of the children had immediately been informed about Wendy's mother's death, they made little verbal reference to it in school. After the first few days they were totally silent about the death for about the next two weeks. In fact, at no time during the remainder of the school year did Wendy's mother's death move clearly into the foreground within the school setting as a major and shared area of conflict for the children. On the contrary, avoidance of talk and denial of feeling about it seemed to prevail within the group.

Initially, all the children showed a behavioral reaction to the death. Separation from mothers at the beginning of the school day

2 Further details about the role of the nursery school teacher in helping children to understand death have been reported by McDonald (1963).

3 Robert Furman (1964) has reported the case of a kindergarten boy whose mother died during his analysis.

resulted in openly expressed anxiety and regressions to previously abandoned behavior, such as thumb sucking and clinging to dolls and blankets. Many children anxiously rushed to greet their mothers at the end of the school day. Inability to tolerate ordinary frustrations, to play in a group, or to be in control at the lunch table were common findings during the days immediately following the death. Many children experienced marked anxiety about the fate of a teacher who was absent with an illness for a few days during the week after Wendy's mother's death. Wendy and Eddy, a boy whose parents were both older and in poor health, anxiously inquired whether anyone would do the work of the absent teacher, e.g., set up afternoon activities. The teachers tried to help the children with their anxiety, which was expressed in regressive behavior, by interpreting for them how their behavior reflected their worry and sadness about the death. They repeatedly reviewed the facts about Wendy's mother's unusual illness and death, as well as about death in general. Repeatedly they reassured the children that death was not expected to strike again.

David was the first child to break the silence which had set in a few days after the death. He made a direct reference to the death about two weeks later. This also happened to be about two weeks after the time David had first learned that he would be moving out of town. For the next several weeks until David departed there were only a few references to the death and these frequently seemed to indicate, for David as well as for the other children, a confusion between moving away and dying. The teachers attempted to correct this confusion with an explanation of facts. However, they stressed that both death and moving away caused people to have feelings of sadness. It was our impression that David's departure (two months after the death) was such a source of anxiety for both David and his schoolmates that his move obscured many of the children's reactions to the death of Wendy's mother. Some excerpts from the teachers' reports of this period illustrate the close relationship between the death and the move:

Wendy said at the lunch table, "We're moving to New York —Daddy, Winnie [her two-and-a-half-year-old sister] and me." [This was fantasy, not fact.] David asked why their mommy wasn't going. I reminded him that he knew why. David then replied that Wendy was feeling sad because *he* was going to leave.

[David and Wendy had both attended other nursery schools before coming to our school.] At the lunch table David said that he did not like the nursery school he used to go to because there were a lot of children there and no one played with him. He said he likes his school now much better. Wendy brought up her old school and said that her mother had brought her there. David said that her mother had died, and then started getting excited. [Excitement was a defense which David used to ward off feelings of anxiety and sadness.]

David misunderstood a comment about a mother and said, "But Wendy's mother is dead." Stewart said, with head down, "Yes, I know Wendy's mother is dead." Winnie [who was visiting the school] echoed Stewart's words. I was with Wendy, who just listened and looked stunned. I spoke with her about how hard this was for her, since the children had never before talked this much about her mother's death in the group. [The teacher then added her own impression.] I think Wendy denies the death quite often when she is in school, and this incident confronted her with it at school. [A further note says,] This situation was repeated in an almost identical way at the lunch table the next day. Again, it started with David.

After David moved away, the children seemed to make more references to the death of Wendy's mother, and to death in general. In retrospect it seemed that with the death of Wendy's mother, death itself had become a "taboo" topic in the nursery school. Now this taboo seemed gradually to be lifted and the children could be heard to make rather ordinary and spontaneous references to animate and inanimate objects as being alive or dead.

Excerpts from teachers' notes and verbal reports, during the weeks following David's departure:

Mary spoke to Wendy as she was coming out of the bathroom. I heard her say, "Someone called to tell my mother that your mother was dead." Wendy didn't respond.

Two of the children, Ruth and Stewart, on different occasions have stared in disbelief at the sight of Wendy's aunt, who strongly resembles Wendy's mother. Stewart stopped in his tracks at the sight of her. Though the children did not ask, the teachers explained each time that it was Wendy's aunt and not her mother.

On the playground one day the children spontaneously invented a game of "playing dead." Mary was lying down and Ann said teasingly that Mary was dead. Wendy, who was nearby, appeared to ignore the play—though at other times she never misses a thing that she wants to hear. Carol and George joined the game by pretending to be dead. Then a lively discussion developed about how to prove that the "dead" children were not really dead —by detecting their movements, breathing, etc. The game was repeated the next day and again on several later occasions. George in particular plays "dead" often.

Some of the children were making figures with clay. Ann said, "You wouldn't put a face on it when it's dead." Wendy just asked for more clay and appeared to ignore Ann.

Steven and Ruth were playing together in the doll corner. Both pretended to be mommies. Both were complaining of being "so tired" [a pronounced symptom in Wendy's mother's illness] and both were drinking medicine that would "kill" them.

## REACTIONS OF INDIVIDUAL CHILDREN

The teachers learned of Wendy's mother's death as soon as it happened, in mid-afternoon just after the children had left school for the day. Within a few hours they (or in a few cases, the therapists) called each of the mothers of the other children to inform them of the death. Although the mothers and children all knew that Wendy's mother was very ill and in the hospital, her death came as an unexpected and overwhelming shock. Consequently, most of the mothers reacted with a feeling of anxiety and confusion about how (or even, whether!) to talk with their children about it, and they welcomed advice from the teachers.

With each of the mothers the teachers stressed the great importance of immediately informing her child about the *fact* of the death and of giving some education about the reality of death. (Although a few mothers added abstract religious explanations beyond the comprehension of a child, with the therapists' help they were later able to give more attention to the observable and more easily understood facts about death.) The teachers, through their prompt action, afforded the mothers some immediate relief from their own anxieties about the death, and succeeded as well in setting an example for them to follow with their children. Every mother (with one exception, to be mentioned later) in turn was able to inform her child promptly and truthfully about the death.

The teachers also tried to prepare each mother to expect that her child would experience unpleasant *feelings* of anxiety and sadness in response to the news. Further, they stressed that such feelings were appropriate and normal responses to the reality of the death, and that a child should not be shielded from these feelings any more than he should be shielded from the realistic facts about the death. Like the facts, the feelings too would require discussion with the children.

The teachers predicted for the mothers that each child's anxiety probably would be expressed by two questions:

1. "Who will take care of Wendy now?"
2. "Will my mother die too?"

They encouraged the mothers to give not only factual answers—Wendy's father and grandparents would care for her; their own mothers did not have the unusual disease Wendy's mother had had and would live for a very long time before they died—but to give them in as reassuring a manner as possible.

In response to their mothers' honest presentation of the fact that Wendy's mother had died, every child sooner or later asked essentially the same question. This was the first question we had predicted they would ask, namely, "Who will take care of Wendy now?" (Another version, asked by one child, "Who will be Wendy's mother now?") Most children also asked other questions, which had in common with the first question the fact that they all centered upon Wendy and her fate. We regarded all of these questions as an indication that every child was able, in response to being told simply and truthfully about the death, to face the difficult news and to consider its implications for Wendy.

Beyond the point of this universal initial response the reactions of the individual children differed markedly—as did the abilities of their mothers to help them to cope with their anxiety-laden conflicts about the death. In reviewing our findings the children's varying reactions appeared to us to be classifiable into four general groups, as presented below. These groups are distinguished by the manner in which the children dealt with the second question we anticipated they would ask—"Will my mother die too?"—and by the degree of symptomatic reactions which the children developed in order to cope with the death.

In a few children special personal problems commanded attention and overshadowed or confused their reactions to Wendy's mother's death. The most obvious example was David, who first learned of his forthcoming move in the same week that the death occurred. Another example was Mary, who was occupied with the transition from a medically restricted to a normal dietary regime. Donny, who had shown a marked reaction to the death, had to cope with the unexpected death of his godmother three weeks after Wendy's mother died.

## Group I: Ruth, Mary, Carol

These children were all very bright and able to express themselves well in words. Their first distinguishing feature as a group was that, besides being able to discuss with their parents how the death of her mother affected Wendy, they could take one very important additional step. *These children could permit themselves to consider how death might affect their own lives.* Each child was able to consider the possibility that, like Wendy, she too could lose her mother through death. Thus, each child was able to verbalize the second question, "Will my mother die too?" With aid and assurance from parents, many of the child's fantasies about death could then be contrasted with reality. Each child could learn that her own mother's colds, tiredness, etc., were different from the very unusual illness which had afflicted Wendy's mother, and that her own mother would not die for a long time. It so happened that each of these children had experienced the death of a grandparent, and each used the death of Wendy's mother as an opportunity to recall the grandparent's death. This recall seemed to renew the struggle to understand the reality of death and to cope with the psychic reality of the sad feelings it caused.

The second characteristic of this group was that *these children did not appear to develop either marked anxiety or symptoms as a reaction to the death.* In general this group seemed to make the best adjustment to the trauma of the death. However, we learned from therapists' reports that there was one area of psychic life which these children had to wall off from the reality experience of the death. Each of these girls, for various reasons, struggled against the expression of aggressive feelings toward her own mother. To learn that a mother could really die must have meant to them that a child's death wishes could come true. The anxiety stirred up by such a connection would seem to have been so great that thoughts and feelings about it could not be permitted to reach verbal expression. With their difficulty in verbalizing aggression these children probably failed to master the fact that aggressive thoughts and feelings do not cause people to die.

Ruth verbalized great concern that her mother might die because she had a bad cold following Wendy's mother's death. Her mother was able to reassure her about herself and also to discuss the death of Ruth's grandparents, which had occurred when Ruth was an infant. Ruth's particular difficulty with death was that she regarded it as a punishment. Several months previously an adolescent boy in the neighborhood had seduced Ruth. When the seduction was discovered he was sent away to school. In talking with her mother, Ruth revealed her fantasy that death, like being sent away, must be a punishment for badness. Ruth also showed a marked sympathy and affection for Wendy following her mother's death. She was observed to follow her about at school and to hug her and pat her head affectionately. For a short time she tried to imitate Wendy, by carrying a baby blanket with her and sucking her thumb, as Wendy did.

After the death, Mary began talking about her grandfather's death which had occurred two years earlier. She seemed to try to verbalize her sad feelings when she told her father that she still thought a lot about her grandfather. At one year of age Mary had developed a mild form of a chronic and potentially serious childhood disease. The medical management of her illness required her to be on a very restricted and rigidly enforced diet for a period of almost three years. At the time of Wendy's mother's death Mary seemed to have completely recovered from her own illness and her diet was cautiously being expanded to a normal one. But the strict diet, about which Mary had always been extremely cooperative and uncomplaining, left her with a particular difficulty in having excessively to inhibit any aggressive feelings. Now Mary recalled that her parents had once, long ago, told her (in an effort to be truthful and to enforce the necessary diet) that she might die if she failed to conform to her diet. She asked her mother not only about whether her mother could die, but also whether she herself could die from her own illness, as her grandfather and Wendy's mother had died from their illnesses. Her mother was able to reassure her that her illness was an entirely different one and that she was recovering completely from it. At school Mary was especially solicitous of Wendy for a while after the death. That she continued to struggle with her feelings about the death was illustrated by her occasional references to it at school. Weeks after it had happened she told Wendy that someone had called her mother on the telephone to tell her of Wendy's mother's death. Another time she informed George's mother that Wendy's mother was dead.

Carol, with help from her parents, wrote a note of sympathy and mailed it to Wendy. She talked about her own grandmother's death which had happened a year earlier, and she seemed to renew her struggle to understand death. She wanted to write a note to her grandmother, even though she seemed to have understood the fact of her death and to have felt marked sadness about it. Now she appeared to try to master the "foreverness" of death. In the "playing dead" game at school she pointed out many reasons why the children were not really dead. But Carol's reaction to Wendy's mother's death seemed abbreviated by the fact that she could not tolerate any connection between death and angry feelings. Though her parents recalled the entire family's occasional angry feelings toward the dead grandmother, Carol had to deny that *she* had ever been angry with her. Carol's current struggle with aggression toward her mother stemmed from her normal oedipal attachment to her father, with her wishes to have her father all for herself. In her letter to Wendy she had expressed not only sympathy for her mother's death, but had added that she was glad her daddy was going to take care of her.

*Group II: David, Joe, Victor, Stewart*

The children in this group, although all of good or superior intelligence, lacked the ability of the Group I children to express themselves verbally, particularly when under stress. In response to the death they could not spontaneously ask whether their own mothers could also die. This failure to verbalize the "second" question indicated to us that *they were unable to take the step of allowing the idea of death to come into contact with their own personal lives.* Their verbalization about the death in general was minimal. Thus they were handicapped in acquiring a mastery of the facts about the reality of death, and in permitting in consciousness any of the inner reality of fantasy and feeling produced in response to death. Both the children and their parents made prominent use of the defense mechanism of denial. In a few instances a mother, with considerable help from the therapist, could verbalize for her child the fear he must be trying to ward off that his own mother might die. In one case (David) it eventually proved possible to make considerable progress in helping the child to face facts and experience feelings. In other cases, while some progress seemed to be made through the mother-guidance sessions, a large measure of denial still prevailed. With this group of children their denial was "successful" in that *they did not appear to develop significant anxiety or symptoms as a reaction to the death.*

Victor had never lived with his father, who deserted his home and lived nearby in the neighborhood with another woman. Victor had never been able to talk about this reality, and would maintain to the other children at school that he lived with his father. He could say practically nothing about the death of Wendy's mother, beyond asking who would take care of Wendy. Although he was a good friend of David's, Victor answered his mother that he did not know which child at school was moving away.

David's parents relied heavily upon intellectual explanations about death and could not recognize or permit unpleasant feelings about it. His mother had been "too busy" to feel sadness about several miscarriages she had had preceding David's birth. Only with the therapist's help could she reassure David about who would care for Wendy and her sister. The week of the death she began to present their forthcoming move to David. At first she excited him with the many attractions of the new city, before finally telling him the fact that they would be moving to it. In his initial excitement and confusion David told his school that he had a "secret," but he did not know what it was. Not until the following week was his mother able to inform the school about their move. The next several weeks were spent by David and his family in a struggle to deny sadness about moving away. In the beginning the efforts of therapist and school to relieve this denial seemed largely futile. However, the therapist who worked with David's mother reported that he had later met with rather surprising success in his work as the date of the move approached.

Joe seemed at times to feel some sadness for Wendy, but for the most part he maintained his characteristic smile even when directly confronted with the fact of Wendy's mother's death. At school he would refer to Wendy's mother as though she were still alive. His bland response to the teacher's confrontation of his denial would be, "Oh, yes. I forgot." When his own mother had been hospitalized a year earlier, he and his siblings were reported to have had no reaction to the event. They were said to have been happy with the relatives who had cared for them. Joe himself had an organic defect. Neither he nor his parents could allow themselves to acknowledge that his defect presented a problem or led to unhappiness. Joe's mother had been orphaned as an infant. She was the only mother in the school who delayed informing her child about the death. This delay was prolonged for about a week, until Joe returned to school following his absence because of a cold. He had been absent at the time of the death.

One month before the death Stewart had gone through a successful operation for a tumor which had been feared to be malignant but proved to be benign. He never was able to talk about his operation at school or at home, and similarly, he was never able to talk about Wendy's mother's death to any great extent. (It is possible that he discussed both events with his brother in kindergarten, who was a patient in analysis.) Although Stewart appeared to rely heavily upon the defense mechanism of denial, his reaction to the death was rather difficult to assess. Unlike the other children in this group he never appeared to "forget" that Wendy's mother was dead. Sometimes he mentioned it at school, as an isolated fact. Following the death he seemed to avoid Wendy, as though he feared there might be something contagious in her personal tragedy. Several times he remarked to his mother, "Wendy's not my friend!"

*Group III: Donny, Eddy, George, Amy*

*These children appeared to try unsuccessfully to keep the idea of death away from their personal lives.* Often they could be observed to rely heavily upon denial, either of the death itself or of any anxiety that their own mothers could die. But it also seemed that this defense afforded them insufficient protection (in contrast to the children in Group II), so that they could not escape verbalizing the "second" question, and at times being greatly disturbed by the death. *They experienced both frank anxiety and marked symptomatic reactions.* (Amy's reaction is of particular interest since death was a pronounced source of anxiety for her before Wendy's mother died. Strictly speaking, however, Amy does not conform to all of the characteristics which typify the children of this group. Her denial of the death protected her from conscious feelings of anxiety or from having to ask the "second" question, but it did not spare her a symptomatic reaction.)

Donny, one of the two five-year-olds, was a very large boy for his age. His excitability and aggressiveness were the result of much physical stimulation and little verbalization of feelings in his home. The generations were very confused for Donny. He showed a marked sibling rivalry toward his parents' grandchildren, who were his contemporaries in age. Donny's mother once reported that they called him "kissing boy" because "he seems to have it in his head he is not five years old and talks about getting married." When Donny was two years old, his mother was hospitalized for a month for back surgery. Shortly after her discharge his father was hospitalized with a heart attack. Three weeks after Wendy's mother's death, Donny's godmother was found dead in her home, where she had lived alone. The therapist who worked with Donny's mother reported that Donny's reactions to both deaths were profound. On the night following each of the deaths he awakened very frightened and openly expressed his fear that his mother might die. He developed marked separation anxiety and did not want his mother to leave him to go to her nighttime job. He became very anxious about his mother's cold and other physical complaints. For a time he constantly followed his mother about the house. But at other times Donny strongly denied any anxiety at all, and would reject his mother's attempts to discuss the deaths with him or to reassure him about himself. At school Donny tried to frighten other children with talk about violence and death. Though he tried to scare them by saying that there was a skeleton in the closet, in reality he himself was terrified of just such a possibility. But in spite of all of his symptomatic reactions Donny usually maintained that he had no worries about death.

Eddy, like Donny, had been exposed to much physical stimulation and little verbalization of feelings in his home. Sleeping arrangements changed frequently, and for a while Eddy slept at the foot of the bed where his half brother and his bride slept. Eddy's mother was deeply affected by the death of Wendy's mother because Eddy's father suffered from a moderately advanced case of the same illness. In addition, she greatly feared that she herself would not live until Eddy grew up, and therefore she found it very difficult to reassure him that neither she nor his father would die. When Eddy understood what had happened to Wendy's mother, he replied that he was glad it was not *his* mommy who had died. For a few weeks he showed intense separation anxiety, increased withdrawal at school, and marked regression in his behavior—to thumb sucking and a desperate clinging to a toy he had for the most part been able to give up. He became very provoking of other children and talked excitedly about cemeteries, hearses, and burying people. Later he talked about his dog which had died. Together with Donny he threatened to kill the teacher by burning her up. At times he seemed to identify with his sick father by complaining that he was tired, that he did not feel good, or that his hip or legs hurt. Sometimes Eddy "forgot" that Wendy's mother was dead. Three weeks after her death, Eddy announced in school that Wendy's mother had come to pick her up. The teacher told him it was Wendy's grandmother and reminded him that her mother was dead. Eddy replied, "Wendy's mommy is sick. She's in the hospital." Only with much help from the teacher could Eddy finally say, "Oh! She *was* sick. I know. Wendy's mommy is dead." Eddy showed a marked resistance to talking about the death. After his mother had recovered from a cold he told a teacher, "I hope I won't have to talk about how my mommy is feeling any more. She's all well now and can go back to work." (In many situations Eddy seemed unable to identify his own feelings and he often reacted with a general excitement rather than with a specific, appropriate feeling.)

George suffered from many fears and from a sleep difficulty. At school he often was aggressive to other children. Sometimes he withdrew and talked busily to himself as he played alone. He differed somewhat from the other three children in this group in that his denial was not so apparent initially but seemed to develop later on as a prominent defense. The degree of his symptomatic response also seemed considerably less than was the case with Donny and Eddy. George's mother found it difficult to discuss anything about the death with him. A few months earlier his goldfish had died and she had flushed them down the toilet. Neither she nor George mentioned the missing fish. When George first heard of the death of Wendy's mother he burst into tears and showed a very appropriate sadness. (Two weeks later, when his mother, with help from the therapist, was also able to tell him about the death of his goldfish, he again burst into tears.) Following the death he clung more to his mother when she came for him at school. The day after the death he did not eat anything at school all day, and he said that he did not like anybody because nobody liked him. In his comments he showed his worry that he himself would die. He repeatedly chattered, "My birthday will never come!" When his mother asked whether he was worried about Wendy's mother, he agreed and repeated that his birthday would never come. (Wendy's birthday was only two days before the death of her mother.) But later on, George appeared to deny the fact of the death. When Mary announced to George's mother one day that Wendy's mother had died, George's mother could not speak but put her arm around Mary. George stood by, looking "absolutely expressionless" and appearing not to have seen or heard anything. At another time George said that Wendy's mother was sick and she would come back when she was better. When the children at school began the "playing dead" game, George was an active participant. He also played it much more by himself than did the other children. At times he said he wanted to be dead. In reality he seemed very afraid that he himself could die, and the therapist reported that he was trying to master his fear that death could happen to him by actively enacting his death. About a year after

Wendy's mother's death, George entered analytic treatment for help with his many problems.

Amy was a shy little girl who had difficulties both in separating from her mother and in having to ward off her feelings—especially her aggressive feelings. At three and a half years of age Amy had witnessed a nearly fatal accident to a younger sibling, which had occurred at a time when her parents were away. This incident was the most recent and the most impressive source of her difficulties, and it had served to crystallize them for her. Although her parents had tried to help Amy with the experience, she subsequently developed pavor nocturnus. With the death of Wendy's mother Amy experienced an exacerbation of her sleep disturbance, and she made increased use of her already prominent defense mechanism of denial. Her reaction to any attempt to discuss the death with her was blocked by her denial, or at times by a "pretended" agreement, which aimed at ending the unpleasant conversation. However, with the combined efforts of the therapist and her parents Amy could be helped gradually to verbalize and to master some of her conflicts about death.

### Group IV: Ann, Steven

Like the children in Group I, Ann and Steven were able to discuss death not only as it affected Wendy but also as it might affect their own lives. *But in spite of being able to verbalize well, these children showed very marked anxiety and symptomatic reactions.* Beyond this point they could not really be considered as a group, since their reactions were very complex and intimately interwoven with their own problems. Ann and Steven both entered psychoanalytic treatment later in the year, for problems antedating and not especially related to the death.

Ann was able to speak about the death as well as any of the children in the school, and her mother proved capable of giving her considerable help with it. Ann could discuss general facts about death and could also consider how death could touch her own life. She expressed fear that her mother would die because she had a cold. She discussed with her mother and the teachers how Wendy's mother's hospitalization reminded her of her own hospitalization. At two and a half years Ann had been hospitalized for a week for study and treatment of her recurrent bladder infections. But her excellent verbal ability did not suffice to give Ann a mastery of her feelings. Although she said she understood that sickness and death were not caused by bad behavior, she seemed to feel otherwise. At times she behaved very badly and then needed reassurance that she would not be sent away from school because of her behavior (as had happened to her at another nursery school). When the teachers and Wendy were writing a letter to Wendy's mother in the hospital, Ann had kept up a constant verbal interference by worriedly telling that her own mother was sick (which was not true). The note of one teacher (who was very fond of Ann) describes Ann on the day following the death. "Ann's behavior was absolutely abominable. She fussed, fumed, kicked, and cried over many little things, and at the end of the morning she had to be isolated in the playroom alcove where I sat holding her to prevent further destruction. She denied that her behavior was caused by worry about the death. I said I knew her mother had told her about the death and wondered whether she was clear about it. She replied, 'My mother was very clear about it.' I then asked Ann if she could tell what she herself was clear about. She replied, 'I'm clear that roses are red, violets are blue, I like carrots in my stew!'" Several days after the death another child's mother happened to admire the "angel" doll Ann had brought to school with her. Ann, who had at first been told that dead people go to heaven with the angels, clutched her doll and replied sharply, "We don't like angels here!" For a month following the death, Ann at times cried and appeared to be in a panic when her mother left her at school. More and more frequently the slightest frustration in the course of her busy day reduced her to tears and angry outbursts. She announced in school that her big brother was going to give her a real gun and that she was going to bring it to school to kill all of the teachers and some of the children.

Steven, the other five-year-old in the school, was a very stimulated boy who easily got out of control. He presented a most difficult management problem for the teachers and he often exasperated them as well as his classmates. He was an only child, born by Caesarean section, after twelve years of marriage. In her anxiety about his care his mother had kept him an infant; she kept him in diapers at nap and at night, and she continued to wipe him until he came to our school. At other times his mother seemed to treat Steven as another adult.

At school she kissed him good-by as though he were her lover rather than her son. During Steven's third year of life his father had been hospitalized for ten months because of a severe depression. His mother visited his father daily, and left Steven, without any explanation, in the care of relatives or neighbors. Steven saw his father—at the hospital—only a few times during this period. Of all the children in the school, Steven, next to Wendy herself, appeared to be the most overwhelmed by Wendy's mother's death. He appeared stunned when he heard about it, and asked many questions about why it had happened and who would take care of Wendy. Like Ann, he was able to verbalize as well as any of his classmates about the death. At first his mother was not very reassuring with him. When he asked whether he himself could die, she anxiously replied that it was possible for children to die and that was why their parents protected them when they crossed the street. Or, she made statements such as, "We never know when we are going to die. Everybody is going to die sometime." With help from the therapist Steven's mother gradually became more reassuring about the death. However, Steven seemed to get little relief from his intense anxiety. He was very alarmed about the possibility that his mother would die. But perhaps even more than his mother's death Steven feared that he himself would die. The slightest illness, such as a cold, intensified his fear. To him, death, like being left, was a fate which bad people deserved as a punishment, and Steven knew very well how often his behavior had been very bad. At times Steven seemed to ask endless questions about Wendy's mother's death. But his predominant reaction seemed to be one of excitement and aggression. At school he often required isolation. At home he called his mother a "dumb bastard" and said to her, "I can make you go away and die!" Once he openly taunted Wendy by loudly asking the teacher, who was reading a story about what mommies do, "Why don't you ask Wendy what *her* mommy is doing now!" When Eddy said that his father did not come to school for him because he was "too tired," Steven taunted him with, "You don't have a mommy and a daddy! They are dead!" In typical retaliative behavior which Steven provoked from other children, Eddy lunged at Steven and shouted back at him, "Shut up! I do too have a mommy and a daddy!"

## Summary

The reactions of a class of nursery school children, both as a group and as individuals, to the death of a classmate's mother have been presented. All of the children appeared initially to meet the trauma with defenses of denial and regression. Transitory separation anxieties and behavioral disturbances appeared to be universal. The move of one child to another city two months after the death occurred was an event that became confused with the death. It served to obscure and complicate the children's reactions to both events.

All of the children were told promptly (with the exception of Joe) and truthfully about the death by their own mothers. In response to their mothers' explanations all of the children (with the possible exception of Amy) were able to ask questions about what would happen to Wendy, the child who had suffered the loss. The children who appeared to achieve the most successful mastery of the trauma— with minimal anxiety and symptom formation—were able to take a second, very important step beyond considering how death could affect Wendy. They could also permit themselves to consider how death might touch their own lives. They could ask whether their own mothers, or they themselves, might die, and consequently they could verbalize both fact and fantasy in relation to themselves. (Each of these children, having already achieved some mastery of the facts about death through a previous death of a grandparent, was perhaps better prepared to cope with feelings about death when Wendy's mother died.) A second group of children relied "successfully" upon denial in order to prevent the idea of death from coming into contact with themselves. But even though they had minimal anxiety or symptoms, their denial prevented verbalization and mastery of their feelings about the traumatic experience. A third group also tried to use denial to keep death separate from their own lives. At times they denied any worry about death, but in periods of panic they seemed driven to verbalization of their anxiety about how death could touch their families or themselves. This verbalization, in the midst of panic, did not appear to be in the service of the ego's attempt to master the trauma. Both their denial and verbalization were "unsuccessful" for these children in that they developed marked anxiety and symptomatic reactions. A fourth group of children, already suffering from conspicuous difficulties of their own, appeared to be so greatly affected by the death that, in spite of their readiness and ability to verbalize about how it could affect their own lives, they were unable to master their anxiety. Instead they experienced both open anxiety and marked symptomatic reactions.

The following conclusions might be drawn from this study. When a young child is witness to a traumatic event (in this case, a loss through death), his ego is confronted with the dual task of understanding the facts about the event and experiencing the feelings it produces. Only when his ego can assimilate both facts and feelings will the child be able to achieve a true mastery of the trauma. In this work of mastery verbalization of both fact and feeling is of paramount importance (A. Katan, 1961). In order to learn about the facts the child needs, of course, to have them explained and discussed with him. In order to experience, tolerate, and master his feelings the child must be able, through identification, to experience the traumatic event "on trial"—as though it had happened to himself. This "trial" trauma is best felt in a miniature dosage so that the child's ego does not become overwhelmed by it. Then the ego has the best opportunity to work through all of the ensuing "trial" conflict situations which arise for the child. When such mastery can be achieved, channels of communication with both external and internal reality do not become defensively narrowed. On the contrary, rather than becoming constricted, the child's personality structure gains in depth through the experience.

## BIBLIOGRAPHY

Barnes, M. (1964), Reactions to the Death of a Mother. *This Annual,* 19.
Furman, E. (1957), Treatment of Under-Fives by Way of Their Parents. *This Annual,* 12.
Furman, R. A. (1964), Death of a Six-Year-Old's Mother during His Analysis. *This Annual,* 19.
Katan, A. (1959), The Nursery School as a Diagnostic Help to the Child Guidance Clinic. *This Annual,* 14.
—— (1961), Some Thoughts about the Role of Verbalization in Early Childhood. *This Annual,* 16.
McDonald, M. (1963), Helping Children to Understand Death: An Experience with Death in a Nursery School. *J. Nursery Educ.,* 19.

# DEATH OF A SIX-YEAR-OLD'S MOTHER DURING HIS ANALYSIS

ROBERT A. FURMAN, M.D. (Cleveland)

Billy was just past six when he began his analysis. Two weeks later his mother had a recurrence of the malignancy which had necessitated a radical mastectomy the year before. Her disease ran an extremely rapid course, and she died within three and a half months.

This report covers the first seven months of Billy's analysis and is intended to focus on the technical problems raised by the unfolding of this tragedy. The material will be presented chronologically, the problems discussed at the points at which they arose. The work of the three months after the mother's death is included to follow Billy into the beginning of his mourning.

Billy first came to the Hanna Perkins School (A. Katan, 1959) at age four and a half because of persistent enuresis, finger sucking, and teasing his brothers five and seven years older. Two years of treatment by way of the mother (E. Furman, 1957), which began six months before he started school, was carried out by Miss Marion Barnes. It was marked a year after its inception by the mother's radical mastectomy. Billy's enuresis did not yield to this work, and, in addition, a strong feminine identification became more prominent. This was evidenced by his preference for girls' activities, toys, man-

---

This paper is meant as a companion to those reports which evolved from the death of the mother of a four-year-old girl who was attending the Hanna Perkins Nursery School. McDonald (1964) has studied the responses of other nursery school children. Barnes (1964), who had been working with the mother around the little girl's difficulties, has focused primarily on her work with the father and family after the mother's death. Billy was attending kindergarten at the Hanna Perkins School and was a month away from beginning his analysis at the time of the death of this little girl's mother. The deaths of both mothers occurred within the same school year.

This paper, in an abbreviated form, was presented at the 1963 Annual Meeting of the American Psychoanalytic Association, St. Louis, Missouri.

From the Department of Psychiatry, Western Reserve University School of Medicine, and from the Hanna Perkins School, Cleveland, Ohio.

nerisms, and his defensive choice of girls as his companions and friends.

The unrelenting enuresis at age six and the difficulty with the bisexual conflict seemed adequate indications for an analysis (A. Katan, 1946; A. Freud, 1945). When the parents wanted an analysis for him, the only question was that of the mother's health, and this constituted the first problem. At that time it seemed there was a certainty, Billy's need of an analysis, as opposed to an uncertainty, the mother's life expectancy. I felt that any analytic work that could be done before her death, should she die during his analysis, could only assist him in coping with the loss. It even seemed quite possible that he might pursue his analysis without the mother's illness presenting any further complications. On this basis and aware of the risk involved, as it was then understood, Billy was accepted for analysis.

In presenting Billy's difficulties both parents emphasized the bed wetting, avoiding and denying the effeminacy although this had been stressed with them as one of the indications for referral for analysis.

In the initial exploratory contacts with the mother, it was clear that she was very anxious, preoccupied with a fear of dying. She related enough facts about herself to make this most understandable. She stated that she had been in analysis prior to Billy's birth because of a cancer phobia. Both her parents had died of cancer. She had had some chest surgery herself at age two and, as a child, had been involved in an accident that had resulted in the loss of an eye of one of her four brothers. So in addition to the frightening reality, cancer, surgery, amputation, all had specific meanings to her that could only rekindle old anxieties.

But it was also clear that her preoccupation with death was being used to escape certain everyday realities. For example, she wished me to schedule Billy's hours so as not to interfere with her golf dates because she was not sure how much golf she had left to play. Despite an uneasy feeling, I took the position that I was sorry she had such dreadful worries but we had a job to do in Billy's analysis, and this seemed to relieve her.

Two weeks after Billy started seeing me she became alarmed about her right breast. This was found by her physician to be normal, but a small nodule was noted at the operative site on the left. The biopsy was positive and a course of X-ray initiated. Seven weeks later she was hospitalized, and a month later, halfway through her hospitalization, an exploratory laparotomy revealed widespread abdominal metastases. She died one month after the abdominal exploration.

From the time of the biopsy until the abdominal surgery she was constantly near panic. This provoked many uncontrolled crying episodes before the children. From these I was able to learn two valuable points about her ways of dealing with feelings. She felt it was important to have the feeling whenever it occurred, that it would not be "honest" to control her tears in front of the children. And, when they would cry in response, she would encourage them to "get out" the feeling with no explanation of anyone's sadness.

In my relationship with her, I maintained weekly interviews until eight days before her death, seeing her when she was in the hospital, talking by phone the few times she was confined at home just prior to hospitalization. After the biopsy, in addition, I phoned her weekly between interviews and suggested that she call me when she felt I might be of help. Ultimately we always focused on Billy, how best to manage his reactions to her upsets. It seemed to help her to be encouraged to control, to explain, to answer questions. Even in our last contact, when she was able to talk for but five or ten minutes, she continued to stay actively involved in Billy's treatment, supplying history, asking for progress reports, seeking advice in managing her contacts with him; a truly remarkable accomplishment in the midst of her great suffering. It seemed important to maintain the original focus of my contacts with her, as if there could be no question about her being able to continue these. My purpose, besides the realistic gains to Billy's analysis, was thus to encourage and then support the denial that was so hard for her to achieve (Eissler, 1955).

When Billy came for his first analytic session he was familiar to me and I to him because of the weekly visits I had been making for years to the nursery school and kindergarten. He was small, somewhat fragile in appearance, with short straight brownish hair and rather large expressive brown eyes. Somehow in his first sessions he seemed terribly, terribly small to me, as if he were only two feet tall, and I guess he felt that way.

Initially there was a shallow, timid denial of any apprehension about me or about separating from his mother. Those large brown eyes said otherwise, however. When he commented on my height, he said I was not really very tall; but as he spoke, he slowly measured my height with his eyes, sweeping from the top of my head to the tip of my toes, as if I were seven feet tall. His first pictures were of a giant and of a pliers man, the latter "like the one who took out Mommy's lump." He played he was stick-up man, with me the victim; and to my comment that he did seem to be showing me that he had had some concern about what I might be like or might do, he wondered if it was all right when boys liked boys.

He brought his first dream on the day before the recurrence of cancer was discovered. "Three bad men came to my house. A scary woman who had one eye washed down the floor of the garage. My friend saw her. It was too scary for me." He said his mother once washed down the garage, and acknowledged that he knew the little girl with a sightless eye who had been a patient of mine. But no more would he say about the dream, leaving for the bathroom.

This dream plus two reports of the mother's made me suspect strongly that he not only knew of the breast amputation, which he had not been told about, but had probably seen the operative scar. The mother described his nuzzling between her breasts with his head and his inspecting her special brassiere. She also reported an anxiety attack of his the previous summer on seeing a picture of the cruci-fixion. When Billy told me of the picture he described wounds at the left breast. The boys had been told the year before that a small lump had been removed from their mother's chest wall.

The day of the discovery of the recurrence and of the decision for immediate biopsy, the parents called to inform Billy while he was in his session with me. When told, he burst into tears and was insistent that "only Daddy" come for him. In his great distress as we waited by the window to watch for their car, he explained he wanted Mommy not to come because the ride might make her sicker and because "she letted me see it once. The skin was all wrinkled."

The day after the biopsy he came in full Indian regalia and frightened himself in a tiny mirror in an overhead light. He wanted to play a nose-cutting-off game with me. I interpreted his fear of seeing the mother's operative site again and his fear that I might do to him what he felt mother's doctor had done to her.

Despite my earlier thinking, I considered discontinuing the analysis at this point because I had worked with Billy for such a short time. I was not then aware that this advice is frequently given in control sessions during times of such extreme stress from reality crises. But it would have been most difficult for the mother to accept such a decision of mine, and I just could not bring myself to leave Billy. Discontinuing his analysis would not only have made the months ahead even more difficult for him, but also, I felt, would practically have precluded any future trusting analytic relationship.

During the next three months Billy's sessions had a characteristic pattern. He was hyperactive and angry, doing things he knew were forbidden, such as marking up the wall calendar, pulling on the curtains. The verbal material would come in disconnected staccato bursts, and he could stay on any one theme for only a moment or two. He made constant demands for paper, paper clips, scotch tape, staples, crayons, but could only break, tear, or use them up; he seemed unable to make constructive use of them. There was much yelling of "B.m., b.m., you stinky" and some spitting when he was really enraged.

On my side, in this period there was continual uncertainty. Was the biopsy positive? When it was, what did this mean as far as life expectancy was concerned? When the last hospitalization came, was it carcinomatosis or hepatitis? When the exploratory laparotomy revealed the widespread metastases, how long could his mother live? There were other questions: when to prepare Billy for the summer vacation, the ending of kindergarten, and the separation from the Hanna Perkins School, all of which ultimately were to come just six weeks after his mother's death? Also, I knew the father very little indeed, and this was such a difficult time to begin a relationship.

The necessity for the biopsy made more contacts with the father mandatory. He is a successful, resourceful professional, active in civic affairs, a man of broad interests. He is, like his son, small and wiry and appears younger than his forty plus years. As I was getting to know him, he was trying to cope with his wife's medical care as well as trying to help her, supervising the motherless household and earning a living.

When the bad news came about the biopsy, he recalled a much more guarded prognosis at the time of the original surgery. He was at this time very firm with me about one point. He would cooperate with me in any and every way to support Billy's analysis, but if it ever became a question of Billy's needs conflicting with his wife's needs, hers would have to come first. "After so many years of marriage, I cannot do otherwise." Although I knew this eliminated for a long time any discussion with Billy of the amputation, because the mother could not tolerate this, I could only respect his position. My reasoning at first was to do everything to maintain my relationship with him to preserve Billy's analysis.

But as I thought further, I felt he was more correct than I initially realized. How would Billy feel if his need for explanation of the amputation, for example, produced a period of uncontrollable anxiety in his mother? How guilty after her death this would make him. On this basis, the principle of mother's needs first seemed in the long run in Billy's best interests.

After the biopsy the father and I were faced with what to tell the boys. We decided the only reality possible was the mother's reality: that is, we could not expect the boys to know something their mother did not know and to try to keep such a horrible secret from her. We decided that all direct questions would be answered with "the doctor says" or "the doctor told mother that."

With these two problems clarified, it was possible for me to enlist the father's help in getting the subsequent X-ray therapy realistically explained to the boys in the same way as it had been to the mother (to prevent any more lumps coming). The father was pleased with and helped greatly to establish the new principle with the mother of trying to control her feelings before the children. Very soon I became aware of the father's great depth of understanding of his children and their feelings as he reported how he told his sons about the biopsy news, seeking their feelings and anxieties as well as explaining to them the facts as the doctor had told them to their mother.

I had to clarify another problem: I wondered what role I should play with Billy. But as the father helped me, so did Billy. In the midst of an angry, out-of-control session he suddenly told me a story of some animals who were fighting a fire. The fire got out of control and they needed help in controlling it. He then promptly got out of control himself. I told him he was asking for my help with his out-of-controlness. I told him I could help him with this by helping him to understand his feelings. He replied by switching to playing girls' games and by telling me of his nightmares about fires.

I was a bit chagrined to realize that the "role" Billy wanted me to fill was that of his analyst. As I wondered then why I had ever searched for a "role," I became aware of the anxiety engendered in being unable to do anything active to avert the tragedy that was unfolding. It was a tremendous help to me to feel in a small measure what this family was forced to feel and endure in such a large measure.

It also helped me to realize that I should interfere as infrequently as possible with the family's ways of coping. What was happening was one of the major events of Billy's life, and his parents should deal with it basically in their own ways. Any unfamiliar attitudes they might be encouraged to assume could confuse and perhaps becloud the true picture for Billy. Whatever happened I might try to guide, but basically I should be content with the knowledge that we could analyze Billy's reactions in due course.

I was naturally struck with the fact that what seemed best in dealing with the mother was to follow conventional child analytic technique for work with the mother of a young latency child; that what seemed the best rule in managing situations with the father was the conventional analytic principle of supporting what was best in the long run for my patient; that what Billy wanted me to be was his analyst.[1]

In the seven-week interval between the brief hospitalization for the biopsy and the final hospitalization there were three main themes discernible in Billy's hours. These were presented within the angry, out-of-control framework that I described above as characterizing this period.

The first of these was a sorting out of my role. "Why can't Daddy help me solve my problems? Do you help your children with their troubles?" And in another vein: "Why did Mommy call you when she cried? Why did she say you help her?" At this point I dealt with

[1] I am indebted to a colleague, Miss Elizabeth Daunton, for the pertinent observation that the word "conventional" requires clarification. The type of work with parents referred to in this paper is conventional for the child analytic group in Cleveland which has been influenced by Dr. Anny Katan's Child Analytic Seminars. The literature suggests that there is a wide variety of techniques for working with the parents of early latency children in analysis.

the latter questions by stressing that I tried to help Mommy understand what Billy felt when she was so upset.

The second theme was his anger which came more and more in messing and in anal words. We saw this as a reaction to anxiety, that it made him angry to be so worried, primarily about mother, secondarily about me. He told me one day that his mother was very much better, but in the next sentence alluded to the little nursery school girl whose mother had died. When I said the mention of the little girl's mother made me doubt whether he really felt Mommy was better, he was furious and I could show him how angry it made him to know how worried he really felt. The other source of his anger was a defense against the sadness of missing mother, first in her worried withdrawal because of her sickness, later in the hospitalization.

The third theme was his femininity, manifest in giving tea parties, wanting to take dolls home, representing himself in drawings as a girl. This was interpreted to him as a wish to be a mother so as not to miss mother or as a manifestation of his jealousy of all the attention he felt mother was getting from father and me.

This period of work yielded a partial control of his messing and uncontrolled behavior, and enabled him to tell me that at night he tried to put out the angry fires he dreamed about. Outside the hour the teasing interaction in school greatly diminished, as it did at home, and he became completely independent about dressing himself. His parents were surprised and pleased by the appearance of more age-appropriate maturity.

With the advent of the mother's last hospitalization, he did not regress outside the hour but did at once within the hour. We tried to rework the previous sources of anger, and he sadly told me one day that he feared there would be many more hospital trips. He visited his mother weekly in the hospital with his brothers and father, and spoke to her by phone every other day or so.

During the next four weeks he pretended many things: that his parents were in Europe; that he was on a trip with them or without them; that he had new parents. And he played many magic games. I only sympathized with him how hard it was to have such worries and offered no interpretations, because his pretending seemed to constitute a conscious wish that things were different rather than a denial of the reality.

He was angry with the mother once in a tea party game, saying, "I don't want her tea," and he immediately followed this by asking me very sadly something his mother used to ask him daily: "Did you brush your teeth today?" He could then say with much feeling how greatly he missed her. He asked for a doll from me. After a little discussion, I gave him a soldier which he took home and promptly lost. This losing of "presents" coupled with a demandingness for them had just been discussed with me by the mother. I took the losing as an expression of how angry he was that I did not give him what he wanted. I wondered later with other requests, such as for extra paper which he would promptly throw away, whether he did not ask for presents when he was angry to make sure I was not angry in return and that his anger broke through again in the throwing away.[2] His response was, "B.m., b.m." I said he did to me with my presents as a child who is being potty trained feels his parents do to him with his b.m. presents when they flush them away.

Billy told me two stories then, the first about a boy who was sad because his parents were angry about an accidental mess; the second about a boy who was sad because his dog was given away. I could now tell Billy what I had learned from his mother: that his fears had started just after he was potty trained, when the family had moved to a new house and he had lost a beloved maid and a beloved dog all at the same time, and I made a very definite point of where this information had come from.

It was at this point in the analysis that the laparotomy was performed, an event which immediately caused the father to raise the questions when to stop the boys' visits and when to tell them their mother was dying. The visits continued as long as the mother wished them, the last one two and a half weeks before her death. The visits became quite brief. She had no drainage or infusion tubes at these times, but she did look haggard and changed. The last scheduled visit was ten days before her death, but this was canceled when she required too much morphine just prior to their coming. She last spoke by phone to Billy five days before she died. She asked about what clothes he had chosen to wear and why he had not called her that day. We decided we would tell the boys that she was dying only

---

[2] I am indebted to my wife, Mrs. Erna Furman, for the understanding of this crucial and, to me, puzzling mechanism.

when we were certain they would no longer be in contact with her, using the same reasoning that had prevailed earlier.

With Billy I did add a definite goal to the work in the last month of the mother's life. He had been allowing all contact to be initiated by his mother and had not given or written to her. I realized full well that his demandingness and his inability to give were long-standing symptoms whose resolution would require many, many months of analytic work. But I feared that if I could not actively interfere here and help him to set aside his symptom temporarily, it would make his guilt after his mother's death too great to cope with. One day he offered me candy his mother had sent him. I refused to take any, saying I knew they were too precious to him when he was missing her so. "I do miss her now and I think I'll have a piece." I suggested he write her to tell her how he missed her and he did. He was dry that night for the first time in his analysis. He next made a card box to hold her "get-well" cards: she thanked him not just for the present but mainly for giving something to her. His last letter to her was simply, "Dear Mommy, I love you, I love you, I love you. That's how much I love you."

After his last visit to her he told me she was better, but then immediately got out of control. I said I knew he was worried, but wouldn't he rather do something for her than just be out of control? He made a silhouette of himself for her because "maybe she's forgotten me." I wondered whether he feared forgetting her. "She looks so different, maybe she won't come back." I said that hard though it was, maybe it was better to know this worry and to face it than to try to pretend it wasn't there and be out of control.

There were two new games this month. In one he hid, and I called in vain for him. When the passive-into-active was interpreted as a defense against his sadness, he told me his older brother, Bert, now thirteen, had said it was sissy to be sad and that he did not miss mother. We discussed his brother's defense and how different things felt at six and at thirteen. The other game involved a bank; he made massive withdrawals from me the teller, robbing the bank of large sums when I tired of writing out the endless bank notes. I just sympathized with how empty and poor he felt when he missed Mommy so much.

Eleven days before his mother died, the other brother, Peter, now eleven, asked his father whether the mother was going to die. The father replied by saying what the doctors had told Mommy. Afterward the father felt badly about this and five days later told the two older boys the truth, explaining why he had not told them before and why they should not yet tell Billy. He told them what he later told Billy the day before the mother died. He stressed that their family would always stay together right in their own home, that he saw a great deal of sadness ahead for them all, but nothing to fear, and that there was no feeling they could not discuss. Peter cried for Billy and the father, and then confessed an angry death wish toward mother just prior to her hospitalization. Bert feared, first, that he would try to get sympathy from others and, second, that if he was sad, he'd go crazy he'd be so sad. When his father then cried, he did so too, saying that if Daddy could, he could, and he thanked his father for crying.

In the analysis I felt I detected an unconscious awareness on Billy's part of his brothers' knowledge, as evidenced by remarks about a secret place where animals died and about the father not telling the mother of a friend's death in a recent plane crash. But when the father called early for Billy the day before the mother's death, Billy stoically told me he knew that Daddy was going to tell him about "Mommy's not coming home." Months later, Billy told me directly that Peter had told him before the father had. When· Billy was told, he asked that it not be true, and he cried when his father said he could not make it different. Although told of her death by the father at school the next day, Billy cried only when alone with his father or with his brothers.

The father brought Billy to his hour Friday, the day after the mother's death, primarily to tell me of his last few moments with his wife. Billy evidenced little wish to see me, and we walked around the block for about ten minutes. The funeral was that day, and Billy was back in school and in analysis on Monday. I went to the funeral.

My attendance at the service I did not discuss with Billy beforehand, although subsequently it did come up. I went because of my relationship to the mother, clearing it with the father lest my presence embarrass him. The service was a large one, attended by many people, and I did not see Billy or his father. Because of Billy's fear of forgetting what his mother looked like, as evidenced in part by the material presented above, I have, with his knowledge and my full explanation, kept available in the office for him the newspaper clipping of the obituary notice because it included a picture of his mother. I have no further explanation for these things nor for the walking with Billy the day after the mother's death. They just seemed appropriate things to do at the time.

There was, of course, the question of the boys going to the funeral. Although the father left the choice of attendance up to each boy, I believe he communicated his need for Bert to accompany him. Once I knew the service would be closed casket, that the father would prepare the boys for the service, and that they would not go to the interment, I saw no reason to interfere. Since Peter elected to go with Bert and the father, Billy did likewise. I have since learned that during the burial time, while waiting for his father's return, Billy walked around the block with his aunt.

After the mother's death, little changed in the management of the home: most of the changes had already evolved during the two months' hospitalization. A relatively young colored maid, who had been with the family for two years, prepared lunch and dinner, the father managing breakfasts and on Sundays. An aunt took care of food ordering and, under the father's direction, such things as haircuts and getting clothes. Transportation to Billy's hours was not a problem, because my office is in the same building as the kindergarten. During the last month we stopped a large car-pool arrangement (five children) when it appeared that the group could not cope with the strain of Billy's situation. All of the children knew that Billy's mother's condition was serious, some knew just how serious, and there were some instances of joking about death. The father then took over bringing Billy to school, he or an uncle or an aunt or a friend picking him up.

The only change that occurred after the mother's death was that the father now wanted to take over almost all of the transportation and the ordering of food. He made it clear to everyone that it was his family, that he was the boss, and that when help was needed he would ask for it. In the fall, with the advent of public school, transportation to and from Billy's new afterschool analytic hours was worked out by hiring the maid's unemployed husband for just this job.

It was new to Billy to see his father enjoying social relationships without his mother being present. These relationships, like a long week-end fishing trip with friends just before the end of school, seemed much more like a diversion from the strain of coping with the boys' feelings and with the management of the home rather than a flight from coping with these problems. Business trips and one particular relationship later came into focus as defenses against parts of the father's own mourning. Yet mourning never seemed absent. Rather, it was held partially in abeyance until the realities of the motherless home had been clarified and managed.

A further word about the father seems in order. By allowing his sons to attend the service, by not answering at once Peter's direct question about the mother's dying, by excluding his in-laws from the management of the home, by the relationships mentioned above, the father has received honest, direct criticism from friends and in-laws. I was not overly distressed by these things. I felt that they did not detract from his main goal of keeping his family together, that with all that was demanded of him, some allowance had to be made for his personal needs. In addition, I have never witnessed before a more appropriate use of defenses than he demonstrated, of which one example may suffice. I tried to discuss the funeral plans with him shortly after the laparotomy. He denied that this was a question we needed to consider, still clinging to a hope that his wife would rally. When I approached the topic again two weeks later, he said, "I cannot bear to discuss it, with her fighting so hard just down the hall, but we must discuss it. I have to face it now." The *now* seems the important word. When the defense had to be surrendered, he would surrender it, not allowing the defense to carry a situation beyond recall.

I cannot avoid mention of something that was difficult for me as the analyst during the last few weeks. I was aware of the father's denial but not yet fully certain of his appropriate use of this defense. I was apprehensive of my denial. Ten days before the mother's death, I heard indirectly that she was in coma; and nine days before her death, that she would die any moment. On returning from my visit with her eight days before her death, when we had discussed Billy and the analysis for, say, ten minutes, I heard a report that she was dead. Once my anger subsided, I realized that these premature statements were the result of pathological defenses adopted against the apparently unending anxiety of a mother's dying. By contrast, I could appreciate the healthy and effective defenses that were at the father's disposal.

There was a six-week period between the mother's death and the summer separation. During this time Billy remained cooperative and in control at home and began playing more with boys his age rather than with girls. He seemed to be able to have his sad feelings at home when the others did, seldom just on his own. In the sessions the uncontrolled behavior and the anal messing continued, but less intensely. Each day there was some material relating to the loss of the mother, but there was little affect with it, and there seemed no other themes or trends discernible. It was more like the repetitious expression of the same thoughts over and over in many different ways —I wish I had a mommy; I am angry that I don't.

On the Monday after his mother's death he came to his analytic session with the same toy soldiers that he had brought the first day he had seen me, when his mother had been waiting just outside. He became angry with a little girl classmate whose mother had just returned home from a hospitalization. He was afraid of her father, something hard to understand until he sang "America" for me, ending with "Land where my father died." In the first two instances I sympathized with the obvious and painful wishes. In the third I put his feelings more into words—the frightening thought that sometimes he maybe even wished it had been Daddy instead of Mommy who had died. He was angry at all babies, most especially the very new baby of his former kindergarten teacher—babies have mothers. In the sessions he wanted to mix up his drawings and special toys with those of my other patients, as if to say, let us all be one big family, sharing parents. Knowing I have two daughters, he wanted to bring my son a present, and then played some games about being kidnapped. Again I took this as a wish to belong to a family that had a mother.

The money games returned, plus a new one in which he was a repair man who could fix everything. There was some gibberishlike talk, which I understood only when it became connected with the reported burial of a pet turtle to which he had not been keenly attached. "This was a sensible burial, with food." We discussed the

Hebrew at mother's service, which I assured him he had not been alone in not understanding. He was truly sad only a few times, such as one day when I was late and he was early and had missed me. He readily agreed it was the "Mommy-missing feeling."

What was striking to me was the relative absence of denial. Rather, it seemed a period in which he tried to accustom himself to a reality he had accepted. He did wonder whether his father would remarry. But his verbalized anxiety seemed so healthy: "What would she think of me peeing the bed?"

The bed was dry four times during this period. The first was after he asked his father who would take Mommy's place. The father answered that no one would or ever could take Mommy's place in their feelings, but that he would see to it that Mommy's many jobs would always be done. The other three dry beds occurred during his father's week-end fishing trip when he shared Peter's bedroom, sleeping in the twin guest bed. Before the father left, Billy had been able to express his anxieties about a plane crash during the trip. When I related this fear to his anger with father leaving at this particularly hard time, he added that maybe father might slip while fishing and drown.

His aggression also seemed available to him regarding my vacation. He wanted me to bring him back a gun "that really shoots," and he enacted a puppet show in which the one who was leaving got shot, and the one who returned also got shot. The one who returned got shot for being the wrong one to return. He wanted to take all his drawings home on our last day. When I pointed out his anxiety that I might not return, and related this to his anger with me, he stuffed the things back into his box, saying, "O.K., you nice head."

While I was away, I wrote every ten days a card or a brief letter. He answered just once, dictating to his father that he was telling all his troubles to Peter and signing himself with "Thank you for listening."

The six weeks after vacation were very different from the six weeks before. The main material consisted of the missing of mother, now accompanied by much more sadness. This appeared daily, either explicitly or indirectly in an out-of-controlness, the meaning of which would unfold to us after a few days' work. Weaving through this material were two anxieties, that of substitutes and that of me as a doctor.

The missing of mother came up in every place where a six-year-old first-grader would ordinarily feel his mother's presence: in starting school, in being driven to school, in coming home for lunch, going back to school, coming to his hours, going home in the late afternoon, getting clothes, getting father's birthday present, being ill, or a time of analytic progress. Each instance had to take its turn in a process that was not to be accelerated. It was his brother, Peter, incidentally, who picked up the fact, and reported it to the father, that Billy was not bringing school papers home and that it was because there was no mommy at home to whom the papers could be shown.

These times of "Mommy-missing" would present themselves as an anger or an anxiety until we could get to the source of the trouble. Billy was angry at first when he had a cold, but then was very worried about himself because father had just felt his brow, and how could he know whether Billy had a temperature if he did not use the thermometer as mother always had?

This very feelingful "Mommy-missing" convinced me that his mourning was well under way. I wondered when and even whether he could have achieved this without the analytic work which constantly supported his painful reality awareness and prevented current reality events from augmenting the guilt his neurosis would bring to him.

It was hard to follow the trends of his anxieties because I never knew whether the material he brought related to the "Mommy-missing" over some daily want or to one of the two anxieties mentioned above. He played school often, Billy being the teacher, I the pupil. We got to know this as a defense against me as the doctor, and him as the patient. Sometimes it told that there was a substitute teacher at school that day. Also, it reported a day when the teacher had told the children that if they did not stop misbehaving, she would probably get sick. Incidentally, although Billy had been told that the father had informed the teacher of mother's death, he denied that she knew and pretended to her that he did have a mother at home. He did this by asking for P.T.A. tickets for both mother and father, and by drawing a family picture which included mother.

These events occurred just toward the end of this period and seemed to introduce a new trend in the analysis.

What I have called the anxieties about substitutes took a long time to unravel even partially. He became very worried about a minor respiratory infection Peter contracted. On days when father would pick him up after his hour, he had to keep checking to see if father had arrived safely. Then he had a substitute teacher at school of whom he seemed really terrified, although there was no reality reason for this fear. It took a bit of time before he could acknowledge his aggression toward the substitute, who seemed such a poor substitute for his well-liked teacher. The picture further clarified itself one day when I was late and he was visibly shaken. He explained, "I get so angry when you're late. I get scared to death." I could then show Billy that he was angry with all those who he felt were substituting for Mommy—father, brother, me—because we seemed such poor substitutes for the mother he so much missed. If he knew how angry he was, and why, maybe then he would not be so worried about our safety, so frightened of the substitute teacher.

He often wanted to spend his hours going for walks with me, which I allowed a few times on an exploratory basis. On one of these walks he insistently demanded popsicles from me. As we explored this demandingness, it became clear that a present from me would mean I was not angry—not angry in return when he was so displeased with me as the poor substitute. The wish to walk was obviously connected with the mother's death (he had walked with me the morning after mother died, and walked with his aunt while waiting for father to return from the burial), but we could not gain further insight at this time.

During this period a complicating factor was the father's social contacts, which for a while kept him out of the home for large parts of many evenings. As the father and I reviewed this, it seemed wise to make a rule that only business requirements would keep him away from home for the dinner hour and early evening. There seemed no material to suggest that the substitute anger was aimed also at those who were with the father socially and who in this sense substituted for the mother. Rather, it seemed that father's times away were giving too much reality to Billy's complaints about him as a poor substitute.

The other anxiety concerned me as the doctor. It made its appearance the day following a booster shot, for which, unfortunately, he had been little prepared. The preceding session he had been able to bring enough of the substitute anger to knife me with a paper knife. It was a bit rough to have the doctor "shoot" him right afterward. He subsequently came dressed in his brother's safety patrol outfit, focused on damaged toys, and then brought a book containing a children's rhyme about a man who fell apart into many pieces. When he brought the book the second time, he sang a ditty he had in part made up about someone in a "teeny Bikini." The school game or the wish to take a walk would follow these bits of material frequently enough for us to be aware that there was something scary about me as a doctor, something which he greatly wanted to avoid. My feeling was that this material ultimately would lead us back to the amputation.

## DISCUSSION

In selecting the analytic material I have had the twin goals of following Billy's mourning and outlining the technical problems of the analysis. During this period the mourning seems to have unfolded in two distinct phases, the painful acceptance of the reality loss (the period before the vacation) and the beginning painful decathexis of the inner-world representation (the period after the vacation). As mentioned above, I was struck by the relative absence of denial during these phases. It was just appearing toward the end of the last month's work I have described (his reactions at school to his teacher's knowledge of his mother's death).

In the weeks that ensued this denial became more intense and was directly associated with Billy's guilt-laden fear that his anger had caused his mother's sickness and death. I mention this aspect of the subsequent course of the analysis because the question has been asked: Was Billy's anger, prior to his mother's death, also a confession of his fear that he had caused her illness? I offered this interpretation a number of times with no effect or significant response. I felt at the time that he was too much in contact with the horrible and frightening reality to allow this fantasy into consciousness.

It is of interest that the period of the analysis characterized by the denial and guilt never reached its peak until the mourning work had passed its high point. It was at this time, five months after the mother's death, that Billy asked his father, "Is it all right that I don't think about mother all the time? Sometimes now when I play, I just play and don't think about her. I used to [think about her] all the time."

If it seems that I have included a great deal of the work with the father and some of its associated problems, it is because this work absorbed a great deal of my attention. I felt it essential for Billy that the father allow himself to mourn fully because only then could he understand and support Billy's feelings. But the demands on the father were tremendous. There were the exacting reality demands as well as the emotional ones of his and his three sons' grief. When the demands became too great his response was to withdraw, either physically or in feeling or both. Usually the purpose of the withdrawal was to obtain a temporary respite so that he could more fully meet the demands on his return. At these times no interpretations were necessary. A few times an apparent temporary withdrawal represented a serious flight from and denial of his many troubles. Such withdrawals I had to interpret to the father, but distinguishing between the two was often technically very difficult. I believe his mourning took longer to reach its high point than did Billy's, both because of the extra demands upon him as well as because of his own occasional diversions. It took a great deal of energy to understand and support the father in weekly sessions under these circumstances. But it seemed to me a cardinal part of my work.

And now a word about the work with Billy. All through the period described in this report I felt that a process was unfolding on its own within Billy and that he was asking my help in keeping his defenses from interfering with this process and with his conscious contact with it. I did not feel that I brought the reality or the mourning to him—he brought them to me, and I basically confined my work to interpretations of the defenses his neurosis offered him to ward off his pain. I deviated from this role only when I encouraged his giving to his mother. This I did specifically to prevent his guilt after her death from being so unbearable as to interfere with his acceptance of the loss and hence his mourning.

I do not feel that my role was one of supporting him in enduring his pain. Some support was, of course, inevitable, but the main support he received was from his father and his brother, Peter. In terms of support, I extended my effort toward enabling his father fully to give to Billy the sensitive understanding of which he proved so capable. I believe Billy recognized this by sharing his affects with them more than with me. I felt that this was most appropriate.

In one of the few cases at all similar to Billy's that I can find in the literature, Shambaugh (1961) began therapy with a boy because his mother's death was imminent. He clearly states that this was for the purpose of studying the child's reaction to loss. He does not specify the impending loss of a parent as an indication for treatment, and neither do I. My point is simply that, if there are valid indications for an analysis, I would not be deterred by the possibility of a parent's death.

I am sure there are many instances when the death of a parent is anticipated to occur within a matter of months or years. In these situations I think some of the factors to be considered would be the realities of the child's neurosis, availability of analytic vacancies, duration of life left to the parent. Perhaps it could go without saying that treatment should not be considered just because of the imminent death of a parent. In this latter instance the analyst would be in danger of allowing himself to become a replacement in reality for the lost parent, and this would probably preclude successful analytic work. Instead, work with the surviving parent would seem indicated until the death had occurred and the circumstances sufficiently clarified to make treatment indications clear-cut.

## Summary

This report covers the first seven months of the analysis of a six-year-old boy whose mother died four months after he began his treatment. The terminal phase of her illness started just two weeks after his first analytic session. I have tried to outline the technical problems which came in the wake of this tragedy and how they were approached. In this particular instance I was impressed with how little variation seemed necessary from the basic child analytic technique appropriate for a child of his age.

I have tried to present sufficient material to follow this boy through his gradual acceptance of the reality loss to the beginning of his mourning. I believe the material substantiates the validity of the decision not to interrupt the analysis despite the reality crisis.

## BIBLIOGRAPHY

Barnes, M. (1964), Reactions to the Death of a Mother. *This Annual*, 19.

Eissler, K. R. (1955), *The Psychiatrist and the Dying Patient*. New York: International Universities Press.

Freud, A. (1945), Indications for Child Analysis. *This Annual*, 1.

Furman, E. (1957), Treatment of Under-Fives by Way of Their Parents. *This Annual*, 12.

Katan, A. (1946), Experience with Enuretics. *This Annual*, 2.

—— (1959), The Nursery School as a Diagnostic Help to the Child Guidance Clinic. *This Annual*, 14.

McDonald, M. (1964), A Study of the Reactions of Nursery School Children to the Death of a Child's Mother. *This Annual*, 19.

Shambaugh, B. (1961), A Study of Loss Reactions in a Seven-Year-Old. *This Annual*, 16.

# A CLINICAL CONTRIBUTION TO THE STUDY OF NARCISSISM IN INFANCY

## SAMUEL KAPLAN, M.D. (Boston)

Our current longitudinal study, under the leadership of Beata Rank and Marian Putnam, is focused on the investigation of the development of object relationships, and more specifically on the development of communication. In an effort to gain a more precise understanding of the deviant pattern that became so painfully obvious in one of the infants, we were stimulated to re-examine the concept of narcissism as it applies to the study of personality structure in infancy. In his paper "On Narcissism" (1914) Freud stated: "The disturbances to which a child's original narcissism is exposed, the reactions with which he seeks to protect himself from them and the paths into which he is forced in doing so—these are themes which I propose to leave on one side, as an important field of work which still awaits exploration" (p. 92). It is our hope that an examination of Daphne's early development may shed some light on the vicissitudes of narcissism in infancy.

To avoid semantic confusion of theoretical concepts, we follow Hartmann (1950b) who has differentiated the terms ego, self, and personality; I shall insert the appropriate terms in Freud's last definition of primary narcissism (1940): ". . . the ego [self] in which the whole available amount of libido is at first stored up. We call this state of things absolute, primary narcissism. It continues until the ego [infant] begins to cathect the presentations of objects with libido —to change narcissistic libido into *object libido*. Throughout life the ego [self] remains the great reservoir from which libidinal

Presented as part of the Symposium on Narcissism at the Boston Psychoanalytic Society and Institute, Inc., on April 22, 1962.

This research was supported by U.S.P.H.S. Grant #M3026, "A Developmental Study Centered on Mutual Communication," at James Jackson Putnam Children's Center, Roxbury, Mass.

cathexes are sent out on to objects and into which they are also once more withdrawn, like the pseudopodia of a body of protoplasm" (p. 24f.). We thus define narcissism as the libidinal cathexis of the self, conceptualize the original state as one of maximal (absolute) concentration of cathexes on the self, and delimit that segment of libido which eventually accrues to the *ego* by identification as "secondary narcissism" (Hartmann, 1950b). We did explore and attempt to utilize other theoretical models of narcissism, but came to the conclusion that this formulation was most applicable to our observations of infants, since our focus was on the relationship between narcissistic libido and object libido. Theoretical difficulties stemming from Freud's original concept of primary narcissism have led some authors, e.g., Jacobson (1954), Bing et al. (1959), to question the validity of this hypothesis. However, it does seem useful, in attempting to conceptualize psychological functioning in the young infant, to hypothecate the existence of an original reservoir of psychic energy which is only gradually shifted from the self to the outside, a process which is influenced by the infant's experiences.

The question to which I shall first address myself pertains to some aspects of Daphne's innate equipment as assessed during the first week. I shall then summarize some of the observations on this infant and her family which led us to suggest that an infant can respond to excessive "pain," i.e., to deprivations, trauma, or organismic distress, by a persistence to an excessive degree of the cathexis of the self. The interrelated and demonstrable impact upon the budding ego structure and on the incipient capacity to form an object relationship will be highlighted.

## CLINICAL OBSERVATIONS

Daphne was delivered by low forceps after a long (forty-eight hours), but mild labor, during which Mrs. T. received minimal sedation. The baby was thus subjected during delivery to an influx of stimulation without the protection afforded by sedation. At birth, Daphne breathed immediately, cried lustily, had a minimum of acrocyanosis, practically no mucous to cope with, and was given a superlative rating on our observational scales. She was neurologically intact and gave every indication of being an alert baby with a readily available apparatus for responding to auditory and visual stimuli.

From the multitude of observations recorded during the first week, I shall highlight those responses which were unique to this infant and significant in terms of her subsequent development.

From the beginning, she showed a range of responses to mild visual stimuli. Thus, when presented with the colored ring, she hunched her shoulders, got her hand to her mouth, and showed increased motor activity, but often did not fix and follow the stimulus. On the fourth day, she seemed to respond to the visual stimulus by focusing on her hand instead of the ring, and then getting the fists to her mouth. Although these were not consistent responses, they were suggestive, especially when followed on the fifth day by an actual closing of the eyes in response to mild visual stimulation. On the last day in the hospital, we noted a more consistent turning away of her head as her way of not responding to the visual stimulus. On a more clinical level, we contrasted Daphne's responses with those of the other babies in this study who by the fifth day tended to show a noticeable increase in responsiveness and a quality of participation. We were therefore led to speculate that this baby was indeed demonstrating a prototype of an avoidance reaction as her response to visual stimuli.

Daphne was highly responsive to auditory stimuli, and could readily be awakened from a sleep state by a whisper. However, and again in contrast to most babies who respond positively to a rattle by the end of the first week (i.e., turn to it and quiet), Daphne reacted with tears, wrinkles and other motor evidence of distress. We noted too that loud noises, usually evoking startle reactions in other babies, only elicited a moderate response in Daphne. Indeed, she was outstanding for the paucity of startles or other evidence of jitteriness, for the quality of moderateness in her states and in response to many stimuli. I emphasize that the amplitude of her responses was almost always muted. The outstanding exception was her reaction to position change. Invariably she cried and showed marked evidence of distress when she was placed in prone, lifted, or sat up. Once she could be safely encased in the examiner's arms, she quieted down nicely and snuggled in. The observers were left with the impression that the exposure to changing kinesthetic and proprioceptive experiences was the basis for her marked distress.

In essence, then, we were left with the impression that this baby began life with a capacity to avoid visual or auditory stimuli or to tone down her responses to them, and that she tended to respond to unfamiliar, relatively unsupported, positions with marked distress.

To round out this brief glimpse of Daphne's first week of life, we note that she lived in a rooming-in arrangement from the second day. Her mother adopted an attitude of great casualness combined with a striking efficiency that was quite unusual to see in such a young woman. As will be developed, her responses seemed to be more a function of her basic personality structure rather than the relatively temporary outcropping of her struggle to achieve new solutions in response to the developmental crisis posed by pregnancy and delivery (Bibring et al., 1961). She gave us hints of her orientation toward minimal handling of the infant and of her philosophy of a minimal exposure of the baby to sights and sounds. She was quite unable to share with the observers their enthusiastic responses to this very beautiful, wide-eyed, cuddly infant. She would either respond with exaggerated casualness or would absent herself from the scene upon the arrival of the observer. There was a noticeable absence of tender exchanges between mother and baby, and she apparently never held the infant "just for the fun of it."

In presenting the clinical data in a condensed form, I shall perforce highlight those observations of mother and infant which are relevant to the thesis of this paper and omit the data pertaining to the normal aspects of this baby's development.

Home visits confirmed reports from Mrs. T. that Daphne settled into a static routine in which the baby was successfully insulated from stimuli. She spent most of her time in the quiet solitude of her bedroom, enclosed in a small bassinette which reposed within a larger car bed with screened sides. She was in a position from which she could hear sounds but was unable to see anything out of her bed. The crib was not equipped with dangling toys or any other source of pleasurable visual or auditory stimulation. Daphne was never fussy during the early weeks and gained well on breast feeding. At age five weeks, it was stressed that she had wide-open bright eyes, would single out people with her eyes, and visually hold onto them, seemingly staring. The early promise of a good visual apparatus seemed to be fulfilled. When held on the observer's lap, she stared fixedly and intently at his face for an unusually long period of time, and was not distracted by the multitude of other stimuli impinging upon her. This capacity to stare fixedly at an object, first noted at this time, was to become an important feature of Daphne's waking life. This baby continued to evince distress in response to any change, including the postural changes involved in being picked up.

When seen on a home visit at seven weeks, Daphne's skin was very mottled, presumably due to the cold and her relative inactivity. The baby was sucking on her fist, eyes wide open, *staring* at the corner of her crib pad. When the observer spoke to her, there was no response to indicate that she had heard. The observer then walked to the other side of the crib, but Daphne did not look at him; she continued to suck on her fist and to stare at the crib pad. The mother emphasized Daphne's unresponsiveness to people, trying to rationalize it on the basis of the baby's tendency to become excited by stimulation. She confirmed the picture of a bare, spartan, routinized, and isolated existence that was being offered to her daughter. At no time during this visit did she openly express any pleasure in the baby, and nothing in her actions revealed any feeling of enjoyment or any wish to be close to her daughter.

It is by now commonplace to relate aspects of an infant's development to specific maternal practices or attitudes. A specific formulation, directly applicable to our understanding of the interaction between Mrs. T. and Daphne, is to be found in a discussion by Robert Waelder at the symposium on "Problems of Infantile Neurosis" (1954): "Miss Freud . . . widen[s] the problem of maternal rejection, on the one hand by considering both rejection and stimulation, and on the other by differentiating between the reactions of the same mother to the various activities of the child. This approach . . . gives us . . . the realistic picture of mothers rejecting some trends in their children and stimulating others . . . the environment has a selective influence upon the development of the constitutional endowment, by encouraging some trends and discouraging others . . . the environment in large measure controls which of the inborn drives of the child—or his ego attitudes—are encouraged, which discouraged . . . the personality of the child may in turn change the mother" (p. 56). We add to this familiar orientation the emphasis placed by Rank (1949a) and her co-workers on the impact of the mother's unconscious conflicts on the development of particular trends in each of her children. This concept was recently brought sharply into focus by Lichtenstein (1961) in elaborating his hypothesis concerning primary identity.

In this study, parents were not in analysis and we had to be content with interview material and an interpretive appraisal of the behavioral patterns as they became manifest and impinged themselves upon the infant. To some extent, we were able to trace out the connections between observed behavior and psychological data supplied by the parents during the interviews, and we did become acquainted with some of the major conflicts and anxieties influencing parental orientation toward the baby. Thus, and in very brief summary, we can describe Mrs. T. as a very efficient, successful, independent, reserved, stoic young woman, with an obsessional character structure. She impressed us as being very well defended, with a great need to control, and a tendency to deny the existence of disturbing situations until after they had been resolved. *Post facto* she could half-jokingly acknowledge her anxiety. An outstanding and very relevant characteristic was her frequently verbalized and strongly felt need for peace and quiet. She was an avid reader, was almost never seen without a book, and apparently relied on books to help her ward off and in other ways control feelings, especially anxiety.

It was in accordance with our anticipation that Mrs. T. promptly proceeded in the post-partum period carefully and methodically to arrange life, so that she could anticipate and feel prepared for each step in Daphne's development. Her initial success at imposing a clockworklike schedule on Daphne exposed her own ambivalence. In the context of an episode of "colic," the mother revealed her desire to be able to predict and to establish rigid controls and schedules, but also her fear of robbing her daughter of her "character" and imposing her own image on Daphne.

Mrs. T. did breast-feed her infant, but a closer examination of the actual process again helps us to see this mother's ambivalence. Consciously she wished to provide well for her daughter, and she did not voice any objections to the *idea* of breast feeding. However, she managed to convert this presumably intimate period of tactual and emotional communication into a library hour for herself, tending thus to emphasize the mechanics of breast feeding and somehow to establish a gulf between her and the infant. The quantity of breast milk was indeed ample, but the quality of the breast-feeding experience left very much to be desired. Brody (1956) reports from her study that infants held for either breast or bottle feeding do tend to gaze at their mothers' faces in those situations where the mothers were free to look at, smile at, or speak to their infants. Otherwise, the infants tended to become drowsy or gazed unwaveringly at an object high on the wall or ceiling, or at their own hands, or at a close part of the mother's body. We are here reminded of Daphne's pronounced tendency to stare fixedly at the corner of her crib pad, or at some minute, stationary object.

Two separate but interconnected forces were already influencing Daphne's development, i.e., Mrs. T.'s studied casualness and emotional detachment from the infant, and her creation of an aseptic atmosphere, heavily laden with drabness and silence. The immediate effect of this impoverishment was to limit the baby's opportunities for pleasurable sensory experiences and thus to set up an early barrier to a shift of libidinal cathexis from the self. Implicit in this statement is the thought that a direct relationship exists between an adequate discharge of instinctual tension via the sensory modalities, with its attendant gratifications, and the strengthening of a baby's cathexis of sensations. An important place is thus assigned to this early cathexis of sensory experiences as a bridge between the initial cathexis of the self and the eventual cathexis of the object. The hypothecated pleasurable cathexis of impulses and sensations should pave the way for the wish to repeat the cycle of tension rise and fall. A baby who is deprived of this opportunity for satisfying sensory experiences, for example, by being kept for many hours of the day in a lonely, drab room, devoid of colorful objects to arouse his visual interests, might indeed surrender a portion of his perceptual sensitivity and be forced to search for more primitive bodily gratifications as provided by sleeping, clutching, rocking, or simply staring (Brody, 1956). Indeed, this is precisely the direction in which Daphne is beginning to move.

It has been emphasized by many investigators of child development (Escalona, 1953; Kris, 1951b; Spitz, 1950a, 1959; Ramzy and Wallerstein, 1958; and others) that twelve weeks is an important maturational milestone. Previously imperceptible or less well perceptible functions become integrated and can be observed. The basic neurophysiological prerequisites are now available for coordinated functioning and for the beginning differentiation of the self from the nonself. This is an early decisive moment in the infant's development toward an object relationship.

In our studies, we have become accustomed to see, at about twelve weeks, the emergence of various behavioral correlates of the beginnings of object relationships and of a more definite ego organization. Daphne's performance at this age is therefore particularly striking, since the observations emphasize her relative retardation and her relative unresponsiveness to and disinterest in people. Mrs. T. reports on her baby's persisting tendency to focus her gaze on small and relatively stationary objects. During the psychological test, Daphne concentrated her gaze on her own feet, rather than on the examiner who was talking to and smiling at her. When fretful, she would characteristically quiet much more readily when she was *not* in visual contact with her mother. At no time during the examination was it possible to describe Daphne as "merry." She was showing a marked preference for her third and fourth fingers, and would occasionally bring her free hand to her ear while sucking.

These tendencies built up to a crescendo of sufficient volume as to leave the members of the research group with a growing feeling of uneasiness. At fourteen weeks, the following observations are to be highlighted. The pediatrician held Daphne on his lap so she could see his face and tried in his most persuasive and gentle manner to elicit a smile. Daphne studied him for several minutes, during which time he was uncertain as to whether she was about to smile or cry. The tension culminated in prolonged high-pitched wailing which could be quieted only by the mother's putting the baby over her shoulder. Similar reactions to strangers and new stimuli were repeatedly observed in subsequent weeks. Throughout this morning, Daphne was very vulnerable to the slightest amount of stimulation and was not easily comforted by her mother. The most effective quieting stimulus was this position on her mother's shoulder, staring at the corner of the room, away from people. The only object that really interested her and that elicited a positive response in the form of increased activity and animated facial expression was the movie camera. In general, she seemed to be extremely passive, never initiated social contact, and was outstanding for her lack of responsiveness

to overtures initiated by observers or by her mother. Mrs. T. reported
that the baby was now sleeping fifteen hours at night and was on
three regular meals a day.

A home visit made when Daphne was sixteen weeks old served
to validate the impressions gained during the above observation made
at the Children's Center. It was noted that she was singularly socially
unresponsive, rarely looked at people, and was definitely more comfortable when she was staring at inanimate objects. It was extremely
difficult for her to accept and to adapt to change, and she was quite
unable to tolerate new, albeit mild, stimuli. We were reminded of
the compelling need manifested by many of the older atypical children for constancy and sameness, and of their arrest at a very early
stage of an identification with an inanimate object. There was evidence of restriction in Daphne's functional and adaptive use of her
arms and legs. Body activity was at a very low ebb, and her passivity
was striking. On occasion, she would stare at her raised, flexed legs for
long periods of time, and in this sphere she was precocious. Her
finger sucking was of great importance to her. She frequently mouthed
two fingers of her left hand, with her right hand resting on her head
or brought to rest on the left hand which was being sucked on. She
also clutched at her clothes or at an object placed in her hand, but
rarely did she reach for anything. The mother again commented on
the very many hours spent by Daphne in her crib, either asleep or
"contentedly" staring off into space.

As we pause and note the unhappy state of Daphne's progress to
the age of four months, it would be my inclination simultaneously
to discuss the fate of her instinctual development, the quality of her
object relationships, and the state of her ego organization. However,
since the focus of this presentation is on narcissism, I shall seek to
highlight two considerations:

1. Daphne provides us with a very sharp contrast to the developmental sequences which are readily traced out in the other infants
in this study, and which fit in with psychoanalytic propositions concerning the positive influence exerted by the mother in the gradual
shifting of cathexis from the self to the object. Thus far, I have
demonstrated that Daphne has responded to the particular external
forces impinging themselves upon her by a persistence of the original
narcissistic cathexis, with distortions and deficiencies already begin-

ning to manifest themselves in the areas of her ego formation and in the development of her object relationships. The apparent "stranger anxiety," so vividly demonstrated by Daphne at a precocious age, can perhaps better be understood as "stimulation anxiety." Proceeding from her very early distaste for postural change to her developing intolerance for new sights and sounds (very much fostered by the mother's intense quest for a library type of peace and quiet and her minimal handling of the baby), Daphne did indeed show a pronounced negative response to people by twelve weeks. However, it is our impression that this anxiety type of response was not so much the function of her differential response to mother versus other adults; it represents, rather, a peak in her inability to respond to any change and to cope with the new and the unfamiliar.

2. It is of vital importance from both the theoretical and clinical points of view to consider the implications of such a persistence of a narcissistic cathexis for a child's future development. In this presentation I shall describe Daphne's development to nine months, stopping at that point because of major changes in the environment which substantially influenced the pattern of her development in the subsequent months.

On the occasion of our first contact with Mrs. T. following the summer vacation, she was able to review her concern over the baby's alleged stranger anxiety of the previous few months. As indicated earlier, it is characteristic of this mother that she is only able to acknowledge her anxieties *post hoc*, and so she could now discuss this phenomenon because she felt that Daphne was "getting much better about strange people, places, and noises." Mrs. T. had taken Daphne to visit friends and the baby had responded to the hubbub by screaming continuously for an entire day. However, she had then become less frightened and more responsive.

Daphne was seen at home when she was twenty-three weeks old. The mother placed Daphne on her back on a play-pen pad. The baby remained almost immobile, did very little reaching, but occasionally twirled her hands and feet. She gazed at the observer for prolonged periods, unresponsive in either a positive or negative direction. Her motor responses left much to be desired. She had a floppy quality to her body, and when pulled to sit, she showed no adaptive postural response. This was also noted when she was placed on her feet. She was completely unhappy on her belly and just put her head down into the pad, whimpering. Daphne was interested in her own hands, looking at them and mouthing her middle fingers. She also pulled her feet up to her mouth. When the baby was offered colored rings by the observer, she did become more active, her face momentarily brightening and legs kicking. However, there was no attempt to reach; she soon lost interest and went back to her toes. This lack of persistence was striking and was repeatedly demonstrated.

Mrs. T. again emphasized the baby's placidity, and commented happily on the extraordinary number of hours Daphne spent in her crib, asleep or staring out the window (sixteen to eighteen hours daily). Daphne could be kept contented by being in the room with the relatively immobile cat, and would spend long periods of time just sitting and watching this "baby sitter." When she was placed out of doors, she was again contented to watch the slight movements of leaves, bushes, or even grass! Somewhat uneasily, Mr. T. told of an incident in a supermarket when another woman, in all seriousness, asked her, "Why are you carrying a doll around with you?" It was characteristic of this casually attired woman to dress her daughter in exquisite, dainty, very feminine clothes. The atmosphere emanating from this doll-like infant expressed the mother's unconscious invitation: "Look, but do not touch."

At twenty-five weeks, Daphne was observed during a psychological and a pediatric examination. When she was put on her back, she went into her usual inert position, absolutely motionless. Throughout the psychological examination, she maintained a sameness of mood and demonstrated a marked degree of inflexibility. When the ring was presented to her, she looked at it, waved her arms, but did not reach toward it until it was brought very close to her. She continued to demonstrate a very cautious attitude with unfamiliar objects. Her attention to her mirror image was prolonged and she seemed to become fascinated and facially more expressive as she looked at herself. Her vocalizations were prominent and seemed to be a source of gratification to her. We also saw the beginning of what was to become a characteristic gesture, i.e., from time to time she would put a fisted hand up to her eyes and rub vigorously, as if she were sleepy. (It is in the interest of an attempt at clarity and simplicity that I defer until another occasion any considerations relevant to a discussion of the aggressive drive.)

The following week (twenty-six weeks old) she demonstrated a new peak in what we were beginning to conceptualize as her auto-erotic activities, and a step in the development of an interest in people. In the group situation, she remained very quiet for a long time, watching another baby or the photographer. After a while she rolled over easily, still sober-faced. She showed poor space perception, missed objects which she did reach for, and was unable to correct her hand position in regard to the object. She was still unable to sit unsupported, and when pulled to standing, she did not support any weight. In all this time, there was no positive response to people. The observer then presented the baby with a furry rabbit puppet whose ears were rhythmically moved by the puppeteer. Suddenly, Daphne came to life, began to laugh at the puppet, and showed a good deal of vigorous motor activity, waving her arms and kicking her feet. When the puppet was removed, her expression faded, her activity ceased, and without any kind of protest or distress, she returned to her inactive state. As soon as the puppet was reintroduced, she again laughed and became animated. After a while, she began to respond positively to the puppeteer, independent of the puppet, laughing and kicking in response to overtures.

The range and intensity of her autoerotic preoccupations had become more and more impressive. She was wont to do a good deal of hyperflexing, looking at, and touching her feet and legs. She sought tactile contact at every opportunity, so that she could often be seen touching and stroking the sheet on which she was lying, or her own body, especially her face. Her finger sucking had become even more elaborate. Characteristically, she would bring her left hand up to her mouth and explore, prior to sticking her third and fourth fingers into her mouth. As she sucked, she brought her right hand to rest on her left, as if to support it and hold the fingers in her mouth. Then she put her right hand into her mouth with an exploratory type of gesture, after which the left hand was pulled out with a loud pop as she continued sucking on the right one. She looked at her left hand, felt it all over, and back in it went. This was repeated over and over again with minor variations. Thus, at times she used the right hand to explore herself, touch her face, ear, etc., while sucking the left. She also seemed to enjoy looking at, touching and feeling the observer's hand or lips as she sucked, finding in him a mirror of her own activities. She found the caress extremely gratifying. When the observer would cease, she reached for his hand with her fingers and started him stroking her again, holding onto his hand during the process. When thus preoccupied (sucking, stroking, etc.) she seemed to shut out people and appeared to be entirely focused on herself. The person's hand, not the person, was used by Daphne as the agent of gratification, almost as if this hand were an extension of herself. At other times, however, in the setting of a one-to-one relationship, she was more responsive and manifested her interest and pleasure by appropriate vocalizations, smiles, and motor reactions. However, if the adult's attention wavered, the baby would immediately withdraw into herself and did *not* initiate contact.

When her mother went out of the room, the baby showed little evidence of distress. Her equanimity was in striking contrast to the varied reactions of distress displayed by the other babies. This placidity was accompanied by the eye-rubbing gesture previously described. When her mother returned and spoke to Daphne from across the room, Daphne responded only with a widening of her eyes and a dilation of the pupils. She seemed to be immobilized and gradually began to suck her fingers as she watched her mother very intently. When the mother came over and picked her up, Daphne dissolved into tears.

At twenty-eight weeks Mrs. T. reported her intention of gradually weaning Daphne to a cup and commented that the baby was very irritable "because of a cold and her second tooth." She was indeed very distressed during the entire morning, grasping her feet, rubbing her eyes, sucking her fingers, and bursting into fretful, high-pitched tears. Mrs. T. attempted to console her by piling one toy on top of another near Daphne, none of which the baby could focus on. The mother was defensively aware of Daphne's relative retardation, e.g., in sitting, and tried to explain it away. Later in the morning, Daphne, on the mat, began to scream in her high-pitched, inconsolable way, trying to hide her eyes or stuff her mouth with her hands. Her crying was disconcerting in that it would be turned on or off without any apparent relationship to what was going on around her. She found some comfort in her fingers and by bringing her feet to her mouth as she clutched the undersides of her bare thighs. She was by now extremely adept at weaving intricate patterns in the air as her fingers, hands, and wrists went through complicated gyrations. She demonstrated an increasing interest in her hand activities, as she contentedly focused her gaze on the delicate movements of separate fingers. She frequently turned from a toy to a mouthing of her fingers, indicating a preference for the autoerotic gratification.

At thirty weeks, Mrs. T. reported that Daphne spent most of her time playing with her hands and feet, and this often consisted of just sitting and looking at them. In the group observation, Daphne was more actively interested in the other two babies, turning her head from side to side to observe them. At one point, however, she was inadvertently pushed by another baby and began immediately to cry in a high-pitched shriek, holding her hands over her eyes as if to shut out visual stimuli. She would occasionally look at her mother from behind a toy, with a renewal of her gurgly screams. Whenever the other baby began to crawl in her direction, Daphne again dissolved into distressed wails.

I shall bring my description of Daphne's development to a close with a report of a visit to the Center at age thirty-four weeks and a home visit three weeks later. At the Center, Daphne looked very sober, and when she was sat down on the mat, she was rigid. Another baby crawled over and took her hand, but Daphne did not respond. She sat motionless and stony-faced for twenty minutes. Another mother handed her a toy with the comment, "She has been staring at this." Mrs. T. replied testily, "Well, let her go after it!" When another baby bumped into Daphne, she simply toppled over, cried briefly, and then just lay inert on the floor. This seemed to be her response to any sudden stimulus. After lying inert for a few moments, she would begin to watch her fingers go through some gyrations, and would then rub her eyes—a process which could perhaps be more accurately described as "stuffing" her eyes with her fists. It is noteworthy that the mother was now able to comfort Daphne, and the baby did begin to cry as soon as her mother was out of sight, either behind her or out of the room. At such times, she was most readily consoled if she was able to fix her gaze at the window and stare at the trees.

During the home visit when Daphne was eight and a half months old, Mrs. T. commented on Daphne's extreme sensitivity to sounds, and noted that in general Daphne seemed to enjoy minimal sensory stimuli more than gross ones. Mrs. T. lifted Daphne from her crib and plunked her in the middle of the floor, handing her a cloth book to look at. The baby sat motionless, fingering her book as her eyes remained very wide and staring. She remained immobilized in this position, with her hands rotating, clasping and unclasping. Mrs. T. indicated that Daphne was just as much immobilized on her stomach as she was in the sitting up position. This was immediately verified as Daphne, in prone, quickly arched herself with her head off the floor, so that she was left in a typical airplane position. In general, her activities were extraordinarily restricted and there was a striking absence of manifest enjoyment.

Spitz (1959) comments on the spectacular progress in the areas of perception, cognition, memory, object relations, the manifestations of the emotions, which is to be expected around eight months. The expected development toward more complex and meaningful social relationships, toward shadings in affective responses, toward increasing discriminations and expressed preferences, toward definite indications of an identification with the major libidinal object—all these indices of a smoothly coordinated and mutually supportive interchange between maturation and psychological development are not yet demonstrable in Daphne.

## DISCUSSION

We are all too familiar with those extreme deviations in development which we have studied and treated at the Children's Center. In connection with one such child, John I., whom we described (Putnam et al., 1951), we formulated the hypothesis that the libido remains exclusively invested in the self, and traced out the environmental forces which, we felt, could account for the very faulty development of the ego and of object relationship in this child. Today I described a far less pathological situation where we can see, in *statu nascendi,* much milder but definite deviations in a child's development. In essence, Daphne substituted autoerotic activities for object contact; i.e., she retained an unusual degree of investment in the self for a prolonged period of time.

In describing the development of a baby in terminology appropriate to a theoretical concept such as primary narcissism, I am of course attempting to correlate those phenomena which can actually be observed in an infant with an intangible, nonmeasurable, and only assumed quantum of psychic energy. The vital characteristic of this psychic energy highlighted in this presentation is its potential capacity to flow from its original storehouse (the self) to an ever-widening range of objects in the outside world (the nonself). It is not my intent to reflect upon the philosophical and psychological questions which lie at the root of the controversy concerning primary narcissism versus primary object love (for a scholarly discussion of these problems, see Lichtenstein, 1961). It seems to be that the neonate's situation can best be conceptualized as an extension of the very recently relinquished state of being inseparably intertwined with his mother. There is no original basis for a feeling of separateness—on the contrary, there is only basis for a feeling of unity. Any and all of the neonate's experiences could therefore be conceptualized as being felt by him as an extension of the original state of affairs. It would not be necessary for the baby to have any awareness of a separate self in order for us to hypothecate a concentration of psychic energy on the self. Rather, we would understand by the term "self" in this early period of life that fusion of self and mother which is biologically germane only to the intra-uterine state. The more usual definition of self as reflecting an awareness of separateness from the nonself is, of course, acquired only gradually during the first months of life. This is the essential prerequisite for and correlate of the shifting of cathexis from the original self-and-mother unit to the mother as a nonattached, only sometimes available, separate entity.

Mrs. T. is a young woman who is by no means devoid of a capacity to form meaningful relationships. However, her significant and close relationships, e.g., with her husband, represent the kind of sharing which is enjoyed by two companions who have a mutuality of interests, such as reading, golf, etc. By word and deed, she impressed us with her need to attain a companionable, practical, but not too highly charged or intimate relationship with her daughter. I have described the spartan atmosphere created by Mrs. T., and the way in which she kept body and emotional contact down to the barest acceptable minimum.

If we permit ourselves to speculate about Mrs. T., we proceed from an awareness of the extremes to which this mother went in her very persistent endeavor to protect the child from stimulation. We would have to assume that such an insistent and persistent emphasis has a deep-rooted instinctual basis. It is quite likely that she used books as a prop to help protect her against visual and other stimulation. It thus becomes part of my speculation that this woman's neurosis includes a very strict, staunch defense against stimulation, and that an original compulsion to ward off sexual stimuli reflected itself in the unconsciously motivated and well-rationalized campaign to "protect" her daughter against all stimuli. This is certainly not an atmosphere in which cathexis is enticed away from the infant's body onto the object!

In terms of the model of narcissism I am utilizing, the libido remains in its original storehouse of the self, and cathexes are only sporadically and infrequently sent out onto objects; i.e., the pseudopodia are only minimally in evidence. It is in this context that we can understand some of the specific manifestations of Daphne's autoerotic orientation as the baby's attempts to provide herself with pleasure or solace by substituting a part of her own body for the absent, or only minimally available, meaningful and gratifying contact with her mother. Thus, we see the gradual development of her finger sucking into an elaborate ritual, accompanied by stroking or rubbing of the ears, face, etc., supplemented by a range of other preoccupations with her body. In all of this we would again be forced to the conclusion that the great bulk of this baby's libidinal cathexis was not shifted to the image of the object but remained focused on the experience of satisfaction and relief via her own body. It was also our repeated observation that for Daphne the autoerotic activity did not constitute a self-arousal device (Escalona, 1954) but rather aided her in screening off the environment. In a footnote dealing with the impact of maternal behavior on the development of perceptual style, Escalona and Heider (1959) state: "Those infants whose mothers tended to maintain a good deal of distance from their children, both physically and emotionally, furnished the most extreme examples of infants who rely on motor habits and more narrowly autoerotic behavior for the re-establishment of equilibrium.

That is, the great majority of babies who conspicuously engage in stroking and pinching of their own skin, rhythmic body motion, peculiar and often rhythmic vocalizations without communicatory or expressive meaning, etc., almost all had mothers who were distant, or mothers who were singularly inept in comforting their babies. The one exception in our Infancy data was excessive thumb sucking, which occurred both among this group of babies and also among those who enjoyed a particularly close relationship with the mothers" (p. 77).

The persistence of such a state of narcissism has obvious implications for ego development. It is beyond the scope of this paper to discuss these aspects of Daphne's development in detail. Suffice it to say that our observations, supported by periodically repeated formal psychological tests, demonstrated progressively more pronounced deficiencies in this baby's ego apparatus.

This can best be illustrated by recalling the very particular ways in which Daphne used her hands. I described the intricate patterns created by this baby as she spent endless hours gazing "contentedly" and with self-absorbing preoccupation at her own movements. I must assume that she was indeed the recipient of a good deal of gratification resulting from this visual and proprioceptive sensory experience. The position of the fingers and hands throughout all of these gyrations was essentially nonfunctional. Though she had a well-developed motor capacity, she used her appendages only expressively. Concomitantly, there was a striking lag in the development of those hand abilities which we associate with an infant's growing capacity to deal with the environment. Daphne did not reach out, pick up, explore with her hands, etc.; i.e., her hand movements did not become integrated into a functional process. In so far as we see this as a reflection of a state of affairs in which the libido retains its narcissistic focus, i.e., there is an elaboration of gratifying but nonfunctional hand movements, we make the assumption that psychic energy is not being utilized for the development of those capacities which are associated with the ego's tasks of adaptation and mastery.

Daphne's development provides us with many opportunities to demonstrate the thesis that specific components of an infant's evolving personality structure represent the outcome of the mother's (and father's) conscious and unconscious selection of and emphasis on particular innate capacities, with the concomitant rejection or minimization of others. Thus, Daphne was impressive for her quality of moderateness—as stated, the amplitude of her response was almost always muted. She was remarkably free of startle reactions as a neonate and fell into the category of infants with a low activity level. From another study, it is reported that "variability and range in bodily activity, and such characteristics as restlessness or the capacity to remain quiet, are relatively more stable traits than is activity level as such" (Escalona and Heider, 1959, p. 73). Furthermore, there was some evidence that Daphne had an initial aversion to new experiences. Conspicuous by its absence was any attitude of striving or pleasure in connection with maturational phenomena. These parents, for different reasons, yearned most passionately for a quiet, good, undemanding infant. In innumerable ways, they sought to insure this type of development, thus imposing definite limitations upon the patterning of the infant's perceptual and motoric behavior, and insuring the baby's decreasing capacity for enjoying that which was at all unfamiliar (Brody, 1956). Daphne's lack of persistence, coupled with a lack of decisiveness, contributed to a placid passivity which made it all too easy for the mother to distract Daphne or divert her into a meaningless staring into space or a contented gazing on a crib pad, puppet, etc. During psychological tests, Daphne was impressive for her minimal capacity to reach out, to focus on the presented task, or to solve the age-appropriate problems assigned to her. There was thus an unhappy concordance of innate potentials and environmental demands, resulting in the development of a non-complaining, self-focused, passive infant.

A full discussion of the problem of anxiety would take us too far afield. I merely wish to refer to Hoffer's discussion (1950) of the specific ways in which the earliest experiences in perception and motility may be linked with pleasure and pain. Hoffer points out that the greater the failure of the mother in her efforts to relieve the infant in distress, the greater will be his helplessness ("silent trauma"), and the more will he react by a withdrawal of cathexis, or by a surrender to helpless crying, or by both. An infant is repeatedly engaged in the process of effecting gradual transformations of instinctual demands into ego-controlled activities. ". . . the ways in which the persons in the infant's environment react to such tiny acts . . . and to normal tensional behavior from day to day may be decisive for the infant's freedom to perceive reality, freedom to exercise motoric capacities, and freedom in general from an anxiety which would necessarily consume energies otherwise available for adaptive functions" (Brody, 1956, p. 373f.). Many of the mothers in our project spontaneously and often ingeniously devised ways of helping their infants meet the challenges of such maturational tensions as reaching, rolling over, sitting up, crawling, etc. Mrs. T. was unhappily reduced to one formula: "Daphne will do it herself sooner or later." Once again I must call attention to the impact of specific maternal attitudes on particular inherent capacities (or incapacities). I have already alluded to Mrs. T.'s ambivalent wish not to impose her own forceful personality upon the baby, and I would suppose that this contributed to her laissez-faire attitude toward Daphne's maturational problems. On the side of the innate, I remind the reader that Daphne from the beginning was unhappy with changes of position, being lifted, turned over, etc. It is a speculation shared by others that infants who are distressed when exposed to spatial disorientation and who do not have the capacity to make the necessary compensatory postural adjustments may find it more difficult to engage in "bodily exploits which subsequently serve to establish comprehension of spatial relationships and anchorage in space" (Escalona and Heider, 1959, p. 83). Indeed, Daphne remained moderately retarded in important areas of spatial orientation. As she found herself deficient in this sphere of her ego functions she was further hampered in her capacity to master the unfamiliar. It is conceivable that the resultant anxiety (or organismic distress) did interfere with Daphne's freedom to explore, helped reduce her zest for new experiences to the vanishing point, contributed to the perpetuation of a narcissistic investment of the self, and inevitably minimized her capacity to cathect sensory experiences and eventually the human object. A conspicuous symptomatic expression of this process was the development and elaboration of a complex series of autoerotic phenomena which helped foster her withdrawal into herself.

## BIBLIOGRAPHY

Benedek, T. (1938), Adaptation to Reality in Early Infancy. *Psa. Quart.*, 7.

Benjamin, J. (1960), Some Developmental Observations Relating to the Theory of Anxiety. *J. Amer. Psa. Assn.*, 9.

—— (1961), The Innate and the Experiential in Development. In: *Lectures on Experimental Psychiatry*, ed. H. W. Brosin. Pittsburgh: University of Pittsburgh Press.

Bergman, P. & Escalona, S. K. (1949), Unusual Sensitivities in Very Young Children. *This Annual*, 3/4.

Bibring, G. L., Dwyer, T. F., Huntington, D. S., & Valenstein, A. F. (1961), A Study of the Psychological Processes in Pregnancy and of the Earliest Mother-Child Relationship. *This Annual*, 16.

Bing, F. J., McLaughlin, F., & Marburg, R. (1959), The Metapsychology of Narcissism. *This Annual*, 14.

Bowlby, J. (1960), Grief and Mourning in Infancy and Early Childhood. *This Annual*, 15.

Brody, S. (1956), *Patterns of Mothering*. New York: International Universities Press.

Escalona, S. K. (1953), Emotional Development in the First Year of Life. In: *Problems of Infancy and Childhood*, ed. M. J. E. Senn. New York: Josiah Macy, Jr. Foundation.

—— (1954), In: Problems of Infantile Neurosis: A Discussion. *This Annual*, 9.

—— & Heider, G. M. (1959), *Prediction and Outcome*. New York: Basic Books.

Fenichel, O. (1945), *The Psychoanalytic Theory of Neurosis*. New York: Norton.

Freud, A. (1946), The Psychoanalytic Study of Infantile Feeding Disturbances. *This Annual*, 2.

—— (1952), The Mutual Influences in the Development of Ego and Id: Introduction to the Discussion. *This Annual*, 7.

—— (1954a), Some Remarks on Infant Observation. *This Annual*, 9.

—— (1954b), In: Problems of Infantile Neurosis: A Discussion. *This Annual*, 9.

—— (1960), Discussion of Dr. Bowlby's Paper [Grief and Mourning in Infancy and Early Childhood]. *This Annual*, 15.

Freud, S. (1895), Project for a Scientific Psychology. *The Origins of Psychoanalysis*. New York: Basic Books, 1954.

—— (1905), Three Essays on the Theory of Sexuality. *Standard Edition*, 7. London: Hogarth Press, 1953.

—— (1911), Formulations on the Two Principles of Mental Functioning. *Standard Edition*, 12. London: Hogarth Press, 1958.

—— (1914), On Narcissism: An Introduction. *Standard Edition*, 14. London: Hogarth Press, 1957.

—— (1915), Instincts and Their Vicissitudes. *Standard Edition*, 14. London: Hogarth Press, 1957.

—— (1920), Beyond the Pleasure Principle. *Standard Edition*, 18. London: Hogarth Press, 1955.

—— (1923), The Ego and the Id. *Standard Edition*, 19. London: Hogarth Press, 1961.

—— (1925), A Note upon the 'Mystic Writing-Pad.' *Standard Edition*, 19. London: Hogarth Press, 1961.

—— (1926), Inhibitions, Symptoms and Anxiety. *Standard Edition*, 20. London: Hogarth Press, 1959.

—— (1940), *An Outline of Psychoanalysis*. New York: Norton, 1949.

Greenacre, P. (1952), *Trauma, Growth and Personality*. New York: Norton, Chapters I and II.

—— (1958), Toward an Understanding of the Physical Nucleus of Some Defence Reactions. *Int. J. Psa.*, 39.

—— (1960), Considerations Regarding the Parent-Infant Relationship. *Int. J. Psa.*, 41.

Hartmann, H. (1950a), Psychoanalysis and Developmental Psychology. *This Annual*, 5.

—— (1950b), Comments on the Psychoanalytic Theory of the Ego. *This Annual*, 5.

—— (1952), The Mutual Influences in the Development of Ego and Id. *This Annual*, 7.

—— (1956), Notes on the Reality Principle. *This Annual*, 11.

—— & Kris, E. (1945), The Genetic Approach in Psychoanalysis. *This Annual*, 1.

—— —— & Loewenstein, R. M. (1946), Comments on the Formation of Psychic Structure. *This Annual*, 2.

Hendrick, I. (1942), Instinct and the Ego during Infancy. *Psa. Quart.*, 2.

—— (1951), Early Development of the Ego: Identification in Infancy. *Psa. Quart.*, 20.

Hoffer, W. (1950), Development of the Body Ego. *This Annual*, 5.

—— (1952), The Mutual Influences in the Development of Ego and Id: Earliest Stages. *This Annual*, 7.

Jacobson, E. (1953), The Affects and Their Pleasure-Unpleasure Qualities in Relation to the Psychic Discharge Processes. In: *Drives, Affects, Behavior*, ed. R. M. Loewenstein. New York: International Universities Press.

—— (1954), The Self and the Object World: Vicissitudes of Their Infantile Cathexes and Their Influences on Ideational and Affective Development. *This Annual*, 9.

Kris, E. (1951a), Opening Remarks on Psychoanalytic Child Psychology. *This Annual*, 6.

—— (1951b), Some Comments and Observations on Early Autoerotic Activities. *This Annual*, 6.

Lichtenstein, H. (1961), Identity and Sexuality: A Study of Their Interrelationship in Man. *J. Amer. Psa. Assn.*, 9.

Lustman, S. (1957), Psychic Energy and Mechanisms of Defense. *This Annual*, 12.

Mahler, M. S. (1954), In: Problems of Infantile Neurosis: A Discussion. *This Annual*, 9.

Mittelmann, B. (1954), Motility in Infants, Children, and Adults. *This Annual*, 9.

Nacht, S. (1952), The Mutual Influences in the Development of Ego and Id: Discussion. *This Annual*, 7.

Orr, D. W. (1942), Is There a Homeostatic Instinct? *Psa. Quart.*, 2.

Putnam, M. C., Rank, B., & Kaplan, S. (1951), Notes on John I.: A Case of Primal Depression in an Infant. *This Annual*, 6.

Ramzy, I. & Wallerstein, R. S. (1958), Pain, Fear, and Anxiety. *This Annual*, 13.

Rangell, L. (1961), The Role of Early Psychic Functioning in Psychoanalysis. *J. Amer. Psa. Assn.*, 9.

Rank, B. (1949a), Adaptation of the Psychoanalytic Technique for the Treatment of Young Children with Atypical Development. *Amer. J. Orthopsychiat.*, 19.

—— (1949b), Aggression. *This Annual*, 3/4.

—— & Macnaughton, D. (1950), A Clinical Contribution to Early Ego Development. *This Annual*, 5.

Ritvo, S. & Solnit, A. J. (1958), Influence of Early Mother-Child Interaction on Identification Processes. *This Annual*, 13.

Rubinfine, D. L. (1961), A Survey of Freud's Writings on Early Psychic Functioning. *J. Amer. Psa. Assn.*, 9.

Schur, M. (1960), Discussion of Dr. Bowlby's Paper [Grief and Mourning in Infancy and Early Childhood]. *This Annual*, 15.

Spitz, R. A. (1945), Hospitalism: An Inquiry into the Genesis of Psychiatric Conditions in Early Childhood. *This Annual*, 1.

—— (1950a), Relevancy of Direct Infant Observation. *This Annual*, 5.

—— (1950b), Anxiety in Infancy. *Int. J. Psa.*, 31.

—— (1953), Aggression: Its Role in the Establishment of Object Relations. In: *Drives, Affects, Behavior*, ed. R. M. Loewenstein. New York: International Universities Press.

—— (1955), The Primal Cavity. *This Annual,* 10.
—— (1959), *A Genetic Field Theory of Ego Formation.* New York: International Universities Press.
—— (1961), Early Prototypes of Ego Defenses. *J. Amer. Psa. Assn.,* 9.
—— & Wolf, K. M. (1949), Autoerotism. *This Annual,* 3/4.
Waelder, R. (1954). In: Problems of Infantile Neurosis: A Discussion. *This Annual,* 9.

# THE PARENTS' ROLE IN THE ETIOLOGY OF LEARNING DISABILITIES

## EDITH BUXBAUM, PH.D. (Seattle)

### I

In the course of working with school-age children who suffered from learning difficulties of varying degrees, we had the opportunity of studying not only their relations to their parents but also their parents' relations to them. There are only a few references to the parents' active and continued participation in their children's learning difficulties in the psychoanalytic literature. Robert Koff, reviewing the psychoanalytic literature on a panel on "Learning Difficulties in Childhood" (1961), summed it up in the following way:

It seemed to me that the greatest agreement and understanding has been in the areas of the content of the fantasies of people having a disorder of learning. The nature of the conflicts, the dynamic tendencies and countertendencies, are most clearly described. Starting with Freud's concept of inhibition of function, the id-ego-superego conflicts are elaborated and related to instinctual development on oral, anal, phallic, and genital levels. Regressions to early types of mental operations are described.

The next point of view is the consideration of the nature of the ego itself, especially the quality or mode of the energy utilized in the learning process. The essence of learning is in the process of abstraction, of conceptualization, and the ego utilizes a sublimated form of energy, as well as a shift of aim to accomplish this. Regression to sexualized and aggressivized modes of energy is characteristic of learning problems.

Finally, there is the huge puzzle about the nature of lan-

I am much indebted and grateful to the staff of the Northwest School, Eve Smith, M.A., and Mrs. Octavia Burton, and to the therapists of the Northwest Clinic of Psychiatry and Neurology, Francis S. Bobbitt, M.D., Charles A. Mangham, M.D., and Adolph M. Gruhn, M.S.W., for their material and discussions, which I have included in this paper.

EDITH BUXBAUM

guage itself. Learning problems in children most often seem oriented about learning to read and write a language, because words are the symbols by means of which we communicate.

Some authors believe language is originally derived from a symbol-forming tendency inherent in the human mental apparatus. Likewise, speech is said to be genetically determined. There must exist some point in development where the need to communicate is the organizing principle which joined the originally separate symbol-forming tendency with speech to create language.

Thus, the literature on learning difficulties is almost exclusively concerned with intrapsychic processes and conflicts. The interpersonal conflicts of childhood are only implicitly considered as contributing to the symptom of learning disability. Yet for some time analysts have been aware of the fact that parents participate in a most important way in the etiology of learning difficulties. Spitz and Wolf (1946), Joyce Robertson (1962), and Ernst Kris (1962) have described and discussed the interaction between mothers and infants that may delay the desire to be held, to touch, to grasp, and the smiling response, which are expressions of the first social contact. Vocalization may be promoted or delayed by the mother's response. Preverbal communications and subliminal perceptions on the part of both mother and child are intricate and complicated; only prolonged observation and contact allow some understanding of them.

Ego functions mature in the climate of their environment like flowers that require certain climate and soil conditions for growth. They may develop normally, subnormally, or hypernormally. As is generally true, it is easier to study the conditions of abnormality than to find out those which assure normality. The delayed and retarded development of infants as it is described by the above authors seems to be due to a deficiency in the relationship between the mothers or their substitutes and these children. Lack of stimulation as well as unrelieved pain and frustration are the rule for those infants whose mothers are unable to read the signals with which the children communicate their needs.

Another type of retarded development has been described by Margaret Mahler (1952), who has coined the term, "symbiotic relationship," to describe a relationship between mother and child which results in making them each other's prisoner. They seem to be unable to live with each other and unable to live without each other. Ilse Hellman (1954) has made similar observations on mothers of children with intellectual inhibitions.

Analysis makes it possible to understand, and often to dissolve, the noxious tie between mother and child. I have found that such mother-patients often develop a strong, overly dependent transference. They are unhappy at any interruption of treatment, afraid to be left alone by the therapist; silence on the part of the therapist is hardly bearable for them; they are afraid that they or the therapist might die at any separation. They expect that the therapist will fulfill all their needs and often think that their troubles would be over if they only had a penis. They expect fulfillment of that wish, too, and are angry and disappointed when the reality is pointed out. At times they show an inability to express themselves adequately—but they expect that the analyst will understand them without words.

The relationship of these mothers to their children shows the same characteristics, only in reverse: the mother requests that the child stay with her lest one or the other, or both, might die. The understanding between mother and child must remain wordless, as it was in infancy, in order to ensure their insoluble oneness. Such more or less complete symbiosis of mother and child leads to severe, massive disturbance of the child, usually of a psychotic nature, which Margaret Mahler has described.

I consider partial symbiosis to be the etiological basis for functional deficiencies which encompass not all areas of behavior and functions but are confined to specific ones. Among these is inadequate speech. Such children may say just a few words and mostly indicate their wishes by gestures. The mother, and sometimes siblings, understands these gestures and fulfills their wishes, thus making speaking unnecessary. Or the children talk baby talk, which again is understood by somebody in the environment; this baby talk then serves as a secret language between two people from which everybody else is excluded. The mutual dependency is upheld in the area of speech. An example of the mother's investment in her child's deficiency in speaking was a mother who brought her four-year-old boy into therapy because he spoke very poorly and only to her. She did not bring him back, however, after he had talked to

the therapist the first time in whispering tones—and had said within mother's hearing, "I don't want to go home!" She preferred him
not to talk rather than love somebody else; she was afraid he might
leave her.

Food is another of those areas. The child refuses to take food
from anybody except one person and in addition is extremely selective about the kind of food he will eat; very often he eats only two
or three kinds of foods. The mother again is concerned and upset,
but secretly she is delighted to be the only person from whom the
child will take nourishment. This reveals itself in the mother's visible disappointment when the child eventually likes somebody else's
food.

Another area of such partially symbiotic mother-child relations
occurs in regard to sphincter control: in one way or another, the
child whose mother is preoccupied with the child's, and usually
also her own, defecation remains dependent on his mother in de-
fecating. Some soil, some are constipated, but they all cling to their
mother's ministrations, by demanding enemas or by wanting to be
wiped, to be asked to go to the toilet, or to be asked whether they
have had a bowel movement. The same is true for control of urina-
tion.The child needs to be reminded or awakened for urinating
long past the time when children normally are able to control themselves. He insists that his mother participate in this function. The
mother, on the other hand, satisfies her own needs as much as those
of the child: the genital or anal area of the child is touched, looked
at, cleaned, and fondled, allowing the mother direct and vicarious
satisfactions of old, infantile, forbidden pleasures, which have been
repressed for a long time. The mother who wants to have a penis
of her own insists on participating in the handling of the son's penis
in order to fantasy that she owns it.

The child's reluctance to dress himself or to play by himself or
with another child is often due to the same kind of relationship
between mother and child which tends to keep the child dependent
exclusively upon the mother.

The child who suffers a functional deficiency of the kind described is often unable to learn in school. His inability to function
independently carries over into the area of academic learning. I
consider an all-pervasive learning difficulty a disturbed ego function

which is based upon a partially symbiotic relationship between mother and child.

The child whose academic learning difficulties are pervasive is disturbed not only in the area of learning but also in the area of behavior. He is unable to tolerate any pressure, for example, to sit on a chair longer than he wants; his attention span is extremely short; he is unable to tolerate any frustration, but bursts into tears or temper tantrums at the slightest difficulty. He is also unable to let anybody show him or teach him how to do something. He is engaged in a constant love-fight with his mother: he clings to her desperately, sometimes to the point of being unable to separate from her for any length of time. His school attendance is likely to be poor. He is often sick or is kept at home for other reasons. The mother herself is desperate; she alternates between tolerating or promoting the child's demands, and losing patience and punishing him in wild outbursts of temper. She participates excessively in the child's school performance. She considers his success or failure her own; she checks his work, tests him, and bribes and threatens him, carrying on the old fight in a new field. The child in turn feels unable to function alone in his work, as in other areas of his life. The ability to learn in school—or to study in any situation—has become another area of a partially symbiotic relationship.

All-pervasive learning disorders are different from circumscribed, symptomatic learning disorders. All-pervasive learning disorders, like primary behavior disorders, are the result of a continuing conflict with the mother. Symptomatic learning disorders are to some degree the result of internalized conflicts, although here, as in other neuroses of childhood, the battle with the environment continues and shapes the child's behavior.

## II

We had an unusual opportunity to study the interaction between parents and children in regard to their learning difficulties in the Northwest School,[1] which was housed by the Northwest Clinic

[1] The school was supported by the members of the Northwest Clinic of Psychiatry and Neurology in Seattle, Washington, and a teaching grant from the National Institute of Mental Health. Tuition fees were on a sliding scale.

during the past ten years. The school was intended to teach children between the ages of six and twelve who were unable to attend the public schools because of their psychological difficulties and who were in treatment. All of these children showed learning disabilities of varying degrees, which were an integral part of their disturbances.

Most of the children were treated by the therapists of the Clinic (Drs. Bobbit, Buxbaum, Mangham, and Gruhn, M.S.W.), some by outside therapists. The proximity of therapists and school allowed for a degree of cooperation between teacher and therapist which went beyond that of the regularly scheduled individual and staff conferences. Sidewalk consultations between teacher and therapist proved to be most helpful because it was possible for each to keep the other perfectly posted from day to day. Cases treated by outside therapists served as an unplanned control group: their progress was slowed down by the lack of immediate communication.

The school consisted of one schoolroom which could be sub-divided by movable walls. There were two teachers, Miss Eve Smith and Mrs. Octavia Burton. The number of students varied between three and eight; eight was the largest number the teachers could handle.

Most children in the Northwest School were two or three years behind in their grade achievement. They had been promoted in the public schools, despite their difficulties, as a result of public school policy based on the philosophy of making social promotions. With these particular children this policy had failed. The children did not fit into their classes socially, although they were kept within their peer group. They did not play with other children, nor had they attained the academic achievement of the other children. Social difficulties had been added to their academic difficulties so that many of them were expelled from school.

We considered it to be the role of the Northwest School to keep the children in school and on their achievement level. Many of them had been frequent truants from their other schools. We found that truancy practically did not exist in the Northwest School. In public school these children had at times been sent out of the classroom or sent home for punishment, but this disciplinary measure usually had had little effect. In contrast, at the Northwest School the children felt punished and deprived when they were asked to leave the school temporarily or for good. The school represented a certain security from failure and from being ostracized by other children.

The combination of school and treatment in one building created a type of relationship comparable to that which patients develop in a hospital setting. The school may be compared to a six-hour-a-day hospital which enhanced and facilitated the psychotherapeutic process. Frequently we found that the children would hang around the Clinic before and after schooltime. Everybody in the building from secretary to janitor, including all the doctors, had a part in the relationship. There were certain limits which had to be kept, and these were enforced by everybody in a consistent way.

In the schoolroom minimal standards of behavior and of academic achievement were permissible. The teachers reduced their demands to the point where the child could produce. From this level on, demands were made vigorously and it was expected that they would be fulfilled. Failures to produce in any one subject or in general were constantly brought to the awareness of the student and of the therapist, who then could deal with them as he saw fit.

The possibility that a child could slide through without learning or with cheating of any kind was excluded in this school. Thus the school served as a differential diagnostic means, in the same way as the nursery schools discussed by Anny Katan (1959). At the same time the school was an adjunct to treatment since it could either insist on or dispense with certain performances.

The teacher had conferences with the parents, calling their attention to certain actions and attitudes that were adverse to the children's progress. Some of these were: not bringing the children to school on time or bringing them irregularly; calling for them late and keeping them waiting; forcing them to come to school alone and go home alone or preventing them from doing so; participating in their children's homework in various ways, by asking about it, checking and correcting it, doing it for the children; teaching them in ways which differed from the teacher's methods and thereby disturbing them; and also preventing the children from doing their homework by deciding that they should do other things or use their time in other ways.

These conferences between teacher and parents included an aspect of parent education. Most of the parents were seen by a therapist either for their own difficulties or in connection with their children's difficulties. Whatever was discussed with the teacher could eventually be continued in their discussions with the therapist.

The following cases will demonstrate the interaction between parents and children and their therapy.

## III

*An All-pervasive Learning Disability*[2]

Henry, age nine, was a shy, quiet boy, who was unable to function in school, had no friends, and did not play with other children. He appeared younger than his age, in size as well as in behavior. Both parents were in psychoanalytic treatment and denied as long as they could that their son was in need of help. Henry was skillful in drawing. He was inventive with paper and wood, Tinker Toys, and plasticine. Psychological tests revealed that he was of "at least average intelligence." He did not read, write, or do any number work. He said and demonstrated that he could not remember. He did not know his street address, his birthday, or his age. His mother brought him to the clinic and called for him. The oldest son in the family had drowned at the age of five before Henry was born. He was the youngest of three children. Supposedly he knew nothing of the death of the oldest son.

Henry's analysis started with his setting up a scene: a house in the woods. There were no animals and no people. At the end of the session he quietly dismantled the whole thing and put it away. This went on for many hours. Only gradually, animals and people were added to the scene. The people were in their beds; it was night. The beasts were quietly in the woods, with all their heads directed toward the house. Nothing was ever said, nothing ever happened. At every session the setting was dismantled. The dismantling, however, became more and more violent. Although it was timed to happen at the end of the session, it became the climax of the play; it was staged as a sudden, frightening outburst of impersonal destruction—a catastrophe that destroyed everything and everybody. Gradually this catastrophe moved from the end of the session into the session itself. The

[2] Therapist: Edith Buxbaum, Ph.D.

people got up from their beds and started fighting; the animals moved toward the house and attacked the people. The setting became less important than the fighting and eventually gave way to another fantasy.

It was clear at this point that Henry represented himself as the wild animal, who observed quietly what was going on at night in the parents' bedroom. He saw every action, his own as well as those of others, as utterly destructive. The masturbatory quality of the fantasy as well as Henry's anxiety were obvious.

This fantasy was followed by that of the "Superbaby." The Superbaby could conquer and destroy all people, animals, and monsters. He was almighty. He would as a last resort drown his enemies, and eventually drown himself; however, he would come to life again while his enemies died. Of course, once he had come back to life, the fight would start all over again. He never got older and never died.

When the therapist asked Henry about the boy who had drowned, he knew all about him—the family had talked about the accident, and Henry had heard. He thought of himself as the boy who had drowned when he was five years old. The brother had never gone to school, had not learned to read and write. He lived eternally in his and other people's fantasies. So Henry did not want to go to school, he did not want to read or write or learn, in order to remain magically five years old and continue the fantasy of living the life of his brother.

Henry could not swim and refused to learn how to swim. His refusal to learn how to swim was a mixture of the fantasy of magically being able to swim and his fear of drowning. When he was able to admit his fear, he also had to give up his fantasy of being the Superbaby, who did not die and who, since he was omnipotent, never had to learn anything. The first thing he learned was swimming—and he became an excellent swimmer. Moreover, this resolution of his conflict and fantasy in regard to swimming opened the door to an interest and desire to learn other things as well: he now wanted to go places alone in order to play with boys with whom he had made friends. He did not want his mother to take him every place—he found it embarrassing to be treated like a baby and wanted to be like the other children. In order to be able to use the bus, he had to know his address, how to read the numbers on the bus and the street signs, and how to make change. Reading and arithmetic became knowledge that was necessary in order to get away from his extreme dependency on his mother.

When Henry learned to swim, he gave up the fantasy of being the Superbaby and revealed his various anxieties. His fear, lived out in the fantasy of the Superbaby, was a fear of dying himself, which he denied by his fantasy; it was also fear of destroying those around him, which he acted out in his repeated dramatic play. Kill and be killed was what he saw in the world around him: this was what his parents did to each other, what they did to him—or did they do it to his brother?—and what he felt he wanted to do to them.

His fantasy of the Superbaby was full of feelings of revenge. Another fantasy revealed this feeling more clearly: he played at being a dentist, the therapist being the patient. He made two models of jaws with teeth out of plaster of Paris. Then he proceeded to drill through the upper teeth into the brain, and through the lower teeth all the way through the body into the penis. In this way he demonstrated of what he was afraid at the dentist's, and for what he held his parents responsible. At one point he casually said, "See my finger? My mother smashed it in the car door!" This had happened when he was two years old, and one finger was shorter than normal. The finger, which was crippled in reality, represented to him far more than a finger: it was his penis, his masculinity, his ability to function with his mind and his body.

Henry's not learning was his accusation of his parents for crippling him in mind and body, while at the same time he punished them by remaining the (drowned) Superbaby, who would take revenge for his death. Helplessness and omnipotence were thus mixed in his fantasies, and both were represented in his learning disability.

The parents' part in creating, promoting, and prolonging Henry's inability to learn in school was considerable. Although the family lived within ten minutes' walking distance from the Clinic, the mother insisted on bringing the nine-year-old boy and taking him home. When I suggested that she allow Henry to come alone, she burst into tears, saying she could not face losing him too in an accident, as she had lost her oldest son who had drowned. She had never let him get out of her sight. The problem was compounded by the fact that the Clinic is located near a lake. The mother eventually overcame her fear in her own analysis and allowed Henry to learn to swim, to come to the Clinic alone, and to go other places by himself.

Henry's father referred to him as "the little guy"; he gave him whatever he desired. One time, when Henry was working on a model boat with a motor, the father brought home for him a bigger and better boat, already put together. He saw no reason for "the little guy" to work so hard if he could buy him a better boat. He also saw no reason to give Henry an allowance, since he could have as much as he wanted any time. He took him out of school whenever he wished to go fishing, hunting, or on a vacation. When the therapist and the teacher protested, he told them that it was quite unnecessary for Henry to be a student because he would inherit the family business and fortune anyway. Even if he could not read or write, other people would do the work for him—so why shouldn't his father go on a vacation with him if he wanted to!

Henry had no allowance. He did not know the value of pennies, nickels, and dimes; he never bought anything. When Henry wanted to make model ships or airplanes, I bought them for him in order to work on them during his session. Henry was concerned that I be reimbursed; since he had no money, he would have to ask his parents. The question of an allowance came up in this connection. But Henry was not interested—he said he did not need any money because his parents bought him whatever he wanted.

The question of money came up again at Christmastime. The idea of giving anybody a present had never occurred to Henry. But when the children in school started talking about it, he told me that he thought of giving his mother a wristwatch. I asked how he would manage to do this since he did not have any money. Henry said off-handedly that of course his father would buy the watch, but it would be his present. The question of what was his father's or his mother's possession, and what was his, led finally to his wanting to give a present that came from himself. He asked his father to give him some money to buy his mother a present. The father thought this was a "cute idea" but said that they would go shopping together and buy mother something "really nice." Henry gave up at this point and was satisfied to fall back into his role of the "cute," dependent, little boy.

I then discussed this matter with the father. It turned out that the father was opposed to giving an allowance of a quarter or a dollar a week because that was not enough to buy what he might want and "he could get anything he wanted by just asking for it." On the other hand, the father did not want to give Henry five or ten dollars a week because he had no idea about the value of money and would probably lose it. The reluctance of Henry's father to give him an allowance was in part due to his need to keep exclusive control over money, on which he based his position in the family. He felt threatened by the idea that his son might not need to ask him for something, as if in this way he, the father, would become expendable.

Eventually the father saw that his attitude was preventing Henry from learning how to deal realistically with money, and decided to give Henry fifty cents a week, a sum that was appropriate to his age and was as much as the other children in school received. After a short time Henry learned what he could buy with his allowance; he learned to make change, and his arithmetic skill took an upward swing. But, even more important, he felt more independent and grownup because he could go places on the bus with his money if he wanted to without having to ask somebody for transportation, and he could save money and buy presents for others, instead of always receiving.

Both parents had different reasons for keeping Henry "a little guy." Both of them used magic means to keep him alive. Both parents used this unrealistic overprotection for ambivalent reasons. Henry, in his refusal to learn, lived out the fantasy of the Superbaby, which they supported.

Every attempt on Henry's part to give up the role of the baby was blocked by one or the other parent. It took the therapist's intervention and the parents' therapy for Henry to give it up. The parents' reluctance to allow realistic gratifications appropriate to Henry's age made it unnecessary and even undesirable for Henry to seek them. The pull toward unconscious gratification in fantasies of magic and omnipotence was reinforced by the parents. To mature against his own infantile wishes and against those of his parents was not possible for Henry: he stood still in his development. This, too, was represented in the eerie scene at the beginning of his analysis—time was supposed to stand still, as in "Sleeping Beauty," keeping the strivings of life in abeyance together with the powers of the bad fairy.

Henry's analysis shows in what way the partial symbiosis with his mother can be considered as the basis for his reluctance and inability to grow up, which would mean separating himself from her. One part of his learning disturbance was an aspect of his partially symbiotic relationship with her. Another part of his learning inability was in different ways related to his father's attitude and Henry's relationship with him. This will be discussed at a later point.

## A Success Neurosis of Childhood[3]

Martin was brought for treatment by his parents because of severe anxiety—his learning difficulties became known shortly after the beginning of treatment. He was nine years old, shy, small, and of average intelligence. He suffered from nightmares and was afraid to play with children in the neighborhood or in school. The public schoolteacher liked him, but said he was too quiet and a poor student; however, since he did not give her any trouble, she was not concerned.

Martin was seen three times weekly; his mother was seen once a week by the same therapist. Martin dreaded going to school. Every day, when it was time to go to school, Martin refused to go. His mother drove him to school because he refused to walk. When they arrived at school he refused to get out of the car, and this resulted in a lot of pushing and pulling. When his father took him to school, he went without offering any resistance.

One of the reasons for Martin's fear of going to school was his inability to do the work. He could not read, spell, or do any arithmetic, although he was in the fourth grade. When this state of affairs became known, it was decided by the parents and the therapist that Martin should attend the Northwest School, where he could get tutorial help, in order to catch up to his grade level.

Martin's difficulties with going to school continued for a while after he came to the Northwest School, although his inability to do the work was no longer the reason, since he was now given work that he could do. In guidance work with the mother, and in therapy with the child, the idea was developed that the fights they had about

3 Therapist: Adolph Gruhn, M.S.W.

coming to school were a game in which both participated. The mother decided not to play the game any more, and she was able to convey this decision to Martin so that he soon began to come without difficulties, and even to come alone on the bus.

The teacher drew Martin's attention to his reading mistakes, and she reported them to the therapist. They became understandable in the course of his therapy.

Martin was not really unable to read, but he read hesitatingly and made peculiar mistakes. He stopped completely when he came to a word with any kind of aggressive connotation or when he associated an aggressive meaning with the word. An example was the word "tank." In the particular context, the word referred to a water tank. Martin, however, took the word in its military meaning and refused to read it either to himself or out loud. It was obvious from his behavior that his difficulty was not in reading but rather in his refusal to pronounce words with aggressive connotations.

Martin's father was a reserve officer, absorbed in the study of arms and weapons of all kinds; he had a private arsenal in a locked room. These weapons were extremely interesting for Martin, but they were absolutely forbidden to him; he was not allowed to enter his father's armory or even to touch the weapons, which were father's toys. Martin took this prohibition against handling aggressive weapons into other areas: he was unable to fight or to compete in any way, unable to express aggression in words, and consequently unable to read any aggressive words.

Martin's difficulties with arithmetic were similarly meaningful. Most of his mistakes were miscalculations by one, either one too many or one too few. They were connected with his mother's lack of one finger, which she concealed so skillfully that it was not immediately noticeable.

It also became obvious that Martin always left his work unfinished or made at least one mistake in otherwise perfect work, and this troublesome behavior proved to be most difficult to understand and to handle. In observing his working with models, which he wanted to do very much, we began to understand the meaning of his need for imperfection. As long as a model was not perfectly finished, it had to be left in the school or in the therapist's office; this was one of the rules in school and one of the rules the therapist had set up.

Martin managed never to finish anything, and therefore never took anything home. His fear that his younger brother might destroy his models was discussed, but apparently this was not the decisive reason. What seemed to bring about a change was the analysis of the following situation.

The father worked in a store that sold models, among other things. He sometimes brought models home for Martin and, when Martin had finished one, took it back to the store where it was displayed as an advertisement. If Martin wanted to keep a finished model, the father demanded that he pay him a part of the cost of the model. This meant that an unfinished model remained Martin's, while a finished model cost him either the model or some money—he did not know how much money, since his father's prices were somewhat unpredictable. This, too, had something to do with Martin's difficulties in arithmetic. But, even worse, Martin considered it dangerous to finish any work. This became connected with the idea that if he finished anything, he would have to lose something. That he did not know what he would lose made the danger even greater. It could be anything—something he cherished, or part of his body like the finger his mother had lost, or perhaps even his life.

Discussions with the father revealed that he saw no harm in taking things from the store, like the airplane models he brought home for Martin. He did not think that he ought to pay for them, although he did not think that Martin should have them without paying for them. His armory, too, contained things that he had kept from the army; his reason for keeping Martin out of that room was not only that he feared for Martin's safety, but also that he did not want Martin to question his ownership of the weapons.

The father came to recognize the inconsistency and dishonesty of his petty thievery and decided that it was not worth the trouble it made for Martin or the money it cost him in therapy. He rectified his handling of the models by allowing Martin to keep them. He also decided to pay for the models himself and consequently was able to set a fair price on them if Martin wanted to buy one.

The private armory remained a closed room for Martin until one day he burglarized it, stole the stolen goods, and distributed them to his friends. His courage scared him almost to death; his father felt sufficiently guilty himself so that he did not punish him severely.

When Martin's fears became clearer, his reasons for not finishing or for making mistakes became conscious, and making mistakes became a willful act instead of an involuntary one.

As often happens with people who suffer from one type of anxiety or another, Martin was not yet willing to give up his defenses without help. The teacher had to insist that Martin finish his work without mistakes. Only then could Martin realize that it was possible to be successful without danger to life and limb.

The teacher's observation and her interference were needed in order to pinpoint Martin's learning difficulties. They provided clues which enabled the therapist to look for certain relationships between these symptoms and others that he already knew, or which made the therapist aware of connections not previously known to him. In this way the teacher's observations became an important stimulus for the therapeutic work, which was considerably speeded up by this close cooperation.

When the therapist and the child came to an understanding of the reasons why Martin could not learn in certain areas, the teacher offered a proving ground for the validity of their conclusions. The teacher and the school represented a reality situation that did not yield to Martin's fantasied anxieties. Omitting words helped him to avoid dangerous fantasies; making mistakes in numbers was a symbol of his castration anxiety, as was his attitude of avoiding success. None of these devices—defenses in the dynamic sense—was accepted by the teacher. Failures in reading, as well as not finishing or avoiding perfect scores, were at first unconscious; later on they were conscious forms of avoidance and denial. The teacher's insistence that Martin did know, and that his mistakes be corrected and a perfect score be achieved, proved to Martin that he could risk the achievement of perfect scores upon the insistence and with the approval of authority. Eventually he became able to achieve perfect scores without this means of ego support. Martin became able to work up to his capacity and be successful; he also gained the ability to play with children and to be openly aggressive if necessary.

## Discussion

Martin's learning difficulty was a symptom of his success neurosis. The success neurosis of children is to be differentiated from symptomatic learning disorders, which can be resolved by the analysis of the particular symptom. Martin's making arithmetic mistakes by one was a symptom that yielded to the analysis of his mother's missing finger. His success neurosis, however, forced him to continue making less definable mistakes. He belonged among those children who have to substitute one failure for another in order not to be entirely successful. Many such children are known to teachers: they may do creditable work in general, but spoil their scores during tests; they may not finish their work or may lose part of it, forget their assignment or do the wrong one, continuously failing in small ways so that their teachers are forced to grade them down.

The picture these students present is similar to that of adult patients who complain that they have just missed a promotion, or that they are afraid of promotion because they may not be able to do the job. This may be so even when they have already been doing the job as "acting" director or "acting" secretary; when they get the actual title, or are offered it, they either collapse or fear that they will collapse. This symptom has been described by Freud (1915) under the heading "Those Wrecked by Success."

Children with these specific types of failures also try their best to remain unsuccessful and not to be promoted. In the American school system of today, this is extremely difficult. Children get promoted in what we call "social promotions," which prevent teachers, parents, and children from recognizing their particular difficulty for what it is. Such children get into treatment mostly because of difficulties other than learning ones, as in the case of Martin.

The attitude of Martin's father contributed to his learning difficulty. He was able to rationalize keeping his arsenal for himself and forbidding Martin to use any part of it by pointing to the danger of the weapons. Similarly, other fathers find more or less valid rationalization for forbidding their children the use of tools ranging from pencils to power saws. Obviously it is necessary to forbid children the use of objects that are dangerous to handle. There is also something to be said in favor of allowing fathers a certain amount of private ownership. Yet, these possessions are overdetermined in the minds of the men; they are regarded not only as useful tools but as symbols of status and masculinity, and it is for just this reason that they are desperately desired by the sons. The sons need to identify

with their fathers in the area which they consider a masculine prerogative. Another area that Martin's father considered his prerogative
was money, as we have seen. The fact that Martin did not know
how much money he could call his own, or how much his father
would take from him, was reflected in his arithmetic mistakes and in
a deeper sense symbolized his castration anxiety.

Martin's reluctance to go to school was a love fight between him
and his mother. It afforded them both a certain amount of body
contact—enough to make Martin feel extremely guilty and afraid of
his father. It was necessary for Martin to give up this physical relationship with his mother before any further progress could be made.

We can see in Martin's case that the area of failure was determined by the interaction between father and son. The son backed away
from an area that the father had staked out for himself, symbolized
in a room containing all the father's instruments of aggression and
symbols of manliness, from which Martin was excluded. Henry, too,
was not allowed to know the value of money, which was the area of
his father's strength and authority.

Martin and Henry could not resolve their difficulties with the
help of therapy alone as long as their fathers continued their attitudes, which were opposing their sons' attempts at competing with
them. An isolated learning difficulty may be considered a symptom,
i.e., an intrapersonal conflict, and as such may be resolved in analytic
therapy. When a child's symptom is being created and maintained
by a parent, the child needs the parent's permission—manifested in
a changed attitude—in order to give it up. In learning difficulties it
is, as a rule, necessary to explore the possibility of such adverse parental influence and to deal with it.

It is generally expected that great men will not bring forth great
sons, but that, on the contrary, well-endowed sons are likely to be
handicapped by their great fathers.[4] A study of some geniuses has
suggested the idea that these men had fathers who devoted all their
knowledge, time, and love to their gifted children while they themselves remained in the background, not making any claim to fame
except that of being the father of a successful son. Eissler (1959) has

---

[4] There are exceptions: Bach and his sons; Breughel, father and sons; but perhaps
these exceptions are in the fields of art, music, and artisanship, areas where family
traditions and schools are involved.

described this kind of relationship in his study of Goethe. Other examples might be John Stuart Mill, Mendelssohn, and Mozart. The corollary of this idea that a father may play a role in bringing out his son's abilities to the fullest is our clinical experience which shows that he can also significantly disturb his son and prevent him from using and developing his abilities. And unused abilities, like unused limbs or tools, deteriorate.

When a father says to his son, "When you finish this airplane model, either I will take it back to the store or you will have to pay me for it," he implicitly forbids his son to accomplish what he set out to do.

When another father says to his son, "I never went to college, and if you don't get to college you'll have the money anyway," and when, in addition to this attitude and these words, he takes his son out of school any time the father wants to take a vacation then he is actively preventing his son from striving to be better than he is.

It is rare that we find the father's feelings expressed so clearly outside of analysis. However, analysis of fathers makes us aware that the father's feelings toward his son are just as strong and rivalrous as the son's feelings toward his father. In fact, they are derived from the father's own oedipal feelings. In a reversal of feelings, the father sees his son as dangerous, as he used to see his father. Now that the father is stronger and more powerful than the son, he can do to the son what he could never to to his previous rival, his father, and he wins at the expense of the son.

Ernst Kris (1955) has said that the learning process functions best in the conflict-free area. Both Martin and Henry bore this out by their inability to learn. For Martin, the learning process was laden with conflict and anxiety, pertaining to his rivalrous competitive feelings toward his father. To some extent Henry's disability had a similar genesis.

Both these boys were so intimidated by their fathers that they were unable to function normally in the areas in which the fathers were relatively strong—areas which the fathers reserved for themselves. These boys resolved their oedipal conflicts by forgoing the ability to compete and to be aggressive with their fathers in the areas of their fathers' strength. They gave up their ability to function by becoming passively aggressive in these areas. They surrendered to their fathers by not exercising some of their ego functions, which they considered aggressive and competitive, and which their fathers acknowledged as a threat to themselves.

Success neurosis has been discussed in the psychoanalytic literature beginning with Freud. Such patients, as adults, may fail when they meet with success in their work, and also when they have succeeded in obtaining the love of a desired woman. They are very often, if not always, impotent. The surrender to the father occurs not only in their ability to function in their work but also in their ability to function as men. In children this impotence is expressed in their castration anxiety, which forbids them to function in areas reserved by their fathers for themselves, and which prevents them from being normally aggressive and competitive.

## IV

In recent years ethologists have pointed out that the development of imprinting occurs during a very critical period of time in the early development of the organism. The end of this critical period seems to be when the organism shows fear responsiveness (Lee Salk, 1962; Charles Kaufmann, 1960). Learning, too, can progress best at "critical times"; i.e., when an organism is ready for action. Ernst Kris remarked in his paper, "Decline and Recovery in a Three-Year-Old" (1962), ". . . that a function that had matured, but was not being used, led to retardation." When a child suffers severe deprivation and lack of stimulation in early infancy, as in the example described by Spitz (1945, 1946), incorrigible retardation and eventual deterioration of constitutionally normal capacities takes place.

In contrast, most of the children with all-pervasive learning disorders were amenable to therapy and became able to learn to some degree. It is significant that the children suffering from all-pervasive learning disorders, as we have seen them in the Northwest School, are children tied to their mothers in a partially symbiotic relationship. They were not physically deprived and left without stimulation. Rather, to the contrary, they were overstimulated and too much taken care of, in so far as their mothers did too much for them in certain areas.

When the kitten or the puppy is ready to feed himself, the mother does not insist on continuing to nurse it. When the human infant is ready to be weaned, the mother may or may not recognize his readiness to take other foods and may continue to nurse him. Some of the difficulties of weaning are due to wrong timing. The readiness of children to take in knowledge may be compared to food intake in more ways than one. We talk about people who "devour books," who "drink in everything." One of the children in the Northwest School refused to learn from a white teacher, but accepted a Negro teacher; she reminded him of a nurse who had fed him when his mother had deserted him for the birth of his sister. He refused to take food from his mother when she returned. Henry insisted on going home for lunch to be fed by his mother, although the other children stayed in school. Only when his mother packed his lunch, telling him that she would not be home, did he stay in school and eat with the others—and he also began to learn with them.

Ernst Kris (1955) stated that learning takes place most effectively in the "conflict-free sphere." When a function has matured, the child feels the need to use it. When he is prevented from doing so, a conflict develops between the child and the person who is preventing him, and this leads to frustration and aggression. I have pointed out (1947a) that children who have been restricted in making use of their maturing functions become extremely frustrated and express their angry feelings in various forms of aggression. The children whose learning disturbances were all-pervasive were often openly aggressive toward their mothers, from whom they were inseparable; all of them were preoccupied with fantasies of destruction of others as well as of themselves.

As long as the child is prevented from functioning by another person, his anger is directed against the outside. Only when outside intervention is removed, do anxiety and inhibition become apparent as signs of the ongoing introjection. What used to be on the outside is now on the inside; e.g., Henry's fear of drowning became apparent after his mother no longer prevented him from learning how to swim.

We think of inhibitions as the result of phase-specific traumata. We consider them one-time occurrences which disrupt the progression of libidinal phases and bring about regressions to fixation points of previous developments. We expect that, once an inhibition is removed, recovery will occur. This is true in those cases where normal development has taken place, where functions have been established. For example, a child who has learned to talk, walk, be continent may give up these functions due to traumatic experiences, but quickly resume them when these experiences have been mastered. This is not the case with the child in whom the development of these functions has been disturbed through the repeated intervention of the mother or her substitute. Ego functions that have been squelched in their beginnings and have never been established independently from the mother can be disturbed to an extent that approaches destruction; and along with them, developmental progression as well as libidinal development are retarded and distorted. In Giovacchini's words (1963): "If the external world does not supply the gratifying experience that leads to learning at a time when the physical apparatus has acquired the ability to master certain skills, a defect occurs which is reflected in the structure of the ego and later in character."

In the child whose disturbances are rooted in his partially symbiotic relation to his mother, certain functions remain dependent on the mother's help. The child is unable to function alone. The cooperative relationship between mother and child continues in the particular area; it is necessary for the mother as well as the child to relinquish their functioning together before the child will be able to function independently of her.

Anna Freud, in the introduction to Kata Levy's paper, "Simultaneous Analysis of a Mother and Her Adolescent Daughter" (1960), says: "Where the neurotic symptom, the conflict, or the regression of a child is anchored not only in the young patient's own personality but held in place further by powerful emotional forces in the parent to whom the child, in his turn, is tied, the therapeutic action of analysis may well be slowed up or, in extreme cases, made impossible." The disturbing factor is not so much the mother's active and conscious interference as a general attitude she displays toward the child. Henry's mother was afraid to lose this child, as she had lost her oldest son. She kept Henry with her to the exclusion of other children; she transported him every place and did not teach him, or allow him, to find his way home. She prevented him from becoming oriented in place and time as well as with people. She prevented him from thinking and doing for himself. These things need not invariably occur together, but, as is the case with inhibitions and phobias, the affected area has a tendency to enlarge itself and to encompass other than the original areas.

The partially symbiotic relationship between mother and child maintains the child's feeling of not being able to function alone in the particular area of his mother's cooperation; when he is left alone he becomes anxious to an extreme degree because he feels helpless. On the other hand, he "feels great" when he is together with his mother. He has her at his disposal, his feeling about himself includes her. He feels as big, strong, powerful, able to do things as they both are together. She functions as his complementary ego. His feeling about his ability to function in the area of his partially symbiotic relationship is either a feeling of helplessness or a feeling of great strength—both unrealistic—both expressed by Henry in his fantasy of the Superbaby.

Moreover, these two feelings are not restricted to this one area, but are carried over into all other areas: if the child cannot do something, he feels furious and anxious and expresses this in temper tantrums; he expects his mother to come to his rescue at this point. He will not attempt to learn anything he cannot do, since he is used to having his mother do for him or with him whatever he cannot do himself. When he is together with her, he has the feeling that he can do anything, without even trying. He cannot assess his own ability or his own strength, and not knowing his own strength or weakness makes it impossible to gauge that of others. His view of the world is distorted, he cannot adapt himself to it, he cannot learn.

Mother and child are tied up in a relationship in which each expects and demands miracles from the other. Miracles—magic, either good or bad—are both wished for and feared, and this brings about an extremely ambivalent relationship in which mother and child are afraid to let got of each other for fear that they will be mutually destructive. The child feels all-powerful as long as he dominates his mother. When the mother is removed from him, he feels threatened by the world onto which he projects his own aggressive fantasies. He now feels as helpless as he felt almighty before. The child who feels all-powerful cannot learn, because learning is itself an admission of not knowing—an admission of weakness. It presupposes logical thinking and an acceptance of reality, which debunk the fantasy of omnipotence. Reality is distorted according to the fantasies of the child.

The fantasy of omnipotence and its opposite, the fantasy of helplessness, are fantasies related to the mother. They are part and parcel of the learning difficulty itself, which is rooted in the partially symbiotic relationship. The mother often seems to be transferring her fears of her own mother onto her child and making him the feared mother person. The child becomes a demanding, aggressive person who threatens his mother as she was threatened in her childhood. When the child feels he can threaten his mother, he feels powerful while she feels helpless like she did as a child; when he feels helpless and dependent on her, she feels indispensable and powerful. His belief in her power lends her fantasies the illusion of being real; this is the reason why she continues the role she plays with him, however inconvenient it may seem to be.

Freud (1911) wrote about the magical thinking of the infant. He discussed the child's inclination to believe that fantasying something makes it come about. He says, "Since the later care of children is modelled on the care of infants, the dominance of the pleasure principle can really come to an end only when a child has achieved complete psychical detachment from its parents" (p. 220). The transition from magical thinking to reality-oriented thinking is a long-drawn-out process, which at best is resolved together with the resolution of the oedipus complex. However, the children who are arrested in a partially symbiotic relationship do not reach the oedipal phase; they remain in the preoedipal phase, and their thinking remains magical to a large degree. Not being able to progress toward reality, they regress further into magic and fantasy.

The child's all-pervasive learning inability is a derivative of a partially symbiotic mother-child relationship which prevents the child from becoming completely independent of his mother. He is dependent on his mother in the function which she has taken over for him, and this results in a defective ego function of the child. When he depends on his mother to interfere with reality on his behalf, he is unable to judge it, deal with it, or adapt himself to it; he cannot think, and he cannot learn. His learning ability, one of his most important ego functions, has been crippled and is defective and disturbed.

Learning difficulties which are rooted in the relation to the father are usually limited to certain subjects. They are success neuroses—failures due to the child's fear of competing with a powerful adversary. This was the way it appeared in Martin's case in regard to his reading, which was connected with forbidden aggression; in arithmetic, which was connected with money; and in his inability to finish a task. His castration anxiety was displaced from his genitals to his ability to function intellectually.

As it happened, all the cases with this particular syndrome were boys. The corollary of it is the woman who forgoes beauty and attractiveness to men because of guilt feelings toward the mother. Marjorie P. Sprince (1962) described a patient, an adolescent girl, who "avoided successes" in the intellectual field because her mother claimed them for herself. In our cases the child chose the location of this displacement in obedience to the father—in Sprince's case, to the mother—and in respecting their expressed prerogatives. In a paper on "Fathers of Sons with Primary Learning Inhibitions," Grunebaum et al. (1962) discuss a number of cases in which sons, in obedience to the unconscious wishes of their unsuccessful fathers, developed specific learning difficulties. The area of their difficulties was not stated. The onset of Martin's learning difficulty was in the oedipal phase and was a symptom expressing his conflicting feelings toward his father. The inability to learn was his way of foregoing aggression and submitting to father. This adversary, however, is potent in reality; the relationship is based upon existing power, however distorted by anxiety and ambivalent feelings it may be. The threats of Martin's father were real ones. Martin's anxiety was to some degree justified.

The children who suffer from success neuroses are the little Oedipuses, who fight their fathers—unsuccessful though they may be —from the vantage point of the oedipal-genital developmental phase. Realistic concepts are in the foreground. In both aspects they differ from children whose learning disabilities are all-pervasive: their libidinal position is preoedipal, and they are preoccupied with fantasies of magical power. In the success neuroses of children we encounter the active participation of the parents in the child's neurosis; in the neurosis of adults, on the other hand, the parents' roles are internalized in the demands and prohibitions of the superego.

## Summary

The cases presented in this paper are representative of two types of children who came to the Northwest School during the past ten years: the child who suffers from an all-pervasive learning disorder is tied to his mother in a partially symbiotic relationship which prevents him from functioning independently of her or from recognizing his abilities and limitations, and his reality orientation is impaired.

The other type is the child whose learning disorder is limited to certain areas. We consider him a success neurosis of childhood, based upon an oedipal conflict.

In both types of cases the parents' continued attitudes and actions prevent the child from gaining control over his ego functions, particularly his learning ability.

### BIBLIOGRAPHY

Buxbaum (1947a), Activity and Aggression. *Amer. J. Orthopsychiat.*, 17.
—— (1947b), *Your Child Makes Sense.* New York: International Universities Press. Republished under the title, *Understanding Your Child.* New York: Black Cat Edition, 1962.
—— (1954), Technique of Child Therapy: A Critical Evaluation. *This Annual*, 9.
Eissler, K. R. (1959). Notes on the Environment of a Genius. *This Annual*, 14.
Freud, A. (1960), Introduction to Kata Levy's Paper. *This Annual*, 15.
Freud, S. (1911), Formulations on the Two Principles of Mental Functioning. *Standard Edition*, 12. London: Hogarth Press, 1958.
—— (1915), Some Character-Types Met with in Psycho-Analytic Work. *Collected Papers*, 4. London: Hogarth Press, 1925.
Giovacchini, P. L. (1963), Integrative Aspects of Object Relationships. *Psa. Quart.*, 32.
Grunebaum, M. G., Hurwitz, I., Prentice, N., & Sperry, B. M. (1962), Fathers of Sons with Primary Neurotic Learning Inhibitions. *Amer. J. Orthopsychiat.*, 32.
Hellman, I. (1954), Some Observations on Mothers of Children with Intellectual Inhibitions. *This Annual*, 9.
Katan, A. (1959), The Nursery School as a Diagnostic Help to the Child Guidance Clinic. *This Annual*, 14.
Kaufmann, C. (1960), Some Ethological Studies of Social Relationships and Conflict Situations. *J. Amer. Psa. Assn.*, 8.
Koff, R. H. (1961), In Panel on: Learning Difficulties in Childhood, reported by E. A. Anthony. *J. Amer. Psa. Assn.*, 9.
Kris, E. (1955), Neutralization and Sublimation: Observations on Young Children. *This Annual*, 10.
—— (1962), Decline and Recovery in the Life of a Three-Year-Old; or: Data in Psychoanalytic Perspective on the Mother-Child Relationship. *This Annual*, 17.
Levy, K. (1960), Simultaneous Analysis of a Mother and Her Adolescent Daughter. *This Annual*, 15.
Mahler, M. S. (1952), On Child Psychosis and Schizophrenia: Autistic and Symbiotic Infantile Psychosis. *This Annual*, 7.

—— & Gosliner, B. J. (1955). On Symbiotic Child Psychosis: Genetic, Dynamic, and Restitutive Aspects. *This Annual*, 10.

Robertson, J. (1962), Mothering As an Influence on Early Development: A Study of Well-Baby Records. *This Annual*, 17.

Salk, L. (1962), Mother's Heartbeat as an Imprinting Stimulus. *Trans. N.Y. Acad. Sci.*, Series II, Vol. 24, No. 7.

Spitz, R. A. (1945), Hospitalism: An Inquiry into the Genesis of Psychiatric Conditions in Early Childhood. *This Annual*, 1.

—— (1946), Hospitalism: A Follow-Up Report. *This Annual*, 2.

—— (1951), The Psychogenic Diseases in Infancy: An Attempt at Their Etiologic Classification. *This Annual*, 6.

—— (1959), *A Genetic Field Theory of Ego Formation*. New York: International Universities Press.

—— & Wolf, K. M. (1946), The Smiling Response. *Genet. Psychol. Monogr.*, 34.

Sprince, M. P. (1962), The Development of a Preoedipal Partnership Between an Adolescent Girl and Her Mother. *This Annual*, 17.

# THE DEVELOPMENT OF A PRESCHOOL SYMBIOTIC PSYCHOTIC BOY

MANUEL FURER, M.D. (New York)

The purpose of this case report is to describe some of the processes by which a preschool-aged psychotic child reinvested the object world and the world of reality, and some of the consequences in his personality development.

## REVIEW OF LITERATURE

The following brief review is concerned with theoretical conclusions about normal development in the earliest period of life which seemed to be helpful in understanding the case material. Margaret S. Mahler's clinical and theoretical contributions to the understanding of child psychosis are implicit throughout.

In Freud's original formulation, the ego evolves out of the id under the impact of reality. Instead of this formulation, Hartmann, Kris, and Loewenstein (1946) introduced the concept of an undifferentiated phase out of which both id and ego are gradually formed. According to them, this structural differentiation depends on the ability of the infant to distinguish between his self and the world around him. They point out that partial deprivation is probably an essential condition for this piece of development; on the other hand, this distinction does not seem to be possible unless a certain amount of gratification takes place. The theory states that an object in the external world is experienced in the beginning as part of the self; in economic terms, that the object partakes of the narcissistic cathexis of the infant. When the distinction has been made, the

Supported by National Institute of Mental Health Research Grant M-3353 "Investigation of Symbiotic Child Psychosis," Principal Investigator, Margaret S. Mahler, M.D.; carried out at the Masters Children's Center, New York City.

Medical Director, Masters Children's Center.

object, now experienced as independent of the self, has retained this cathexis, even though separated.

Jacobson, in her paper "The Self and the Object World" (1954), attempted to clarify some of these issues. In dealing with the distribution of psychic energy, she conceives of the state of primary narcissism and primary masochism as one in which there is both a continuous low-level discharge of energy toward the inside of the body through physiological channels and, at the same time, a discharge to the outside through feeding and excretory functions. She considers the latter as the precursor of object-related discharge. In psychosis, she points out, the semistuporous states represent a regression to this inner discharge, except that in the psychotic there is a generally pervasive destructive quality which contrasts with the libidinal quality of normal sleep. She suggests that psychic energy is still in an undifferentiated state at the beginning of life and that it develops into two kinds of drives, partially under the influence of external stimulation (their potential form is predetermined.)

To solve the problem of secondary investment of the ego with psychic energy, Jacobson proposes, as had Hartmann (1950), the concept of a self representation as opposed to an object representation. Both result from memory traces of the infant's experiences, as distinct from the system ego, which is made up of certain functions. The self image is, of course, first fused and confused with the object images, and consists of fluctuating memory traces of inner sensations and experiences.

Finally, Jacobson points out, the repeated unpleasurable experiences of frustration, deprivation, and separation from love object not only aid in the differentiation of the self, but also induce fantasies of incorporation of the gratifying object, thus expressing wishes to re-establish the original unity of self with pleasurable ministrations of the mother. These are the foundations upon which all future types of identification are built.

The infant progresses from wishes for total incorporation to fantasies of only partial oral, anal, visual, and respiratory incorporation of the love object. True ego identification, although ultimately derived from the early infantile wish to achieve oneness with the love object, partakes of a change of function, which she calls partial introjection. In this process, the self image is modified through the assumption of certain characteristics of the object, becoming like that object, and no longer striving for union with the object *in toto*. In the transitional stage there are constant shifts of libidinal and aggressive energy from object to self and back again, reflected in introjective and projective mechanisms based on fantasies of oral incorporation and anal ejection of the love object.

Margaret S. Mahler has written extensively about the earliest formations of entity and identity (1958). She states that in early infancy the young organism is beset by potentially traumatic stimuli, both from without and from within. Protection against the stimuli from without is provided by the relative lack of cathexis of the perceptual conscious system, which sets up the stimulus barrier. Inner stimuli have no such barrier. Both outer and inner stimuli must be organized for the infant by the symbiotic partner's nursing care, in order to prevent organismic distress that might jeopardize the development within the ego of the distinction between the self and the object world. Primitive undifferentiated drive energy, she states, is vested mainly in the visceral abdominal organs. The buffering, protective action of the nursing mother is necessary for this energy to progress toward a gradual libidinal cathexis of the periphery of the self, as well as for the centrifugal direction of the primitive aggressive discharges away from the early body or self image. In psychosis, one finds a defusion of drives and a preponderance of aggressive cathexis of the primitive self.

Winnicott, in his paper on transitional objects and transitional phenomena (1953), describes what he calls the intermediate area of experience, that is, the experience having to do with the infant's first awareness of an external world. In terms of behavior, it is the experience that occurs between the thumb- or fist-in-mouth activities (which constitute a psychically complete part of the reflex functioning of the body at birth) and the attachment to a teddy bear which is clearly a representative of the outside world. For example, the infant's babbling, especially the tuneful babbling before going to sleep, is part of this transitional experience. Winnicott claims that this area of existence is never challenged for the infant, because it represents a resting place for "the individual engaged in the perpetual human task of keeping inner and outer reality separate yet inter-related." In describing the self-comforting of the infant, he points out that thumb sucking is accompanied by other activities—the rubbing of an object with the other hand, the production of certain noises—and postulates that thinking and fantasy gradually become linked with these experiences. He states, in addition, that the transitional object (the first not-me object) may also stand for the infant's feces and that transitional objects may later develop into fetish objects, which occurred in the case to follow.

## CASE STUDY

### Evaluation

Malcolm was first seen at our Center when he was three years five months of age. His family had sought help because of the child's isolation from people, his extreme stubbornness, the retardation in his speech, his head banging, the breakdown of his toilet training, and his general inaccessibility.

The mother said that during the first half of his first year, he had been a friendly, happy, smiling baby, and she recalled playing peek-a-boo with him when he was about eight months old. When he was seven weeks old, a hernia was discovered in the left inguinal region. The physician decided to postpone surgery until Malcolm was half a year old. His mother was taught to reduce the hernia, but there were at least three occasions on which she was unable to do so and the baby screamed with pain until the mother could get him to the doctor, who then reduced it. He was operated on when he was five and a half months old. The mother stayed with him the first day, but was allowed to visit him only once in the subsequent five days he stayed at the hospital.

We have little information about his experience in the hospital; he did not appear overwhelmed, but was rather indiscriminately friendly to adults. The mother feels sure that at five months Malcolm recognized her and distinguished her face from others', and at that time was not particularly interested in his father.

In the second half of his first year, Malcolm became increasingly sluggish, to such an extent that at about eight months his pediatrician gave him thyroid. He sat quietly in his crib, engrossed for a long time in some tiny object he had happened to pick up; he would not reach for toys put in his crib.

During the second and especially the third year of Malcolm's life, his mother had difficulty in handling him, carrying him, and dressing him because she had severe low back pain. Consequently his father, who had a store in the building in which they lived, took over much of the physical care of the child. Gradually Malcolm developed an intense, demanding, clinging relationship to his father; he went into wild tantrums and banged his head whenever his father left him.

Malcolm had never seemed to want to walk (though he began at fourteen months) and had insisted on being wheeled in his carriage, even for short distances, until three years of age. His extreme stubbornness may have started as early as the second year of life; it was well established by the third year. When his mother asked him to go outdoors, he would accompany her; but as soon as he reached the outside, he would stop and refuse to move, and remained this way for periods of over an hour. When his mother forced him, he would have a tantrum and bang his head. This happened also in response to a changing street light; when the light changed, preventing him from continuing, he would stand still for many changes, refusing to move on.

The head banging had started when he was about two years of age, probably when the stubbornness became apparent, and was in general a response to frustration; it always occurred when his mother was angry with him. In the third year of life, after his mother had started to worry about him, Malcolm apparently protected himself by putting his hand between his head and the cement sidewalk when he banged his head in the street.

Malcolm had been toilet trained, after several attempts, at two years ten months. In the summer prior to coming to us, there was a regression in his toilet habits, to which his mother responded angrily. When she reprimanded him for soiling, he banged his head on a windowpane, breaking it. It was this event that had brought her to seek treatment. By the time Malcolm came to us, he seemed indifferent to his bowel functioning, and was withholding and soiling without apparent awareness.

His mother did not recall any speech in this child until he was eighteen months of age, when he began to use single words to name objects. There seemed to be no progress in his speaking until the summer prior to admission, when his mother, now anxious, tried to teach him and he began to repeat and echo speech that he heard from her or his older brothers. It was with this type of echolalic speech that he appeared.

When Malcolm was first seen at the Center at the age of three years five months, he was withdrawn, lethargic, with an empty, lusterless expression. Most of the time he seemed preoccupied with his sensations—placing his eye almost against the edge of the arm of a chair, pulling at his eyelids, his head cocked to listen to the radiator, or rolling any object available back and forth with his hand. If directly approached, he became sullen and irritable and avoided one's glance. If he wanted something, however, he directed one's arm toward it, as if it were an extension of himself. He named objects in a desultory manner and repeated what was said to him in an exact imitation, including the inflection. The first time he seemed to make overt contact, he climbed onto the window sill, threw a ball down and then fell down himself, perhaps with the expectation that the therapist would catch him, as she did. The therapist was a woman. His immediate reaction to the presence of the male supervising analyst in the therapy room was to form a bridge with his body, his back and head in the analyst's lap and his legs on his mother's lap, while he rubbed the analyst's tie and sucked his thumb.

## Discussion

In the initial evaluation of preschool-age psychotic children, for the purpose of prognosis and of determining the therapeutic methods to be applied—or, rather, of determining where, along the line of object relationship, the therapist may start—many factors have to be taken into account. To begin at the pessimistic end of the spectrum of psychotic phenomenology, there are children among the group that are seen at the Center who almost completely avoid the outside world, primarily the human, animate outside world. Attempts to impinge upon the isolation of these children generally result in severe panic tantrums.

Even these children, however, will show some relationship to an inanimate object. We have come to call this object colloquially the "psychotic fetish." Whatever interest these children may have in anything outside their bodies seems to be directed toward such objects as a baby bottle, a jar, a piece of cloth, or the edges of furniture, boxes, etc., as in Malcolm's case. They may voice no words at all, or, if they do, it is in imitation and with no apparent communication intended. They show a great deal of random movement, which we have learned to recognize as a reaction to physical discomfort or slight, deep pain, and which seems to be a motor discharge in response to the internal stimulus, with little organization. In hospitals, I have seen more deeply regressed children whose entire waking day is spent in continuous autoaggressive or kinesthetic stimulating activity, such as whirling about or head banging, with no relationship to external objects at all, not even inanimate ones.

Malcolm belonged in the group of children who form a fleeting contact with animate objects; this contact is revealed in an altered expression when the eyes of such a child meet those of the observer. Usually there is also speech, in the form of echolalia, though among more disturbed children this echolalic repetition is usually speech heard from nonanimate sources, such as television or records. Among the less severely disturbed children who have a better prognosis, there seems to be some interposition of thought or fantasy between, for example, bodily distress and its external manifestations. In Malcolm's case, the hallmark of distress was a kind of back-and-forth movement of the hand; later he held a toy (a train car) at such times. In our observation this movement seemed to represent an awareness of the downward movement of feces. Later we learned that he feared the expulsion of feces and also had connected the word "broken" with it.

The conceptualization of these phenomena in terms of ego development and psychic structure can only be speculative. What we observe at the outset can be explained by a combination of a disordered development, a very deep regression or lack of development, and a very primitive defense organization.

Some of the phenomena suggest primitive levels of ego-id functioning; for example, what appears to be the immediate motor discharge in the entire body of any slight internal discomfort, or what would appear to be a somewhat more organized attempt to combat this discomfort by the production of other sensations as seen in the whirling and head banging. It is difficult to find any thought content for this activity, although subsequently, when the child's ego development in general appears to be more advanced, these movements and activity become organized in symptoms such as tics or play activity, the psychic content of which we are able to understand. Another striking feature in this regard is that the mother, as well as other observers, find it very difficult to anticipate what the child will do when he approaches her—whether he will bite or kick, or press his lips against her (without any of the puckering or sucking involved in a kiss), which seems at least more affectionate. The observer's inability to understand the child's intentions may possibly be caused by the child's having regressed to a stage at which the drives lack differentiation. Moreover, at such times, one seems to be unable to empathize with the distress which the child appears to be in, whereas in a later period of treatment the mother and therapist both have the feeling that the child is pathetic and in need of them when he cries, and become quite sure of his intentions on approaching them. These changes, which appear to be in the children rather than in the observer, are among the most heartening events for the mothers.

The psychotic child suffers from extreme panic and anxiety, and at first cannot be comforted. The source for this anxiety is not always clear, though the frequency of self-stimulating and body-defining activities such as rubbing the body with sand, or head banging (see Greenacre. 1954), as well as the wild aggressive outbursts, have led many to speculate that such behavior has to do with the fear of loss of body boundaries and with the lack of capacity for binding aggression.

The most prominent defensive maneuvers are the withdrawal from reality, especially from the animate or human external world, or deanimation as Mahler (1958) has called it. Any awareness or involvement with a human object that is separate from the self seems to be beyond the capacity of the most severely disturbed children, and can be sustained for only short intervals by children like Malcolm. When a more sustained involvement with an external human object occurs, it appears to be in the form of a primitive identification in the sense of an omnipotent mother-child dual unity.

There are many indicators of what appears to be an incomplete

separation of self from object: the echolalia; the use of the other
person, especially parts of that person's body as extensions of himself; the expectation of the omniscience and omnipotence from the
other person in response to the most minimal cues; and, as will be
described, the imitation of inanimate objects. At the outset, one
cannot find meaning, in the sense of communication, in the repetitive phrases or actions. However, the echolalic speech later begins
to be used in an appropriate context; for example, "good-by, Chet,
and goodby, Dave," imitating a portion of a TV newscast, is used at
the time of leaving. Later on in the treatment, such phrases are integrated into more complex communications of feelings and
thoughts.

Although the investment of actual human objects is in the most
severe cases almost completely withdrawn, cathexis of the mental
representations of these objects, merged with self representations,
seems to be maintained in the children with better prognosis. I
believe this is shown by the investment, often the intense investment, in the inanimate object, "the psychotic fetish." In our experience, the children who come to the Center with such a focused activity have a better prognosis. Other, more regressed children must
first develop some awareness of the therapist and mother before such
an organization and focusing of behavior occurs; when it does, it
shows itself most often in an involvement with inanimate objects.
In the course of treatment the child will make both destructive and
loving gestures toward such a "fetish"; and, even more important,
there will often be long periods in which the child plays the game
of throwing the object away, with the expectation that the therapist
will return it. Such activities are indicative of the growing differentiation between self and object and the attempt to master the fear of
loss. Still later, when the investment returns to the mother and separation anxiety appears, this object can substitute for her, as one sees
in normal development.

Malcolm arrived with a preoccupation with edges, that is, the
edges of any object, whether a piece of furniture or a piece of wood
or part of a toy; he had to be able to touch the edge with his finger,
or with his body as a whole if it was large enough, as he did over the
large apex of the roof of a doll house, and almost touched it with
his eyes, as it were. From evidence in his later behavior, I am inclined

to think that he was attempting to fuse his body or self image with a form of object image; this fusion was probably represented physically by an act of incorporation through touch and vision, modalities which may not have been clearly differentiated in his mind.

This preoccupation with the inanimate object and, as it seems to me, with his own bodily sensations that accompany what he does with this object has a close relationship to the "intermediate area of experience," which Winnicott has labeled transitional; that is, though the object concerned is a "not-me object," it remains for the child a fused representation of experiences of his own body and of the external world. Most important, it seems to me, is the fact that this preoccupation with "the psychotic fetish" contains within it some residue of gratifying mothering experiences and thus allows for the possibility of reviving them or bringing them closer to consciousness. These cathected inanimate objects seem to me to represent the remnants of a tie to the maternal object; they are evidence that a mental representation of the maternal object has been cathected, that this cathexis has a predominantly libidinal quality, and that it has been preserved.

Malcolm's preoccupation with edges seemed to contain memories of the gratifying experiences of being carried by the mothering person, who in this case was his father. Later in his treatment, when his attachment shifted to his mother, he developed an insatiable demand to ride the subways with her. Also, as will be seen in what follows, during treatment there was a transition from these preoccupations with edges and riding trains, in which it appeared that self and object were not differentiated, to make-believe play with toy trains, when it appeared that this differentiation had been accomplished.

*Early Phases of Treatment*

The therapeutic procedures adopted in Malcolm's case cannot be described here in detail. Each child treated at Masters Children's Center is seen, together with the child's mother, for two to two and a half hours, three to four times a week. The child's therapist makes herself part of his experiences and of those dimly perceived, not-me forces which bring comfort to the child; for example, she joins him in his rocking or rocks him herself when it seems appropriate. The therapist thus becomes part of the symbiotic dual unit as a comforting agent. She is there when the child omnipotently expects her to be; for example, when he jumps or falls into her arms.

In another sense, she can be called his auxiliary ego; she performs certain ego functions that his own ego is not able to do. For example, she protects him in innumerable little ways from being hurt. The communication between them is essentially a signal communication; i.e., it takes place within the symbiotic dual unit. The child signals and the therapist is part of the result of that signal, not really a separate being. Whatever may be said by the therapist in helping the child understand his actions cannot at first have the same function as in work with a neurotic; to the psychotic child, it is a signal from another part of the dual unit. His initial capacity to withstand inner distress without being overwhelmed seems to come from the strength supplied by the therapist as part of the dual unity. She performs the reality testing of which the child is incapable and thus corrects his reality sense. The first interpretations supply a primitive education, simply giving the child words for his actions or moods.

The disintegration of Malcolm's functioning was extreme, especially in terms of his lack of awareness of his sensations and his emotional needs, and the connection between them. It is probably this disorganization that made empathy with him so difficult during the early part of his treatment.

Later, the organization of his experience by the therapist's intervention, especially by the therapist's supplying of words to which past and present similar experience could be connected, is also an important part of treatment. Later phases of therapy involve many aspects of mastery of anxiety through play as well as through the therapist communicating her understanding of the meaning of the child's behavior. The special importance and place of the mother in this treatment has been reported in a preliminary observation (Mahler and Furer, 1960), and will not be considered in this report.

The next steps had to do with the participation of the therapist and the mother in the focused "transitional world" in which the child had now begun to live and out of which his individuation would take place. In the period prior to that described in the next section, he spent a great deal of time fascinated with the edges of furniture, running his fingertips over them, putting his eyes almost in touch with them, and pulling at his eyelids, the latter seeming to distort his visual image of these edges which he later came to call train tracks.

## The Discovery of "Self"

Malcolm's conscious discovery of the "I" as separate from the external world took place after one and a half years of treatment. This was a culmination of various trends in his therapy. At the time there were a number of interweaving developments: (1) a shift of the symbiotic relationship from father to therapist and mother, in which he had to be physically carried by the therapist and taken for endless rides on the subway by the mother; (2) at first there had been a total bodily imitation of inanimate objects; this was replaced by a shift of interest from the body to the toy; (3) an awareness of bowel functioning and a struggle over bowel retention.

The therapeutic team gradually became aware of the fact that much of Malcolm's behavior seemed to consist of a total body imitation of various inanimate objects. At this time the "symbioticlike relationship" to the therapist (more as a whole being rather than as voice or arms) had been established; he rarely responded with complete withdrawal, and frequently behaved as though the therapist were a part of his actions. His body represented a train which he moved across the floor, setting up bridges for it to cross and tunnels for it to go through. He stopped, we learned from his mother, in response to various imagined lights. A peculiar waving movement of his body as he stood still turned out to be an imitation of the flag in the playground. A bizarre movement of his head as he ran represented the police cars that have a rotating red light on the roof. It should be made clear that this behavior was not a playful imitation, as seen in very young children; this bodily activity occupied him continuously most of the day, and was often accompanied by a return to the lusterless expression seen on his first arrival. All of this greatly alarmed the mother because she felt, as she said, that at those times he had again withdrawn from her. He did not play with toys, that is, with toys as representations. Instead, there was a kind of externalization of body sensation via imitation; for example, he rolled the toy train car back and forth with increasing rapidity when he was in apparent distress, as his body tried to move his feces out and he tensed to retain them. At that time we could not yet make him consciously aware of his bowel sensations or of his conflict (as we later understood his behavior).

In the course of the treatment Malcolm seemed to develop a growing awareness of therapist and mother as separate whole persons who could supply his needs—and not simply as extensions of himself which he steered toward these supplies. In conjunction with this new awareness of separateness, Malcolm showed varying degrees of anxiety which he attempted to combat by having the therapist copy his activities or, even more reassuring to him, carry them out as though they had done them together. For example, another child who began to write, first numbers and then his name and his mother's at the age of five, would do it only if the therapist's hand were on top of his as he made the lines. Such observations are regularly made in the treatment of these children. The growing awareness of separateness is regularly accompanied by manifestations of anxiety, and the defenses against that anxiety include the attempt to regain a state of fusion with the object—an indication, at the same time, that the object is now perceived as separate from the self.

As Malcolm emerged from his shell a striking change was manifested in his intense, almost insatiable desire to ride the subways with his mother. When his father was home over week ends, Malcolm would leave his father only if he could take a subway ride with his mother. She felt both so guilty toward her son and so grateful for his loving interest that she spent many hours traveling the subway system with him. The other area of their closest interchange during this period was in the bathroom, where Malcolm agreed to defecate if his mother drew him pictures of trains or, later, told him about the rides they had already taken.

During the same period, if random motor activity did not appear during distressing bowel pressure, the child sometimes developed the same blank facial expression that had been an indication of his earlier autistic withdrawal. As treatment progressed, this expression occurred only when he had been frustrated and probably enraged.

Severe anxiety began to appear when he could no longer withhold and feces appeared in his pants. It should be mentioned that although the mother had been angry with him several times after he had begun to soil about a year before we saw him, the attempts to train him had not been accompanied by severe demands or threats. In the treatment, soon after the appearance of this anxiety a period began when he seemed preoccupied with his feces and the functioning of the toilet. He endlessly played a game with the therapist through the swinging Dutch door at the entrance to the bathroom. The therapist had to put her fingers under the door, he swung at her fingers, then she took her hand out and showed it to him; he would be delighted and the process would be repeated. On other occasions, he would emerge from under the door and return, and he made her do the same. Finally, he put his own hand into the toilet bowl, repeatedly flushing the toilet and taking his hand out to look at it. At one point he defecated on the ground and insisted by gesture upon his mother's touching the feces, after which he touched them. Direct libidinal and aggressive behavior toward mother and therapist had previously appeared in the form of spitting.

After a period of this repetitive game, a differentiation of the self image seemed to develop rapidly, and was accompanied by the appearance of more fully personal communicative speech and the use of toys as symbols. Instead of moving his body as a train, Malcolm began to push a chair around the room, refusing to allow his hat to be removed (we later learned that his hat indicated that he was the engineer); and soon thereafter he admitted the therapist into the game as a passenger.

The next step seemed to center around his imitation of the playground flag. His mother was always upset by his bodily imitation of objects, because she could then feel how withdrawn he was. She made toy flags out of paper and sticks and offered them to him again and again. Then, during a therapy session, he discovered a small cloth flag in the treatment building. He had acquired communicative speech, but from echolalic sources as described; that is, he used phrases imitatively but in an appropriate context; he now asked for what he wanted; on the other hand, he continued to mix his pronouns, using "you" for "I" and often using his name instead of "I." When he found the therapist's flag, he said "*I* have a flag." Later he said, "This is a real flag," and then, "This is mine." With great astonishment shortly thereafter, he discovered that the toy trains were not real trains such as he had seen near the treatment building; and finally he began to play with the toy train, that is, he used it as a representative symbol for the actual train he saw outside. He then became afraid that the cars of the train would be separated from one another and insisted that they be securely fastened together—a return, we thought, to his concern about the loss of body parts and his feces, now displaced into a true toy.

These expressions of self awareness—although followed by a temporary state of anxiety and regression to a clinging, demanding attitude, wanting to be constantly in touch with mother and therapist—represented a momentous step in his development and heralded a change which has remained intact to the present day, about four years later. He never again showed his particular kind of withdrawal and "autism" in relation to human objects, nor did he return to a state, previously so prominent, in which he apparently had lost his self in the environment. Also, from then on we were consistently able to empathize with him because of the change in his facial expression and the quality of his communications; finding it so difficult to feel along with her child or to console and comfort him had previously caused this mother great distress.

*Discussion*

When this child emerged from his autistic withdrawal, he lived in what I would like to call a "transitional world" and in a static state. By this I mean that in his waking life he behaved more or less continuously in a manner one might consider to be similar to that phase of early development where, though external objects are recognized, the psychic images of self and object are not adequately separated. His situation was also static as compared to normal development where this is, as Winnicott calls it, a transitional stage. In our experience, many psychotic children, either spontaneously or in treatment, seem to progress and regress back and forth from this state to that of autistic withdrawal, but rarely proceed further in development.

During this period his body did not seem to be fully separated from his inanimate environment. Either he imitated the inanimate object or, later on, was often found in a state of rapt fascination as he beheld it (trains and tracks as derived from edges). In this state of fascination, which recurred later during his period of fetishistic behavior, it also seems likely that there are fluid boundaries between the mental images of the self and of the object observed (Bernfeld, 1928). One may speculate that this state provides the psychotic child with the "resting place" Winnicott describes for the infant.

In the case described here, the therapeutic efforts of mother and therapist seemed to set a progressive development in motion. This began with Malcolm's acceptance of the human object—what might be called a gratifying transitional object, and what may be a universally important form of a not-me object that carries and moves the child. The experiences Malcolm demanded were probably connected with memory traces of previous libidinally invested experiences which, as noted, had occurred after his first year, particularly with his father. The mental images are assumed to derive from the early gratifying interchanges taking place in a mothering person-child unity. In these interchanges the psychotic child is in an almost totally passive state, and often molds his body to fit that of the carrier. At a later time the child's behavior alternates between this passive molding and an active pushing away, which indicates the conflict over the beginning awareness of separateness. During the time of self-object unity I have hypothesized that the child experiences the therapist not as a whole person but only in terms of isolated qualities, such as the voice, or a feeling tone, or the supportive body.

In Malcolm's case, the anal sphere seemed to play a highly important role in the process of differentiation of self and object. The feces (also spit and urine) are parts of the body that make a complete transition to the external world, concrete representations of the experience that what may be inside can become outside. Moreover, the feces are a source of inner bodily sensations which, as noted previously, cause such distress in these children. In the course of their further development, connections are set up between these internal sensations, their concrete representations, i.e., the feces, and the self- and object-directed feelings once such representations of self and object are organized.

The struggle with the experience of bowel functioning seemed to reflect the process of self differentiation. The role of the aggressive drive in this differentiation can be seen, I believe, in the withholding of feces and in the fear of losing the feces from the body. For these children, loss of a body part seems to be equivalent to destruction.

In our contacts with psychotic children we repeatedly observed that, as the child begins to emerge from his autistic shell and to make aggressive and libidinal investments in both therapist and mother, he regularly withholds feces. Once again one can see that in the child's mind feces have the characteristics of a transitional object; i.e., it is the focus of the libidinal and aggressive cathexis of poorly differentiated images of self and object and at the same time indicates the beginning formation of this differentiation. This image, and the feces representing it in reality, acquires importance to the child because of its increasing libidinal cathexis; the retention of this bodily product may then be explained as an attempt to prevent its loss by destruction; i.e., to protect it from a predominating and overwhelming aggressive cathexis which would cause the loss of the beginning representation of both self and object (to some degree separate from each other). We seem to be dealing here both with the fear of the loss of the object, that is, of the beginning cathexis of the object representation, described by many authors in relation to schizophrenia, and with the fear of extinction or dissolution which has been connected by others to the fear of loss of the self representation. The narcissistic investment of the feces in psychosis was noted by Stärke (1919) and von Uphuijsen (1920). There may be a regular relationship in early normal development between awareness of bowel functioning, a clearer differentiation and increase in intensity of the aggressive drives, and the differentiation of self from object.

This material does not provide any explanation of the causation of the psychosis. The role of the early painful bodily experiences in what may be a constitutional predisposition is suggestive. The mother, we felt, could be included in the category of "ordinarily devoted mothers" and did not have a narcissistic or depressive illness.

In the process of recovery we see again the intimate and mutually dependent relationship between ego functioning and object relationship. As has been noted in previous studies on prognosis (Eisenberg and Kanner, 1956), the functioning of communicative speech is crucial for a development in the direction of recovery. In Malcolm's case we see that the appearance of communicative speech was part of the last steps in differentiation of self and object. This differentiation may also be facilitated by the neutralization or binding of the aggression so that separation-individuation was not equivalent to the destruction of both self and object. Words and meanings derived from and made possible by the developing object relationship now could be put in the service of reality testing. As Freud (1911) stated in discussing the reality principle, with the conversion of freely displaceable cathexes into "bound cathexes," a person's thinking becomes endowed with "further qualities, perceptible to consciousness [through connection] with verbal residues" (p. 221), which result in a vast expansion of his appreciation of both outer and inner reality.

*Further Development*

The foregoing covers the first year and a half of treatment. Malcolm has been at the Center for another year and a half, and will continue at least one further year. Some aspects of his later development are worth mentioning because they illustrate changes in his over-all functioning and in his self identity.

As noted, when he withheld his feces, his mother was able to obtain an evacuation first by promising another subway ride, then by drawing pictures of trains and signal lights. Later, he accepted his mother's verbal account of a previous experience on the subway. After his "self" discovery, he evacuated his feces in exchange for his mother's wiping his anus, revealing, it seemed to us, that the libidinal gratification from his mother had become predominant. In the subsequent year, except for transient regressive reactivations, the anal sphere seemed to become less invested, and he carried out the toileting on his own without any fixed ritual.

In the third year of treatment, the material centered on intense oedipal conflicts, showing manifestations of both feminine and masculine strivings, and, for a period of some months, of a fixation to exhibitionistic and fetishistic activities. He was now five and a half years old, was fully verbal, and had grown to be a tall, muscular boy. The sequence of events was roughly as follows. The manifestations of his oedipal conflict seemed to coincide with the loosening of his teeth, which he inspected with fascination in front of the mirror, and during this period of time several teeth fell out. He first became preoccupied with the problem of where babies come from. He then again retained his stool, which at that time seemed to be a masturbatory equivalent because he obviously became genitally excited by the sensation, and talked about having babies himself. He expressed fears that his body had come loose and that his head might come off. He gradually became jealous of his brothers, his father, and the analyst who interviewed his mother, and had fantasies of their death. In these, they usually dropped into a river and were washed away and drowned. Sometimes, however, he saved them by drawing them back, at the same time exhibiting his great power (as over his own feces). In contrast, his passivity was illustrated by a dream of this period: he is standing on the bank of a river and a strong wind churns up the waves which reach higher and higher, finally up to the boy, dragging him down into the river's depths. His mother comes after him and saves him. At a later date, he developed a fear of tornadoes.

This period was followed by one in which the overt sexual preoccupation disappeared and instead there came into prominence various delusions of grandeur. One, in which he could stare down the sun, alternated with the delusion of omniscience of his therapist, who should know everything, and if she did not, he was furious. He fantasied that when he had feces within him, he was bigger and a creature of great power, which was lost when he passed the feces.

At about this same time, seeing his mother on the toilet and in the shower, he said, "Mommy has a penis in her tushy," after which he made a bowel movement in his pants, a rare occurrence during that period. He then insisted that his mother take the "duty" out of his pants, put it on the floor, and then put it back into the pants. The feces here seemed to represent a penis for his mother as well as for himself.

Overt genital masturbation appeared while he was riding with his mother on the subway train, especially when the train moved into the station. A transient toilet ritual appeared in that he wanted stories about what he would be like when he was grown up and bigger. He shifted his interest from riding in trains to fans, and later, to the bathroom fans that he looked at with clear scoptophilic interest.

Finally, he arrived with a flag that he had asked for after having seen the flag outside of his brother's school. The following months were spent in preoccupation with this flag, preening it, building a flagpole for it outside the treatment building, constantly worrying about the effect of wind and rain upon it, and when he became acutely anxious, wrapping his body in it and seeming to fall asleep. At other times he took the flag and its flagpole out of the window and, holding it against the lower part of his body, marched back and forth in front of the mirror as he observed himself. Most of the time was spent in gazing in rapt fascination at the flag while he masturbated. Although he was obviously self-preoccupied at these times, none of the observers felt that the quality of his facial expression indicated the kind of withdrawal with which he had originally come to the Center.

At the end of the year a series of neurotic symptoms appeared: fear of the dark; fear of automobiles crashing, especially if his mother was driving; fear of airplanes crashing; fear of death and of being buried. He continues to show primitive functioning in his feeling of the great power of either himself or the people around him (at six years of age, when he is accidentally hurt, he still turns with rage upon his mother as though she had caused his injury, or he hits the offending piece of furniture); and he still insists that the therapist or mother knows everything, and becomes panicky and angry if they deny this. He also retains a concretistic kind of thinking, a vulnerability to narcissistic hurt, and a propensity for primitive defenses like denial. Recently, for example, when he was given a flag by a neighbor and brought it to his therapy session, he discovered that the flag he had brought was larger than the one he himself owned. He developed one of the typical panic tantrums until the therapist explained that even though an object may be smaller than another, it can still be stronger, such as the tugboat which pulls the ocean liner. For a month therafter, he was preoccupied with strength rather than size.

## SUMMARY

In Malcolm's case, therapy was begun by bringing the child from his withdrawn state into a primitive relationship with the therapist as a need-satisfying object, chiefly through her communication to him of her empathy with his needs and their gratification. At the same time, she became a part of his omnipotent dual unity. Gradually she helped him to organize his experience and to explore reality, in this way fostering the libidinal cathexis of herself. A previously static state in his psychosis, liked to the resting place of Winnicott's transitional experience, and in the mother-child relationship which was reflected in the therapist-child relationship, was altered and progressive changes ensued. When we first saw him, he was already capable of delaying, of interposing thought and fantasy between instinctual pressure and discharge, and showed some organization of his psychic life, at least in the preoccupation with the "psychotic fetish," which in his case were the edges of inanimate objects. However, there appeared to be a profound disorganization in his instinctual and affective expressions. Gradually, however, his reactions became more differentiated and understandable to observers, when he began to show aggressive responses to frustration and libidinal responses to gratifications from the therapist and mother. There were indications that the human object had become invested, though self and object seemed not yet to be distinguished. Despite this lack of complete differentiation, a coalescence of memory traces of separate object images and a separate self image took place. In this period the child's previously chaotic behavior became better organized and we saw a flowering of life and interest in the "transitional world," which now included the human object, and the appearance of a variety of understandable symptomatic behavior.

It seemed that both the emerging self and object images were invested predominantly with aggressive energy. The child only gradually mastered the anxiety which seemed to be related to this aggressive investment, and which was eventually focused on his feces and anal functioning. His anxiety seemed to concern the loss not only of the image of a need-satisfying love object but also of the self representation. It was warded off by total incorporation which seemed to be represented by the bodily symptom of fecal retention.

Along with the progressive development in object relations, there occurred a differentiation of the self from both the inanimate and human objects, and the conscious discovery of "I" as a separate entity. There were also changes in the direction of greater organization and integration of his ego functions, an increased libidinization of his activities, and increased ego strength in such things as the control of his rage and the capacity to withstand frustration.

In the last year of Malcolm's treatment, oedipal conflicts appeared, which resulted in symptoms. These indicated that various levels of ego functioning and various levels of defensive functioning were present. On the one hand, there were periods in which there was an intensification of his feelings of omnipotence, sometimes delegated to others and sometimes to himself. On the other hand, a fetishistic interest in the flag seemed to arise from an attempt to resolve the castration fear associated with these conflicts. It is noteworthy that this fetishistic interest was centered upon an object, the flag, which had played a prominent role during the time when his behavior had been dominated by imitation of inanimate objects, and which was also involved in his experience of the discovery of "self."

Toward the end of the year, Malcolm became more sad than angry, often telling both mother and father to go away and leave him alone. He seemed to be increasingly aware of internal conflict. On close observations, some of his movements and sometimes his vocal inflections are strange; on the other hand, those who see Malcolm for the first time now are no longer impressed by his severe disturbance, which had previously been apparent even on cursory observation.

## BIBLIOGRAPHY

Abraham, K. (1924), A Short Study of the Development of the Libido. *Selected Papers on Psycho-Analysis*. London: Hogarth Press, 1927.
Bak, R. (1954), The Schizophrenic Defence against Aggression. *Int. J. Psa.*, 35.
Bernfeld, S. (1928), Über Faszination. *Imago*, 14.
Brodsky, B. (1959), Self-Representation, Anality, and the Fear of Dying. *J. Amer. Psa. Assn.*, 7.
Eisenberg, L. & Kanner, L. (1956), Early Infantile Autism. *Amer. J. Orthopsychiat.*, 26.
Freud, S. (1911), Formulations on the Two Principles of Mental Functioning. *Standard Edition*, 12. London: Hogarth Press.
Greenacre, P. (1954), In: Problems of Infantile Neurosis: A Discussion. *This Annual*, 9.
Hartmann, H. (1950), Comments on the Psychoanalytic Theory of the Ego. *This Annual*, 5.
—— Kris, E., & Loewenstein, R. M. (1946), Comments on the Formation of Psychic Structure. *This Annual*, 2.
Jacobson, E. (1954), The Self and the Object World. *This Annual*, 9.
Mahler, M. S. (1958), Autism and Symbiosis: Two Extreme Disturbances of Identity. *Int. J. Psa.*, 39.
—— & Furer, M. (1960), Observations on Research Regarding the 'Symbiotic Syndrome' of Infantile Psychosis. *Psa. Quart.*, 29.
—— —— & Settlage, C. (1959), Severe Emotional Disturbances in Childhood: Psychosis. *American Handbook Psychiatry*. New York: Basic Books.
Stärke, A. (1919), The Reversal of the Libido-Sign in Delusions of Persecution. *Int. J. Psa.*, 1, 1920.
van Ophuijsen, J. H. (1920), On the Origin of the Feeling of Persecution. *Int. J. Psa.*, 1.
Winnicott, D. W. (1953), Transitional Objects and Transitional Phenomena. *Int. J. Psa.*, 34.

# THE ANALYSIS OF A BOY WITH TRANSVESTITE TENDENCIES

## A Contribution to the Genesis and Dynamics of Transvestitism

MELITTA SPERLING, M.D. (New York)

There are comparatively few psychoanalytic studies of transvestitism. The classical concepts of this perversion have been developed by Fenichel (1930). According to Fenichel, the transvestite has not been able to give up the belief in the phallic nature of women and, in addition, he identifies himself with the phallic woman. Fenichel drew attention to an important accidental factor in transvestitism, namely, "that, as a rule, contemporaneously with the identification with the mother, there exists in another more superficial, psychic-stratum, a similar identification with *a little girl*." He believed that this identification occurs when "a sister has at an early period to a great extent become a mother-substitute." He assumed a special bisexual disposition in his patient, and wondered what the specific circumstances might be which lead to this outcome.

The psychoanalytic study of a child with overt transvestite behavior could provide an opportunity to learn more about the circumstances under which such behavior develops than is possible in the analysis of an adult transvestite, where significant childhood experiences are often not fully recovered and, at best, have to be reconstructed.

I had the opportunity to treat, in long analyses, two tranvestite boys, one of prelatency and one of latency age. In both cases I had their mothers in analysis prior to treatment of the child. I have also treated two adolescents with marked transvestite behavior, and three

Clinical Professor of Psychiatry, State University of New York, Downstate Medical Center, Division of Psychoanalytic Education.

adults with transvestite tendencies. Two had episodes of transvestite behavior prior and during the early part of their treatment. The third one, who had overt transvestite episodes in adolescence, had polymorph perversions, particularly exhibitionism and voyeurism.

Since, in my opinion, the presentation of detailed analytic material is indispensable for a convincing demonstration of the unconscious fantasies and conflicts underlying the clinical manifestations, I have decided to limit myself here to the report of one case, and I shall have to restrict myself to those parts which are essential to my thesis. I have selected the case of the prelatency child for three reasons: (1) His mother came into analysis for depression when he was six months old, and I could observe indirectly the development of the transvestite behavior from its very beginning. (2) He was only four years and ten months old when he began analysis, and the rich dream and fantasy material was obtained with unusual freshness. (3) I could follow up his development to adolescence.

## CASE PRESENTATION

### Preanalytic History

Of the wealth of material on Tommy obtained through his mother, only very little can be reported here. Up to the time he was two years old, the mother did not think that he presented any problems. She was too preoccupied with the difficulties of Tommy's sister, five years his senior. Because she felt that she had rushed her daughter's toilet training, she was reluctant to train Tommy, and when she did, she was ambivalent and inconsistent. Tommy was still enuretic when he came into analysis, and his enuresis proved to be a very stubborn symptom. An outstanding phenomenon in the analysis of the mother was her need to conglomerate both sexes in herself and in her children. She was a sturdy woman who wore a short, straight haircut and tailored clothes. Her husband was a small, frail-looking man with delicate features. Paula, Tommy's sister, was sturdy and strong like her mother. She was a tomboy. Tommy was frail-looking and small like his father. He liked to wear his sister's clothes, especially her panties, nightgowns, and pajamas. This, his mother thought, was very cute. This behavior had started when he was three years and four months old, shortly after an aunt, who had just given birth to a baby girl, had stayed at their house with the baby for several weeks. Tommy, who was very curious about this baby, seemed to be resentful and jealous of her. At that time he would say, "All people are born girls. Then they turn into boys. I was born a girl." He would frequently say: "When I was a girl. . . ." This fantasy, openly expressed at the age of three and afterwards repressed, was one of the basic fantasies operating in his transvestite behavior, as will be seen later.

As a little boy he had had ample opportunity to see his mother in the nude. Observing her after a shower (when he was not quite three years old), he asked, pointing at her breasts, "What's that?" "My breasts," said the mother. "Will I have breasts when I grow up?" he asked. "No," said the mother, "you are a boy." "Take the brown stuff away and let me see your penis," he demanded. "I don't have a penis," the mother said. "What do you have?" "A vagina," she replied. "Will I have a vagina when I grow up?" he asked. "No, you are a boy," was her answer.

He started nursery school at four. He behaved very babyishly, disturbed the other children, and was considered a nuisance. He could not hold his own with the other little boys in his neighborhood and, instead of fighting, he would run away and play by himself. Even at the age of three and a half or four, he would help himself to money from his mother's purse and make up fantastic stories. This tendency to pseudologia fantastica became more pronounced later. He also had all kinds of accidents and continually hurt himself. A conversation he had with his mother at the age of four and a half when a classmate had a tonsillectomy indicated that he was, at that time, obviously struggling with castration anxiety.

Tommy: How do they take out tonsils?
Mother: They cut them out.
Tommy (puts both hands over his mouth): I wouldn't let them.
Mother: They put you to sleep. You don't feel it.
Tommy: I won't go to sleep any more. Why do they have to cut them out?
Mother: If they are diseased and make people sick . . . when they have a lot of colds.
Tommy: I won't go outside any more so I won't catch cold.
While this discussion was going on, the mother was preparing

carrots on the kitchen table. Tommy took a carrot and put it to his belly button, saying, "This is my tonsil."

Mother: Tonsils are not in the belly button.

Tommy: Oh, yes they are.

## Tommy's Analysis

Tommy's analysis started when he was four years and ten months old, shortly after his mother had finished her analysis. He exhibited a peculiar mixture of babyishness and alertness. On some days he would crawl from the waiting room into the playroom like a baby, talking like a baby. On other days he would come in a cowboy outfit and pretend to be riding into the playroom on his big horse. This was his first dream: He slept with his father, his mother slept in his sister's bed, and his sister in his bed. This dream, which was not interpreted to Tommy, gave immediate insight into Tommy's unconscious (fantasy) life. The role which he wanted and which, by the changes in the sleeping arrangement, he had managed to assume in his dream, was that of the mother and the sister. *He* slept in bed with his father in place of the mother, and, in his bed, in his place was his sister. As sometimes the first dream of an analytic patient contains the patient's basic conflict, which, in its full significance, may be understood and worked upon only much later in the analysis, so Tommy's first dream revealed some of his wishes and conflicts.

Tommy had a need to make his father into a "strong man." He would tell me that his father was an athlete and that he had been a gym teacher at one time and a famous fighter. Unfortunately, his father was nothing of the kind and, at that particular time, was in very poor physical health. When his father was in the hospital, Tommy glorified this by making him a "hero." However, when he drew a picture of his family for me, his mother appeared as the biggest person. Mother and sister seemed the important people in the family, father was "bossed" by mother.

He complained about his mother: "She never buys or gives me what I want." Actually, his mother bought and gave him things rather readily. Yet, there was a great deal of truth in his feelings, because she really did not want him to have "boyish" things, as she had not been able to let Paula have really "girlish" clothes and playthings. Once he asked his mother whether she would buy him a doll.

She immediately agreed to it, but then he did not want one because "real boys don't play with dolls." Yet sometime later, Tommy became an ardent collector of dolls, thus picking up his mother's cues.

A dream about a snake in his bed which was spitting from its mouth at his sister and father, who first tried to run away but then were killed, brought into the analysis the aggressive, sexual aspects of his bed wetting and also his jealousy of his father and sister as rivals for his mother. In connection with the dream Tommy began to talk about some of the activities between his sister and himself. Up to the age of five (Tommy was now six years old), they had been taking baths together, and his sister would ask him to make his penis wiggle. He was still frequently going into her bed at night.

There were noticeable changes in Tommy's behavior after some of this material had been worked through. He was becoming more aggressive and was beginning to fight back with the boys. He had some dry periods, but this progress was not yet a sustained one. It was only then that the emergence of the positive oedipus complex manifested itself in Tommy's overt behavior. One could detect a quality of chivalry in his attitude toward his mother and sister. There was a lessening of the infantile behavior and a decrease in the over-compensatory cowboy and Superman play. For a while Tommy almost behaved like a real little boy of his age, but his transvestite behavior continued; he was more careful, though, in concealing it. He was still wearing his sister's panties steadily. He also liked to put on her leotards and wanted to wear her jewelry and sometimes her discarded dresses. He was very observant of her development and would make remarks such as, "She will soon need to wear a girdle. Her nipples are getting big." He wondered why boys could not use makeup, and he sometimes liked to paint his eyebrows with an eyebrow pencil.

In the sessions he played a game in which he was shot by an imaginary attacker. He would drop to the floor shouting, "I have a bullet in my vagina." He had gone shopping with his mother and chose a red sports jacket. On the way home he said, "The boys will call me a girl." His mother suggested that he return the jacket, but he said, "What's wrong with being a girl?" He did not return the jacket. It was during this phase of analysis that he began to express thoughts about "whether girls never had a penis," and revealed this fantasy: "If there are girls in a car and boys are crossing the street and are run over and cut into halves, and the girls are also cut into halves, and then the halves get mixed up and the upper part of the girl is put together with the lower part of the boy, then in this way they would be half boy and half girl."

He had a dream in which he knocked over a big dinosaur. He told me that he had actually seen dinosaurs a long time ago when he had been to a museum with his parents. His reaction to seeing a dinosaur had come up in his mother's analysis. He had been particularly interested in the dinosaur's belly and had repeatedly asked, "Could I fit into its stomach?" "Could it eat me up?" When we discussed that he did not like his father and mother to sleep together and that he was angry that his father had his mommy (the big dinosaur), he replied, "But I have Koko and she is going to have babies." Koko was his cat to whom he was very attached. He considered her a member of the family, calling her by the family name. He behaved as though he considered himself the father of Koko's babies, but he also identified himself with her. This was brought out in a dream about a cat which was in his bed, licking his face, jumping around, and pulling at him. While this was going on, everybody came into his room; his sister, his father and mother. The cat said, "Can't we have any privacy?" He told me that his mother did not like the cat to touch his face because of her dirty paws. The night preceding the dream, he had gone into his father's bed. I learned from the mother that he had been jumping around in the bed and, in the course of this horseplay, had touched his father's penis. The father, startled by this, had mentioned it to his wife.

Tommy was very much interested in babies and baby-making, and he told me that he had known for a long time that Koko would have kittens because her breasts felt big. His mother's friend was pregnant at that time and had told him about babies. He had asked, "What would happen to a baby if the food went in and hit the baby's head?" Although she had explained to him that there were two different places in the mother's belly, one for food and one for the baby, he had the idea that this would kill the baby. He had asked his mother whether she had urinated while giving birth. He had the fantasy that the baby could drown. He also thought that the baby came out through the navel. He asked me whether I had ever had a dead baby. His mother had told him that she had had one before he was born. He brought home two little dolls which he called "babies." He played with his friend and they were looking for the dolls' vaginas. When he went to the bathroom with his friend that afternoon, he wet all over the bathroom floor. He explained to his mother that it had happened because he had laughed so hysterically. Analysis revealed that he had acted out a fantasy of giving birth by urinating.[1]

He played a game with puppets in the play session. The excitement with which he played and the fighting between the male and female puppets left no doubt about the sexual nature of this game. First the woman was attacking; she was a witch and she was lifting the male puppet up, saying, "Rise in the air," and then she would drop him. Then the male puppet attacked the female; he jumped upon her and threw her down. In the end, both puppets dropped from the edge of the little table on which the fight took place and were killed.

Sexual activity was dangerous for both the male and female (the parents). Nevertheless, Tommy seemed to come closer to an identification with the male. A story he invented about a lion was revealing: This lion, who was the king of the forest, felt that he needed a lioness to be his wife. He got the wife; they were king and queen and had six children. When the king became old, he devised a test to see who should be king. The young lions had to jump off a cliff. The first one drowned, four more shared his fate, the last one did okay and became King Tommy. King Tommy needed a wife; he went out of the jungle, came to a circus where he saw the most beautiful lioness, except for his mother. He married her and she began to eat a lot and had sixteen children and then the story repeated itself. Only one could be king and the others had to die.

During this phase, he would ask his mother such speculative questions as the following: "What would happen if you back out the car and my bike was in the driveway, and you hit it but it doesn't break?" He had a period of absent-mindedness; in his daydreams he was engaging in dangerous actions. He managed to injure himself in the most obvious ways. Once he actually cut himself deliberately

---

[1] The analysis of his bed wetting will be reported in detail elsewhere.

with a knife. He was provocative in his behavior, inviting punishment upon himself. He was more careful, though, in concealing when he was wearing his sister's panties and nightgowns.

He reported the following dream: He was driving in a car with his friend, Fred. At first he could not drive and Fred was driving. But then he could drive. He went to live with Fred, who was married. It seemed to be safer not to *be* a man but instead to live with one (his father). His conscious attitude was much different. He would now make statements such as, "I'll grow up and I'll be a daddy," or "I'm glad I am a boy. I can plant the seed for the babies." To his father he said, "Now I know how you make babies." Earlier in his analysis he would say, "I won't get married. I don't want to be bossed." Talking to another boy he once said: "Girls are lucky. They grow up to marry a boy." The other boy replied, "Boys are lucky. When they grow up they marry a girl." He made up stories of clearly oedipal content and he wondered why he could not marry his sister.

Tommy began to display considerable interest in girls. He declared that he was in love with one little girl. He would say, "Now that I have a girl friend, I don't have any fears any more." Similar to an adult patient, Tommy was attempting, with the exaggerated interest in girls, to demonstrate and to prove his masculinity as a cover-up and overcompensation for his feminine wishes. He now talked, although with reluctance, about the special games he played with the children. In these games the girls were included. They would pull their pants down and look at each other's bodies. Exhibitionism and voyeurism played a great part in his games, fantasies, and dreams. He had a fantasy that his girl friend was at his house. He undressed her. All the boys from his class were looking, and he took a shot with the camera of her vagina. This theme (of voyeurism and exhibitionism) was repeated in innumerable fantasies and dreams. One dream sample: His girl friend came into the house with her friend. His pants fell down in front of the girls. He awoke.

The analysis, now in its third year, took on a different flavor. He had stopped the bed wetting and was making determined efforts to stop the transvestite activities. It was the most fruitful and decisive phase of his treatment, during which Tommy had settled down to work. While before he had been hyperactive in the playroom, he now became interested in his dreams and introspective. He disclosed his masturbation fantasies and practices. A phenomenon which he mentioned for the first time brought into the analysis his castration fears and his reactions to the sight of the vagina. Let me briefly reconstruct some of the events of this phase. Tommy had related several dreams about a ball. In one dream he had thrown a ball at the teacher. The teacher did not give him back the ball, but kept it. His associations made it clear that the ball represented his genital (he called his testicles penis balls) and that the teacher also represented myself (and his mother). In another dream his father had given him a ball, a very precious ball (there were only three or four such balls in the whole world, he said). The ball fell into the sewer. He went down into the sewer to get the ball. He got wet. He awoke dry. In association to this dream, he related the following two experiences. The night before the dream, a little girl cousin had slept over at his house. She had told him that when she touched her vagina with her finger, it smelled. They had played a game of touching each other's genitals. And then, with signs of great disturbance, he spoke of an experience which seemed to concern him very much. He said that he experienced things twice, as if the very same thing had happened before, and yet he knew that it had not happened. Tommy described in detail and with great affect a *déjà vu* experience. He was anxious and expressed fears about his sanity. "I think I am going coocoo; maybe I should have my brain examined."[2]

I could show him that he was afraid of heterosexuality because this meant that he would lose his penis; the teacher, I, mother, would take it away from him if he were sexually aggressive. To be a girl would be preferable, but this idea was very frightening, because girls have a vagina, but no penis. Tommy proceeded to tell me that he liked the behind better than the front, in girls as well as in boys. He told me that, wearing his sister's nightgown, he would slap himself on the behind and that this felt very good and gave him great pleasure. It tickled all the way down his legs. To my question as to when he had started this activity, Tommy answered by making up the following fantasy: "When I was born and came out of my mother's belly, she slapped me with a board which had a nail on it

[2] I have encountered *déjà vu* phenomena in two of my other transvestite patients (one latency and one adolescent boy). It is my impression that there is a specific connection between *déjà vu* and transvestitism. This is a subject which cannot be dealt with in this presentation but one which I intend to investigate further.

on my behind. That's why I like it." He said that the two people who slapped him on his behind in reality were his mother and his sister. I knew from the analysis of his mother that she had been in the habit of slapping him on his behind (her mother had done the same to her). He then revealed his leading masturbation fantasy and practice. He told me that he would put on his sister's dress and go into the crawling place in his house and imagine the king was beating him. This gave him the greatest pleasure.

There is a striking similarity between Tommy's behavior and that of adult transvestites observed and described by Boehm (1923), Fenichel (1930), and other investigators (Alexander, 1928; Burchardt, 1961; Fessler, 1934; Greenberg et al., 1958, 1960; Grotjahn, 1948; Gutheil, 1954; Hirschfeld and Tielke, 1912; Hora, 1953; Karpman, 1947; Luhianowitz, 1960; McKenzie and Schulz, 1961; Wilson, 1948). The leading fantasy is one of being beaten on the behind. In the cases of adult transvestites, the beating person is always a woman.

The origin of Tommy's beating fantasy could be traced back to age three and a half to four, the same age when he had expressed his fantasy of "All people are born girls." A fuller analysis of the genetic and dynamic function of these fantasies and their role in his transvestite behavior, and particularly of the dynamic function of the beating fantasy in relation to the primal scene and to the oedipal conflict, will be given in the discussion, following the case presentation. At this point, I want to draw attention to Tommy's masochistic needs, which manifested themselves in overt behavior and in his accident proneness. This is a feature characteristic of and prominent also in adult transvestites. Even when he was not really injured, Tommy sometimes would put on bandages and pretend that he had hurt himself. He once asked whether one could be punished for trying to commit suicide (he had once jumped out of a second-floor window "playing fire drill"). He wondered whether the punishment would be to be sent to a reform school and gave this as his version of what a reform school is like: "They give you a hammer and you break up stones six days a week. On Sunday as a special treat you get bread and castor oil. Every day you get bread and water. On Christmas everybody is excited and what do you get: a new hammer."

New and significant aspects of his transvestite behavior were brought into the analysis and could be understood with the help of dreams and his associations. I have in mind here a series of dreams, which Tommy termed "funny"-crazy dreams. In one dream, a boy in school had a bottle. He drank from it. He grew a vagina. He went into the boys' bathroom. His pants changed into a dress. His hair got long. He had no belt and the dress fell down. When he went back into the classroom, the vagina changed into a penis again. The girls took a hatchet and wanted to chop it off. He awoke at this point. In another dream he had a certain suit (he was actually to get a new suit and this time he had decided to buy a "real boy's suit"). It was a magic suit. By magic it made him what he was wearing. In the first dream it is a magic potion which transforms him from a boy into a girl. In the second dream this magical quality is clearly attributed to the clothing, to something that he could put on and wear on his body. This, Tommy had been practicing in his transvestite behavior; by wearing his sister's panties underneath his own, he could maintain the illusion that he was both a boy and a girl at the same time. Similar to certain types of behavior in adults, who, although they use their genitals in their sexual activities, derive sexual gratification only with the help of pregenital fantasies (penis equals breast, vagina equals mouth and anus) and with special techniques (fellatio, cunnilingus), so Tommy, by his exaggerated interest in the genitals, was hiding the fact that, under the threat of castration, he had shifted his interest from the front to the rear and from below to above. He derived sexual gratification from stimulating his buttocks and anus and was very interested in looking at breasts.

The analysis of Tommy's persistent enuresis cannot be dealt with here except to indicate that pregenital fantasies entered into its dynamics. Urine, on one level, was milk and sperm, and, on another level, poison and feces. He had a dream about a boy who was born without a "tuschie." The b.m. (feces) kept coming out of his penis. He then became the boy in the dream. His pants fell off and his girl friend said, "Wear a tuschie." Repressed memories from his traumatic oedipal phase were mobilized in the analysis of this dream. He did not remember the change in sleeping arrangements during the time his aunt and baby cousin stayed at their house (I knew from his mother that he had slept in the parental bedroom then), but he remembered that he would awaken in fear during the night and go into his parents' bedroom. This was later replaced by going into his sister's bed. He actually had suffered from a sleep disturbance which subsided when his enuresis became fully established. In the dream of a boy born without a "tuschie," Tommy's fantasy, "all people are born girls," returned in a different version. It was found that "tuschie" as well as "wear" had a double meaning. "Tuschie" meant not only the behind but also the front and was both the male and female genital; and "wear" was a play on words (a favorite game of Tommy's) and also meant "where?" In the dream, the calamity of a boy born without a "tuschie" proved to be no calamity because, first, he had a penis which took over such functions, and, secondly, he could remedy the situation easily by the transvestite mechanism of dealing with such a problem, i.e., by wearing a piece of clothing designed for intimate contact with a girl's body on his own body. In this way he magically acquired parts of or the whole body of a girl. This was the essence of his transvestite behavior. Since he was a boy and had a penis, he could, by wearing his sister's panties and night-gowns, gain in addition everything she (a girl) had. While in the manifest dream Tommy had the girl say, "Wear a tuschie," further analysis revealed that on a deeper level Tommy was asking the girl the fateful question, "Where is your tuschie-penis?"

Tommy's concept of the vagina was that it was an asset like the breasts and the pubic hair. The emphasis was shifted away from what girls did not have (and he could lose), namely, the penis, to what girls had or could grow later, namely, pubic hair, breasts, and babies. In the dream in which the magic potion transforms him into a girl, this is manifested by his growing a vagina, long hair (pubic hair), and by the change of the pants into a dress.

Tommy still insisted that men also grow breasts. He told me that he had seen the big breasts of his gym teacher (a cover for the big penis of his father). In the profile of a woman he drew, the equation of breast-penis was very obvious. The breast actually looked like a big penis. Concomitant with the flow of this material, there was a change in the character of Tommy's drawings. He was now drawing himself as a muscle man with tremendous biceps, but also with big breasts. He still wanted to have everything a man and a woman have.

There were marked changes in Tommy's behavior after the working through of this material. When he terminated his analysis at the age of nine, he had given up his transvestite activities completely, had settled down to work in school, had friends, and became interested in sports. He not only acted but he felt like a real boy. I saw Tommy again for a short period at age thirteen because of some difficulties he had in school. I found that his sexual development had progressed very satisfactorily and felt that I could leave him on his own. Tommy came to see me one year later just to report that he was doing very well. He had worked himself up to the upper third in his class and took pride in his achievement. He had grown and put on weight, and he was pleased with his appearance. He had made new friends, both boys and girls. He had become quite athletic and was a member of two teams in school. He had little conflict about masturbation and thought that he had less need for it than some of his friends. It appeared to me that Tommy showed a very good ability for sublimation. He had also taken up his music more seriously and obviously was doing very well at it. He had not only maintained but also consolidated these gains further when I saw him at age fifteen and last at age sixteen.

A few remarks about the technique of treatment seem indicated, particularly since no successfully treated case has been reported in the literature and because transvestite behavior is not a rare phenomenon in children or adults. That so few cases are known is due to the fact that parents usually do not ask for help unless the behavior of the child exposes them publicly and they are compelled to do so. Similarly, adult patients do not come for treatment because of their transvestite behavior (which they reveal reluctantly only later), but usually for accompanying symptoms, most often depression. It was my experience in many years of work with children with deviate sexual behavior that no satisfactory results could be obtained without concomitant treatment of the mother, and in some cases of both parents (Sperling, 1959). A case such as Tommy's would have gone untreated or treatment might have been requested at a later time for other problems, e.g., learning and school problems, but not for his basic problem had his mother not been in analysis. I have developed a technique whereby I preferably work with the mother first in preparation for the treatment of the child. This makes it possible to work with the child with very little contact with the mother, and also quickly to resolve resistances which otherwise might lead to withdrawal of the child from treatment.

The case report of Tommy may give the impression that he was an easy patient to treat. He definitely was not. This was true also for the nine-year-old transvestite boy, whose mother was in treatment with me for three years prior to his analysis, which was successfully concluded after four years with three years of follow-up. In such a treatment, one gets a taste of the difficulties of treating adult perverts. It is essential for a successful outcome that the treatment be carried out in an atmosphere of instinctual deprivation. The analyst cannot be a party in the child's transvestite acting out in the treatment situation. The child has to know that he is in treatment because of the transvestite behavior, that the analysis will help him understand the reasons for it and enable him to give it up and find more satisfactory and more appropriate gratifications. It is essential also to establish with the mother of the child patient what I call the "superego alliance," which assures that the child has only one direction in which to go in his analysis. It also insures that the changes and gains made in the analysis will not be undone but maintained after treatment is terminated.

## DISCUSSION

Although there seems to be a close relationship between transvestitism and fetishism on the one hand, and transvestitism and homosexuality on the other, transvestitism is a distinct perversion with its own well-delineated features. From the psychoanalytic point of view, the most significant difference lies in the choice of the love object, which in transvestitism is a heterosexual one. The transvestite, in order to achieve sexual gratification, has to have an article of female clothing, which is not limited to one fixed piece of clothing, on his body and in close proximity with it or certain parts of it. The fetishist, on the other hand, requires a very specific fixed article, the fetish, which may or may not be a piece of female clothing, which is not worn by the fetishist but usually by his love object. We would expect, therefore, to find different dynamic constellations in each of these conditions, and it should be possible to define specific factors which would account for these specific outcomes.

We know that bisexuality plays an important role not only in transvestitism but also in other types of perversion as well as in the neurotic, psychotic, and even in the normal person (Freud, 1909; Kubie, 1954; M. Sperling, 1950).

On the basis of clinical material, I shall attempt to identify certain factors which might account for the persistence and intensity of bisexuality and its specific outcome in transvestitism in certain cases. In the simultaneous analysis of children with deviate sexual behavior and their mothers, I have found that the relationship between mother and child, which I have described (1959) as the perverse type of object relationship, was a genetic factor in the pathological ego and super-ego functioning of the child. The fact that the parent-child relationship leads to specific superego pathology and thus is an important factor in the genesis of perversion has been noted by other observers (Gillespie, 1952; Johnson and Szurek, 1952; O. Sperling, 1951). The role of primitive mechanisms and identifications and of preoedipal conflicts particularly in fetishism has been stressed in numerous contributions (Bak, 1953; Balint, 1935; Friend et al., 1954; Gillespie, 1952; Greenacre, 1953; Socarides, 1960). From this point of view, the analyses of the mothers of the two boys with transvestite behavior are of interest. Only a few details of this material can be given here. Both women had older brothers who excelled intellectually, whom they envied, and with whom they had been in rivalry. Tommy's mother's brother died suddenly in his late teens, and she took up the education and career intended for him. She vied with both men and women, and it was equally important for her to be considered bright and efficient (like a man) and soft and attractive (like a woman). After the birth of her first child, she willingly gave up her career and devoted herself to her household and child. She recalled with great pleasure in her analysis an episode from childhood. Once, in a summer resort she met a boy on the first day of her arrival; this boy mistook her for a boy. She fooled him for an entire day about her true sex and enjoyed this experience tremendously.

The mother of the latency boy who showed transvestite behavior liked to wear slacks and short coats with big pockets. She never carried a (woman's) handbag. Her mother would say to her, "If you'll start wearing skirts, your boy would stop wearing dresses." The analysis of these mothers revealed that, unlike the latent homosexual, they did not suffer from an unconscious conflict concerning sexual identification; this type of behavior was rather a conscious playfulness and pretense of being both sexes in certain situations in the sense of a "controlled illusion" (O. Sperling, 1956). Both mothers encouraged similar behavior in their sons.

Friend and his collaborators (1954), in an interesting study of transvestitism in three boys, have noted the confusion of sexual roles in the families of these children. Yet, such confusion of roles and similar family constellations are not uncommon findings in a great variety of neurotic disturbances. Even in those cases where the overt attitude of the mother would seem to encourage feminine behavior in her son, the development may lead rather to homosexuality or other forms of sexual deviation than to transvestitism. I have found that there was not a confusion of sexual roles, but rather a *fusion* of roles with an emphasis on being both male and female in one. Both mothers functioned adequately sexually and enjoyed being women. The role of a woman was not depreciated; in fact, certain feminine activities, and especially maternal functions, were highly valued. In comparison, the role of the man appeared to be less important in some respects because he was not entrusted with the care of the children. Both women considered themselves, and were regarded by their husbands, as intellectually superior and were the leaders of the family. The outstanding features of the mothers of these boys were their strong oral fixation and a bisexual orientation. The fathers did not seem to present any specific problems related to their sons' behavior. Tommy's father went into treatment shortly after Tommy began his analysis, as I understand, primarily for psychosomatic complaints. The father of the other boy appeared to function well and did not present any difficulties in the treatment of his son.

Tommy's bisexual wishes were aptly expressed in his fantasy of boys and girls being cut into halves and these halves being mixed up and put together again so that they were half boy and half girl. The nine-year-old patient referred to previously revealed an identical fantasy during one phase of his analysis. Boys and girls should be cut into half and the upper half of the girl put together with the lower part of the boy. A ten-year-old boy with transvestite tendencies revealed the following fantasy: "It would be best to be half boy and half girl. One side should be a boy and the other side a girl." He explained that then he would not have to worry about getting married. He would be married from birth on. Possessing everything his mother had, he would not need her and would be able to take care of himself. He had also thought of a way in which this could be accomplished: a man and a woman would get together so closely that they would become like one. Their children would be born half boy and half girl.

What is the source of this intense wish of the transvestite to be not only male but also female? Fenichel (1930) put the emphasis on castration anxiety and on the identification with the phallic mother; yet the belief in the phallic mother as a denial of castration is a phenomenon met with frequently in conditions other than transvestitism. In fact, fetishism has been considered by Freud (1938) the classical perversion in which this particular feature, namely, that the fetish represents the illusory penis, is a decisive dynamic factor. Friend's study (1954), in which transvestite behavior had been observed in a one-and-a-half-year-old boy, seems to indicate that transvestite behavior can occur in the prephallic phases before castration anxiety proper is active. My experience from the analyses of children and adults with transvestite tendencies leads me to believe that, in addition to the specific mother(parent)-child relationship and castration anxiety, two factors have to be present which contribute to the persistence of bisexuality and would seem to account for the specific outcome in transvestite behavior.

In 1950 I introduced the concept of the pregenital father; that is, the father with breasts (equation of penis = breast). I could show that the particularly intense positive oedipal conflict of the girl, in certain cases, covered up for an unresolved negative oedipal conflict, whereby the pregenital father represented a mother with penis, breasts, and babies, from whom the girl expected everything that her mother had not given her. The intensity of the castration conflict and of the penis envy in the patients described in this 1950 paper stemmed from their unresolved oral conflicts. They had cathected the penis with oral libido and the intensity of the wish for a penis was derived from an actual event: the birth of a younger brother which had been experienced as a loss of mother to the baby. The primary source for the fantasy of the loss of the penis (castration) in these cases came from this loss and from the unwillingness to accept weaning, i.e., separation from mother. The cathexis of the penis with oral libido was found to be a significant factor also in the dynamics of genital exhibitionism (M. Sperling, 1947).

We can now identify those two factors which, in my opinion, in a given situation, may account for the development of transvestite behavior. The first factor is a strong oral fixation with unresolved oral conflicts. Tommy's orality manifested itself in his intense envy and greed. This is characteristic also of bisexual fantasies. To be both a man and a woman means to possess everything that both have. A dream, which Tommy dreamed under anesthesia when he had a tooth pulled, illustrates this orality. In this dream, in place of his teeth which had been pulled out, the dentist gave him a crazy set of teeth over which he had no control and which snapped at everything. The urgency and impulsivity which characterizes oral personalities was also very apparent in Tommy's behavior.

The second factor is the reaction to the primal scene, which, in such a case, not only intensifies castration anxiety but is experienced as an abandonment by both parents and reactivates separation anxiety.

Tommy developed overt transvestite behavior at the age of three, shortly after he had been confronted with the fact that girl babies do not have a penis. Tommy had had ample opportunity for sexual explorations in his play with his seductive sister and his exhibitionistic mother. In his previous observations he had seen his mother's pubic hair, her big buttocks and breasts; his sister had long hair and was beginning to develop physically. Growing long hair and breasts played an important part in his dreams and fantasies of magical transformation into a girl. This lent itself to support his fantasy that there was something hidden ("Take off your fuzz," he said to his mother once upon seeing her nude) that eventually would develop and become visible. The shock effect of the sight of the baby girl came from the fact that he could plainly see that she had *nothing:* no penis, no hair, no breasts, no teeth. He counteracted with the confabulation, "All children are born girls." He could say, "I too was born a girl," because he was the actual possessor of a penis. That he was very much aware of this fact was brought out in a little incident which occurred about that time. He saw a little girl dancing; apparently he was envious that she could dance and said to her, "I have a penis and you don't, and I can urinate with my penis."

By the fantasy of "I too was born a girl," he could only gain. He could grow hair, breasts, and babies like his mother (aunt) and sister. By equating the (missing) penis of the baby with the as yet missing but later developing breasts, he could retain the fantasy of a female penis in a rationally acceptable form. The importance of the penis was displaced to the breast. Since he had a penis and girls did grow breasts, he could not only deny castration but support his bisexual fantasy.

Tommy was very curious about, but also very jealous of, the baby and of his mother who was very taken by the infant. He feared that he might be replaced by the baby. At that time his mother actually contemplated having another baby. He manifested regressive behavior particularly in speech and an intensification of his greed and envy. He wanted to have everything his mother and his sister had (he stole from his mother and sister but not from his father).

It seems to me that the emphasis in transvestite tendencies is equally as much on the man with breasts as it is on the woman with a penis. The fantasy material and the drawings of Tommy clearly indicated this. He persisted in the belief that men had breasts and that he, too, would grow them. He drew the breast of a woman in profile elongated and appearing like a big penis, and he would draw men with big penislike breasts.

Tommy expressed his positive oedipal wishes quite openly, especially in the displacement to his sister: "If I can't marry my mother, why can't I marry my sister?" he would ask. His dominant sexual orientation was heterosexual. The negative oedipal wishes were repressed and found expression and gratification in the transvestite behavior, especially in the beating fantasies and practice. Of interest is the fact that, although in reality his mother and sister were the ones who liked to slap him on his buttocks, in his fantasy he was beaten by the king. One adult patient with transvestite tendencies and with fantasies of being beaten by a woman remembered in his analysis a dream from childhood (during the oedipal phase). In this dream he was a slave and the king was beating him. He could permit himself the gratification of being beaten by a man only in a dream. In the beating fantasies which he developed in adolescence, the king was replaced by a woman. It would appear that hidden behind the woman in the manifest beating fantasies of transvestites is a man: the king-father; and that such a distortion may be a regular occurrence in the development of these fantasies. This patient, as my other patients with transvestite behavior, lived a full heterosexual life. He had never had any homosexual relationship and no conscious thoughts or fantasies of such a nature. Analysis, by bringing his unconscious passive homosexual wishes to the fore, did not transform him into a homosexual but, to the contrary, enabled him to gain more satisfaction and enjoyment from his heterosexual love relationship. I would not consider, as some authors seem to do (Friend et al., 1954), transvestite behavior as a defense against homosexuality or as a transitional phase in the development of homosexuality; I consider it a distinct perversion with a specific genesis, dynamics, and aim.

Reference has been made in the literature to transvestites who seek surgery so that they can actually live as women (Burchardt, 1961). In my opinion, this behavior alone would invalidate the diagnosis of transvestitism in these cases. The transvestite wants to be a man primarily and, at times, also a woman and have what a woman has. He does not want to be either one; he wants to be both. Tommy wanted to be his mother and he wanted to marry her; he wanted to be his sister and he wanted to marry her. He wanted to be the baby and he wanted to have babies. At the same time, he wanted to be a bigger boy and a father. He was the slave and the king. Yet, Tommy never really thought that he was a girl; he always knew that he just pretended.

The analysis of an adult patient with transvestite behavior revealed that the deeper meaning of this behavior was the re-enactment of the primal scene. He, too, was playing both roles; the male and the female in one. It would seem that the transvestite patient is re-enacting an *actual* trauma (the abandonment felt in reaction to the primal scene), and by himself representing both parents in the sexual embrace as one person with the attributes of both, he attempts to bring his conflict to a successful solution in the transvestite act.[3] This becomes particularly clear in the cases where the transvestite

[3] The need for episodic transvestite activity was clearly precipitated by a sudden reactivation and increase in separation anxiety in one patient. This activity had the earmarks of an emergency action, rather than one designed purely for the procurement of sexual pleasure and gratification. This behavior was similar to that observed in other types of perversion, but also in addicts and impulse-ridden (oral) characters (Bak, 1953; M. Sperling, 1947).

act takes place in front of a mirror (Greenacre, 1953). In this way the viewing of the primal scene and the unsolved puzzle of whether the parents in embrace are just one or two people is repeated. This would seem analogous to the hysterical fit in which Freud (1909) recognized that the patient is playing both roles, the male and female, in sexual intercourse.

Not every "dressing up" of a little boy in girl's clothing can be considered as true transvestite behavior. In fact, the public masquerading of males in female clothing is more indicative of certain types of homosexuality than of transvestitism. Only if such dressing-up behavior continues through or originates during the oedipal phase, increases in intensity, and continues into latency and is practiced with a certain degree of secrecy as sexual activities would be, could it be considered as transvestite behavior. Tommy was careful to conceal those activities which were really important to him and became even more careful as he grew older. When he would put on his sister's dress during the daytime to indulge in his beating fantasy and practice, he would hide in the crawling space of the house or in other secret places. He would hide his sister's panties and nightgowns in his bureau drawers, and he did not want other children to know about his behavior. In order to differentiate whether such behavior indicates the beginning of a homosexual or of a transvestite development, it would be necessary to know the fantasies underlying it. The dominant fantasy of these children with transvestite behavior was the "half and half" fantasy, that is, to be half boy and half girl; a fantasy which would seem characteristic for transvestite behavior. Characteristic, also, was a certain plasticity, playfulness, and imagination which permitted displacement from the important to the less important, i.e., from the primary sex characteristics, the genitals proper, to the secondary sex characteristics, the breasts, the anus, pubic hair, and hair in general; from below to above, from the front to the rear, and from the body itself to the clothing and all the female accoutrements.

I found a striking richness of fantasy life and creative imagination in the children as well as in the adults. Tommy's parents permitted freedom of thought, playfulness, imagination, interchangeability of sexual roles and acting out of fantasies. He was a fantastic storyteller even at the age of three or four. He was able later (and I like to think that this was a result of his analysis) to sublimate these tendencies and actually wrote stories and poems. He could permit himself the controlled illusion of being *also* a girl in the transvestite act (O. Sperling, 1956).

In summary, it can be said that the equation of penis with breast and the emphasis upon the breast are special modes of dealing with castration anxiety, holding out the promise for gain rather than the danger of loss. To the concept of identification with the phallic mother, considered to be the basic mechanism in transvestite behavior, can be added the concept of the pregenital father, the man with breasts. Both are expressions of the fantasy of "half and half"; man and woman in one. In the final analysis, this fantasy and the transvestite activity are the result of the child's reaction to the trauma of the primal scene, expressing his feelings that the parents in embrace are one person with the attributes of both.

Tommy's behavior, while it could not be considered a perversion in the true sense, was an indication of a serious deviation in his psychosexual development, which, I believe, without therapeutic intervention, would have led to an actual perversion in later life. The nine-year-old boy, whose treatment was not reported in this paper, began his transvestite behavior at the age of three. Because of its persistence and increase, the family sought psychiatric treatment when he was five years old. He was in play therapy for one year, and his mother was seen once a week during this time. There was no improvement in the child's behavior, and, because it was felt that the mother could not be reached in therapy, the case was referred to me. I treated the mother for three years before I began his analysis, and I am convinced that I could not have been successful with him without this preparation. At the start of analysis, he was withdrawn, distrustful in a paranoid manner, had no friends, and did not function well in school. He was phobic and bizarre in many ways, and had frequent *déjà vu* experiences. His transvestite activities were now a well-guarded secret and not easily accessible in the analysis.

From the analysis of the adolescents and adults with transvestite behavior, I gained the impression that there had been certain experiences and certain behavior in their early lives to indicate the probability of transvestite behavior in the future, even though manifest and active transvestite practices may not have been present. In the case of one adult, an episode, which occurred when he was between three and four years of age, had a direct bearing on his transvestite behavior later. His first overt transvestite episode occurred in early adulthood, and was a re-enactment of this early experience. This tendency, first noted during the oedipal phase, had remained latent through all these years, and emerged in a situation which unconsciously represented to him a repetition of the experience of that phase.

I intend to deal with certain structural aspects of the ego and superego, the *déjà vu* and other phenomena of ego regression in transvestitism at a future date.

## BIBLIOGRAPHY

Alexander, F. (1928), Ein Fall von masochistischem Transvestitismus als Selbstheilungsversuch. *Almanach.*
Bak, R. C. (1953), Fetishism. *J. Amer. Psa. Assn.*, 1.
Balint, M. (1935), A Contribution on Fetishism. *Int. J. Psa.*, 16.
Boehm, F. (1923), Bemerkungen über Transvestitismus. *Z. Psa.*, 9.
Burchardt, J. M. (1961), Struktur und Soziologie des Transvestitismus und Transsexualismus. *Beiträge zur Sexualforschung*, 21. Hamburg: Ferdinand Enke.
Fenichel, O. (1930) The Psychology of Transvestitism. *Collected Papers of Otto Fenichel*, 1. New York: Norton, 1953.
Fessler, L. (1934), Ein Fall von posttraumatischen Transvestismus. *Arch. Psychiat. & Nervenkrank.*, 100.
Freud, S. (1905), Three Essays on the Theory of Sexuality. *Standard Edition*, 7. London: Hogarth Press, 1953.
—— (1909), Some General Remarks on Hysterical Attacks. *Standard Edition*, 9. London: Hogarth Press, 1959.
—— (1927), Fetishism. *Collected Papers*, 5. London: Hogarth Press, 1950.
—— (1938), Splitting of the Ego in the Defensive Process. *Collected Papers*, 5. London: Hogarth Press, 1950.
Friend, M. R., Schiddel, L., Klein, B., & Dunaeff, D. (1954), Observations on the Development of Transvestitism in Boys. *Amer. J. Orthopsychiat.*, 24.
Gillespie, W. H. (1952), Notes on the Analysis of Sexual Perversions. *Int. J. Psa.*, 33.
Greenacre, P. (1953), Certain Relationships Between Fetishism and Faulty Development of the Body Image. *This Annual*, 8.
Greenberg, N. H. & Rosenwald, A. K. (1958), Transvestism and Pruritus Perinei. *Psychosom. Med.*, 20.
—— —— (1960), A Study in Transsexualism. *Psychiat. Quart.*, 34.
Grotjahn, M. (1948), Transvestite Fantasy Expressed in a Drawing. *Psa. Quart.*, 17.
Gutheil, E. A. (1954), The Psychologic Background of Transsexualism and Transvestitism. *Amer. J. Psychother.*, 8.
Hirschfeld, M. & Tielke, M. (1912), *Der erotische Drang zur Verkleidung.* Berlin: Pulvermacher.
Hora, T. (1953), The Structural Analysis of Transvestitism. *Psa. Rev.*, 40.

Johnson, A. M. & Szurek, S. A. (1952), The Genesis of Antisocial Acting-Out in Children and Adults. *Psa. Quart.*, 21.

Karpman, B. (1947), Dream Life in a Case of Transvestitism with Particular Attention to the Problem of Latent Homosexuality. *J. Nerv. & Ment. Dis.*, 106.

Kubie, L. S. (1954), The Drive to Become Both Sexes. Presented at the American Psychoanalytic Association, St. Louis.

Luhianowitz, N. (1960), Two Cases of Transvestism. *Psychiat. Quart.*, 34.

McKenzie, R. E. & Schulz, I. (1961), Study of a Transvestite: Evaluation and Treatment. *Amer. J. Psychother.*, 15.

Sperling, M. (1947), The Analysis of an Exhibitionist. *Int. J. Psa.*, 28.

—— (1950), The Structure of Envy in Depressions of Women. Symposium on Feminine Psychology: Its Implications for Psychoanalytic Medicine. New York Medical College at Flower and Fifth Avenue Hospitals.

—— (1959), A Study of Deviate Sexual Behavior in Children by the Method of Simultaneous Analysis of Mother and Child. In: *Dynamic Psychopathology in Childhood*, ed. L. Jessner & E. Pavenstedt. New York: Grune & Stratton.

Sperling, O. (1951), Illusions, Naïve or Controlled. *Psa Quart.*, 20.

—— (1956), Psychodynamics of Group Perversions. *Psa. Quart.*, 25.

Socarides, C. W. (1960), The Development of a Fetishistic Perversion. *J. Amer. Psa. Assn.*, 8.

Wilson, G. W. (1948), A Further Contribution to the Study of Olfactory Repression with Particular Reference to Transvestitism. *Psa. Quart.*, 17.

CONTENTS OF PREVIOUS VOLUMES

# CONTENTS OF PREVIOUS VOLUMES

## VOLUME III/IV, 1949

## VOLUME X, 1955

## VOLUME XI, 1956

## VOLUME XII, 1957

## VOLUME XIII, 1958

## VOLUME XIV, 1959

## VOLUME XV, 1960

## VOLUME XVI, 1961

BENJAMIN SHAMBAUGH—A Study of Loss Reactions in a Seven-Year-Old
ALBERT J. SOLNIT AND MARY H. STARK—Mourning and the Birth of a Defective Child
HELEN D. WALLACH—Termination of Treatment As a Loss
I. HYMAN WEILAND AND ROBERT RUDNIK—Considerations of the Development and Treatment of Autistic Childhood Psychosis

# VOLUME XVII, 1962

K. R. EISSLER—On the Metapsychology of the Preconscious: A Tentative Contribution to Psychoanalytic Morphology

HEINZ HARTMANN AND R. M. LOEWENSTEIN—Notes on the Superego

GEORGE S. KLEIN—Blindness and Isolation

JEANNE LAMPL-DE GROOT—Ego Ideal and Superego

JOSEPH SANDLER, MARIA KAWENOKA, LILY NEURATH, BERNARD ROSENBLATT, ANNELIESE SCHNURMANN, AND JOHN SIGAL—The Classification of Superego Material in the Hampstead Index

JOSEPH SANDLER AND BERNARD ROSENBLATT—The Concept of the Representational World

ANNA FREUD—Assessment of Childhood Disturbances

ILSE HELLMAN—Hampstead Nursery Follow-up Studies: 1. Sudden Separation and Its Effect Followed Over Twenty Years

ERNST KRIS—Decline and Recovery in the Life of a Three-Year-Old; or: Data in Psychoanalytic Perspective on the Mother-Child Relationship

SEYMOUR L. LUSTMAN—Defense, Symptom, and Character

JOYCE ROBERTSON—Mothering as an Influence on Early Development: A Study of Well-Baby Clinic Records

DAVID L. RUBINFINE—Maternal Stimulation, Psychic Structure, and Early Object Relations; with Special Reference to Aggression and Denial

RENÉ A. SPITZ—Autoerotism Re-examined: The Role of Early Sexual Behavior Patterns in Personality Formation

JOHN C. COOLIDGE, ELLEN TESSMAN, SAMUEL WALDFOGEL, AND MARY LOU WILLER—Patterns of Aggression in School Phobia

AARON H. ESMAN—Visual Hallucinoses in Young Children

JEROMA KAVKA—Ego Synthesis of a Life-Threatening Illness in Childhood

SAMUEL D. LIPTON—On the Psychology of Childhood Tonsillectomy

MARJORIE P. SPRINCE—The Development of a Preoedipal Partnership between an Adolescent Girl and Her Mother

MARTIN WANGH—The "Evocation of a Proxy": A Psychological Maneuver, Its Use as a Defense, Its Purposes and Genesis

M. KATAN—A Causerie on Henry James's "The Turn of the Screw"

# VOLUME XVIII, 1963

JAY KATZ—On Primary Gain and Secondary Gain

SEYMOUR L. LUSTMAN—Some Issues in Contemporary Psychoanalytic Research

LEO RANGELL—The Scope of Intrapsychic Conflict: Microscopic and Macroscopic Considerations

LEO RANGELL—Structural Problems in Intrapsychic Conflict

JOSEPH SANDLER, ALEX HOLDER, AND DALE MEERS—The Ego Ideal and the Ideal Self

JOSEPH SANDLER AND HUMBERTO NAGERA—Aspects of the Metapsychology of Fantasy

SIBYLLE K. ESCALONA—Patterns of Infantile Experience and the Developmental Process